Material Politics in Turkey

BIAA | BRITISH INSTITUTE AT ANKARA

Understanding Turkey and the Black Sea

Contemporary Turkey

The *Contemporary Turkey* monograph series is a joint initiative by the British Institute at Ankara (BIAA), internationally renowned for its support of independent academic research, and leading publisher of Middle East and Turkish Studies I.B. Tauris, an imprint of Bloomsbury Academic.

The series publishes cutting-edge research monographs and edited collections from a new generation of scholars working on modern Turkey across the social sciences and humanities. In bringing to light new data and insights directly from the field, this series is distinguished by its emphasis on innovative approaches that challenge established ways of examining Turkey.

Published Titles

The Politics of Education in Turkey: Islam, Neoliberalism, and Gender, Zühre Emanet

Architectures of Emergency in Turkey: Heritage, Displacement and Catastrophe, edited by Eray Çaylı, Pınar Aykaç and Sevcan Ercan

Political Violence in Turkey, 1975-1980: The State at Stake, Benjamin Gourisse

Mobility and Armenian Belonging in Contemporary Turkey: Migratory Routes and the Meaning of the Local, Salim Aykut Öztürk

Police Reform in Turkey: Human Security, Gender and State Violence Under Erdogan, Funda Hülagü

Material Politics in Turkey

Infrastructure, Science, and Expertise

Duygu Kaşdoğan, Ekin Kurtiç, Mehmet Ekinci

I.B.TAURIS
LONDON • NEW YORK • OXFORD • NEW DELHI • SYDNEY

I.B. TAURIS
Bloomsbury Publishing Plc
50 Bedford Square, London, WC1B 3DP, UK
1385 Broadway, New York, NY 10018, USA
29 Earlsfort Terrace, Dublin 2, Ireland

First published in Great Britain 2025

Cover design: Adriana Brioso
Cover image: A steel arch bridge over the River Euphrates in Anatolia, Turkey, c. 1950. © Keystone/Getty Images

A catalogue record for this book is available from the British Library.

Library of Congress Cataloging-in-Publication Data

Names: Kas¸dog?an, Duygu, editor. | Kurtic¸, Ekin, editor. | Ekinci, Mehmet, editor.
Title: Material politics in Turkey: infrastructure, science, and expertise / [edited by] Duygu Kas¸dog?an, Ekin Kurtic¸, Mehmet Ekinci.
Description: London; New York: I.B. Tauris, 2025. | Series: Contemporary Turkey | Includes bibliographical references and index.
Identifiers: LCCN 2024027859 (print) | LCCN 2024027860 (ebook) | ISBN 9780755647880 (hardback) | ISBN 9780755647927 (paperback) | ISBN 9780755647903 (epub) | ISBN 9780755647897 (ePDF)
Subjects: LCSH: Infrastructure (Economics)–Turkey. | Materials–Political aspects–Turkey. | Science and state–Turkey. | Technology and state–Turkey. | Turkey–Economic policy.
Classification: LCC HC495.C3 M38 2025 (print) | LCC HC495.C3 (ebook) | DDC 338.9561–dc23/eng/20240909
LC record available at https://lccn.loc.gov/2024027859
LC ebook record available at https://lccn.loc.gov/2024027860

ISBN: HB: 978-0-7556-4788-0
ePDF: 978-0-7556-4789-7
eBook: 978-0-7556-4790-3

Typeset by Deanta Global Publishing Services, Chennai, India

Contents

Figures

On Materiality and Politics in Turkey

An Introduction

Duygu Kaşdoğan and Ekin Kurtiç

As we write the introduction to this book, the political scene in Turkey once again boasts awe- and wonder-generating representations of a large-scale technological system, reinforcing the "technological sublime" (Nye 1996) that has been central to the nation-state's past and present. The construction of what is being praised as a technological marvel, the country's tallest dam, was finalized approximately ten years after its groundbreaking ceremony in 2013. On November 22, 2022, several television channels broadcast live the inauguration ceremony of the Yusufeli Dam and Hydroelectric Power Plant, which took place at the resettlement site of the soon-to-be-submerged town of Yusufeli, with public speeches by President Recep Tayyip Erdoğan, the Minister of Energy, and the Minister of Environment and Urbanization. Erdoğan's public address was a carefully crafted blend of an emphasis on the project's material achievements—such as the sheer scale of the dam, the unprecedented length of its tunnels and roads, and the expanded size of the new town center—of an expression of his love for the nation, as well as his gratitude to the Yusufeli inhabitants for their praiseworthy sacrifice for the sake of the nation's future;[1] and of a stress on the government's fight against terrorism and for democracy. His speech, in other words, showcased how a material-affective-political assemblage can be leveraged for the construction of political power and authority in Turkey.

On the night of the inauguration ceremony, the public television channel TRT broadcasted a documentary about the dam, as part of the TV series titled "Turkey's Giant Structures" (*Türkiye'nin Dev Yapıları*), which documents "the engineering marvels that push the boundaries and put a signature on the future."[2] In conveying a particular story of the dam's construction, the documentary highlighted two interrelated factors as the defining characteristics of the construction process: first, the harsh geographic conditions on site, entailing very steep mountains with a heterogeneous geological composition and a fiercely flowing river that created a deep valley; and, second, the "native" (*yerli*) Turkish engineers' experience, prowess, and creativity in carefully engaging with, responding to, and mastering this challenging landscape. The fact that the construction took place as the result of a constant, dynamic relationship with the challenging geological and hydrological conditions on the ground further reinforced the sense of technological awe conveyed in the documentary. The process was presented as a co-construction of infrastructure, environmental knowledge, technoscientific expertise, and political power, in a geography that is cast as harsh but bearing great potential. In other words, the particularities of the material landscape constituted a core reference point throughout the documentary, highlighting the importance of the engineering experience and skills, coupled with a sense of national prowess and technopolitical power.

Materiality matters. This saying can be traced from ancient philosophical discussions to the rise of materialism as a historical movement (e.g., within the terms of Marxist historical materialists). The turn to the question of "materiality" in recent decades—following the historical shift to information as an analytical tool and object of research, alongside the population of the field of cybernetics in the 1940s—has been an investigation into how information has lost its body (e.g., Hayles 1999). However, this turn was not simply a reiteration of the importance of materiality in understanding societal organizations, or a spotlight on "reality," "corporeality," or "concreteness," or any connotation of materiality as a word.[3] Scholars working, for example, in science and technology studies (STS), anthropology, philosophy, geography, and architecture have taken new approaches to retheorize and unpack why and how materiality matters, while also revisiting other big questions and themes, such as what humans become; the relationship between nature and culture, subject and object; and agency, sociality, objectification, representation, power, and politics. This line of thinking has paved the way for divergent conceptualizations in understanding the changing dynamics of societies and the different constructions of humans. These conceptualizations range from "posthumanism" over "transhumanism" to "new materialism" and mark new orientations to study matter and the materiality of multiple worlds in the aftermath of the Second World War.

Navigating such a diverse and complex field of "materiality studies" across multiple disciplines, the basic question with which this collection begins is the following: *Why is it important to put emphasis on materiality while studying politics in modern Turkey?* Multiple answers may emerge. It is important "to avoid being caught up in the description and qualification of 'perspective'" (Woolgar and Lezaun 2013) and "not to ignore things" (Olsen 2007). Drawing attention to "the stuff of politics" (Braun and Whatmore 2010) goes beyond representational understandings of politics and shows the multiplicity of reality-in-practice (Mol 2002). This approach works as an invitation to complicate any simplistic distinction between ontology and epistemology (Barad 2003), and between sociality and materiality (Law and Mol 1995). As we shift our attention to matter in understanding politics, we ask once again: *How do infrastructures, expertise, and scientific knowledges come to matter, materialize, and manifest in, through, and of particular politics?*

The chapters in this edited collection contribute to unpacking this question, addressing the different ways in which infrastructures, scientific and expert knowledges, and practices come to matter in various political contexts—for example, forestry, water and wetland management, energy and food production, and the military. They provide specific analytical approaches to study politics in Turkey and show what becomes visible when we attend to materiality. The analytical approaches employed in each chapter build on diverse and different scholarly interests in the questions of materiality and politics (such as new materialism, posthumanism, actor–

network theory, material culture, materialist political economy and history, and more-than-human geographies). However, they all come together in the primary framework of this book—namely, *material politics*.

Andrew Barry, in his book titled *Material Politics: Disputes Along the Pipeline* (2013), has explored in detail the entangled relationship between information and materials by focusing on the knowledge controversies around the BTC pipeline. His approach to "material politics" informs this book's framework. Barry has differentiated his study of materiality from other accounts on the role of material agency in political life, accounts which take for granted that materials in themselves have political agency or a form of political significance. His work has attended to the specificity of materials and explored their political importance through closely studying their relational, practical, and contingent achievements (Barry 2013, 183). Such an approach neither attributes a political agency to materials, nor claims that politics is always shaped by material relations. Instead, "material politics" as an analytical approach draws attention to the coproduction of materials and politics in empirical terms—that is, by focusing on particular practices and processes unfolding in specific times and spaces. It is very much in line with Timothy Mitchell's (2002, 42–3) definition of technopolitics as an amalgam, "a technical body, an alloy that must emerge from a process of manufacture whose ingredients are both human and nonhuman, both intentional and not [. . .]." Therefore, this approach does not take for granted general meanings attributed to the materials and politics under investigation; rather, it aims to show how materials and politics take their form, their meanings, and their force in contingent relational practices.

Such an empirical focus speaks to what Ingold has called "an ecology of materials"—namely, an approach that takes materials as ineffable: materials cannot be reduced to existing categories; rather, they can be described through observation and engagement with what is there, by following them (Ingold 2012, 435). Producing material worlds, then, is not "the imposition of preconceived form on raw material substance," but a meshwork (ibid.). Ingold underlines that this meshwork is also historical, as materials are histories: "To understand materials is to be able to tell their histories—of what they do and what happens to them when treated in particular ways—in the very practice of working with them" (ibid.). The chapters in this collection address the production of material worlds, by closely exploring how divergent actors work with similar materials in different and, most of the time, contingent ways. The stories that these chapters tell are thus histories of materials as part of modernization processes in Turkey. As such, they explore material worlds as more than a background, or a passive element upon which political, social, and economic relations are built, reinforced, negotiated, or challenged. In so doing, this book builds upon Timothy Mitchell's (2002, 29) powerful critique that "it is not that social analysis necessarily ignores disease, agriculture, chemicals, or technology, but that these are externals—nature, tools, obstacles, resources—whose role is essentially passive." As the book's contributors collectively show, material worlds do not constitute a ground on which political regimes, ideologies, conflicts, and relations get materialized. Rather, the material worlds explored in this collection—such as water infrastructures, coal and gold mines, oil fields, forests, wetlands, and military bases—play a dynamic role in shaping the political processes. Yet, this does not mean attributing a separate, autonomous force to materiality, a force that is assumed to be independent of human practices. We foreground the formative role of material entities and processes entwined with the meanings, values, and power relations in political processes of infrastructure construction, scientific knowledge production, and the transnational manufacturing of technique and expertise in Turkey.

Overall, the selection of "material politics" as the main framing of this edited collection is not arbitrary and differs from analytical concepts such as "political materiality," "political materials," and "material powers" in those works that explore the relationships between materials, politics, and power. For example, Pilo and Jaffe (2020) in their studies on the political materiality of cities emphasize "the role of objects in mediating relations of power between humans" (9). Such a framework does not directly take an interest in the agency of materials and/or develop an ontological approach to studying their politics. Scholarly works that stress "political materials," however, focus more on the agency of material worlds. In his essay surveying divergent meanings given to political materials in scholarly works, Jensen (2015) has drawn attention to the multiplicity of political materials: in his study, these refer to climate models, trees and rivers, apples and salmon, genes and energy flows, anaconda ancestors, and spirit rivers. Such an emphasis on "political materials" renders visible the "invisible activities of the materials out of which environmental infrastructures are composed, and the invisibility of forms of action that fall outside the scope of the ordinary and vernacular" (Jensen 2015, 28). Attention to "political materials" points to the importance of studying emergent ontologies, so as to experiment with alternative ways of infrastructuring the manner in which we cohabit this world with multispecies. To us, the notion of "material politics" provides a more balanced look at politics and materials, providing a framework for the contributions of each chapter, a framework that unpacks the coproduction of material worlds and political worlds by adopting different focal points and introducing multiple understandings of politics.

The reading of politics in these chapters does not limit itself to the question of power relations,[4] but invites us to rethink the modern state and political transformations in modern Turkey. Throughout the book, we populate the realm of politics with a variety of actors and forces to show that the making of infrastructure, science, and expertise does not merely consist of top-down processes of the consolidation of state or corporate power. By joining recent scholarly works that offer a detailed examination of politics in Turkey beyond the contours of the central state actors' discourses and practices (Açıksöz 2019; Babül 2017; Massicard 2022), the authors in this volume examine a diverse set of actors, including state and governmental officials, engineers, scientists, experts, city dwellers, farming communities, dairy producers, and military actors, as they enact politics through and with material landscapes.

Understanding Politics in Turkey through a Material Lens

The exploration of political transformations through the lens of material practices and processes is not a new line of research in the context of Turkey. Since the nineteenth century, from the Ottoman Empire to republican Turkey, the material change of the built environment has been at the core of the project of "modernization" and "Westernization," as spearheaded by the increasingly centralized political rule. As Tekeli and Ilkin (2004) have noted, efforts to integrate the Ottoman Empire into the world economy took place through the introduction of new agricultural technologies and machines; factories and industries such as gunpowder, textile, and paper factories, as well as ironworks; the expansion of communication technologies such as the telegraph; and the construction of transportation infrastructures such as railroads and highways. The making of a centralized, "modern," "Westernized" empire was a material process, as much as it was social, economic, and political.

As the modernization project was carried over to the republican period—a process defined by Tekeli and Ilkin (2004) as a transition from a "shy modernity project" to a "radical modernity project"—sociopolitical transformations continued to happen on material grounds. Studies of the built environment, especially in urban contexts, have provided fertile ground to trace material manifestations of changes in political power, socioeconomic relations, and cultural values and meanings. Architectural historians have paid close attention to urban material transformations in the making of the nation-state, reflecting on the priority given to architecture and urbanism as a form of "visible politics" by the modernizing national elites (Bozdoğan 2001, 9). In her work on the history of architectural culture in Turkey, Bozdoğan (2001, 6) has explained that architecture in early republican Turkey can be seen "as a literally 'concrete' manifestation of the high modernist vision." As a vision that draws on the allure of technical prowess and scientific progress to make reality legible and controllable, this high-modernist ideology, as Bozdoğan has shown, appealed to the architects and planners in their endeavor to construct a modern, Westernized nation-state through changes in the built environment. Yet, understanding the case of Turkey, as Bozdoğan has contended, also requires going beyond the framework of high modernism in order to attend to the contradictions, ambiguities, and complexities that the actualization of this imported ideology entailed on the ground. As a result, the buildings constructed in the early republican period were material manifestations of the modernist Turkish architects' aim of nationalizing the modern.

Similar ambivalences and complexities also lie at the core of Zeynep Kezer's (2015) exploration of tangible spaces and sites for creating a unitary nation-state through both constructive and destructive forces. The political construction of a homogeneous nation-state and national identity was inextricable from the material construction of the built environment: the making of a new capital city, Ankara, allowed for "inscribing the structural transformation of the state into the physical landscape" (Kezer 2015, 17), while the expansion of physical infrastructural projects and public works such as schools, roads, railroads, hospitals, and bridges aimed to "instill in the population a sense of unity and continuity as a people with a common history and a united destiny living on a shared piece of land" (158). Yet, remaking the material landscape in practice, as Kezer has shown, was a messy and untidy process composed of unfinished or changed schemes, due to reasons varying from financial constraints to social resistances, reflecting the messiness of a seemingly coherent and solid political project of modernization and nation-state building.

The growing field of environmental humanities has recently offered a rich analysis of how the construction of the modern nation-state in Turkey took place through changes in environmental relations and processes. From the drainage of swamps to eradicate malaria and modernize the rural population (Evered and Evered 2012), to the foundation of scientific forestry and the valorization of verdure (Özkan 2013), to the struggle against locusts and for the control of the Kurdish population (Özbilge 2020), nation-state building has materialized through the co-constitutive aim of conquering and taming nature and society. Yet, instead of a linear progression toward ever-expanding and consolidating governmental control over nature cultures, unruly ecologies, conflicting aims and interests, competing interventions, and limitations to power and resistances have rendered this "process a project, not a secure accomplishment" (Li 2007, 10). Even the construction and maintenance of large dams—the epitome of the centralized nation-state's endeavor to control waters and conquer frontier landscapes (Stahl 2019)—is shot through with material complexities and unruliness on the ground, as exemplified by the problem of soil sedimentation in reservoirs (Kurtiç 2023). Similarly, as Caterina Scaramelli (2021, 11) has shown the making of Turkey's wetlands into objects of knowledge and management is a multivalent process where, "in their contestation over how to preserve and manage wetlands, and how to live with them, different social groups wrestle with what it means to be moral ecological subjects at a time of political and climatic uncertainty."

Recently, in studies of Turkey, the question of how politics takes place through material practices and discourses has gained renewed attention beyond the analytics of nation-building, and invited us to understand the role of infrastructure, extraction, and construction projects in enabling authoritarian rule and populist power (Erensü 2018; Bulut, Can, and İleri 2020; Paker 2017; Hoyng and Es 2020); in fostering neoliberal developmentalism (Adaman, Akbulut, and Arsel 2018); in enacting a state effect (Harris 2012); in developing modern bioeconomies (Kasdogan 2017); in building hegemonic and counter-hegemonic mobilization (Dissard 2017; Islar 2012; Yıldırım and Haspolat 2020); in forging violence, racialization, and dispossession in and through material landscapes (Çaylı 2021; Evren 2021; Yıldırım 2022); and in shaping the notions of and interactions with time and history (Arican 2020; Suni 2023; Navaro et al. 2021). This scholarship shows the limits of methodological nationalism (e.g., Beck 2007; Pries 2009; Wimmer and Glick Schiller 2002) and reveals how material politics take shape in Turkey through multiscalar relations and processes—a central theme that runs throughout this book.

"Things are not one thing," as Puig de la Bellacasa (2017, 144) has underlined, hence, it is crucial to recognize the specificity of the political and ethical concerns arising from engagements with diverse nonhuman others, either the organic "natural" world or technological entities. Accordingly, this book attunes to the multiplicity of material worlds and their particular politics—ranging from muddy forests to urban water provision, from oil fields to transnational encounters at a military base, from unruly and contested wetlands to the global expansion of gold extraction. In doing so, this collection builds on and contributes to the three intertwined lines of literature outlined above: studies on the built environment and architecture, environmental humanities, and infrastructure studies. While Part I stands in close conversation with the rising field of infrastructure studies and offers a renewed focus on the material configuration of Turkey's infrastructures, Parts II and III provide new analytical and conceptual lenses for the study of material politics in Turkey, in that they focus on questions of scientific and expert knowledge and transnational flows and relations.

Overview of the Volume

Material Politics in Modern Turkey is composed of three parts. Each part ends with a commentary that unpacks the main analytics of its chapters and provides a reflection on the chapters by weaving them together. Each commentary is designed to situate the chapters within broader discussions and diverse perspectives in scholarly analyses of interplays between the material and the political, therefore, offering readers frameworks that are required to make sense of the unfolding of these divergent interplays. These commentary texts serve as a tool to slow down, pause, and reconsider what these chapters teach about the complex modernization processes in Turkey.

Part I, "The Politics of Infrastructure," explores the political processes of state- and space-making through an analytical focus on infrastructure-building. The chapters in this part elaborate on how state rule and presence, city governance, multispecies relations, and regional boundaries shape and are shaped by the practices of constructing physical infrastructures. Overall, the chapters of Part I foreground the relevance and significance of infrastructural analysis for understanding the formation of political power, as the latter is entwined with material constructions; they reveal the fragmented, incomplete, and unsettling materialization of politics. Part II, "Making Material Worlds Scientific," presents an inquiry into the politics of negotiation, collaboration, and uncertainty that are imbued in rendering material worlds scientific. The chapters in this part explore the scientific practices and discourses through which forests, cheesemaking, wetlands, and oil in Turkey get to be known, produced, and regulated. Together, they shed light on the force of biophysical and geological entities, as they mediate how politics and science are entangled. Part III, "Translating Techniques and Expertise," broadens the exploration of material politics in terms of scale—that is, beyond the nation-state—and attends to the role that transnational actors and processes play in making sociotechnical expertise in Turkey. The chapters in this part focus on material sites such as a military base, soccer fields, psychiatric hospitals, and a gold mine, in order to shed light on how the contested, uneasy, and institutionalized translation of technologies, techniques, and expertise forges diverse power relations.

Part I: The Politics of Infrastructure

Recently, the renewed attention to the centrality of physical infrastructures in sociocultural, political, and economic life has led to an "infrastructural turn" in the humanities and social sciences. The critical scholarly analysis of infrastructures as technological systems that move things, connect places and spaces, and provide public goods and services has offered close scrutiny of the material configurations of political rule and economic power (Folch 2019; Joyce 2003; Mitchell 2011), citizenship claims and political action (Anand 2017; Fredericks 2018; von Schnitzler 2016); the government of space and nature (Carse 2014; Stamatopoulou-Robbins 2019); and the formation of social identities and belonging, as well as relations of morality and care (Nucho 2016; Scaramelli 2021). Similar to the context of Latin America and the broader geography of the Global South, Turkey is an ideal place to think through infrastructures. Yet, unlike Latin America, where, according to Hetherington and Campbell (2014, 193), "from around 1990, infrastructural investment would no longer be about marking the landscape with monuments to human intervention that might spur sluggish national economies," the approach to infrastructure as a way of marking the landscape continues to be prominent in Turkey (Kurtiç and Nucho 2022).

Infrastructural analysis has particular relevance for and importance in the context of contemporary Turkey: there, the Justice and Development Party's government has been drawing on the trope of serving people through the construction of roads, bridges, power plants, and airports (Paker 2017). In addition to fostering popular consent and support, infrastructure projects in Turkey have become channels for distributing political economic benefits to pro-government construction companies, thereby consolidating government–business relations. While infrastructure projects offer a crucial window into the making of the authoritarian populist regime in the current context, this book expands the temporal and scalar scope of the inquiry beyond the predominant focus on contemporary central state politics. To this end, the chapters in Part I explore past and present forms of region-, city-, and subject-formation through the lens of infrastructure politics. The chapters attend to the ways in which the politics forged and manifested by infrastructure projects take specific forms in different temporal and spatial contexts.

Social scientific and humanistic analyses of infrastructures require tackling the question of materiality since infrastructure projects are made of material components such as pipes, concrete, and iron, "carrying their own promise, transformative potential, aesthetic effect, and affective force" (Harvey 2015). Moreover, they are built in and become part of material landscapes entailing soil, water, and rock, and they are inextricably linked to the broader built environment composed of other technical and infrastructural projects. The material politics of infrastructure, as Andrew Barry (2020, 6) has noted, allow us to consider that "the properties and behavior of its [infrastructure's] nonhuman or material elements are surely irreducible to human interests and agency," while also noting "the ways in which materials are the objects of government, as well as the ways in which infrastructural assemblages have been governed historically" (7). In line with this perspective, Part I offers an analysis of infrastructural politics in Turkey, in that it examines the material composition of the corresponding infrastructures entailing canals, pipes, grids, fountains, waters, and microbial communities as they accrete, change, or persist over time. It also addresses how infrastructure's materiality is designed, controlled, governed, and experienced by technoscientific experts, governmental actors, and ordinary people.

The first chapter by Aybike Alkan examines the water infrastructures built within the scope of the Southeastern Anatolia Project (GAP); it was introduced in the mid-1970s as an integrated river basin project, of which dams constitute major components. By approaching dam-building as a scalar process that entails engineering decisions about the shifting physical constellations of infrastructures, Alkan shows that the prioritization of energy production at the national scale at the expense of regional-scale irrigation purposes has led to the GAP's failure as a regional development project. In doing so, Alkan demonstrates that debates and decisions about material configurations of infrastructures, such as their location, type, and scale, not only reflect but also register political projects such as the recognition and denial of the idea of a *region*—in this case, the Kurdish region. Asya Ece Uzmay's chapter furthers the analysis of water infrastructures and their politics by shifting the focus to the city scale, particularly tracing the political debates and materialities of Istanbul's fountains, water towers, and underground pipes from the early republican period until the 1970s. Uzmay investigates how the materiality of water infrastructures intersects with more-than-human landscapes of disease since the latter shapes the changing visibility of fountains and pipes, rendering them central to the politics of urban modernization. This process of modernization is not a linear progression toward a more centralized governance of water provision; rather, it is a fragmented process with site-specific and ad hoc solutions. In the last chapter of this part, Irem Az examines the constitutive role of thermal energy infrastructures in shaping contemporary Turkey's welfare and labor regimes. By tracing Soma coal's diverse material and symbolic presence in the everyday lives of the miners and their families, Az demonstrates that coal not only constitutes the material substance on which both the energy infrastructure and the authoritarian populist regime depend, but also, importantly, that it has become a pedagogical infrastructure configuring the workers' vernacular knowledge of how to behave as "deserving" laborers and/or "deserving" poor. As Özden-Schilling underlines in her commentary, state-making emerges as a cross-cutting theme across all of the chapters: the politics of infrastructure imply a site of encounter between citizens and states that are not preexisting entities but are themselves produced through infrastructural services.

Part II: Making Material Worlds Scientific

The relationship between science and politics has been one of the main issues of public discussion and—as a point of reference, alongside the questioning of democratic governance practices—has long shaped the imaginaries of nation-building and modernization processes in Turkey. In the second part of this edited collection, we aim to deepen our understanding of the complex relationship between science and politics as it takes shape in Turkey by closely looking at the specific sites of the politics of negotiation, collaboration, and uncertainty imbued in rendering material worlds scientific. Therefore, this part moves beyond analyses that either explore the ways in which science gets politicized or critiques of scientism that reinforce the idea that science is inherently political. The chapters of Part II address the mutual constitution of science, material, and politics on the ground through specific discourses and practices. By showing how material worlds are rendered scientific, they provide pathways for studying the relationships between science and politics in Turkey, thereby contributing to the relevant literature in the field of STS.

STS scholars have largely engaged with the question of politics in their critical studies of science, technology, and society. These studies, drawing on different conceptions of politics,[5] have explored the relationship between science and modern state-making (Prakash 1999), science and nationalism (Subramaniam 2019), science and democracy (Hilgarter, Miller, and Hagendijk 2015), science and the social order (Jasanoff 2006), science and the public (Irwin and Wynne 2004), science and participation (Chilvers and Kearnes 2015), and science and neoliberal globalization (Moore et al. 2011), among other topics. The chapters in the second part of this collection contribute to lines of inquiry that unpack the complex role of science and scientists in the making of societies, states, nations, and publics; they do so by exploring scientists' relations with different actors, questioning scientific authorities, and elaborating on scientists' involvement in the making of material worlds.

The contributors draw particular attention to scientific and expert knowledges and provide ethnographic insights into the relationship between local and scientific knowledges; the work that the indeterminacy of scientific knowledges does for politics, knowledge, and power relationships in environmental governance projects; and state- and citizen-making through scientific discourses. These empirically rich discussions, which add to the expansive literature on social studies of scientific knowledges and scientific research practices, shed light on the force of biophysical and geological entities in mediating how politics and science get entangled in Turkey. As such, they not only introduce particular pathways to study the coproduction of science and politics in Turkey, but also show why and how it matters to attend to the question of materiality in exploring this entangled relationship between science and politics in Turkey's modernization processes. These place-based ethnographic studies furthermore challenge universal understandings of science as well as highlight new knowledge that can be derived from the critical studies of science in and through studying Turkey.

Part II opens with Hande Özkan's chapter, which explores state- and citizen-making through the scientific forestry discourse about the ambiguous materiality of forests, centered mainly on terrestrial and aquatic interpretations of the forest. She shows how discussions about such an ambiguous materiality of forests reveal the complex relationships between state-appointed forest engineers, forest guards, and forest villagers. According to her, the negotiation between these actors teaches us how the modern Turkish state is made via managing and making forests. Fatih Tatari's chapter furthers ways to study negotiations between scientists and local actors, using as a case study *kaşar* cheesemaking processes on the pastures of Kars. Tatari's close ethnographic attention to the relationship between scientists and farmers opens a space to question scientific authority and to learn how science is being made through such encounters in a local place as well as through the materiality of territory. Caterina Scaramelli's study of wetlands follows a similar thread; she analyzes material politics through an ethnography of the negotiations over different forms of knowledges and powers, by adding how failed participation in collaboration processes shapes the materiality of wetlands. The last chapter in this part, written by Zeynep Oğuz, on oil exploration in Turkey invites us to work with the question of indeterminacy as a way to explore material politics. She explores the role that the indeterminacy of material worlds and scientific knowledges plays in politics. All chapters in Part II show that scientists in Turkey have long been collaborating with multiple actors practicing outside the scientific field, leaving us with multiple new questions that can inspire new research, as Knudsen notes in his commentary.

Part III: Translating Techniques and Expertise

The third part contributes to this collection by broadening the scale of the exploration beyond the nation-state and turnsing to the role of transnational actors and processes in making sociotechnical expertise in Turkey. The nation-state as a relevant scale of analysis has been questioned in the social sciences, and several scholars have addressed transnationalism to overcome methodological nationalism in different areas of research, ranging from law and history to political science, cultural studies, and migration studies, among others. While we recognize that the long history of global flows of both people and goods goes back to the sixteenth century, in line with the scope of this volume, the chapters trace the history of flows of material expert practices within the time scale of Republican Turkey. Part III demonstrates that gaining a comprehensive understanding of material politics in Turkey necessitates broadening our analytical horizon by not only considering the role of more-than-humans but also examining human encounters across differences.

The chapters in this part challenge the mainstream studies of technology and expertise transfer that address the question from an innovation and/or developmentalist perspective by highlighting the contested, partial, and divergent nature of these flows. In this regard, the notion of "translation" addresses the role of local material and political processes in embracing, challenging, or resisting new technologies and knowledges (Türem and Ballestero 2014; Savcı 2021). In her book on the production of modernization theory in Turkey within the context of the Cold War, Begüm Adalet (2018, 4) has underlined that "theories do not hover above and independent from their destinations but rather are manufactured in material spaces where they can be worked out, refined, and given more definite form." This process of expertise production in material sites, as Adalet meticulously demonstrates, occurs through encounters between actors within transnational networks of knowledge- and policy-making. Drawing on a line of research that traces such connections through practices and encounters in particular sites (Tsing 2004), the chapters in this part examine the making of material politics by focusing on flows of knowledges, techniques, and technologies across nation-state boundaries that take a particular shape in specific contexts.

Part III opens with Sertaç Şen's chapter on everyday life and material encounters at an American military base in Turkish Thrace during the Cold War. Analyzing how the globally expanding US military presence and nuclear partnership took shape in concrete localities and through material relations between soldiers from different countries, as well as civilian employees and town inhabitants, Şen reveals the production of new political subjectivities and the negotiation of local authority through the circulation of ordinary objects that the American military presence made available in this process. Shifting the focus from a military base and the related everyday objects to the body as a material site of governance, Can Evren's chapter explores in detail the meeting minutes of a large Sports Council that took place in 1946, to trace the debates and negotiations over diverse technoscientific paradigms of athletic nation-building. In doing so, Evren sheds light on the contentions over the transnationally circulating sources of knowledge and practice, to be tapped into by the institutional processes of governing and modernizing the athletic citizen body as a material entity. The result is an analysis of the contentious encounter between biomedical-scientific and *ampirik* visions of expertise and authority in matters of sports governance, as mobilized by the members of different professional domains. Part III closes with another contentious encounter on material grounds, as examined by Tarık Nejat Dinç. This last chapter offers an ethnographic inquiry into the global expansion of gold mining into Turkey in the 1990s, engendering a socio-environmental conflict in Bergama, centered on the technopolitics of risk. By analyzing the material conditions and infrastructures (such as cyanidation) that made the global gold rush possible, while also producing sites of toxicity such as waste dams, Dinç demonstrates how the farming communities of Bergama draw on their long-standing expertise in engaging with more-than-human landscapes of uncertainty and risk in their anti-mining resistance. Altogether, these three chapters close the book with an analysis of material politics beyond the scale of the nation-state and by tracing transnational politics, as they unfold in particular settings and through situated relations. As Adalet states in her commentary, together these chapters contend that the terrain of a transnational material politics is shaped by those who are not passive recipients of exported expert knowledge and technologies, but active agents in transforming them, putting them to use, or challenging them.

Notes

1 For an analysis of the role of sacrificial politics in shaping the process of dam-building in Yusufeli, see Kurtiç (2022).

2 See https://www.trtizle.com/belgesel/turkiyenin-dev-yapilari

3 Anthropologist Tim Ingold's essay titled "Materials against Materiality" (2007) investigates what analysts mean when they speak of "materiality" and underlines the contingent meanings that it takes. In this introduction, we do not aim to directly differentiate between the analyses of "materials" and "materiality." Nevertheless, analytically speaking, it is worth mentioning the "two sides to materiality" (Ingold 2012): brute materiality—that is, materiality in terms of physicality and human beings appropriating this physicality for their purposes (p. 432). Ongoing materiality studies go beyond such a dualistic understanding of materiality (such as the terms of symbolic vs. physical).

4 This also explains why we chose not to employ the concept of "material powers" as a framework for this edited collection. Nevertheless, readers will find parallels between

this book and the volume edited by Bennett and Joyce (2013), titled *Material Powers: Cultural Studies, History, and the Material Turn. Material Powers* is exemplary of what is considered the "material turn" in the social sciences and unpacks how power is made and exercised.

5 For a survey on the conceptions of politics appearing in STS works, see Brown (2015).

References

Açıksöz, Salih Can. 2019. *Sacrificial Limbs: Masculinity, Disability, and Political Violence in Turkey*. Oakland: University of California Press.

Adalet, Begüm. 2018. *Hotels and Highways: The Construction of Modernization Theory in Cold War Turkey*, Stanford, CA: Stanford University Press.

Adaman, Fikret, Murat Arsel, and Bengi Akbulut. 2018. "Neoliberal Developmentalism, Authoritarian Populism, and Extractivism in the Countryside: The Soma Mining Disaster in Turkey," in Ian Scoones, Marc Edelman, Saturnino M. Borras Jr., Lyda Fernanda Forero, Ruth Hall, Wendy Wolford, and Ben White (eds.), *Authoritarian Populism and the Rural World*, 154–77, Oxon: Routledge.

Anand, Nikhil. 2017. *Hydraulic City: Water and the Infrastructures of Citizenship in Mumbai*, Durham: Duke University Press.

Arican, Alize. 2020. "Behind the Scaffolding: Manipulations of Time, Delays and Power in Tarlabasi, Istanbul," *City & Society* 32 (3): 482–507.

Babül, Elif. 2017. *Bureaucratic İntimacies: Translating Human Rights in Turkey*. Stanford: Stanford University Press.

Barad, Karen. 2003. "Posthumanist Performativity: Toward an Understanding of How Matter Comes to Matter," *Signs: Journal of Women in Culture and Society* 28 (3): 801–31.

Barry, Andrew. 2013. *Material Politics: Disputes along the Pipeline*, Chichester: Wiley-Blackwell.

Barry, Andrew. 2020. "The Material Politics of Infrastructure," in S. Maasen, S. Dickel, and C. Schneider (eds.), *TechnoScienceSociety*, 91–109, Cham: Springer.

Beck, Ulrich. 2007. "The Cosmopolitan Condition: Why Methodological Nationalism Fails," *Theory, Culture & Society*, 24 (7–8): 286–90.

Bennett, Tony and Patrick Joyce, eds. 2013. *Material Powers: Cultural Studies, History and the Material Turn*, London, New York: Routledge.

Bozdoğan Sibel. 2001. *Modernism and Nation Building: Turkish Architectural Culture in the Early Republic*, Seattle: University of Washington Press.

Braun, Bruce, and Sarah J. Whatmore, ed. 2010. *Political Matter: Technoscience, Democracy, and Public Life*, Minneapolis, London: University of Minnesota Press.

Brown, Mark B. 2015. "Politicizing Science: Conceptions of Politics in Science and Technology Studies," *Social Studies of Science* 45 (1): 3–30.

Bulut, Ergin, Başak Can, and Nurçin Ileri. 2020. "Cementing Hegemony in New Turkey: The Construction Spectacle in Istanbul and the Rise of Right-Wing Masculine Populism," in Cameron McCarthy, Koeli Moitra Goel, Ergin Bulut, Warren Crichlow, Brenda Nyandiko Sanya and Bryce Henson (eds.), *Spaces of New Colonialism: Reading Schools, Museums, and Cities in the Tumult of Globalization*, 121–40, New York: Peter Lang Publishing.

Carse, Ashley. 2014. *Beyond the Big Ditch: Politics, Ecology, and Infrastructure at the Panama Canal*, Cambridge: MIT Press.

Çaylı, Eray. 2021. "The Aesthetics of Extractivism: Violence, Ecology, and Sensibility in Turkey's Kurdistan," *Antipode* 53 (5): 1377–99.

Chilvers, Jason and Matthew Kearnes. 2015. *Remaking Participation: Science, Environment and Emergent Publics*, London, New York: Routledge.

De La Bellacasa, Maria Puig. 2017. *Matters of Care: Speculative Ethics in More Than Human Worlds*, Minneapolis: University of Minnesota Press.

Dissard, Laurent. 2017. "From Shining Icons of Progress to Contested Infrastructures: "Damming" the Munzur Valley in Eastern Turkey," in Fatma M. Göçek (ed.), *Contested Spaces in Contemporary Turkey: Environmental, Urban and Secular Politics*, 229–57, London, New York: I.B. Tauris.

Erensü, Sinan. 2018. "Powering Neoliberalization: Energy and Politics in the Making of a New Turkey," *Energy Research & Social Science* 41: 148–57.

Evered, Kyle T. and Emine Ö. Evered. 2012. "State, Peasant, Mosquito: The Biopolitics of Public Health Education and Malaria in Early Republican Turkey," *Political Geography* 31 (5): 311–23.

Evren, Erdem. 2021. "Tenses of Violence: Ruination and Accumulation Along the Çoruh Valley," in Yael Navaro, Z. Ö. Biner, A. von Bieberstein, and S. Altuğ (eds.), *Reverberations: Violence Across Time and Space*, 233–254, Philadelphia: University of Pennsylvania Press.

Folch, Christine. 2019. *Hydropolitics: The Itaipu Dam, Sovereignty, and the Engineering of Modern South America*, Princeton: Princeton University Press.

Fredericks, Rosalind. 2018. *Garbage Citizenship: Vital Infrastructures of Labor in Dakar, Senegal*, Durham: Duke University Press.

Harris, Leila. 2012. "State as Socionatural Effect: Variable and Emergent Geographies of the State in Southeastern Turkey," *Comparative Studies of South Asia, Africa and the Middle East* 32 (1): 25–39.

Harvey, Penny. 2015. "Materials," Theorizing the Contemporary, *Fieldsights*, September 24. https://culanth.org/fieldsights/materials

Hayles, N. Katherine. 1999. *How We Became Posthuman: Virtual Bodies in Cybernetics, Literature, and Informatics*, Chicago, London: The University of Chicago Press.

Hetherington, Kregg and Jeremy M. Campbell. 2014. "Nature, Infrastructure, and the State: Rethinking Development in Latin America," *The Journal of Latin American and Caribbean Anthropology* 19 (2): 191–4.

Hilgartner, Stephen, Clark Miller, and Rob Hagendijk, eds. 2015. *Science and Democracy: Making Knowledge and Making Power in the Biosciences and Beyond*, New York, Oxon: Routledge.

Hoyng, Rolien and Murat Es. 2020. "Material Politics Facing Post-Truth: Speculation, Infrastructure, and Ecology in Turkey," *Antipode* 52 (6): 1731–50.

Ingold, Tim. 2007. "Materials against Materiality," *Archaeological Dialogues* 14 (1): 1–16.

Ingold, Tim. 2012. "Toward an Ecology of Materials," *Annual Review of Anthropology* 41: 427–42.

Irwin, Alan and Brian Wynne, eds. 2004. *Misunderstanding Science?: The Public Reconstruction of Science and Technology*, Cambridge: Cambridge University Press.

Islar, Mine. 2012. "Struggles for Recognition: Privatisation of Water Use Rights of Turkish Rivers," *Local Environment*, 17 (3): 317–29.

Jasanoff, Sheila, ed. 2006. *States of Knowledge: The Co-production of Science and the Social Order*, London, New York: Routledge.

Jensen, Casper Bruun. 2015. "Experimenting with Political Materials: Environmental Infrastructures and Ontological Transformations," *Distinktion: Scandinavian Journal of Social Theory* 16: 17–30.
Joyce, Patrick. 2003. *The Rule of Freedom: Liberalism and the Modern City*, London: Verso.
Kasdogan, Duygu. 2017. "Potentiating Algae, Modernizing Bioeconomies: Algal Biofuels, Bioenergy Economies, and Built Ecologies in the United States and Turkey," PhD diss., York University.
Kezer, Zeynep. 2015. *Building Modern Turkey: State, Space, and Ideology in the Early Republic,* Pittsburgh: University of Pittsburgh Press.
Kurtiç, Ekin. 2022. "Living with a Future Submergence: Dams, Temporality and Sacrifice in Northeastern Turkey," *POMEPS Studies: Environmental Politics in the Middle East and North Africa* 46: 15–20.
Kurtiç, Ekin. 2023. "Infrastructural Decay: Maintenance Ecologies and Labor in the Çoruh Basin," *Cultural Anthropology* 38 (1): 142–70.
Kurtiç, Ekin and Joanne Randa Nucho. 2022. "Infrastructural Politics in the Middle East and North Africa: Past, Present: Future," *Environment and Planning D: Society and Space* 40 (6). https://doi.org/10.1177/02637758221114437
Law, John and Annemarie Mol. 1995. "Notes on Materiality and Sociality," *The Sociological Review* 43 (2): 274–94.
Li, Tania M. 2007. *The Will to Improve: Governmentality, Development, and the Practice of Politics,* Durham: Duke University Press.
Massicard, Elise. 2022. *Street-Level Governing: Negotiating the State in Urban Turkey*. Stanford: Stanford University Press.
Mitchell, Timothy. 2002. *Rule of Experts: Egypt, Techno-politics, Modernity*, Berkeley, Los Angeles, London: University of California Press.
Mitchell, Timothy. 2011. *Carbon Democracy: Political Power in the Age of Oil*, London, New York: Verso.
Mol, Annemarie. 2002. *The Body Multiple: Ontology in Medical Practice,* Durham: Duke University Press.
Moore, Kelly, Daniel Lee Kleinman, David Hess, and Scott Frickel. 2011. "Science and Neoliberal Globalization: A Political Sociological Approach," *Theory and Society* 40 (5): 505–32.
Navaro, Yashin, Zerrin Ozlem Biner, Alice von Bieberstein, and Seda Altug. 2021. "Introduction," in Yael Navaro, Z. Ö. Biner, A. von Bieberstein, and S. Altuğ (eds.) *Reverberations: Violence Across Time and Space*, 1–28, Philadelphia: University of Pennsylvania Press.
Nucho, Joanne Randa. 2016. *Everyday Sectarianism in Urban Lebanon: Infrastructures, Public Services, and Power,* Princeton, NJ: Princeton University Press.
Nye, D. E. 1996. *American Technological Sublime,* MIT Press.
Olsen, Bjørnar. 2007. "Keeping Things at Arm's Length: A Genealogy of Asymmetry," *World Archaeology* 39 (4): 579–88.
Özbilge, Nevcihan. 2020. *Çekirgeler, Kürtler ve Devlet: Erken Cumhuriyet Dönemine Yeniden Bakmak,* Tarih Vakfı Yurt Yayınları.
Özkan, Hande. 2013. "Cultivating the Nation in Nature: Forestry and Nation-Building in Turkey," PhD Dissertation. New Haven, CT: Yale University Press.
Paker, Hande. 2017. "The 'Politics of Serving' and Neoliberal Developmentalism: The Megaprojects of the AKP as Tools of Hegemony Building," in Fikret Adaman, B. Akbulut, and M. Arsel (eds.), *Neoliberal Turkey and Its Discontents: Economic Policy and the Environment Under Erdoğan*, 103–19, London: I.B. Tauris.

Pilo', Francesca, and Rivke Jaffe. 2020. "Introduction: The Political Materiality of Cities," *City & Society* 32 (1): 8–22.
Prakash, Gyan. 1999. *Another Reason: Science and the Imagination of Modern India*, Princeton: Princeton University Press.
Pries, Ludger. 2009. "Transnationalisation and the Challenge of Differentiated Concepts of Space," *Tijdschrift Voor Economische En Sociale Geografie* 100 (5): 587–97.
Savcı, Evren. 2021. *Queer in Translation: Sexual Politics under Neoliberal Islam*, Durham, London: Duke University Press.
Scaramelli, Caterina. 2021. *How to Make A Wetland: Water and Moral Ecology in Turkey*, Stanford: Stanford University Press.
Stahl, Dale J. 2019. "A Technopolitical Frontier: The Keban Dam Project and Southeastern Anatolia," in Onur Inal, and E. Turhan (eds.), *Transforming Socio-Natures in Turkey*, 31–51. Oxon, New York: Routledge.
Stamatopoulou-Robbins, Sophia. 2019. *Waste Siege: The Life of Infrastructure in Palestine*, Stanford: Stanford University Press.
Subramaniam, Banu. 2019. *Holy Science: The Biopolitics of Hindu Nationalism*, Seattle: University of Washington Press.
Suni, Anoush Tamar. 2023. "Historical Alchemy: Buried Gold, Buried Pasts," *Anthropological Quarterly* 96 (2): 335–60.
Tekeli İlhan and Ilkin Selim. 2004. *Cumhuriyetin Harcı: Modernin Altyapısı Oluşurken*, İstanbul: Tarih Vakfı Yayınları.
Türem, Z. Umut and Andrea Ballestero. 2014. "Regulatory Translations: Expertise and Affect in Global Legal Fields," *Indiana Journal of Global Legal Studies* 21 (1): 1–25.
Tsing, Anna. 2004. *Friction: An Ethnography of Global Connection*, Princeton: Princeton University Press.
Von Schnitzler, Antina. 2016. *Democracy's Infrastructure: Techno-Politics & Protest after Apartheid*, Princeton: Princeton University Press.
Wimmer, Andreas and Nina Glick Schiller. 2002. "Methodological Nationalism and Beyond: Nation–State Building, Migration and the Social Sciences," *Global Networks* 2(4): 301–34.
Woolgar, Steve and Javier Lezaun. 2013. "The Wrong Bin Bag: A Turn to Ontology in Science and Technology Studies?" *Social Studies of Science* 43: 321–40.
Yıldırım, Deniz and Evren Haspolat. 2020. "Türkiye'de Hegemonya ve Karşı Hegemonya Stratejileri Bağlamında Yol Siyaseti: Fatsa Örneği," *Fiscaoeconomia* 4 (3): 661–704.
Yıldırım, Umut. 2022. "Resistant Roots: Occupation Ecologies on the Shores of Tigris River," *Jadaliyya*, March 21. https://www.jadaliyya.com/Details/43956

Part I

The Politics of Infrastructure

1

Water Pipes versus Power Lines

GAP Between the Promises and Practices of Infrastructure Buildup

Aybike Alkan

In its third five-year development plan (1973–7), Turkey's State Planning Organization (*Devlet Planlama Teşkilatı*, DPT) adopted the term "localities with priority in development" as a step toward eliminating regional disparities. The plan noted that the future development of these localities, each of which referred to single provinces, should be achieved in accordance with the principles of national unity and integrity (DPT 1973, 947–9).[1] Designed after the 1971 coup,[2] the plan was politically more cautious when compared to the previous two plans, and it intentionally refrained from using the word *bölge* (Turkish for region). This was because *bölge* euphemistically signified southeastern Turkey and was used in leftist and Kurdish circles as an allusion to the long-banned term Kürdistan, an administrative unit of the Ottoman Empire, which later on referred to the imagined Kurdish homeland (Açıksöz 2020). In this regard, the introduction of the term "localities" (*yöre*) in itself served as a strategy to avoid regional planning in a political setting, where marking specific regions, even for technical purposes, was considered a threat to national unity. This strategy also supported the decreasing focus on regional disparities and, thereby, the adoption of an economically oriented development approach (Tekeli 1972). Accordingly, the DPT plan stated that investment decisions should be based on national economic growth, and regional disparities should be considered in the long term, so as not to slow down economic development in Turkey (DPT 1973, 122).

Despite all efforts to avoid using a regional scale as the object of development plans, statistics on economic and social indicators, surveys on the population's cultural habits and values, and maps showing the distribution of electoral votes among political parties all delineated Southeast Anatolia as a distinct region. This distinct character was to an important extent derived from the region's ethnic composition. For example, according to a survey on social change in Southeast Anatolia, the region was ethnically very diverse with its Arab, Assyrian, Kurdish, Turkish, and Turkmen communities, and around 70 percent of the village population spoke Kurdish as their mother tongue (Gökçe et al. 2010, 37). When state actors recognized this distinctiveness, they tended to explain this distinct character, as well as the insurgence of Kurdish communities demanding greater political and cultural rights, as a problem of economic underdevelopment. This recognition was also interwoven with the racialization of Kurds and, accordingly, attributed to them racial stereotypes such as a natural propensity to violence, crudeness, hypersexuality, and gullibility (Duruiz 2021). The making of the Southeast Anatolia Project (*Güneydoğu Anadolu Projesi*, GAP) was significantly affected by this dilemma between the recognition and denial of the idea of a *region* together with its different meanings and practices of recognition.

The GAP was introduced in 1977 as a project of integrated river basin planning (IRBP) that refers to the unified multipurpose development of a river basin. Accordingly, it was intended to harness the Euphrates and Tigris Rivers for the multipurpose development of southeastern Turkey. It consisted of thirteen main projects, with seven on the Euphrates and six on the Tigris. The major project was the Lower Euphrates Project, which included the Atatürk Dam, the GAP's centerpiece. Demirel, a US-trained civil engineer, stood as an important figure behind the initiation of the GAP and particularly the Lower Euphrates Project. Between the mid-1960s and 1970s, he formed several governments, and when the GAP entered Turkey's development agenda, he served as prime minister. Yet, justifying the GAP was not an easy endeavor because of the political situation in Southeast Anatolia.

Before the foundation of the Republic of Turkey, Kurds had been able to operate semiautonomously in the region under the rule of the Ottoman Empire. When the Republic's founders adopted Turkish nationalism as the new state's official and hegemonic ideology, Kurds were subsumed under the category of Muslim Turkish citizens (Bozarslan 2008). This new conception of citizenship and the accompanying denial of Kurdish identity not only determined the trajectory of the "Kurdish issue" but also led to a new understanding of the Kurdish-populated regions in Turkey. Although the trajectory of the GAP and the Kurdish conflict cannot be solely explained in relation to each other, the GAP progressed simultaneously with the Kurdish resistance, which led to close combat between the Turkish Army and the PKK (*Partiya Karkerên Kurdistan*, Kurdistan Workers' Party). The first attack by the PKK occurred in 1984, and in the following years, the PKK's attacks intensified in response to the acts of the Turkish state, conducted in the name of either security or development.

In this chapter, I focus on the GAP's water infrastructures and the assemblages formed by them in order to show how Turkey's political dilemmas and the accompanying prioritization of rapid economic growth shifted the geographical scale of development, from what was deemed to be the GAP region, to the scale of the province at times and to that of the nation at other times. In doing so, I argue that the GAP has failed as a regional development project due to the up- and down-scaling of the geographies of infrastructural development. Susan Leigh-Star has argued that infrastructures and the relations around them become visible only when they fail. Uzmay (2025) offers an approach that departs from the visibility versus invisibility dichotomy and shows how states of visibility were in flux during the modernization of Istanbul's water infrastructure. In this chapter, I challenge the notion of visibility as the outcome of failure and emphasize how visible operations of infrastructures can motivate political failure. Apart from this, I use failure as an analytical concept to show what kinds of politics were involved during and after infrastructural development and address the cleavages between how the GAP was designed and what it became, from its inception (the 1970s) until its targeted completion date, as it appeared in the GAP Master Plan (early 2000s). While doing so, I offer an analysis on the basis of a particular scale, the river basin, and in relation to the criteria defined according to the concept of IRBP.

It is not surprising that IRBP projects usually take a longer time than expected due to their large scale and the multiplicity of parameters that include technical, social, and financial aspects of implementation. Over the years, targets are usually revised, as was the case with the GAP. The GAP Master Plan (1989) was followed by several other plans such as the GAP Regional Development Plan 2002, the GAP Action Plan 2008, and the GAP Action Plan 2014. Yet, it remains important to examine what happened between the GAP Master Plan and the succeeding plans, and why the revision became necessary. The existing hydropower literature in Turkey provides valuable insights into this transformation, as it underscores the shift toward neoliberalization in water and energy policies within the country, a shift that commenced in the early 1980s (Kibaroğlu, Baskan, and Alp 2009; Islar 2012; Eren 2018). This study will consider how bureaucrats and politicians responded to a range of parameters that extended beyond purely economic considerations regarding the implementation and what they prioritized in this process. Moreover, temporality is an important dimension for IRBP projects since it is usually the case that one project's output becomes another project's input. In this respect, the failure to implement an infrastructure project in an orderly and coordinated manner means a waste of resources that creates financial difficulties for the continuation of IRBP projects. Therefore, I focus on a specific period of the GAP's history, paying attention to the Master Plan targets.

Since its initiation in 1977, the GAP has achieved several important targets while failing to hit others. In this respect, the GAP's history allows for two contradictory perspectives: one focusing on failures, and the other focusing on successes (Bilgen et al. 2021). This contradiction in itself is telling when explored through the perspective of scale: who benefited from the project and who did not, and what does this differentiation tell us about the scales of development? Several existing studies approach the GAP in terms of its differential effects. Harris (2012) has focused on the issue of resource access to argue that the GAP's water infrastructures led to a spatial differentiation within the project region. Özerol and Bressers (2017) have discussed the effects of large-scale irrigation on the reproduction of social differentiation in terms of the locals' financial capacity and land ownership. There also exist several studies showing how the benefits of irrigation infrastructure turned into agricultural problems due to parts missing from the irrigation assemblages, mainly the lack or slow development of drainage systems (Kudat and Bayram 2000; Jongerden, Sıla Akıncı, and Ayboğa 2021). Examining narratives on the GAP's effects, Bilgen (2018a) has emphasized the situatedness of the evaluations and drawn attention to the connection between the differential experiences of the project and the conceptions of the GAP as beneficial or harmful. This chapter proceeds in a similar direction; it identifies the GAP's differential effects, and it claims that these effects can be read as indicators of failure when considered in relation to the idea of integrated development. It does so by focusing on the physical constellations of energy and irrigation infrastructures and using insights from the recent literature on infrastructure studies.

The field of infrastructure studies, growing at the intersection of sociology, anthropology, and critical geography, shows that infrastructures are both political actors themselves and materialized articulations of political life (Anand 2012, 2017; Appel, Anand, and Gupta 2018; Barry 2020; von Schnitzler 2008). According to this growing literature, infrastructures can enact political action as they are assembled or networked together with nonmaterial, social elements. In this regard, the conceptual framework of the field extensively builds on assemblage theory and actor–network theory (ANT). Although they are sometimes used interchangeably or complementarily (see, e.g., Swyngedouw 2015), assemblage theory concentrates more on the process of "becoming," something that has no prior existence, while ANT concentrates on the relations between already existing elements (Müller 2015). This chapter adopts the perspective of assemblage theory in its effort to show how a given infrastructure becomes different things as it spatially expands. In the context of the GAP, this means a focus on how dams cover larger territories as they are linked with hydropower plants, electricity transmission lines, irrigation tunnels, canals, and pipes.

Kaşdoğan and Kurtiç, in their introduction to this volume, underline different dimensions through which materials can acquire political significance and identify material politics as an approach to focus on the coproduction of materials and politics. This chapter follows this approach, shedding light on how various aspects and elements within water infrastructure converge and undergo transformation into political entities. As Barry suggests, socio-material worlds produced by infrastructures rely on their relations with further infrastructures that have their own materiality and spatiality (Barry 2020, 104). Building on Barry, but with a focus on the assembled spatiality of infrastructures, this chapter draws attention to the connections between the different components of large-scale energy and irrigation infrastructures. In doing so, it shows that infrastructures become political in that they create spatial differentiation and inequality between social groups (McFarlane and Rutherford 2008). Analyzing the processes of infrastructural extension, regardless of that extension's scale, helps us to see how the material interventions in an environment are interwoven with political circumstances when it comes to decisions about their making and the interpretation of those decisions.

In what follows, I first introduce how the materialities of water and electricity, especially in terms of their transportation, link the development of irrigation infrastructure more closely to the idea of regional development. Then, I turn to high-ranking bureaucrats' decisions on infrastructure buildup, which created gaps in the actual construction of irrigation and energy projects. While the first section provides a basis for the discussion in the second part, the latter supports the argument about the GAP's failure as an IRBP project by focusing on the energy bias of high-ranking bureaucrats. It does so by revealing how infrastructural decisions were oriented toward the goal of national economic growth rather than the welfare of the population living within the project's region. Recognizing that the uneven development of energy and irrigation infrastructures cannot be explained solely by the appeal of electricity, the third section provides further explanations for this unevenness. It diagnoses the problems underlying the development of irrigation infrastructure, mainly land ownership issues and the accompanying processes of managing the local population. The fourth part discusses the implications of this unevenness in terms of the reiteration of preexisting inequalities and further emphasizes how infrastructures function as politics of differentiation. Overall, the chapter connects the process of building the GAP's infrastructures to the political reservations of the GAP's designers in terms of thinking and acting at a regional scale. In this light, the material politics of infrastructure appear as enmeshed with a politics of scale, mirrored by the practices of scaling infrastructural assemblages.

This research draws on discourse and content analysis of archival data, semi-structured interviews, and secondary literature. The archives include (1) the proceedings of the Grand National Assembly of Turkey (TBMM), (2) the reports and action plans of the DPT and GAP-Regional Development Administration (*GAP-Bölgesel Kalkınma İdaresi*; GAP-BKİ), and (3) the daily newspaper *Cumhuriyet*. The interviews were undertaken in different periods between 2016 and 2019, in Adıyaman, Ankara, and Urfa (also known as Şanlıurfa) with former or current personnel of the State Hydraulic Works (*Devlet Su İşleri*, DSİ) and the GAP-BKİ. In addition to experts and state officials, I also interviewed village heads and the staff of nongovernmental organizations. The interviewees were chosen based on snowball and sequential sampling techniques; in total, thirty-one interviews were conducted.[3]

Priorities of River Use: (Dis)integrated River Basin Planning

In the post-Second World War era, when ideas of development and regional differences became popular, the concept of IRBP provided an appealing vision for water development. IRBP, as identified by geographer Gilbert White (1957), is associated with three major principles: the multipurpose approach, the basin-wide program, and comprehensive regional development. These principles entail the simultaneous planning of any given river basin in such a way that it includes several construction projects for developmental purposes, ranging from electricity production to irrigation, navigation, and flood prevention. As the principle of regional development implies, regardless of the extent to which they are achieved, river basin projects are projects of scale-making—that is, marking and making a region through both discourse and practice (Molle 2007; Swyngedouw 2015). For this reason, regional development is synonymously used with river development in the context of IRBP projects such as the Tennessee Valley Authority (TVA), the federal corporation established to tackle the problems experienced in the Tennessee Valley, which then became a famous model for river management in the postwar years. For the TVA and the projects that it inspired, the success of regional development depended on the coordinated and orderly implementation of the plan.

Yet, sometimes, one purpose of development dominated over others and violated the idea of integration between different purposes of development; consequently, the boundaries of the river basin were widened or narrowed based on political, social, and economic considerations at hand. This change of boundaries was mostly due to decisions about infrastructure buildup. While some infrastructures benefit the environment in which they are built, the benefits of other projects can be carried to remote environments through interconnected networks of infrastructure, which may create a problem for the principle of regional development. The differentiation that David Harvey has made between territory and place is telling here. According to Harvey, the political economy of territory is about economic projects aimed at improving the conditions of a particular zone, such as housing or education. The political economy of place, however, is at stake when economic projects have an impact on territories smaller or greater than the one within which they are to be implemented (Harvey 1989). This differentiation, to a certain extent, relates to the difference between electricity generation and irrigation projects. Although the benefits of irrigation development (e.g., agricultural products) can be transported to distant places and support industries in faraway regions, water as the immediate benefit of irrigation infrastructure is relatively hard to transport, which means that the territory of agricultural production and employment will depend more on where the source of water is located.

Unlike water, electricity can easily be carried to distant places once the transmission infrastructure is built and connected to the electricity-generating facilities. Since electricity lends itself to long-distance transportation, hydropower dams might undermine the regional development principle of integrated river basin development. Hence, electricity generation may not have a positive effect on the place where the production facility is located, even though the production process usually harms nearby areas due to land use, environmental pollution during construction, and the disruption of ecological relations. Unlike electricity-generating facilities, irrigation systems expand in a limited way, and this limited expansion favors regional development by supporting agricultural production near where that very infrastructure is located. These differences between the materiality of electricity and water when it comes to their transportability provide an entry point for analyzing the politics of infrastructures in terms of (re)producing spatial differentiation in the context of the GAP.

When large-scale river basin projects were announced in Turkey after the 1950s, irrigation was the basis on which state elites justified projects to the residents of the concerned regions. In the context of GAP, both left- and right-wing political parties emphasized the importance of irrigated agriculture for the development of the project's region. For example, Hikmet Çetin, the deputy of the Social Democratic Populist Party, underlined the importance of irrigation for achieving regional development with the following words:

> Energy is a transportable good, you produce it somewhere and then carry it where it is needed, where there are energy shortages. And the places of energy shortage are where the industries are located. Therefore, it does not mean that the energy produced in this region [Southeast Anatolia] will be used here. [. . .] To develop the region, the project needs to focus on irrigation alongside energy production. (TBMM 1988a, 622)

Also, for the right-wing leader Demirel, irrigation was a geographical, social, and economic imperative (Turgut 2000, 63), whereas Özal, who competed with Demirel over the GAP's ownership, referred to its Lower Euphrates component as the most important project in Turkey (TBMM 1984). Nevertheless, the discursive emphasis on irrigation did not match the infrastructural investments, as the uneven completion of energy and irrigation infrastructure projects as well as the prioritization of the latter show.

Regardless of the close connection between irrigation infrastructure and the principle of regional development, the provinces affected by the GAP had already relied on agriculture, making irrigation an inevitable component of the project. Unlike other regions in Turkey where market-oriented and mechanized agricultural production had been developed between 1950 and 1975, traditional peasantry and subsistence agriculture persisted in eastern and southeastern Turkey (Keyder and Yenal 2014, 160). The GAP was the first important intervention by state leaders in the name of overcoming the economic problems persisting in the country's southeastern parts. The project intended to irrigate 1.7 million hectares of land, which corresponds to 20 percent of Turkey's total irrigable land. Accordingly, the discourses around the GAP were constructed by referencing Çukurova, a previous notable example of large-scale irrigated agriculture located in the fertile lands of southern Turkey. This reference was also important since Çukurova had become a source of income for many unemployed people in the GAP region (see Figure 1.1). Now, the promise was to put an end to the locals' migration to Çukurova and to bring irrigation to them. These were significant aspects of regional development as articulated by politicians and bureaucrats.

In this scheme, electricity was to be the input for agricultural production, especially for the transportation of pumped water and for fueling industrial development in the region. The complementary relationship between agricultural and industrial development was also recognized in the Master Plan. The plan stated that advancements in irrigated agriculture would eventually require the establishment of industries that would use agricultural products as raw materials (DPT 1989a, 5). This meant that the hydroelectricity generated there would be used for the development of agro-industries around the river basin, although doing so required simultaneously boosting agricultural production. The equal development of irrigation and energy infrastructure, according

Figure 1.1 Geographical distribution of GAP provinces.

to the Master Plan, corresponded to a basic development scenario. In this scenario, the end goal was to make the GAP region "the agro-related export base," by prioritizing energy and irrigation projects of high importance (ibid.).

Despite the planned targets, the GAP's completion was based on the prioritization of electricity over irrigation. Discussions and practices around the Atatürk Dam (1983–90), one of the largest dams in the world, and the irrigation assemblage of which the dam was a part, provide a representative picture to understand how priorities of development affected the materialization and, thereby, material politics of infrastructures. This is what I will discuss below.

Power Lines and Up-Scaling the Region of Development

The Atatürk Dam, located between the provinces of Adıyaman and Urfa, is a large-scale multipurpose dam on the Euphrates River, planned for both energy generation and irrigation development. Apart from its large power capacity, it is connected to the Urfa Irrigation Tunnel System, the GAP's largest irrigation project (see Table 1.1). The system consists of two parallel tunnels of a length of 26.4 kilometers each. The tunnels take water from the Atatürk Dam reservoir and bring it to a canal system at the beginning of the Urfa-Harran Plain. These two canals were supposed to irrigate more than a million hectares of land, stretching from the Atatürk Dam reservoir through Mardin in the East to the Syrian border in the South (Soffer 1999). In that sense, the development of irrigated agriculture depended on assembling infrastructures that

Table 1.1 Irrigation Projects within the GAP's Scope

Projects	Irrigation area (ha)	Targeted Completion date
Urfa Tunnels Irrigation		
Urfa-Harran Irrigation	*141,535*	1992
Mardin-Ceylanpınar 1st Stage	*230,130*	*1996*
Mardin-Ceylanpınar 2nd Stage	*104,809*	*2000*
Siverek Hilvan Pumped Irrigation	160,105	*2002*
Bozova Pumped Irrigation	69,702	1995
Suruç-Baziki Project	146,500	2000
Adıyaman-Kahta Project	77,409	1994
Adıyaman-Göksu-Araban	71,598	1997
Gaziantep Project	81,670	1997
Dicle Right Bank Gravity Irrigation	52,033	1993
Dicle Right Bank Pumped Irrigation	74,047	1993
Batman Left Bank Irrigation	18,986	1993
Batman Right Bank Irrigation	18,758	1993
Batman-Silvan Project	213,000	2001
Garzan Project	60,000	2002
Nusaybin-Cizre-İdil Irrigation	89,000	2002
Silopi Plain Irrigation	32,000	2002
TOTAL	1,641,282	

Source: DPT (1989b).

would carry the water from the dam reservoir to the plains and from the plains to household lands. Once completed, this unified system would be the largest irrigation system of its kind in the world.

In line with the idea of integrated development, the construction of the irrigation tunnels was to be completed before filling the Atatürk Dam reservoir, because the irrigation water would be ready for use after that point (see Figure 1.2). Yet, even before filling the dam, it was clear that the dam was primarily intended for producing electricity since only one-sixth of the available water amount had been allocated for irrigation.[4] Even the state experts in the DSİ admitted that the energy- and agriculture-related decisions of the high-ranking bureaucrats were biased toward electricity from the beginning, and they introduced the GAP as an irrigation project only because they feared resistance from the locals.[5] Among these decision-makers, the Minister of Public Works and Settlement played an important role in prioritizing energy projects over irrigation development (Bilgen 2017, 108). The order of implementing subprojects in the 1990s also indicated this energy bias. As Dağ and Göktürk (1994) argue, the beginning of construction of another dam on the Euphrates, the Birecik Dam and Hydropower Plant, in 1993 was proof of the government's energy bias, because priority was once again given to electricity production, which meant further delays in the development of irrigation infrastructure (86).[6] Accordingly, by 2002, the targeted date for completing irrigation projects, only 18 percent of irrigation investments from the

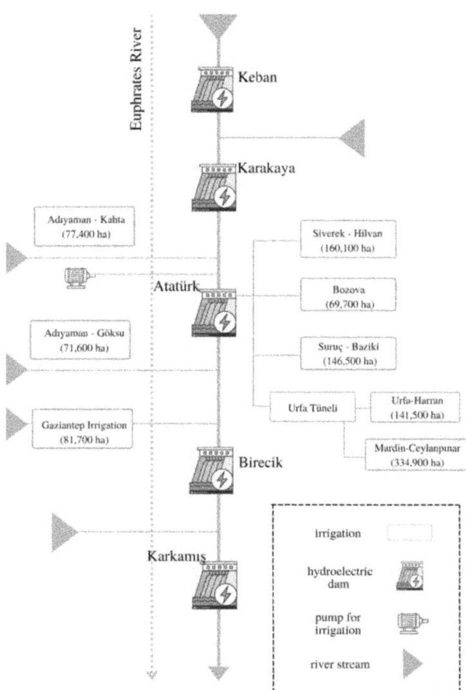

Figure 1.2 Integrated planning of the Euphrates River (drawn by the author using the data from GAP Master Plan 1989).

Master Plan had been realized, while 80 percent of energy projects had been completed (GAP-BKİ 2003).[7]

Turkey was no exception in terms of the planners' energy bias. Electricity generation has been the most important component of basin-wide projects since single-purpose projects gave way to IRBP as the common path for harnessing rivers. Apart from its necessity for the industrial sector and its role as the fuel of modernity, electricity appealed to the state leaders' desire for centralization: electricity can be produced in enormous quantities in one place and then distributed to remote areas. As nation-states strive to achieve a national integration of economy and society, the construction of a national high-voltage grid allows for the national territorial integration of the electricity network, which, in turn, contributes to the former process (Swyngedouw 2015). Still, electricity's appeal was intertwined with several other considerations, leading to different levels of energy prioritization and various implications and meanings for development.

In the case of Turkey, the unbalanced development of infrastructures has exacerbated already existing interregional inequalities because the prioritization of electricity generation has meant greater development of the country's western parts.[8] A deputy from the Republican People's Party, Ayhan Fırat, has summarized the essence of this matter as follows:

> Where are the sites of electricity production? They are in Keban, Afşin-Elbistan, Tigris, Karakaya, and the Atatürk Dam, all of which are located in Southeast and East Anatolia. And where are the sites of electricity consumption? They are in the Northwest of Turkey. The Energy Institution of Turkey will invest 120 billion TL to transport the energy. And consumers in İstanbul are charged the same tariff as villagers in Keban. I ask you: is this social justice? (TBMM 1985, 496)

Fırat's words invite us to follow the pathway of electricity after being produced in southeastern Turkey. Indeed, after the filling of the Atatürk Dam reservoir in 1992, the transmission lines that were to integrate the hydroelectricity plant with the interconnected electricity system had already been ready for operation. The first electricity generation unit was opened in 1992, and by the end of 1993, the plant began operating at full capacity, fueling the industries in Western Turkey (Kıran 2005, 83).

Before the GAP's initiation, when the construction of the first large dam on the Euphrates, the Keban Dam, was launched in 1966, its benefit to the local population had already been a topic of discussion. For example, when the Chamber of Electricity Engineers shared their concerns about the lack of industries as potential electricity consumers in the East, the Ministry of Energy and Natural Resources replied: "Even when we do not consider industries in eastern Turkey, the Keban Dam is still profitable." The chamber demanded a more detailed answer, since the main objective of the Keban Project was to reduce regional inequalities, which meant benefiting the regions near Keban (İMO 1971, 40). The subsequent response of the ministry was once again based on national economic benefits. This communication between the chamber and the ministry was a harbinger of how the GAP would proceed in the following years and how the prioritization of electricity over irrigation would mirror the prioritization of national economic growth over the welfare of people living in the project's region.[9] A clear manifestation of this argument has been the GAP's energy assemblages: through them, the benefits of the subprojects were distributed in a way that deepened spatial differentiations and inequalities within the country. This means that the dams' socio-material conditions and effects changed as they became part of larger energy constellations. Nevertheless, a look at the disparities between the execution of the irrigation project and the completion of the energy project does not provide a full picture of the GAP's effects on spatial differentiation in Turkey. If one side of the coin was the appeal of electricity, which affected the order of implementation and put most of the irrigation projects second in line, then the other side consisted of the difficulties faced before and during the construction of the irrigation infrastructure.

Water Pipes and Down-Scaling the Region of Development

While agriculture constituted the main economic activity in Southeast Anatolia when the GAP was initiated, agricultural production was characterized by an extremely uneven distribution of land. On the Harran Plains, the first place to be irrigated by the Euphrates River under the GAP, 48 percent of the twenty four thousand farming families were landless (Yetkin 1989). The general situation within the GAP region was not different from that of Harran: according to the 1981 Village Inventory Studies, 40.2 percent of the region's population was landless. The distribution of land posed yet another problem in terms of developing infrastructural networks in the region. The spatial structure of ownership was highly fragmented, as the land was divided into small pieces—that is, a farming family often possessed several noncontiguous land plots scattered over a large area. Therefore, at the time when the Urfa Irrigation Tunnels and the Atatürk Dam were under construction, one of the most heated debates around the GAP concerned land reform. Nevertheless, land reform initiatives in Turkey did not gain ground, mostly because of strong opposition from large landowners. Since they were the local powerholders, central state actors relied on them to govern eastern Turkey, especially the southeastern part (Gürel, Küçük, and Taş 2022). Large landowners also had representatives in parliament, which allowed them to oppose any potential land reform program before it could be approved there.[10] Although there existed some attempts to introduce land reform before and after the GAP's initiation, inequality in land ownership and the number of landless families remained virtually static for a long time. To grasp the effects of this failure in the GAP's making, it is necessary to turn our gaze to the institutions involved in the project and how experts conducted their work in conversation with state elites and locals.

Before the establishment of the GAP-BKİ in 1989, the institution responsible for the GAP was the DPT; the latter replaced the DSİ, a state agency responsible for the management of the country's water resources, as the project's administrator in 1986. The initial reservations about making plans at the regional scale persisted under the DPT (Tekeli 2008). As discussed in the introduction, this was mainly due to the political connotations of *bölge*, which often euphemistically referred to southeastern Turkey, a place that state actors perceived as a threat to the state's national unity. In this semantic world, the Turkish translation of regionalism, *bölgecilik*, was a pejorative word, associated with demands for political autonomy and even separatism. Therefore, the establishment of the GAP-BKİ as a result of the project's increasing scale and scope and due to the DPT's administrative failures was an important move in this political context, while also being a politically dangerous act. To minimize this danger, the GAP-BKİ's organizational structure differed from that of its predecessors. For example, the most iconic example of IRBP and the main inspiration for Turkish bureaucrats and politicians in initiating and developing the GAP, the TVA was a semiautonomous regional administration. Since establishing this type of administration carried connotations of federalism in Turkey,[11] the GAP-BKİ remained in limbo as a regional institution that was dependent on the central government for all its activities: even after its establishment, the primary decision-making powers for the GAP remained with the highest-ranking bureaucrats—that is, the cabinet ministers.

The GAP-BKİ's main task was to ensure coordination between different institutions and, more generally, to oversee all development activities within the region. When the GAP-BKİ came onto the scene of regional development, the main responsibility for infrastructure buildup fell on the DSİ, the General Directorate of Rural Services (*Köy Hizmetleri Genel Müdürlüğü*, KHGM), and the General Directorate of Agricultural Reform (*Tarım Reformu Genel Müdürlüğü*, TRGM). In this institutional framework, the responsibility for planning, designing, and constructing large-scale irrigation systems belonged to the DSİ. Once the large-scale infrastructure had been completed, the institution dealt with operation and maintenance without being involved in the construction of subsequent small-scale projects. For on-farm development as well as the planning and construction of small-scale irrigation infrastructure, the KHGM served as the responsible institution. It worked in collaboration with the TRGM to deal with land ownership issues.

The institutional work necessary for building the irrigation infrastructure began with land ownership issues. To be able to use private lands in the GAP's context, state officials usually leased the land for a period of time in order to combine fragmented land parcels and adjust their ownership, a process called land consolidation. In theory, land consolidation should precede any intervention in the land. Yet, TRGM officials sometimes worked on land consolidation only after construction had already started. This meant that they had to stop construction whenever the canal reached a villager's land until an agreement was reached.[12] A DSİ engineer explained this as follows:

> The communication between the DSİ and reform [TRGM] was poor. The DSİ sent the project to the reform, but there were some disputes. After going to the fields and encountering problems, it was demanding from the DSİ to change the projects, and we were trying to do our best. The land consolidation process was getting prolonged, and the state was paying for the citizens' losses. A project that would have been profitable if completed in two years was likely to be profitless if completed in five years.[13]

This quote implies that waste of investment was a serious problem in the GAP's context, as much as underinvestment. The extension of the time frame, necessary to deal with ownership issues, sometimes even led to an invalidation of the subprojects' cost–benefit analysis.

The political power of large landowners vis-à-vis the experts also exacerbated the problems of land consolidation and the accompanying financial deficits.[14] In this respect, even an apparent success story, such as the (belated) completion of the Urfa Irrigation Tunnels, involved a great deal of coordination and administrative problems, which prolonged construction. In the early 2000s, when the GAP's infrastructural development was supposed to be completed, the water flowing through the Urfa Tunnels only reached the province of Urfa and its Harran district. Although the tunnels had been planned to also irrigate the province of Mardin by that date, the canals that would carry the water to Mardin's plains had not been constructed. The problems in constructing and assembling the irrigation infrastructure in an orderly and timely fashion implied a down-scaling of the project benefits in terms of initiating irrigated agriculture, not only in those places that the Urfa Tunnel System was supposed to irrigate, but also over a larger area. Figure 1.3 illustrates the level of this down-scaling for 2002, twenty-five years after the start of the Urfa Tunnels' construction and just three years before the Master Plan's target date for completing all irrigation infrastructure. It does so by showing the proportion of the actually irrigated area in comparison to land available for irrigation; even though Urfa has the largest area of agricultural lands, this proportion was incomparably higher than in the other provinces.

As this section shows, the course of developing the assemblage of irrigation infrastructure has been affected significantly by the material conditions of the project region, such as the unequal land ownership and the spatial distribution of land holdings. This implies an inverse relation between materiality and politics because here it is also materiality that shapes political decisions about infrastructure buildup. The problems posed by the material conditions concern not only the lack of financial and technical means but also how to use and organize them and how to allocate costs and benefits throughout the decision-making processes around the infrastructure buildup.

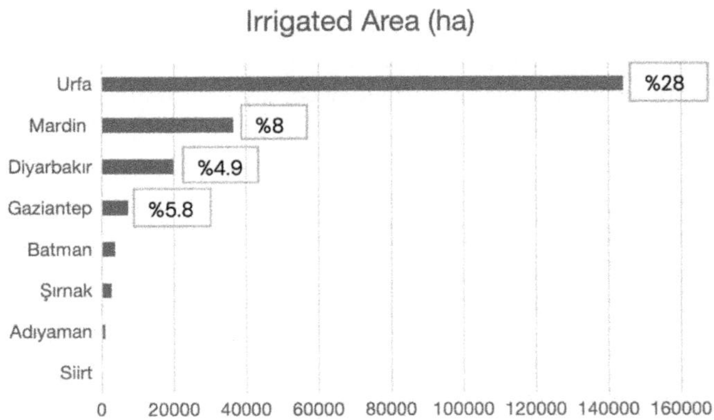

Figure 1.3 The area of irrigated agricultural lands and percentage of irrigated land in proportion to available land by 2002 (GAP-BKİ 2003). Note: The calculation of the irrigated areas is based on irrigation projects under operation. The area of the land to be irrigated is calculated according to the Master Plan targets (DPT 1989b).

The GAP-BKİ, as a regional institution dependent upon the central administration in all of its activities, fell short of ensuring the project's coordinated and integrated implementation at the scale of the GAP's region. Similar to the up-scaling of the electricity network, which intensified the interregional inequalities (between the eastern and western parts of the country), the limited development of the irrigation networks resulted in the project's down-scaling and created intra-regional inequalities. In this regard, the material politics of the GAP's infrastructure were manifested in energy and irrigation assemblages that either went beyond the limits of the GAP region or remained limited to its particular parts, (re)producing spatial differentiations within the country, both inter- and intra-regionally.

The GAP's Implications for Regional Development: Engendering Exclusion and Destabilization

The practices of up- and down-scaling the infrastructural assemblages and their respective benefits are key to seeing how material politics operated through (re) producing spatial differentiation. This also means differentiating between populations included in and excluded from the projects' benefits. The unequal distribution of irrigation benefits, as discussed above, adversely affected relations among locals and between the state and the locals. Whereas a limited segment of the regional population enjoyed the benefits of the Euphrates waters reaching the drylands of Southeast Anatolia, the failure to expand the irrigation network caused a larger segment to resent the project (see Harris 2012). Still, differentiation is as much about the distribution of costs as it is about that of benefits.

The literature on hydropower facilities in Turkey is already extensive, with numerous studies conducted across different regions of the country. These studies consistently reveal the adverse effects of such infrastructure (see, e.g., Islar 2012; Evren 2014; Kurtiç 2023). It comes as no surprise that large-scale hydropower facilities on the Euphrates have caused several social and environmental problems for the locals, who are located far away from electricity-consuming industries (Öktem 2002; Harris 2009, 2012; Hommes, Boelens, and Maat 2016). There was also the issue of resettlement due to the inundation of living spaces: 336 settlements were to be evacuated with the construction of eight dams, leading to the resettlement of approximately 181,000 persons (Jongerden 2007, 112). The problem of dam-induced migration was touched upon by the leader of the Social Democratic Populist Party, Erdal İnönü, in a parliamentary discussion, just after the Atatürk Dam had started to produce electricity:

> We witness an intense migration from Southeast Anatolia. The region is being evacuated rapidly. The latest population census clearly proves this. As a result of the oppression applied to the regional population by government policies, locals are leaving their homes and land and looking for employment and security in other regions. (TBMM 1990, 94)

Therefore, resettlement constituted a problem, made even worse when the local population was sent to remote places. As Deputy Hilmi Ziya Postacı stated, "when you resettle people to places 2,000 km away, it is no longer resettlement, it turns into an exile" (TBMM 1988b, 149). Given these results, one may say that infrastructural development destabilized not only the region itself, but also where its population lived. While electricity flowed from the dams of Southeast Anatolia toward the country's western regions, the locals who had lost their homes and lands scattered to different parts of the country, mostly becoming wage laborers in the industrial sector.

Referring to the uneven distribution of cost and benefit within the GAP's context, the PKK leader Abdullah Öcalan described southeastern Turkey as a colony (Özcan 1999). Building on already existing claims that the region was a colony of the Turkish state,[15] the PKK adopted the view that the state had obstructed the region's development on purpose (ibid., 62). Hence, from its very beginning, the project presented a source of tension between the Kurdish population and the state and contributed to the intensification of the PKK's armed struggle. The first PKK attack occurred in 1984, when the project ramped up due to the construction of the Atatürk Dam and the Urfa Irrigation Tunnels. Turkey's use of the Euphrates also contributed to Syrian support for the PKK's military activities: in the late 1980s, the PKK camps had already been transferred to Syria, and PKK militants infiltrated the Turkish border from those camps (Cumhuriyet 1992).

Strikingly, not only the limited scope of irrigation, but also the way in which it was executed, and especially *where* it was executed, supported claims about the state's malevolent actions toward the Kurdish population. Unlike many other southeastern provinces where the Kurdish political movement was strong, Urfa's population had a high percentage of Arabic-speaking population (about 80–90 percent in the Harran district) and mostly supported the Turkish state (Harris 2009). As explained by a state officer from the TRGM, "Urfa was the buffer zone. Diyarbakır, Mardin, and the rest were the provinces where the Kurdish political movement was strong. In order to not lose their support, the state spoiled the population of Urfa, it spoiled the tribes and large landowners. Here [in Urfa] is the fortress of the state in Southeast Anatolia."[16] In this regard, the political character of the region challenged the modernization processes, through which the transformation of landscapes has usually been about the construction of a new type of citizen in alignment with the ideals of civilization (see, e.g., Özkan 2025).

These were ideas generally accepted among the state officials working in Urfa. Whether they justified the state's actions or not, they pointed to the state's "compassionate" attitude toward the province. This "compassion" was most clearly manifested toward large landowners, which resulted in the maintenance of unequal ownership structures in the region. Referring to the pro-state position of Urfa, Öcalan also claimed that the choice of Urfa for infrastructural development was a politically motivated one. Indicating that the state used dams as a way of showing hostility toward Kurds, he asked: "Why did the irrigation channels not reach Mardin province but only Urfa?" (Öcalan 2015, 13).

Apart from Mardin, Adıyaman also offers a striking example, especially because the Atatürk Dam is located between Adıyaman and Urfa and because the dam raised expectations of irrigated agriculture in both provinces. It should be acknowledged that Urfa was in a more advantageous topographical position for irrigation. Yet, this did not necessarily mean a disadvantage in creating economic opportunities in Adıyaman. Rather, it meant the necessity of building alternative paths:

> Urfa was able to use the water immediately, since the water was flowing easily from high to low levels. So, the aim was to develop agriculture in Urfa and build agricultural industries in Adıyaman, by carrying the agricultural yields there. The previous president of the Chambers of Industry and Commerce built an organized industrial site to develop the textile industry because irrigated agriculture would yield cotton. [. . .] We wanted this place to be the center of production and fashion, but this did not happen.[17]

The economic liberalization and privatization in Turkey throughout the 1980s and 1990s played an important role in the outcome described in this quote from an Adıyaman local. It was evident that the infrastructural development of Southeast Anatolia was not and would not be a concern for the private sector, especially given the close combat between the state and the PKK occurring in the region. For those who advocated for state-led regional development, the rationale was mostly related to the belief that the only solution to the conflict consisted of economic development. Nevertheless, as the head of a businesswomen's association in Adıyaman claimed, state policies fell short of bringing that change:

> After the tobacco quota was imposed upon the pressure of Philip Morris, the government distributed pomegranate saplings to villagers. For years, they put in efforts to produce pomegranates, but when it came to selling their product, they could not do it. They had no connection to markets and no cold storage depots. No one said, let's introduce a new sector to this province. They gave money to large landowners, gave saplings to villagers, and then left them to their fate.

She then added:

> The state should have led the opening of factories at least. [. . .] Adıyaman wanted to produce value-added products, but there was no coordination and synchronization. The state could not inform the citizens; it should have prepared reports and not left the citizens to their fate. [. . .] There is no information on feasibility reports as well. Then I can interpret that the only reason behind the GAP was electricity production.[18]

As Barry has suggested, the material politics of infrastructures should consider the relations between specific infrastructures and the second-order infrastructure of technoscientific knowledge production (Barry 2020, 93). The above quote brings to the fore the importance of this argument. It invites us to further expand our view of irrigation infrastructure in a way that includes other infrastructures related to information exchange. This kind of expansion provides another layer to view the material politics of large dams and their subsequent projects: the assemblages of energy and irrigation are not only about the working conditions of the hardware, but, in order to work effectively according to the promises of IRBP, they also should be supported with administrative components and social networks attuned to the needs of a population larger than was the case for the GAP. In this light, the idea of integrating an irrigation assemblage should consider both agricultural products and how they can serve as input for other projects that could bring welfare to the project region, especially to its most underprivileged populations. While the GAP promised this kind of welfare, its execution led to further differentiation and failed to reconcile the geographical and social inequalities within the region.

Conclusion

As my analysis demonstrates, the material politics of dams is more than the dams themselves; they also include their connections with additional infrastructures. Therefore, the scale of development also becomes a question of how these different infrastructures come together to form assemblages of both electricity production and consumption, irrigation water storage and distribution; which territories these assemblages cover; and how the dam comes to benefit faraway places beyond the territory where it is located. Since the benefit of irrigation infrastructure to its specific location is more obvious, irrigation has served to legitimize IRBP projects in the eyes of river basin populations. Yet, much like these legitimizing claims, the execution of IRBP projects is directly affected by political processes that serve to protect the unified nation-state's structure. In the context of the GAP, these political processes readily went hand in hand with economic motivations; ignorance of regional realities supported the idea of the nation as the fundamental scale of development and shifted the focus from decreasing inter- and intra-regional disparities to national economic growth. This meant further developing the West and, thereby, deepening further the developmental divide between the eastern and western parts of the country. Thus, the GAP dams mostly benefit the economy of those "places" (à la Harvey) where industrial production is concentrated, rather than the "territories" around the dams and the southeastern population.

Despite the high-ranking bureaucrats' energy bias, there were still important improvements in terms of developing irrigated agriculture. The construction of the Urfa Irrigation Tunnels was the most prominent development activity in this respect. The water flowing through these tunnels brought a significant transformation to the agricultural lands on the Harran-Urfa Plains. Yet, these changes affected the local population in different and contrasting ways, along the lines of class and ethnicity. Moreover, irrigated agriculture could not expand in the way that the idea of integration—that is, an orderly and coordinated completion of subprojects—required. This was not a surprising outcome, given the political reservations vis-à-vis thinking and acting at the regional scale, which led to a failure in creating an effective institutional framework for the GAP.

In the end, the enormous discrepancy in the execution of energy versus irrigation projects resulted from both the prioritization of the former—or the prioritization of national economic growth over regional welfare—and incompetence in coordinating the required steps and dealing with the project's increasing expenses. As a result, regardless of the intentions of the GAP's planners, the project had political implications that exceeded the material outcomes of the differentiated distribution of costs and benefits to the local population. Although administrative decisions were made in a way that relieved nationalist anxieties about Kurdish separatism, they bred resentment among the Kurdish population by engendering exclusion and vulnerability, which, in turn, reinforced that anxiety.

Notes

1 Although there existed regional development efforts before this plan, these were mostly planned on the provincial scale, such as the Antalya Project, the Zonguldak Project, and the Çukurova Project.
2 Also known as the coup by memorandum, the 1971 coup occurred in a chaotic setting marked by economic recession, labor strikes, and political assassinations. In the name of bringing order, it led to the brutal repression of unions and strikes and a ban on legal Kurdish organizations.
3 This chapter draws on the data I collected during my doctoral research, which also included interviews with village heads and data from the technical reports of engineers.
4 Personal interview with the president of an Irrigation Association, April 12, 2019, Urfa.
5 Personal interview with DSİ engineers, April 9–11, 2019, Urfa.
6 For a detailed examination of factors behind the GAP's delays, see Bilgen (2018b).
7 According to the GAP-BKİ's latest report, 55 percent of irrigation projects and 91.2 percent of energy projects have been completed. However, the report presents calculations for irrigation projects with respect to the targets of the GAP Action Plan (2008–12). The plan's target for irrigable lands was 1.06 million hectares, whereas in the Master Plan it had been 1.7 million hectares.
8 For detailed information, see Nurçin İleri's article (2021) on the case of electricity in Turkey.
9 For detailed information on the Keban Dam and its politics in terms of electricity distribution and use, see Stahl (2019).
10 One of the most notable examples among them was Kamran İnan, who was a state minister in charge of the GAP between 1987 and 1991. İnan himself owned a village and opposed land reform (Cumhuriyet 1995).
11 For example, the newspaper *Cumhuriyet* (2009) used, in reference to the GAP-BKİ's operations, the headline "Federation [referring to a relatively autonomous Kurdish administration in the region] is arriving with the GAP."
12 Personal interview, April 9, 2019, TRGM, Urfa.
13 Personal interview, April 10, 2019, Urfa.
14 Personal interview, April 9, 2019, TRGM, Urfa.
15 Already in the 1960s, some of the leftist movements in Turkey had adopted the view that the Turkish bourgeoisie exploited eastern Turkey as a colony. In *Doğu*

Anadolu'nun düzeni (The order of East Anatolia, 1969), İsmail Beşikçi provides an in-depth analysis of this view, with a focus on the relationship between capitalism and colonization processes. He then develops his analysis into the thesis that Kurdistan is an international colony (Beşikçi 1990).

16 Personal interview with a TRGM official, April 10, 2019, Urfa.

17 Personal Interview, March 26, 2016, Adıyaman.

18 Personal Interview, March 26, 2016, Adıyaman.

References

Açıksöz, Salih Can. 2020. *Sacrificial Limbs of Sovereignty: Disabled Veterans, Masculinity, and Nationalist Politics in Turkey*, Berkeley: University of California Press.

Anand, Nikhil. 2012. "Municipal Disconnect: On Abject Water and its Urban Infrastructures," *Ethnography* 13, 4: 487–509.

Anand, Nikhil. 2017. *Hydraulic City: Water and the Infrastructures of Citizenship in Mumbai*, Durham: Duke University Press.

Appel, Hannah, Nikhil Anand, and Akhil Gupta. 2018. "Introduction," in Nikhil Anand, Akhil Gupta, and Hannah Appel (eds.), *The Promise of Infrastructure*, 1–38, Durham: Duke University Press.

Barry, Andrew. 2020. "The Material Politics of Infrastructure," in Sabine Maasen, Sascha Dickel and Christoph Schneider (eds.), *TechnoScienceSociety*, 91–109, Cham: Springer.

Beşikçi. İsmail. 1969. *Doğu Anadolu'nun düzeni: Sosyo-ekonomik ve etnik temeller (The Order of East Anatolia: Socio-economic and Ethnic Foundations)* Istanbul: E Yayınları.

Beşikçi, İsmail. 1990. *Devletlerarası sömürge Kürdistan (Kurdistan, an International Colony)*, Istanbul: Alan.

Bilgen, Arda. 2017. "Demystifying the (Post-) Politics of Southeastern Anatolia Project (GAP)," PhD Thesis, Universität Bonn.

Bilgen, Arda. 2018a. "A Project of Destruction, peace, or Techno-science? Untangling the Relationship between the Southeastern Anatolia Project (GAP) and the Kurdish question in Turkey," *Middle Eastern Studies* 54 (1): 94–113.

Bilgen, Arda. 2018b. "The Southeastern Anatolia Project (GAP) Revisited: The Evolution of GAP Over Forty Years," *New Perspectives on Turkey* 58: 125–54.

Bilgen, Arda, Zeynep Akıncı, Antonia Casellas, and Joost Jongerden. 2021. "Is the Glass Half Empty or Half Full? An Appraisal of the Four Decades of Turkey's Southeastern Anatolia Project (GAP)," in Laith Jawad (ed.), *Tigris and Euphrates Rivers: Their Environment from Headwaters to Mouth*, 1511–98, Cham: Springer.

Bozarslan, Hamit. 2008. "Kurds and the Turkish State," in Reşat Kasaba (ed.), *The Cambridge History of Turkey 4*, 333–56, Cambridge: Cambridge University Press.

Cumhuriyet. 1992. "PKK su ile bağlantılı," *Cumhuriyet* (May 21).

Cumhuriyet. 1995. "GAP'ta toprak reformu gereksiz," *Cumhuriyet* (January 17).

Cumhuriyet. 2009. "Federasyon GAP'la geliyor," *Cumhuriyet* (March 2).

Dağ, Rıfat and Atilla Göktürk. 1994. *Gap yeniden yapılanmalıdır*, Diyarbakır: Diyarbakır Ticaret ve Sanayi Odası.

DPT. 1973. *Kalkınma planı üçüncü beş yıl (1973–1977)*, Ankara: Devlet Planlama Teşkilatı.

DPT. 1989a. *The Southeastern Anatolia Project Master Plan study: Final Master Plan Report: Master Plan (Vol. 1)*, Ankara: Devlet Planlama Teşkilatı.

DPT. 1989b. *The Southeastern Anatolia Project Master Plan Study: Final Master Plan Report (Vol. 2)*, Ankara: Devlet Planlama Teşkilatı.
Duruiz, Deniz. 2021. "Erasure and Affect in Race-Making in Turkey," *Pomeps Studies* 44 (6): 827–50.
Eren, Ayşen. 2018. "Transformation of the Water-Energy Nexus in Turkey: Re-imagining Hydroelectricity Infrastructure," *Energy Research & Social Science* 41: 22–31.
Evren, Erdem. 2014. "The Rise and Decline of an Anti-Dam Campaign: Yusufeli Dam Project and the Temporal Politics of Development," *Water History* 6: 405–19.
GAP-BKİ. 2003. *GAP'ta son durum raporu, 2002*, Ankara: GAP-BKİ Başkanlığı.
Gökçe, Birsen, Aytül Kasapoğlu, Nilay Çabuk Kaya, and Zuhal Güler. 2010. *Bölgesel kalkınmanın can suyu GAP: Karşılaştırmalı sosyal ve ekonomik yapı araştırması*, Ankara: GAP-BKİ & Sosyoloji Derneği.
Gürel, Burak, Bermal Küçük, and Sercan Taş. 2022. "Land Occupation as a Form of Peasant Struggle in Turkey, 1965–1980," *New Perspectives on Turkey* First view article: 1–28.
Harris, Leila. 2009. "States at the Limit: Tracing Contemporary State-Society Relations in the Borderlands of Southeastern Turkey," *European Journal of Turkish Studies: Social Sciences on Contemporary Turkey* 10: 1–21.
Harris, Leila. 2012. "State as Socionatural Effect: Variable and Emergent Geographies of the State in Southeastern Turkey," *Comparative Studies of South Asia, Africa and the Middle East* 32 (1): 25–39.
Harvey, David. 1989. "From Managerialism to Entrepreneurialism: The Transformation in Urban Governance in Late Capitalism," *Geografiska Annaler: Series B, Human Geography* 71 (1): 3–17.
Hommes, Lena, Rutgerd Boelens, and Harro Maat. 2016. "Contested Hydrosocial Territories and Disputed Water Governance: Struggles and Competing Claims over the Ilisu Dam Development in Southeastern Turkey," *Geoforum* 71: 9–20.
Islar, Mine. 2012. "Privatised Hydropower Development in Turkey: A Case of Water Grabbing?" *Water Alternatives* 5 (2): 376–91.
İleri, Nurçin. 2021. "Ambitious yet Ambivalent: Electrical Infrastructure and Inequality in Early Republican Turkey," *TRAFO: Blog for Transregional Research*. https://trafo.hypotheses.org/27972
İMO. 1971. "Aşağı Fırat dosyası," *Türkiye Mükendislik Haberleri Dergisi*, June: 26–43.
Jongerden, Joost. 2007. *The Settlement Issue in Turkey and the Kurds: An Analysis of Spatial Policies, Modernity and War*, Leiden: Brill.
Jongerden, Joost, Zeynep Sıla Akıncı, and Ercan Ayboğa. 2021. "Water, Politics and Dams in the Mesopotamia Basin of the Northern Middle East," in Laith Jawad (ed.), *Tigris and Euphrates Rivers: Their Environment from Headwaters to Mouth*, 383–400, Cham: Springer.
Keyder, Çağlar and Zafer Yenal. 2014. *Bildiğimiz Tarımın Sonu*, İstanbul: İletişim Yayınları.
Kıran, Abdullah. 2005. *Ortadoğu'da Su: Bir çatışma ya da Uzlaşma Alanı (Vol. 2)*, Istanbul: Kitap Yayınevi.
Kibaroglu, Aysegül, Argun Baskan, and Sezin Alp. 2009. "Neo-liberal Transitions in Hydropower and Irrigation Water Management in Turkey: Main Actors and Opposition Groups," in Sander Meijerink (ed.), *Water Policy Entrepreneurs: A Research Companion to Water Transitions around the Globe*, 287–303, Edward Elgar Publishing.
Kudat, Ayşe and Mümtaz Bayram. 2000. "Şanlıurfa-Harran Plains On-farm and Village Development Project," in Ayşe Kudat, Stan Peabody, and Çağlar Keyder (eds.), *Social*

Assessment and Agricultural Reform in Central Asia and Turkey, World Bank Technical Paper 461: 255–301.

Kurtiç, Ekin. 2023. "Infrastructural Decay," *Cultural Anthropology* 38 (1): 142–70.

McFarlane, Colin and Jonathan Rutherford. 2008. "Political Infrastructures: Governing and Eperiencing the Fabric of the City," *International Journal of Urban and Regional Research* 32 (2): 363–74.

Molle, Francois. 2007. "Scales and Power in River Basin Management: The Chao Phraya River in Thailand," *Geographical Journal* 173 (4): 358–73.

Müller, Martin. 2015. "Assemblages and Actor-Networks: Rethinking Socio-Material Power, Politics and Space," *Geography Compass* 9 (1): 27–41.

Öcalan, Abdullah. 2015. *Demokratik Kurtuluş ve Özgür Yaşamı Inşa: İmralı Notları*, Cologne: Mezopotamya Press.

Öktem, Kerem. 2002. "When Dams are Built on Shaky Grounds: Policy Choice and Social Performance of Hydro-Project Based Development in Turkey," *Erdkunde* 56 (3): 310–25.

Özcan, Nihat A. 1999. *PKK Tarihi, Ideolojisi ve Yöntemi*, Ankara: ASAM Yayınları.

Özerol, Gül and Hans Bressers. 2017. "How do Farmers Align with the Agri-Environmental Changes in Irrigated Agriculture? A Case Study from the Harran Plain, Turkey," *Irrigation and Drainage* 66 (1): 45–59.

Özkan, Hande. 2025. "The Liminal Forest: Mud, Science and Nationalism in Turkey's Forests," in Duygu Kaşdoğan, Ekin Kurtiç and Mehmet Ekinci (eds.), *Material Politics in Turkey: Infrastructure, Science, and Expertise*, 93–118, London: Bloomsbury.

Soffer, Arnon. 1999. *Rivers of Fire: The Conflict Over Water in the Middle East*, Lanham: Rowman & Littlefield Publishers.

Stahl, Dale. 2019. "A Technopolitical Frontier: The Keban Dam Project and Southeastern Anatolia," in Onur İnal and Ethemcan Turhan (eds.), *Transforming Socio-Natures in Turkey*, 31–51, London: Routledge.

Swyngedouw, Eric. 2015. *Liquid Power: Contested Hydro-Modernities in Twentieth-Century Spain*, Cambridge: MIT Press.

TBMM. 1984. *Tutanak Dergisi* (Term 17, Year 2, Sitting 37). Ankara, December 9.

TBMM. 1985. *Tutanak Dergisi* (Term 17, Year 2, Sitting 93). Ankara, May 1.

TBMM. 1988a. *Tutanak Dergisi* (Term 18, Year 1, Sitting 14). Ankara, January 27.

TBMM. 1988b. *Tutanak Dergisi* (Term 18, Year 1, Sitting 18). Ankara, February 4.

TBMM. 1990. *Tutanak Dergisi* (Term 18, Year 4, Sitting 44). Ankara, December 10.

Tekeli, İlhan. 1972. "Üçüncü Beş Yıllık Plan Üzerinde Genel bir Değerlendirme," *Mimarlık* 192: 26–36.

Tekeli, İlhan. 2008. *Türkiye'de Bölgesel Eşitsizlik ve Bölge Planlama Yazıları (Vol. 2)*, İstanbul: Tarih Vakfı.

Turgut, Hulusi. 2000. *GAP ve Demirel*, İstanbul: ABC Yayınları.

Uzmay, Asya Ece. 2025. "Fountains, Disease, Blueprints: Making the Water Infrastructure of Istanbul Visible" in Duygu Kaşdoğan, Ekin Kurtiç and Mehmet Ekinci (eds.), *Material Politics in Turkey: Infrastructure, Science, and Expertise*, 41–56, London: Bloomsbury.

Von Schnitzler, Antina. 2008. "Citizenship Prepaid: Water, Calculability, and Techno-Politics in South Africa," *Journal of Southern African Studies* 34 (4): 899–917.

White, Gilbert. 1957. "A Perspective of River Basin Development," *Law and Contemporary Problems* 22: 157–87.

Yetkin, İbrahim. 1989. "GAP Gerçeği," *Cumhuriyet* (March 9).

2

Fountains, Disease, Blueprints

Making the Water Infrastructure of Istanbul Visible

Asya Ece Uzmay

Shedding its imperial mantle in the first decades of the twentieth century, Istanbul, the burgeoning commercial center of the newly founded republic, embraced the task of navigating its water resources to meet the demands of its growing populace. This task had been a sociotechnical challenge for various stakeholders since the last decades of the nineteenth century. Every household was to be furnished with faucet water to fulfill the requirements of "civilization," to use the words of Ziya Erdem, the first president of the Istanbul Water Administration (*İstanbul Sular İdaresi*, henceforth İSİ) (Erdem 1948). Yet, almost thirty years after Erdem's statement, according to another report, this time prepared by an international engineering firm, the question of supplying water to every household was far from a reality. "The most striking feature of the water use situation in Istanbul," the report stated, "is the great number of persons dependent on fountain water" (DAMOC 1971a). Indeed, approximately 40 percent of the population of Istanbul as of 1968 was still dependent on the over 1,500 extant water fountains originally built in the twentieth century (DAMOC 1971b).[1]

Fountains were the visible counterparts of a larger network. Scholars have associated modern infrastructural systems and changes in the cities through metaphors such as the "invisible city" (Lewis Mumford cited in Graham and Marvin 2001, 39) or "subterranean counterparts" of the modern city (Gandy 1999, 26). This system would make the city function without breaking or disrupting urban daily life. While doing so, the material systems that facilitate the constant flow of people and goods are often located far from our sight thus they "[disappear] from [the] urban imagination" (Kaika and Swyngedouw 2000, 121–2).

This invisibility is understood in one of the two ways: a *physical absence* of infrastructure or related to its *function*, that is, infrastructures that are hidden in nature become visible when they stop working (Star 1999; Carse 2017). However, not all cities experienced the change toward a networked city similarly. In particular, scholars who focus on the Global South have shown many other forms of water infrastructure regimes that are not necessarily buried and rendered invisible (von Schnitzler 2016;

Furlong and Kooy 2017; Anand 2018). This chapter offers an approach that departs from the visibility versus invisibility dichotomy—which can produce a more static approach, especially in historical accounts—and shows how states of visibility are actually in flux during the modernization of Istanbul's water infrastructure. I will demonstrate the water infrastructure's changing states of visibility by examining its material existence in the urban fabric and the change in contemporaneous discourse around water infrastructure, particularly in moments of diseases.[2]

Here I take two outbreaks of waterborne disease as departure points to show their larger roles in the urban history of Istanbul concerning the city's environmental and housing questions. The first section centers on the 1937 typhoid outbreak in the Fatih neighborhood of Istanbul to explain the dynamics between old and new water infrastructure following the nationalization of the water distribution system and the purchase of foreign water companies. I examine how disease changed the visibility of public fountains and underground water pipes. The second section looks at the discourse on the material aesthetics of this new infrastructure in the city, such as fountains and water towers, by focusing on the 1970 cholera outbreak in Sağmalcılar. Although I draw from the site specificity of these outbreaks, in the third section, I discuss these visibility regimes, which had changed with disease, in relation to the city's larger infrastructural plans. In the last section, I explore a decade of master plan and feasibility studies prepared by experts such as policymakers, engineers, health authorities, and architects to solve "Istanbul's water problem" from the 1950s to the 1970s. These blueprints imagined the city on a regional scale to expand Istanbul's water infrastructure toward its neighboring provinces in the east to include the growing industrial cities Izmit and Adapazarı, so that their respective water needs could be sustained with one centralized system. In such cases, the municipal region was redefined through its water infrastructure and its use of natural resources (Scott 1999). This section discusses the expansion of what constitutes natural resources in relation to diseases of the time, which were perceived as threats to a "better society to come" (Kaika and Swyngedouw 2000, 130).

The 1937 Typhoid Outbreak: Where Disease and Fountains Meet

In July 1937, amid the typhoid outbreak in Istanbul, Kazım, a resident of Hanımefendi Street no. 79 in Şişli, wrote a complaint letter to *Cumhuriyet* newspaper. Noting the open cesspools and mosquitoes in the street, Kazım criticized the authorities for not taking any responsibility for the recurring typhoid outbreaks that appeared over the summer months. Irrigation water, mixed with water from cesspools, was used in *bostans* (vegetable gardens) on his street, thereby prompting him to request the municipality to take measures against the open cesspools (*Cumhuriyet* 1937a).

Typhoid, a waterborne disease, was not foreign to Istanbul. In 1937, however, it started "earlier than usual" and caused more cases than past outbreaks, according to the Minister of Health, Refik Saydam. Typhoid was known to spread through bacteria-infected water and food, and thus, soon enough, consuming *bostan* crops was prohibited by local health authorities and vaccinations began. Rather than being proactive in their attempts at disease control, they acted reactively. Saydam laid this blame on the inadequate infrastructure of the city, stating, "unfortunately, until scientific improvements are made to the water and sewage infrastructure, vaccination will be the only solution for typhoid" (*Cumhuriyet* 1937b). In the past, these scientific improvements to the city were only partially made. For instance, the Terkos water network that opened in 1885 was designed to distribute water to the upper-class and upper-middle class neighborhoods, but not to the lower-class ones, exacerbating urban inequalities in the city (Kentel 2019). Laboratories, where vaccines were developed,[3] as Saydam puts it, would provide an easier solution to the disease instead of undertaking a costly and large-scale improvement in the city's water infrastructure. Thus, laboratories, to some extent, were determinants of urban reforms.[4]

Along with *bostans*, fountains were also associated with disease environments since they were the visible counterparts of the larger water network. During this time, typhoid cases were seen mostly in the Fatih neighborhood, on the west end of the Golden Horn, which was supported by the Kırkçeşme waterways. Coming from water reservoirs in the Belgrade Forest, located just north of the city, the Kırkçeşme main supplied water to intramural Istanbul. Following the outbreak, İSİ declared that typhoid was a result of complications in the sewage and water infrastructure, where the congestion of an old sewage pipe overflowed into one of Kırkçeşme's main galleries (Nirven 1960, 61). As a result, İSİ cut the Kırkçeşme waterways before they entered the city, thereby transforming the public fountains that were connected to the waterways into idle street furniture.[5]

The Kırkçeşme waters were part of a larger system of what was called *vakıf* waters, which were expropriated in 1926 and governed by the municipality of Istanbul (Açıkgöz 2018, 91). *Vakıf* waters remained the main water resources of Ottoman Istanbul until the late nineteenth century.[6] In 1882, a consortium of local and international actors called the *Compagnie des Eaux de Constantinople* (Istanbul Water Company, *Dersaadet Su Şirketi*) undertook the project of bringing water to the city from Lake Terkos, 40 kilometers away from the city, following the stress of increasing population and changes in daily water consumption which the system, at the time, could not handle (Dinçkal 2008, 693–6; Kentel 2018).[7] While electricity, gas, and water were distributed by foreign companies, the Municipalities Law in 1930 expanded the responsibilities of the municipalities such that they had total control over public services, including governance of city water (Kezer 2015, 92). In 1933, *Compagnie des Eaux de Constantinople* was purchased by the municipality as part of the "municipalization" process of governing the city (Tekeli 2013, 129). Public authorities, who discussed purchasing these companies and having a municipal jurisdiction on water distribution in the city, saw the purchase as an example of the democratization of water, that is, to provide affordable and clean water for all citizens as well as having a national control over them (Dinçkal 2008). These purchases empowered municipalities to participate in the distribution of goods through municipalization and monopolization of these services. Ultimately, the governance of modern waterways and the old *vakıf* ways were gathered under a new agency named İSİ,[8] whose aim was to centralize water distribution in the city, despite its partial existence, and can be seen as a subset of the republic's larger project toward technologically led modernization.[9]

The transition from the public fountain to the private faucet in Istanbul has a long and complex history starting from the nineteenth century at the intersection of politics, bureaucracies, technoscience, and aesthetics (Dinçkal 2008; Kentel 2018). These larger structural changes transformed people's relationship with water and its infrastructure, which itself is intertwined with the rhetoric of the political and public spheres and social inequalities of the time. Public fountains, which were condensers of everyday urban life as places of socializing, business, and gathering (Hamadeh 2007), gradually lost significance in urban memory as water became available at homes. Instead, they were seen as artifacts of the "past," a distant history that the new modern republic was moving away from (Dinçkal 2008, 699). While bringing clean water to "a water faucet at home" was considered a necessity of hygienic modernization, it also meant that the fountains previously integral to the social fabric of Ottoman Istanbul became associated with disease environments over time (Erdem 1948, 38).

Infrastructures as built artifacts evoke imaginations about the future and past; about citizenship, technologies, and politics (Larkin 2013). The materiality of these new infrastructural projects was intimately tied to the modernization project, the framework of which was drawn by state officials. As they were symbols of a "better society to come" (Kaika and Swyngedouw 2000, 130), their message was complicated by instances like disease.

Within this framework, public fountains of 1930s Istanbul were not considered desired elements of this new landscape. In his report regarding the first fourteen years after the nationalization of water infrastructure, the first president of İSİ, Ziya Erdem (1933–47), drew a direct relationship between "civilization" and water use. Erdem reiterated the responsibility of İSİ in the making of a "civilized" nation-state. He wrote, "it is possible to *measure* the level of civilization via water consumption of our people" and noted that water consumption in Istanbul as of the mid-1940s had doubled since 1932. "It is also the *necessity* of civilization," he continued, "to cut the need for public fountains and provide easy and affordable water services for people" (Erdem 1948, 38, emphasis added). He pointed out that even though the water comes "clean" from public fountains, the existence of human intermediaries between faucet and direct consumption, whether the people themselves or *saka*s (water sellers), was unlikely or incapable of keeping it clean according to the modern standards defined by the İSİ. In contrast, Erdem stressed that an infrastructural system that is (supposedly) closed, mechanized, and that starts from a water source and ends at "a water faucet at home *(evindeki musluk)*" is needed for "civilization." Human actors within the existing system, whether the consumers or *sakas*, were seen as causes of pollution and as something to be removed from the distribution process. Thus, to him, modern water infrastructure should be sealed and contained. He concluded, "it is impossible to keep the fountain water clean. Hence, we need to stop building new fountains and remove the existing ones" (Erdem 1948, 39). In other words, it was critical for the modern water infrastructural system to eliminate any *visible* counterparts of underground water pipes, like the public fountains, which were now declared as too old to maintain, before they reached the private domain.

In line with this modernization project, in 1933, Burhanettin Berken, a hydrology professor at Istanbul Technical University, envisioned a centralized network for the city to answer the needs of a modern networked city.[10] This plan constituted the base of Istanbul's water-related technoscientific imaginaries until 1947, when, making a break with the past, this plan would put an end to the fragmented infrastructure of the city. Berken focused on improving modern waterways and did not have a structured program for the old *vakıf* waters. Rather, these were neglected and left to decay but at the same time were not decommissioned, therefore becoming *visible* only in moments of disruption, which brings us back to the summer of 1937. After the typhoid outbreak in 1937, Kırkçeşme waters were prohibited from entering the city. Once their connections to the underground waters were cut, fountains were rendered to be reminders of old water infrastructure. However, İSİ did not connect water to private households, as it was envisioned. On the contrary, they built ninety-two new public fountains connected to the Terkos network. These Terkos fountains, rarely mentioned in İSİ publications,[11] represented the failures of the modernization project at large. The construction of new fountains, visible parts of the otherwise hidden underground water system, was therefore rendered invisible in the written accounts in order to create an image of a flawless modernization and centralization process.

While fountains were part of a public debate as to whether they should be maintained or not, the implementation of Berken's plan continued after the postwar period. The application of the plan was delayed due to economic and material shortages caused by the Second World War. The machinery and pipes that were originally planned to be imported from Europe, for example, were unable to be shipped until much later. As another part of Berken's plan, underground water sources in Çırpıcı, Bakırköy, were surveyed in 1939 and became a potential water resource for the city (Erdem 1948, 33). The Çırpıcı water main was connected to the Edirnekapı Water Reservoir, as originally planned, in order to transfer excess Çırpıcı underground waters to other parts of the city and was slated to be completed by 1947 (Esmer 1983, 58). For the first time, the city's water was connected from Bakırköy to Terkos, covering 57 kilometers, as the intended central water network eventually came together, although constructed in a fragmented manner.

However, a centralized water network was not necessarily successful in furnishing every household with faucet water as imagined and aspired. The mayor of Istanbul between 1938 and 1949, Lütfi Kırdar, claimed that by investing in the reform plan, Istanbul expanded its water capacity seven times in comparison to the old water system, aiming to justify the plan's shortcomings regarding equitable outcomes for lower-class neighborhoods. "It was impossible to invest [in the] restoration [of the old water systems] in those circumstances," he argued; "our goal was to remove all public fountains. Water should remain at our disposal in our homes, on every floor. The water carried with dirty containers with unclean hands should belong to the past" (1941, 330). The visibility of the means by which water previously reached most households in Istanbul was not preferred by the government officials and bureaucrats involved in the modernization of Turkey's water infrastructure. In fact, public fountains symbolized the past which the current regime was moving away from as commitment to a larger national project. Thus, the absence of fountains in the streets was associated with civilization.

State officials believed in solving "Istanbul's water problem" through the supremacy of modern technology, which implied a bias against fountains. On the one hand, it changed the people's relationship with the daily consumption of water, while on the other, it created a dichotomy in the city through water's visibility in the urban sphere. Fountains' presence in the streets was believed to be against the medicalized city. However, as we know, public fountains continued to be part of the city's daily life, especially in low-income neighborhoods, for such a long time that they even played a role in the 1970 cholera outbreak, which spread in one of Istanbul's neighborhoods, Sağmalcılar.

1970 Cholera Outbreak: Unpacking the Underground Relations of Istanbul

In the 1950s, Istanbul's population started to increase significantly. Migration to the city was largely due to mechanization in agriculture, hence increasing the average productivity of labor while decreasing the need for a large workforce in the countryside. This gradually freed up capital to be invested for industrial development during the 1960s and 1970s (Keyder 2008; Bozdoğan and Akcan 2012; Pamuk 2014). By 1969, Istanbul's population was almost 3 million, having increased by three times since 1950 (İstanbul Büyükşehir Belediyesi 2001). Consequently, the existing housing stock was insufficient to meet the mounting needs of the new residents. The newly arrived urbanites had to build their own dwellings (i.e., *gecekondus*) on state-owned land in the absence of formal infrastructural systems, such as waste disposal, electricity, water distribution, and street networks.[12] Although these emergent *gecekondu* areas were geographically close to the networked areas of the city, they were disconnected from the rest of the city's infrastructural regime, in contrast with the "modern networked city" ideal. This disconnection resulted in fragmented infrastructures wherein the centralized Terkos water network existed side by side with fountains connected either to the old *vakıf* waterways or to the newly opened underground waters. While the reorganization of water infrastructure was a key site for the materialization of the politics of modernization in urban Turkey, the sociospatial characteristics of the growing city (i.e., the disconnection of *gecekondus* from the growing central infrastructure) led to the emergence of new material landscapes of water infrastructure that challenged the imaginaries and practices of making a modern networked city.

Fountains were designated as diseased landscapes, as we have seen with the 1937 typhoid outbreak, and yet they continued to be the primary source of free water. Although fountains did supply free water, they exacerbated existing inequalities in water consumption since they provided temporary solutions in the absence of permanent infrastructural connections. These less permanent solutions consisted of two types of water resources that were employed in *gecekondu* neighborhoods: fountains, which were connected to artesian waters, and *arazöz* (water trucks), which comes from *arroseuse* in French, that is, mobile water carriers originally used for construction, irrigation, street cleaning, or fire control purposes. In this case, they were adapted to be used as mobile fountains. This made *arazöz* another element in the water distribution system and of the city waterscape. In his canonical essay "Do artifacts have politics?" science studies scholar Langdon Winner looks at the "technical artifacts" that shape the environment and their visible and invisible effects on everyday life and notes that "the invention, design or arrangement of a specific technical device or system becomes a way of settling an issue in a particular community" (1980, 123). Ad hoc solutions like precarious mobile water carriers, artesian wells, fountains, and cesspools gave authorities the freedom to withdraw responsibility from these neighborhoods. As the former mayor of Istanbul Ahmet İsvan emphasized, "building a proper network for *gecekondu* areas weren't considered," thus those areas were left with ad hoc solutions (İsvan 2011, 112). The same trajectory continued with the sewage infrastructure as well, since 80 percent of Istanbul was still dependent on cesspools even by 1971 (DAMOC 1971a). Urban planners like Ilhan Tekeli explain the low priority of sewage infrastructure because of their marginal financial return. Sewage systems, he states, are the type of infrastructure that is neglected the most, as they can be replaced with cesspools at a lower cost. Building a centralized sewage network was prohibitively expensive, as it took a comparatively longer time for this service to pay itself off (Tekeli 2009, 29). Therefore, a combination of poor water and sewage infrastructure resulted in the cholera outbreak in 1970 Sağmalcılar being the epicenter of it.

Cholera, a waterborne disease, came as a result of many reasons. Between 1966 and 1969, the General Directorate of Health had repeatedly brought up the underlying conditions in the neighborhood as being ripe for spreading disease (No Author 1971, 603). Reşit Ülker, a deputy from Istanbul, highlighted that Sağmalcılar was seen as "a laboratory for medical students" to study infectious disease (1971, 612). Unsurprisingly, Sağmalcılar was one of the neighborhoods without proper water and sewage infrastructure, leading to favorable conditions for the spread of disease. The neighborhood was located over the old Halkalı waterways. Although in theory, the Halkalı water distribution system was not in use by 1970, the material conditions in Sağmalcılar were different. Water coming from spring waters was still running through the pipes of Halkalı .[13] Furthermore, one of the springs connected to the Halkalı waterways became a dumpsite for the city.[14] While officially named as abandoned, these pipes carrying water from springs to intramural Istanbul remained hidden underneath the city and left to decay, conveniently forgotten by public officials. Reports written by medical doctors visiting the area show that confronted with the lack of waste disposal systems, residents repurposed the old waterways as sewage canals (Tezok et al. 1970, 7).

Fountains in Sağmalcılar were fed with four underground water sources and hence they were open to underground contamination. But during the cholera epidemic in Sağmalcılar, a water tower was marked as a signifier of the underground relations of water. In *Hayat* magazine, an image of the tower pictured as outstanding over the skyline in the neighborhood contrasted among the residential buildings (see Figure 2.1). It was published along with the words, "Sağmalcılar and its germ-spreading water tower." In a closer image, the concrete water tower is pictured among the street trees and buildings, with people in front of the tower emphasizing its gargantuan scale in the urban environment, with an arrow pointing "source of the trouble started here" (Yarbağ

Figure 2.1 The concrete water tower connected to the underground water source in Sağmalcılar was marked as the source of disease. Courtesy Kutlu Ertuna and Atılay Gülen, "Kolera İstanbul'da Panik Yarattı," *Hayat* no. 43, October 1970, 12. The image is a scanned version of the photograph taken from *Hayat*.

and Koray 1970). This concrete water tower, a typology of the modern infrastructure system to distribute pressured water, was connected to the four underground water collection points in Sağmalcılar. Material conditions that incubated the disease were scattered around the neighborhood and rendered visible with disease.

A central conceptual point laid out in the introduction of this volume by Kasdoğan and Kurtiç argues that the meanings of material artifacts are fundamentally shaped by political processes. Indeed, existing scholarship in Architecture has discussed the materiality of infrastructures through the politics of developing a common techno-aesthetic future for the new nation-state (Bozdoğan 2001; Bozdoğan and Akcan 2012; Demirtaş 2013; Kezer 2015). Novel infrastructural developments such as dams, railway stations, and power plants reached out to the countryside through railways and roads as means for the "construction of a modern, civilized, democratic citizenry" (Adalet 2018, 126), as well as representing the ideals and power of the new Turkish republic (Kezer 2015, 159). By contrast, the lack of infrastructure such as muddy roads, open cesspools, or infrastructures of the past like street fountains gradually came into relief as apparent failures standing against a backdrop of how the modern city is supposed to function. Thus, a water tower found in Sağmalcılar, which has a standardized aesthetic of repetition, gained a new meaning as the municipality's water infrastructure had failed. Its relative place among the other buildings in Sağmalcılar and its visibility as *the* tower marked Sağmalcılar as a signifier of the diseased environment on the urban scale.

Although the historically marginalized conditions of the neighborhood were reiterated in the Parliament and the media, the prime minister of the time, Süleyman Demirel, who was a hydraulic engineer and known as the "King of Dams" (*Barajlar Kralı*), received the news calmly, seemingly ignoring the political and technological conditions that led to the outbreak. During his visit to Sağmalcılar, he claimed, "Disasters like fire, flood and epidemic illnesses are the volition of God. There is nothing to be said. . . . It is pleasing to hear that the disease will end soon. *İnşallah* it will disappear from our conversations as well. . . . Death doesn't care if you are poor or rich, when it comes, it takes you whoever you are" (Bakar 2017, 260). According to official records, at least fifty people died. Residents of Sağmalcılar were ostracized, targeted in public, and deemed contagious in the media, as the medicalization of the city exposed vulnerable populations as subjects of scientific and popular discourse (Yanardağ 2009). Furthermore, the factor of class is a critical aspect of the technopolitics of the neighborhood as it is an example of material politics embedded within technological solutions.

Similar to Demirel's dismissive manner, health authorities shied away from naming the disease. Here I use naming disease in relation to Charles Rosenberg's canonical essay on the topic. He writes, "In some ways disease does not exist until we have agreed that it does, by perceiving, naming, and responding to it" (Rosenberg 1992, 179). Thus, our understanding and handling of disease change through the way it was made visible. Despite the news of cholera's spread from India to Turkey's northern and southern borders and its implied imminent introduction to the country as widely distributed in the media, the first diagnoses were *not* named as cholera. Instead, the authorities called the first instances of disease in the neighborhood as something else to deflect responsibility for the time being. This strategy was used in succession, starting with gastroenteritis and then moving to para-cholera or *El Tor*, which was used as a means of "easing" the public through a "lighter version of cholera" in the media (Bakar 2017, 248–9). This not only affected the mistreatment of the first patients, but it was also a move to avoid a national and international crisis.[15] Cholera made the neighborhood visible, to such an extent that the name, which was associated with these notorious features, was later changed from Sağmalcılar to Bayrampaşa. In the next section, I examine the water problem extensively, where it gets visible in blueprints through the expansion of the city and attempts to prevent the disease.

Expanding Istanbul's "Horizon"

Urbanization and the rapid increase of the city population did not only lead to the development of ad hoc water infrastructures, but it also led authorities to search for new water resources (Esmer 1983, 62). This would, in turn, determine the spatial boundaries of the city toward new sources, including harnessing the abundance of underground waters and lakes at novel distances in relation to the conventional boundaries of the city. Here I use "horizon" in two ways: I use it both in spatial terms to refer to the attempts of expanding Istanbul's boundaries to include new water resources, which requires planning the city on a regional scale, and in terms of expanding the boundaries of Istanbul's technological imaginations through universalized expertise and economic aids exported from international development projects to demonstrate radical change in planning ideology. The former refers to a territory, horizon as a physical boundary, while the latter refers to ideological imaginations. These newly tapped lakes, spring waters, and reservoirs of the city's hinterland are critical parts of Istanbul's modern water infrastructure. Their connection to the city surpasses the municipal boundaries in blueprints drawn by engineers, planners, and policymakers. This expansion of the horizon is important insofar as the representation of technological and infrastructural systems, as compared to their reality, is concerned. As Scaramelli notes in this volume, they are resources in the making, through the contested expertise of different participating actors, that is, for whom these resources are to be used is a political question. As Aybike Alkan also shows in this volume, national development was often prioritized at the expense of the regional natural resources in the Kurdish regions of the republic. Moreover, in order to underline the relations between the built (e.g., water towers and fountains) and natural environment (e.g., lakes and underground waters), historian Sara Pritchard suggests thinking with what she calls "envirotechnical systems" to define an inextricably intertwined relationship between environment and technology (Pritchard 2011).[16] Thinking of these landscapes as part of an envirotechnical system allows us to see these two supposedly separated and closed systems as one which work in relation and transform each other.[17] For instance, stress on Istanbul's water supply had a direct effect on everyday life in Lake Terkos.[18]

Previous plans for Istanbul's water distribution grappled with smaller sites, mainly the residential neighborhoods of the city. Following the increasing numbers in population of the city and the industrial areas, neighboring cities came to be included in the water plan. For instance, the 1937 typhoid outbreak led to the closure of old waterways and the 1970 cholera outbreak showed the fragile nature of underground waters. These waterborne diseases were treated with local solutions. At an international conference held in 1966,[19] Istanbul's water situation was addressed in relation to the "decline [in the] living standards of the society." As the presenters put it, this led to an "increase in water-borne diseases [that] limits the economic growth of the region." They concluded that having a Master Plan can "solve the water problem" (Noyan and Şenoğulları 1968, 845).

In 1958, İSİ published *Istanbul's Water and the Operations of ISI (İstanbul Suları ve Sular İdaresinin Faaliyeti)*. This report was different from the previous ones in that it identified Istanbul's water problem as a regional one. "In our times," the report stated, "before considering the water problem of a village or a city, water problem of the whole region should be considered. In fact in current times, the water problem of the territory, from Izmit[20] to Istanbul, should be the major concern in Turkey" (TC Sular Idaresi 1958, 12). Lake Sapanca, located between the Gulf of Izmit and the Adapazarı Meadow, would be the furthest water source in Istanbul with a distance of 120 kilometers while neglecting local relations established through uses of local water sources.[21] In addition to carrying water from distant geographies, the 1958 report also suggested building a more interconnected network for both Europe and Asia. Yet, by that time, water was far from equal in its distribution. Areas outside of Terkos's reach,[22] such as Sağmalcılar, were dependent on artesian waters. Moreover, even though some neighborhoods were equipped with sufficient infrastructure, water was frequently not available for a full 24 hours a day (TC Sular Idaresi 1958, 13).

Following the 1958 report, in 1961, İSİ published a new program for the city's water plan for the following ten years ("Water Program For 10 Years" 1961). This time İSİ partnered with the State Water Works (DSİ), which allowed them to operate on a much larger scale, as indicated in the last report. Lake Sapanca was still on the radar, and through a projected underground water tunnel in Bosporus, its waters would be transferred to the European side to be mixed with Terkos waters. This way, Istanbul's two sides, Asian and European coasts, would join to work together. Yet the 1961 report showed that a project on this scale would be costly. Even though the problem was first identified in 1958, attempts to have a "Master Plan" for the long-term solution of the inadequate water infrastructure started only six years later.

In 1964, Turkey applied to the United Nations Special Fund for preparing a master plan for water and sewage infrastructure and appointed an engineering and architecture firm from New York, United States, Tippetts–Abbett–McCarthy–Stratton (TAMS), to prepare a feasibility report for "the Greater Istanbul Area" through United States Agency for International Development (USAID) funds (Ministry of Energy and Natural Resources 1964, 42).[23] The application highlighted that access to water was a growing problem due to aggregating industrial areas around Istanbul that created stress on residential water. Areas connected to the old water fountains and new developing sites of the city were using underground water sources. Moreover, they pointed out the 1963 hepatitis and typhoid outbreaks that happened almost every year and explained the cause of these outbreaks by linking them to "contagious special water sources" (Ministry of Energy and Natural Resources 1964, 42–3).

Conclusion

The history presented in this chapter reflects the fragmented, nonlinear, and networked nature of the topic under consideration, Istanbul's water infrastructure. Scattered around the city in varying scales, water infrastructure differs from more visible infrastructural systems, like roads and railways, offering a more dynamic understanding of the (dis)functioning of these systems.

Oftentimes narrated as part of the past from which the city has departed, disease and its relation to the urban context went missing in the history of twentieth-century Istanbul. Following the nationalization of the water infrastructure, İSİ aimed to centralize the existing network through large-scale reform plans and later continued with localized plans, such as site-specific and ad hoc solutions. In the second half of the twentieth century, Istanbul's water problem was regionalized through large-scale network plans. Following the increase in population and the expansion of the city, these new settlements had to use underground well networks, *arazöz*, or new fountains, despite the technological imaginaries of state officials shaped by modernization like Ziya Erdem and Lütfi Kırdar.

Moreover, unpacking forty years of Istanbul's water infrastructure through material relations shows that "Istanbul's water problem" could not be measured only by the number of dams, lakes, and underground water sources. It is entangled with policies on housing, public health, and the city's ecological relations with its expanding hinterland. Furthermore, the dichotomy of visibility versus invisibility is insufficient for the cases outlined in this chapter, including the 1937 typhoid outbreak, the 1970 cholera outbreak in Sağmalcılar, and Istanbul's developmental master plans of the postwar era. Instead, this chapter argues that waterborne diseases were instances that rendered water infrastructure visible, such as water towers and fountains, while at the same time referring to the complications within a larger envirotechnical network. Water towers and fountains became material signals of disease and were associated with unhygienic conditions of the city. Their role and function changed in the public mind and the urban policies, as they became the one-time visible artifacts of disease, which in fact have entangled histories, politics, and aesthetics embedded in them.

Acknowledgment

I am grateful to the anonymous reviewers and to the editors Duygu Kaşdoğan, Ekin Kurtiç, and Mehmet Ekinci. I would also like to thank Sibel Bozdoğan, Ayşe Erek, Murat Güvenç, Esra Akcan, Begüm Adalet, and Suman Seth for their comments on the early version of this research.

Notes

1 Although the number of fountains that were built in the twentieth century is unknown, according to *Tarih Boyunca İstanbul'un Su Davası*, the number of fountains (connected to Terkos) was ninety-three in 1933. This number became 278 in 1949 (*Tarih Boyunca Istanbul'un Su Davası* 1950, 24).

2 This research draws upon the analysis of reports and blueprints prepared by the Istanbul Water Administration and State Hydraulic Works (*Devlet Su Isleri*, henceforth DSİ), in addition to various master plan and feasibility studies made by international engineering firms, together with newspapers, magazines, and official parliament archives. In doing so, I mapped the different phases of the infrastructure in relation to the discrepancies between the discourse surrounding the development of this new infrastructural system at the time and its lived realities, like diseases.

3 These laboratories, located in the Bacteriology Institute (*Hıfzıssıhha Enstitüsü*), which was built under the supervision of Refik Saydam, refer to a larger health infrastructure of Turkey's modernization project (Bozdoğan and Akcan 2012, 57).

4 One hundred and fifty years of sanitary discourse and control over human bodies through controlling streets brought laboratories and cities together again. Bruno Latour discusses this connection in relation to Haussmann's social and political control over Paris through the spatial reconfiguration of the city under the guise of the medicalization of the built environment. The air of professional and scientific knowledge cloaked his political intentions, thereby giving the latter legitimacy. In particular, Latour argues Pasteur's laboratory as a mechanism of control of the microbes and "the masses" (Latour 1999).

5 By 1939, Kırkçeşme waters were first connected to the Mağlova water supply station, where they were transferred to the Kağıthane treatment gallery to be collected, tested, chlorinated, and distributed back into the larger network (Esmer 1983, 55).

6 By the late nineteenth century, the waterscape of Istanbul was a complex array of water infrastructure mains, coming from a variety of sources and ultimate destinations. Kırkçeşme and Halkalı mains were covering intramural Istanbul, Hamidiye main was reaching out to Galata, and the Bosporus was mainly receiving water from Taksim, as well as artesian water coming from local wells, see Çeçen (1988), (1991), (1992), and (2000).
7 Another private company, *Compagnie des Eaux de Scutari et Kadikeui* (Uskudar and Kadıkoy Water Company, *Uskudar and Kadıkoy Su Şirketi*), undertook the project of supplying water to Uskudar and Kadıkoy on the Asian side (Kazgan and Önal 1999, 104).
8 *Compagnie des Eaux de Scutari et Kadikeui* was purchased by the municipality in 1937.
9 For the relationship between technology and civilization and its manifestations on the built environment in the making of the modern nation-state, see Bozdoğan (2001, 106–52).
10 His plan consisted of two phases. First, Berken suggested gradually replacing the existing water pipes in the Terkos main with new ones. Second, in addition to Lake Terkos, Berken proposed using the Çırpıcı underground water reserve to supply water to the Bakırköy neighborhood and its surroundings (Erdem 1948, 9).
11 In my research, I have not encountered any mention of Terkos fountains.
12 The literature on *gecekondu* is too vast to recount in its entirety. For the purpose of this chapter, see Tekeli, Gülöksüz, and Okyay (1976); Bozdoğan and Akcan (2012, 139–69); and Gülhan (2017).
13 Most of the old waterways were abandoned gradually after the 1937 typhoid incident.
14 Former name *Çöp yolu* (Dump way) located in Habipler Village, now named as 2721st Street.
15 Following the news on cholera, a few countries closed their borders with Turkey and quarantined or rejected travelers coming from Turkey (Bakar 2017, 256–9).
16 For a detailed discussion of the "envirotechnical," see Pritchard and Zimring (2020).
17 Similarly, urban geographer Maria Kaika discusses this relationship through dam projects. By situating dams as dialectical "between the production of nature and the production of cities," she writes, "transmuting 'natural' landscapes in their making while making the production and expansion of urban landscapes possible, these technological shrines exemplify the messy dialects between creation and destruction inherent in Modernity's Promethean Project" (Kaika 2006, 276–7).
18 See Kentel (2019, 155–82). This discussion holds its relevance even today, particularly regarding the project called *Büyük Melen Projesi* (Great Melen Project), which brings water from Melen, Düzce, 170 kilometers away from the city. İstanbul's use of Düzce's water resulted in tension between two cities as it led to water shortages in Düzce.
19 In 1966, engineers, policymakers, scientists, and architects reiterated technology's role in peace at the *International Conference on Water for Peace*, held in Washington, with participants from "94 countries and 24 international organizations" (International Conference on Water for Peace 1968, iii). The aim of the conference was to produce universal knowledge about water to prove engineering's transformative power for the better by building alliances through water governance.
20 Izmit, a neighboring city of İstanbul on the east, is 155 kilometers away from Terkos Lake, the main water source of the city at the time.
21 See note 18.
22 Keep in mind that Terkos water was used synonymously with the city's water network.

23 Following TAMS' report, in 1966, a consortium named DAMOC was appointed by the World Health Organization to prepare a water and sewage master plan for Istanbul and the industrial areas nearby. DAMOC was a team of engineering, architecture, and consulting firms: Daniel, Mann, Johnson, & Mendenhall of Los Angeles; Alvord, Burdick and Howson of Chicago; Motor-Columbus of Baden, Switzerland; and Checchi and Company of Washington, DC. This master plan constitutes the base of today's water and sewage infrastructure.

References

Açıkgöz, Ümit F. 2018. *Global Locality, National Modernity: Negotiating Urban Transformation in Early Republican Istanbul*, Houston, TX: Rice University.

Adalet, Begüm. 2018. *Hotels and Highways: The Construction of Modernization Theory in Cold War Turkey*, Stanford, CA: Stanford University Press.

Anand, Nikhil. 2018. "A Public Matter: Water, Hydraulics, Biopolitics," in Nikhil Anand, Akhil Gupta, and Hannah Appel (eds.), *The Promise of Infrastructure*, 155–72, Durham:Duke University Press.

Bakar, Coşkun. 2017. "Kırk Yedi Yıl Sonra Yeniden Bir Salgının Hikâyesi: 1970 Sağmalcılar Kolera Salgınından Günümüze Dersler," *Turkish Journal of Public Health* 15 (3): 245–69.

Bozdoğan, Sibel. 2001. *Modernism and Nation Building: Turkish Architectural Culture in the Early Republic*, Seattle, WA and London: University of Washington Press.

Bozdoğan, Sibel and Esra Akcan. 2012. *Turkey: Modern Architectures in History*, London: Reaktion Books.

Carse, Ashley. 2017. "Keyword: Infrastructure, How a Humble French Engineering Term Shaped the Modern World," in Penny Harvey, Casper Bruun Jensen, and Atsuro Morito (eds.), *Infrastructures and Social Complexity: A Companion*, 27–39, New York: Routledge.

Çeçen, Kazım. 1988. *Mimar Sinan ve Kırkçeşme Tesisleri* Istanbul: ISKI.

Çeçen, Kazım. 1991. *Halkalı Suları*, Istanbul: ISKI.

Çeçen, Kazım. 1992. *Taksim ve Hamidiye Suları*, Istanbul: ISKI.

Çeçen, Kazım. 2000. *Istanbul'un Osmanlı Dönemi Su Yolları*, Istanbul: ISKI.

Cumhuriyet. 1937a. "Halkın Şikayetleri: Bostanlara Akan Lağımlar," July 13, 1937.

Cumhuriyet. 1937b. "Sıhhıye Vekili Diyor Ki: 'Istanbul'da Tifo Geçen Senelerde Görülmeyen Miktara Çıkmıştır,'" June 29, 1937.

DAMOC. 1971a. *Master Plan and Feasibility Report for Water Supply and Sewerage for the Istanbul Region: Report and Study for General Background Studies*, Vol. I. World Health Organization.

DAMOC. 1971b. *Master Plan and Feasibility Report for Water Supply and Sewerage for the Istanbul Region: Water Supply Studies Greater Istanbul Project Area*, Vol. II. Part I. World Health Organization.

Demirtaş, Aslıhan. 2013. "Rowing Boats in the Reservoir: Infrastructure as Transplanted Seascape," in Panayiota Pyla (ed.), *Landscapes of Development: The Impact of Modernization Discourses on the Physical Environment of the Eastern Mediterranean*, 16–35. .Cambridge, MA: Aga Khan Program at the Harvard Graduate School of Design.

Dinçkal, Noyan. 2008. "Reluctant Modernization: The Cultural Dynamics of Water Supply in Istanbul, 1885–1950," *Technology and Culture* 49 (3): 675–700.

Erdem, Ziya. 1948. *Istanbul Sular Idaresinin 1933–1947 Yılları Arasındaki Çalışması*, Istanbul: Halk Basımevi.
Esmer, Kerim. 1983. *Tarih Boyunca Istanbul Suları ve Istanbul Su ve Kanalizasyon Sorunu*, Istanbul: T.C. ISKI Yayınları.
Furlong, Kathryn and Michelle Kooy. 2017. "Worlding Water Supply: Thinking Beyond the Network in Jakarta," *International Journal of Urban and Regional Research* 41 (6): 888–903.
Gandy, Matthew. 1999. "The Paris Sewers and the Rationalization of Urban Space," *Transactions of the Institute of British Geographers* 24 (1): 23–44.
Graham, Steve and Simon Marvin. 2001. *Splintering Urbanism: Networked Infrastructures, Technological Mobilities and the Urban Condition*, London: Routledge.
Gülhan, Sinan T. 2017. "Ezilmiş ve Aşağılanmışlar: 1960'lar Türkiye'sinde Gecekondu Meselesi." *Mülkiye Dergisi* 41 (1): 195–229.
Hamadeh, Shirine. 2007. *The City's Pleasures: Istanbul in the Eighteenth Century*, Seattle, WA: University of Washington Press.
International Conference on Water for Peace *(1967: Washington, D.C.)*, 1968. *Water for Peace*, Vol. I, Washington: For sale by the Supt. of Docs., U.S. Govt. Print. Off.
İsvan, Ahmet. 2011. *Başkent Gölgesinde Istanbul*. Istanbul: Türkiye İş Bankası Kültür Yayınları.
Kaika, Maria. 2006. "Dams as Symbols of Modernization: The Urbanization of Nature between Geographical Imagination and Materiality," *Annals of the Association of American Geographers* 96 (2): 276–301.
Kaika, Maria and Eric Swyngedouw. 2000. "Fetishizing the Modern City: The Phantasmagoria of Urban Technological Networks," *International Journal of Urban and Regional Research* 24 (1): 120–38.
Kazgan, Haydar, and Sami Önal. 1999. *İstanbul'da Suyun Tarihi*. Istanbul: İletişim Yayınları.
Kentel, K. Mehmet. 2018. *Assembling "Cosmopolitan" Pera: An Infrastructural History of Late Ottoman Istanbul*, Seattle, WA: University of Washington.
Kentel, K. Mehmet. 2019. "Nature's 'Cosmopolis': Villagers, Engineers and Animals along Terkos Waterworks in Late Nineteenth-Century Istanbul," in Onur İnal and Yavuz Köse (eds.), *Seeds of Power: Explorations in Ottoman Environmental History*, 155–82, Winwick/Cambridgeshire: The White Horse Press.
Keyder, Çağlar. 2008. "A Brief History of Modern Istanbul," in Reşat Kasaba (ed.), *The Cambridge History of Turkey*, 504–23, Cambridge: Cambridge University Press.
Kezer, Zeynep. 2015. *Building Modern Turkey: State, Space, and Ideology in the Early Republic*, Pittsburgh, PA: University of Pittsburgh Press.
Larkin, Brian. 2013. "The Politics and Poetics of Infrastructure," *Annual Review of Anthropology* 42: 327–43.
Latour, Bruno. 1999. "Give Me a Laboratory and I Will Raise the World," in Mario Biagioli (ed.), *Science Studies Reader*, 141–69, London: Routledge.
Mango, Cyril . 1995. "The Water Supply of Constantinople," in Cyril Mango, Gilbert Dagron, and Geoffrey Greatrex *Constantinople and Its Hinterland: Papers from the Twenty-Seventh Spring Symposium of Byzantine Studies, Oxford, April 1993*, 9–18, Hampshire, Great Britain: Variorum, 1995.
Ministry of Energy and Natural Resources. 1964. "İstanbul Şehri, Büyük İstanbul ve Civarındaki Sür'atle Gelişen Endüstri Sahasının İçme Kullanma ve Endüstri Suyu Ile Kanalizasyon Işlerinin Islahı ve Tesvii Için Master Planı Fizibilite Raporları, Ön

Mühendislik Çalışmaları ve Diğer Teşkilat Etüdleri Yapılması Hususunda Birleşmiş Milletler Özel Fonundan Yardım Temini Için Türkiye Cumhuriyeti Devleti Tarafından Hazırlanmış Talepname," Ankara: Ministry of Energy and Natural Resources, Ministry of Foreign Affairs.
Nirven, Sadi N. 1960. "Istanbul Sularının Tasfiyesinde Otuz Sene," *Tıb Dünyası Dergisi* 33 (2): 59–64.
No Author 1941. *Istanbul Belediye Mecmuasi* 192.
No Author 1971. *Millet Meclisi Tutanak Dergisi* 31.
Noyan, Kemal and Turhan Şenoğulları. 1968. "Domestic and Industrial Water Supply Project for the City of Istanbul and Adapazari-Izmit-Istanbul Industrial Zone," in *International Conference on Water for Peace*, Vol. 6. Washington DC: US Government Printing Office.
Pamuk, Şevket. 2014. *Türkiye'nin 200 Yıllık İktisadi Tarihi*, Istanbul: Türkiye İş Bankası Kültür Yayınları.
Pritchard, Sara B. 2011. *Confluence: The Nature of Technology and the Remaking of the Rhône*, Cambridge, MA: Harvard University Press.
Pritchard, Sara B. and Carl A. Zimring, eds. 2020. *Technology and the Environment in History*, Baltimore: John Hopkins University Press.
Rosenberg, Charles E. 1992. "Framing Disease: Illness, Society, and History," *Hospital Practice* 27 (7): 179–221.
von Schnitzler, Antina. 2016. *Democracy's Infrastructure: Techno-Politics and Protest after Apartheid*, Princeton, NJ: Princeton University Press.
Sayılarla İstanbul. 2001. Istanbul: İstanbul Büyükşehir Belediyesi.
Scott, James C. 1999. *Seeing Like a State: How Certain Schemes to Improve the Human Condition Have Failed*, New Haven and London: Yale University Press.
Star, Susan L. 1999. "The Ethnography of Infrastructure," *American Behavioral Scientist* 43 (3): 337–91.
Tarih Boyunca Istanbul'un Su Davası. 1950. Istanbul: Halk Basımevi.
TC Sular Idaresi. 1958. *Istanbul Suları ve Sular Idaresinin Faaliyeti*, Istanbul: Tan Matbaası.
Tekeli, İlhan. 2009. *Kentsel Arsa, Altyapı ve Kentsel Hizmetler*, Istanbul: Tarih Vakfı Yurt Yayınları.
Tekeli, İlhan. 2013. *İstanbul'un Planlanmasının ve Gelişmesinin Öyküsü*, Istanbul: Tarih Vakfı Yurt Yayınları.
Tekeli, İlhan, Yiğit Gülöksüz, and Tarık Okyay. 1976. *Dolmuşlu, Gecekondulu, İşportalı Şehir*. Istanbul: Cem Yayınevi.
Tezok, Fatih, Kemal Birol, Abdurrahman Koçer, and Nihat Meriç. 1970. "Kolera'ya Genel Bir Bakış," *Mikrobiyoloji Bülteni* 4 (4): 1–20.
"10 Yıllık Su Programı." 1961. stanbul: Istanbul Sular Idaresi.
Winner, Langdon. 1980. "Do Artifacts Have Politics?" *Daedalus* 109 (1): 121–36.
Yanardağ, Pınar. 2009. *The Epidemic, the Prison House and the Global City: Belonging and Identity in Bayrampaşa*, Istanbul: Boğaziçi Üniversitesi.
Yarbağ, Cengiz and Güney Koray. 1970. "Kolera İstanbul'da Panik Yarattı," *Hayat* no 43, October 22,1970.
Yurdakul, İlhami. 2010. *Aziz Şehre Leziz Su: Dersaadet (İstanbul) Su Şirketi (1873–1933)*, Istanbul: Kitabevi.

3

"Not for Sale"

Coal as Pedagogical Infrastructure after the Soma Mine Disaster

Elif Irem Az

One morning in May 2019, I got on the bus that had been rented by a theater group in the town of Soma, in Manisa, Turkey. They had invited me to see their play, "Not for Sale," in the neighboring town of Burhaniye. The text of the play opens with the following words: "(NOT FOR SALE) The truths of our lives in which we find and lose parts of ourselves (the faces that can't be illuminated by the sun). (The foreman appears on stage, he is reporting to his superior on the phone)." The play is an amalgamation of two shorter plays, each written by a different worker, and a short story by Ayşegül K., namely *Olmaz mı?* [Wouldn't it be possible?]. All these texts were written in response to the Soma mine disaster of May 13, 2014. An explosion in the *Eynez* underground lignite coal mine, operated by Soma Mining Co., ignited an underground fire that blocked the exit. As a result, 301 miners died from carbon monoxide poisoning (Union of Turkish Bar Associations 2014, 19). The Soma mine disaster—or the Soma massacre, as it came to be referred to by those who criticized the complicity of the government in the incident—was the deadliest industrial disaster in the history of the Turkish Republic. It sent shockwaves of sympathy and anger throughout the country in the months that ensued. In May 2019, despite the disaster having happened five years before, the play still felt current in the larger Aegean region, and the invitations to perform that the group continued to receive were proof of that. Mehmet[1] asked me to attend the performance in Burhaniye and comment both on the text and the group's performance. He was a coal miner and one of the most active members of the group. Among the actors and crew members were miners, technicians, teachers, thermal power plant workers, and a saleswoman. A sack full of lignite coal was one of the props for the play, which we carried to the bus together. The tag "Not for Sale" [*Parayla Satılamaz*] was printed on it in red as it is printed on all of the sacks of coal distributed to the qualified or "deserving" poor by the government as welfare provision.

It is no surprise that "Not for Sale," written by two workers in response to the tragedies unleashed by the disaster, revolves around the hard lignite coal that is extracted in the Soma coal basin and distributed as Coal Aid for heating purposes by the AKP (*Adalet ve Kalkınma Partisi* [The Justice and Development Party]) government[2]—while the rest of it is used in the region's coal-fired thermal power plants or sold commercially. Soma's lignite coal is referred to as "Soma coal," inside and beyond the basin.[3] And it has long become the symbol of political tensions around the Social Assistance and Solidarity Fund in Turkey (widely known as the Poor Fund [*Fakir Fukara Fonu*]). The tag, "Not for Sale," is semantically and ideologically loaded since it is both a powerful symbolic element of the AKP's iteration of the welfare regime and a signifier of the accusations directed at coal miners and their families due to the widespread belief that all of them continued to vote for the AKP after the disaster—hence, becoming complicit in their own exploitation and subjugation.

In this chapter, I render Soma coal as a microcosm of the contemporary infrastructures of Turkey's welfare and labor regimes, which are both symbolically and materially intertwined with coal extraction. In other words, the materiality, the infrastructural movement, and the broader signifier of "Soma coal" are situated at the intersection of the country's labor and welfare regimes. Increasingly after the Soma mine disaster, Soma coal has become a pedagogical infrastructure in the lives of miners; their family members; and other low-wage, daily-wage, informal, and unpaid domestic workers whose livelihoods—directly or indirectly—depend on mining. This pedagogical infrastructure is composed of material, political, and symbolic elements and processes.

Soma coal is extracted as a substance, and produced as a natural resource. It is central to the energy infrastructure in the region. It is a material and symbolic presence in the work and everyday lives of Soma residents (in different forms among different groups) as a determinant of their experiences of labor and as a heating source, which means it is ambient in the air that they breathe, and thus, present in their bodies.[4] Soma coal is a crystallizing example of how the government's political and economic projects—which programmatically combine neoliberal statism (Tuğal 2023, 461), authoritarian populism, and an ever-expanding extractivist developmentalism (Dinç 2025; Yıldırım 2023)—operate on many levels. In arguing so, I build on the literature on the role of infrastructure, including megaprojects, in manufacturing mass consent under neoliberal statism in Turkey (Tuğal 2023, 458); in urban transformation, development, and governance (Bartu Candan and Kolluoğlu 2008; Dogan and Stupar 2017, 282; Kuyucu and Ünsal 2010, 1484–5; Tansel 2019, 322); and in the country's modes of entry into foreign markets (Uner, Çavuşgil, and Çavuşgil 2018, 801). By extension, my study of Soma coal is informed also by the literature on mega- and other infrastructure projects within neoliberal operations of capitalism or state capitalism in other parts of the world (Grubbauer and Čamprag 2019, 651; Olds 1995, 1713; Rizzo 2020, 1530–2; Wang and Wu 2019, 1658–9).

Meanwhile, it is possible to observe Soma coal as an object, a commodity, an incentive, a symbol, and a rationale in its multifaceted movement due to its relatively small scale and thanks to the ethnographic method. Based on eighteen months of ethnographic research and sixty-eight (recorded) open-ended interviews that I conducted in the Soma coal basin in 2018–19, I conceptually mobilize Soma coal as pedagogical infrastructure because it does not serve merely as a material infrastructure of the government's economic and ideological projects. Nor does it only function as a material and socioeconomic means of coercing the working-class people of the Soma basin into working in the mining sector and/or supporting the AKP. It is a dense nexus of resource extraction, which—through the movement of matter as well as its political and symbolic connotations—reveals how workers who maintain extractivism in the region have learned to endure, navigate, *and* desire it. In other words, Soma coal involves *and* exceeds its infrastructural and socioeconomic function in the market, in the ideological production of mass consent under the AKP, and in the coercive power of mining capital. To show how Soma coal operates as a pedagogical infrastructure, I subsume several interconnected forms of infrastructure in the basin under the signifier "Soma coal." I present them as a complex genre of pedagogical infrastructure that took its current form in the aftermath of the Soma mine disaster.

One strand (or leg) of this pedagogical infrastructure is the Social Assistance and Solidarity Fund, or the Poor Fund, which was established in 1986 by the forty-fifth Turkish government—the first civilian government after the 1980 military coup. The Poor Fund was the first and only government initiative for monetary social assistance. Since 2002, its organizational infrastructure and political orientation have been reshaped by the AKP—with its prioritization of income-based welfare policies over employment-based ones (Yörük 2022, 7), and the involvement of faith-based nongovernmental organizations[5] in the process of distribution (Atalay 2019, 432). Over the same period, the local material infrastructures of coal extraction, production, and distribution began to dominate "the ambient conditions of everyday life" (Larkin 2013, 336) in the Soma basin. "Infrastructures are matter that enable the movement of other matter," and "their peculiar ontology lies in the fact that they are things and also the relations between things," Brian Larkin argues (2013, 329). Soma coal constitutes part of the material of energy infrastructure in the country, namely thermal power plants, as well as part of the infrastructure of the contemporary welfare and labor regimes in Turkey. Soma coal then catalyzes "a moving and a sensing"[6] of neoliberal statism and mining capital through substances, relationships, welfare policies, channels of communication, and subjectivities.

Here I build also on Julie Y. Chu's understanding of infrastructures as "more than just technical apparatuses for the mobilization and conversion of matter into legible human resources," which she argues based on her ethnographic research with residents fighting eviction in Fuzhou, China (Chu 2014, 353). Chu follows Jacques Rancière's thinking in describing how her interlocutors cultivate a "tacit 'common sense' of the world and that world's built-in or proper distribution of life chances and energies" (Rancière 2006; Chu 2014, 353). I follow Julia Elyachar's thinking about "tacit knowledge" and "phatic labor" (Elyachar 2010) while laying out how miners and their family members learn to navigate the welfare and labor networks in the basin by mobilizing their embodied and phatic labor. Through an attention to the enmeshedness of labor, labor networks, welfare policies, coal, and the rest of the material infrastructure in question, I also show how Soma coal—as a complex pedagogical infrastructure—works to subjectivize miners and their family members into working-class subjects desiring coal production.

Soma coal thus hails miners, their family members, and other laborers as "deserving" subjects of the state, and subjectivizes them—rendering them at once subjects of self-knowledge and subjected to relations of power, control, and dependence (Foucault 1982, 781). It shapes the ways in which miners and their families relate to the labor of mining and living, to coal, to the landscape, and to their selves. In emphasizing the role of embodied and phatic labor within this pedagogical infrastructure, I use the concept of subjectivity as intertwined with what Marx calls "living labor," or "labor as subjectivity," which objectifies itself "not as an object, but as activity, [. . .] as the living source of value" (Marx 1993, 272).[7] The authors of the theater play, "Not for Sale," found it fitting to open the play with an emphasis on the truths of their lives in which they find and lose parts of themselves through work, living labor (as bearers of capacity for labor power), suffering, friendship, loss, and grief. Following their lead, I consider "labor as subjectivity," or living as a subject who bears labor as capacity and possibility, entangled with subjectivity as "the means of shaping sensibility" (Biehl, Good, and Kleinman 2007, 14) through an ever-renewed attempt to access the truth of one's self (Lacan 1989; Foucault 2000).

In what follows, I begin by reviewing the origins of and the historical shifts in the welfare system, and Soma coal's infrastructural, political, and symbolic part—crystallized in the tag, "Not for Sale"—within it. I show how these shifts have affected the everyday and work lives of Soma miners, their families, and other residents of the basin. In the second part, I discuss Soma coal's extraction, circulation, and distribution as a locally produced resource; as welfare provision distributed by the government; and as employment-based social aid distributed to miners by their own employers. Finally, in the third part, I trace the effects of the subjectivization of miners and their family members through Soma coal by looking at their changing desires, perceptions of the social, and understandings of post-disaster politics in the Soma basin.

The Welfare Regime and the Symbolic Power of Soma Coal

The origins of the current welfare regime in Turkey date back to 1986—six years after the 1980 coup. On May 30, 1986, *Milliyet* newspaper reported that the Fund for the Encouragement of Social Cooperation and Solidarity, or as it came to be widely known, the Poor Fund [*Fakir Fukara Fonu* or *Fak-Fuk-Fon* in Turkish], was established by the government.[8] Immediately following this announcement was another news article discussing the first stages of the privatization of TEKEL (translates as "single-hand" or "monopoly"), the national institution of Turkish tobacco and alcoholic beverages: "TEKEL goes public." As befittingly placed on the page by *Milliyet* newspaper, macro-level structural and policy changes toward neoliberalization, including privatizations, and the foundation of the Poor Fund were simultaneous because the former necessitated the latter, among other things.

The gradual privatization of TEKEL was part of the postcoup neoliberalization process led by the then-prime minister Turgut Özal. It had a major impact on people's livelihoods in the tobacco-producing region that later came to be known as the Soma coal basin. While agricultural capacities diminished with the introduction of "free market" rules in the coup's aftermath, the production of coal has been free of these same rules. State intervention, subsidies, and purchases enabled the growth of coal mining in the region. The ministries of energy and natural resources supported indigenous coal extraction and coal use to produce electricity royalties through royalty auctions,[9] additional economic incentives, and legal amendments that encourage domestic corporations to invest in the coal sector.

After coming to power in late 2002, the newly elected AKP government revised the fourth article of the Mining Law. As a result, many coal mines were subcontracted (via service procurement agreements [*hizmet alım sözleşmeleri*]) or leased via price-based royalty/*redevance* agreements) to relatively inexperienced private companies. Before TEKEL's privatization radically decreased the value of tobacco, most families in the region had made a living almost exclusively from tobacco farming (Aydın 2010, 171; Özuğurlu 2011; Çelik 2017). As peasant-farmer families of Soma either fully or partially left tobacco cultivation (Adaman, Akbulut, and Arsel 2019; Çelik 2021, 7),[10] most adult men in these families were driven to seek jobs in the coal mines, which came with a relatively steady income and the prospect of a retirement pension. This process continued with an accelerated—yet not total—transition from agricultural labor and tenancy to wage labor after the AKP came to power (Gürel et al. 2019; İslamoğlu 2017, 82–3; Keyder and Yenal 2011, 75).

Meanwhile, the expansion of partnerships between the state, private sector, and faith-based nongovernmental actors as part of the transforming welfare regime included partial or hybrid forms of decentralization and privatization. Sinem Adar and Ayşe Buğra argue that Turkey adopted a "disorganized welfare mix" (Adar and Buğra 2008, 84–93). The strategies of decentralization, diffusion, and privatization of political power allowed the state to reconfigure the combination of actors who carry the burden of labor for social security provision. Some of the central responsibilities of the state were transferred legally to local governments, municipalities, the private sector, nongovernmental organizations,[11] and implicitly, to those who need and seek social assistance. One of the most significant parts of this disorganized mix for the case of the Soma coal basin has been the Metropolitan Municipalities Law, which passed in 2004. This regulation increased the responsibilities of municipalities in the welfare system, and by extension, the amount of phatic labor—"practices of sociality that create a social infrastructure of communicative channels" (Elyachar 2010, 454)—demanded from the potential recipients of provisions who now needed to interact with municipality officials and other local political figures for access to welfare benefits.

There has been an intertwined relationship between the increasing responsibility and knowledge of those who are in need within the workings of the welfare system, and the AKP's "field expertise" about the living conditions and subjectivities of those groups (Tuğal 2009, 85). This relationship is maintained through the AKP's ongoing fieldwork as well as through policy shifts. According to Erdem Yörük, after the AKP came to power, the center of grassroots politics—in other words, the fieldwork sites—of the government has gradually shifted from the formal proletariat to the informal proletariat (Yörük 2022, 7). This has meant increasing prioritization of income-based policies—over employment-based policies—to contain potential or existing political unrest among Kurds and the informal proletariat—which are not mutually exclusive groups—more effectively (Yörük 2022, 167).[12]

In the aftermath of the disaster, Soma coal has come to matter and materialize (Kaşdoğan and Kurtiç 2025) in and through the AKP's politics at the intersection of energy, welfare, and labor. In other words, the material politics of the already consolidated AKP regime required Soma coal to be materialized as a pedagogical infrastructure that depends on and works to shape the tacit knowledge (Polanyi 2009 [1966], 4) of miners, their family members, and other Soma residents about how things work. Julia Elyachar defines tacit knowledge as "unsystematized, unverbalized forms of knowledge that were integrated into the [collective] body itself" (Elyachar 2012, 83). She locates tacit knowledge in communicative channels that are "embodied in collective subjects" (Elyachar 2012, 90) and argues that in Egypt and elsewhere, tacit forms of knowledge have historically been mobilized by the loosely regulated public sector and laid the foundations of neoliberalism, unlike what Western theorists of neoliberalism predicted. The post-1980 welfare system in neoliberal Turkey, too, was built partially on the tacit knowledge of those who seek social assistance.

In the aftermath of the Soma mine disaster, the government found (or invented) a strategic opportunity to reevaluate the impact of the AKP's diverse tools for manufacturing consent and ensuring political containment, including welfare provisions and other forms of social assistance. While thousands of coal miners, their family members, and others in support took to the streets of Soma in protest of the mining companies and the AKP government, new forms of social assistance were fashioned exclusively for the families of 301 miners who died in the disaster (Yumbul 2017, 127).[13] Unsurprisingly, an enduring sense of injustice began to foment among the surviving miners.[14] This persistent sense of frustration toward the government's response catalyzed some changes in the working conditions in the mines. In September 2014, three months after the disaster, a legal amendment was passed to double the wages of miners—double the Turkish minimum wage—though several mining companies refused to implement this change and continued to pay one minimum wage until several miners, including three of my interlocutors, sued their employers. Nonetheless, even in the wake of the disaster, these ameliorations made mining jobs increasingly desirable to workers within and outside the Soma basin.

As the jobs became more desirable, however, they also became increasingly difficult to get. Cemil, who was born and raised in Soma, said:

> Before the disaster, most of the locals [*buranın yerlisi*] wouldn't deign [*tenezzül etmezdi*] to work in the mines. I mean, those who had other sources of income, you know. Now most of us can't get in. People use their connections if they know one or two MPs [Members of Parliament]. Even then it's very hard unless those connections are from the AKP.

Either locals of the basin or migrants from other regions of Turkey—most of whom are also from rural families who gradually lost their agricultural sources of income after the 1980 military coup—learned through experience that there are communicative channels through which one can find a job or gain access to desired forms of social assistance. Cemil and other interlocutors from the villages of Soma and Kınık often talked about how they had to develop relationships and maintain existing connections with the Members of Parliament (MPs) with whom they met in the immediate aftermath of the disaster when politicians were flooding into the region.

All the while, the field expertise and the distribution work of municipalities permitted the welfare regime to infiltrate and gain traction in the greater share of low-income households, including Soma miners.[15] Tahir Çetin, the late president of the Independent Miners' Union [*Bağımsız Maden İşçileri Derneği*], told me about many cases in which, when asked why they are voting for the AKP, miners responded by saying that their children or elderly are on disability benefits, or they have received other forms of social assistance from the AKP government. In most cases, it was not possible to learn the exact types and amounts received by each household since most people did not want to share detailed information out of anxiety over their future interactions in the local channels of welfare provision.

As in the case of Hakan, who was in his thirties, married and had two children, some shared receiving social assistance in the form of cash transfer (Ark-Yıldırım and Smyrl 2021, 73) at least once. In 2012 or 2013—he couldn't remember precisely—Hakan and his brother Ekrem had lost their houses, which were built on the same plot, to an almost deadly fire. As Hakan was recounting the story of how the fire began as an accident inside the house, he casually mentioned that "the Municipality chipped in four thousand Turkish Liras at the time—two for me, two for him [referring to his brother Ekrem]. That's how we rebuilt our houses." Ekrem corrected him, explaining that the person who had "chipped in" from the Social Assistance and Solidarity Fund was not the then mayor Süleyman Kaya from the main opposition party (People's Republican Party [*Cumhuriyet Halk Partisi*]), but the mayoral candidate from the AKP, Sadık Doğruer. Hakan then added that he and his brother had become members of the AKP in order to receive this cash aid from the Fund to rebuild their houses. At the time of our conversation, Ekrem had left party membership while Hakan still hadn't. Hakan's wife Güler rarely spoke but was part of our conversation in their garden. She mildly scolded Emre, implying he was either being lazy or had reason not to renounce his membership. She had a point about her second guess, according to many other miners. Merih, a middle-aged miner who then lived in Savaştepe, for instance, told me that he became a member of the party to find a job in the mines, upon the advice of his miner friends, and he did find one shortly afterward, through his new connections.

The 2014 local elections took place in March, right after Hakan and Ekrem received cash assistance. Sadık Doğruer was elected as the first mayor of Kınık from the AKP, which means it took two terms for the party to establish its voting base in the Alevi-majority town. Doğruer was reelected in Kınık in 2019. When I asked Hakan and Ekrem how they found out about the possibility of such cash assistance in return for membership, they simply said that they knew miners who had done it earlier. A couple of months prior to this conversation, Deniz (one of the organizing experts of the Independent Miners' Union) explained to me that since the disaster, men who wanted mining jobs in Soma had to know an influential MP and/or become a member of the party themselves.

After the disaster, Soma coal gained a broader symbolic meaning on the national level. The Soma mine disaster took place after three successful general elections for the AKP (Table 3.1) and after the effective entrenchment of neoliberal and extractivist policies by its consecutive one-party governments. Scholars hint at the ways in which the party's conservative and populist agenda has always been intertwined with "a

Table 3.1 AKP's Percentage of Votes in Turkey and in Soma

	Turkey (%)	Soma (%)
2002 General Elections	34.28	39
2007 General Elections	46.7	51.2
2011 General Elections	49.8	52.8
2015 June General Elections	40.8	39.9
2015 November General Elections	49.5	49.7
2017 Referendum for Presidential System	51.4	53.1
2018 General Elections	42.56	48.43

Source: Created by author.

strategy of redistributing the benefits of the economic boom [. . .] mainly through social assistance, which, together with the promise of employment, made up the material backbone of the AKP's populism" (Adaman, Akbulut, and Arsel 2019, 521). There was a significant decrease in the AKP's share of votes in Soma as well as nationally in the first general elections after the disaster, in June 2015. Still, the relatively high percentage of the AKP's votes in Soma generated a great deal of contempt for miners and their families among the Kemalist, secularist, anti-AKP circles inside and outside the basin. Though there were approximately 15,000 miners in the Soma mines at the time, amid a local population of 107,075, coal miners became the political scapegoats for the anti-AKP groups' frustration about the failure of oppositional parties to attract larger numbers of voters.[16]

It was in this context that Soma coal became one of the symbols of the AKP's welfare regime, an infrastructure and a tool for manufacturing and maintaining consent, as well as an emblem of the perceived ignorance of working-class and low-income communities who continued to support the party after the disaster (because they were supposedly bought off with Coal Aid). Though the government-led disaster relief payments and other forms of compensation were limited to the families of 301 miners, the material politics of coal production and circulation, including its distribution across the country as Coal Aid, allowed for Soma coal's emergence as one of the national symbols of the AKP's domestic energopolitics (Erensü 2018) and authoritarian populism.

Coal Aid and the Expanded Meanings of Social Aid

How did the infrastructures of coal production and circulation allow for the movement of Soma coal as a substance and as a capacious national symbol that has the capacity to signify Turkey's domestic energy politics, the welfare regime, and the AKP's populism? Bought, used, and distributed almost exclusively[17] by the state, Soma coal is a fundamental component of both the national energy infrastructure's material existence and the contemporary welfare regime in Turkey. Fossil fuels dominate the country's domestic supply of energy. When I arrived in Soma in 2018, more than a third of Turkey's gross electricity production was coming from hard coal (22.4 percent) and lignite (14.9 percent) (EUROCOAL 2018)—including locally produced and imported coal.[18] Meanwhile, approximately 30 million tons of lignite coal has been distributed across Turkey in seventeen years, between 2003 and 2020, as Coal Aid for domestic heating (Turkish Coal Enterprises' official website [*Türkiye Kömür İşletmeleri*—TKİ[19]]).[20] The distribution was implemented by the Social Aid and Solidarity Foundations [*Sosyal Yardımlaşma ve Dayanışma Vakıfları*], which are the faith-based organizations that collaborate with the Ministry of Family and Social Services for the distribution of provisions. Within the same period of seventeen years, a total of approximately 1.198,232 billion tons of lignite coal and asphaltite have been produced in Turkey according to TKİ's "Statistics of Coal Production and Consumption" (TÜİK 2021).[21]

To a significant extent, the transformation of the welfare regime under the AKP rule, which I covered in the previous part, has historically coincided with "Turkey's 21st century coal rush" (Çelik 2021, 3). The state owns approximately 90 percent of the active pits in Turkey. The process of privatization in coal extraction is an extension of the post-1980 military coup process of neoliberalization, but it was accelerated and completed throughout 2000s, after the AKP came to power in late 2002 (Erensü 2018, 149). Through the price-based royalty/*redevance* system[22] that was approved through the 2004 Mining Law amendment, the state—the owner of most mining sites—was authorized to sign five- to ten-year agreements for the extraction and production of coal with private parties/subcontractors (Makhijani 2014, 5; Topaloğlu 2015). In privatization literature, the royalty system is simply called "leasing" (Evyapan 2015). Under this model of monopsony, mining companies focused on minimizing the cost of extraction, mainly through controlling labor, and minimizing its financial cost. This hybrid form of privatization thus inevitably introduced "production pressure" (Çelik 2017, 785) into the work lives of Soma miners since the royalty agreements guaranteed that everything that is extracted—unwashed and unprocessed coal, including the slurry—would be purchased by the state, per ton of mineral.[23]

In the absence of almost any state supervision until the Soma mine disaster, the working conditions in the mines were very harsh, with very few safety measures set in place. My interlocutors often referred to the pressure to produce by mimicking the words of their foremen and other superiors, "Come on, come on!" [*Hadi hadi!*], to which an entire scene was dedicated in the play "Not for Sale." According to my interlocutors who worked underground, the production pressure was not significantly alleviated by the national outrage that followed the disaster. The pressure was only temporarily on pause after May 13, 2014—which significantly reduced coal production as well as the amount of Coal Aid distributed in the following year (SMSP 2015–2019 n.d., 19–20). Domestic energy consumption was on an increasing trend. So was indigenous lignite coal production. Unsurprisingly, then, employment in the mines continued to increase apace in the region (SMSP n.d., 13), and so did the daily profit per employee/miner: from 19.1 TRY in 2004 to 149.3 TRY in 2012 in the overall mining sector, and from 16.3 TRY in 2004 to 34.2 TRY in hard coal and lignite mining (The Economic Policy Research Foundation [TEPAV] and ILO, 2015, 122–3).

The fact that most of the profits made by mining companies were generated through the intensification of exploitation was often mentioned by coal miners. They frequently reflected on the state of their bodies, injuries, and postures both as bearers and parts of the infrastructures of the coal industry. "This 'black diamond' [*kara elmas*] is our sweat and blood, coal aid is our sweat and blood" said Halil, an experienced miner who worked in several coal mines across Turkey. Soma coal is materialized through miners' embodied labor. Miners perpetually anticipate dying in work accidents or surviving accidents with injuries that render them incapable of able-bodied labor. That which is distributed as Coal Aid is, according to Halil and others, miners' sweat and blood. Soma coal, then, operates also through bodies. As an infrastructure of energy, welfare, and labor, Soma coal extends, materializes, and drives life as, through, and into diseases (Uzmay 2025), absences (mostly of limbs), gestures that articulate debility, coal dust in fingernails and other body parts, the breathed and polluted air, and also as ways of carrying one's masculinized and breadwinning body.

While miners complained about their working conditions and the disdainful treatment by some of their superiors, many also perceived Soma coal as a source of pride, including my interlocutors who were coal truck drivers and engineers. This was both because of the actual and perceived quality of coal,[24] and because of the embodied labor they put into the production of coal and the transportation of Coal Aid that is "Not for Sale." This pride is at times ritualized in the form of animal sacrifice,[25] which was performed by the members of the Soma Cooperative of Transporters and Motor Vehicles [*Soma Nakliyeciler ve Motorlu Taşıtlar Kooperatifi*] in 2017—before sending off the coal produced and packaged in Soma as Coal Aid.[26] Since the disaster, the Social Security and Solidarity Fund has continued to reach larger segments of society, as reported by Yörük and the KONDA research company (Yörük 2022, 64).

Soma miners and their families receive another type of social aid in the form of coal: once every year, each miner is given a certain amount of coal as heating aid by the mining company for which he works.[27] The full agreed-upon amount in the basin was 5 tons per miner in 2018–19. The company gives ration cards to the miners and pays the Turkish Coal Enterprises (TKİ), a state institution, for the total amount of coal to be distributed to its workers. Miners then receive their yearly coal rations [*yıllık kömür istihkakı*] from TKİ. This infrastructure of distribution has a pedagogical function. Miners and their families, as well as other worker-residents, perceive the AKP municipality (and the government), the mining companies, and Turkey's Union of Mineworkers [*Türkiye Maden İşçileri Sendikası*] as different limbs of the same organism—not because they conflate them due to lack of knowledge, but through their tacit knowledge of how the connections between them work for the benefit of companies and the high-ups in the union.

Turkey's Union of Mineworkers is the dominant pro-government company union—or "yellow union [*sarı sendika*]" as named in Turkey and elsewhere[28]—and most miners in the region are its members. The yellow union takes both mediating and leading roles in the channels of communication through which miners and their families learn to navigate the networks that provide access to social assistance and mining jobs. The annual coal ration is guaranteed by the collective-bargaining contract signed between the company and the union. The majority of my interlocutors expressed their fear of losing their yearly coal rations if they quit the yellow union. Such a retribution is not possible according to their contract. Refik, a then board member of the Independent

Miners' Union, said that when urged to leave the yellow union and become a member of the Independent Miners' Union, most miners say, "I will do it after the yearly coal rations are distributed."

My interlocutors were either threatened by or witnessed their coworkers getting threatened by the representatives and organizers of Turkey's Union of Mineworkers, some of whom are or were miners themselves. Smoking in the hallway before the inaugural General Assembly of the Independent Miners' Union in December 2018, Raşit, a middle-aged miner, said,

> You know, it seems like they give us coal rations. But it is us who extract this coal. It is us who pay taxes and union dues[29] [referring to the fees collected by the yellow union, *Türkiye Maden İşçileri Sendikası*]. The yellow union does nothing for us—nothing but stealing from us. The ration is much less than what is already ours. It costs way less than the yearly total of union deductions.

Factually, this was not, and still is not true.[30] There is no connection between the union fees deducted from miners' wages by the yellow union and the coal rations provided by companies. Raşit's words, however, still communicate miners' perceptions of the connections between the mining companies and the yellow union.

On April 27, 2019, Nihat, a 28-year-old miner, told me that "the coal list" was up on the notice board. This particular form of coal aid (in the form of an employment benefit) and "the coal list" constitute another pedagogical form that Soma coal takes. It is a list of miners' names accompanied by the amount of coal each "deserved" in the past year. In other words, miners are *graded* on this list over 5 tons of coal, based on the number of days they have worked each year. The collective-bargaining contract signed by Turkey's Union of Mineworkers and İmbat Mining Co. dubs these coal rations "social aid," and states that one cannot receive the full amount of 5 tons unless he works 342 days of the year. Not only is this a tall order, but it also means working during the recognized national and religious holidays. Moreover, the legally protected paid sick leaves are also counted by the foremen and other managers as days not worked, even if one obtains a medical report. This is technically possible since such cases are not specified and are thereby inscribed in the contract as loopholes.

The distribution of yearly coal rations is more systematized since the disaster. Refik said, "miners are very sensitive about their yearly coal rations since 301 [another naming of the disaster]. In a way, it is like the only benefit they receive, you know?" In other matters, though, submissiveness toward authority and willingness to defend and advocate for—either proactively or through passive consent—the practices of superiors are strong factors in a miner's likelihood of receiving all of the job benefits. In my interlocutors' experiences, the forms of "social aid [*sosyal yardım*]" listed in the collective-bargaining contracts or accessed through tacit knowledge and personal connections depend upon their political dispositions, their personalities, and their attitudes toward colleagues, foremen and other superiors. Miners, and often their family members, have to extend and expand their productive capacities—"living labor"/"labor as subjectivity"/"living source of value" (Marx 1993, 272)—in order to access not only social assistance and mining jobs but also their employment benefits.

Coerced, ideologically contained, or willing, miners who perform the necessary phatic and embodied forms of intersubjective labor have more access to different forms of social aid and job benefits.

Learning to Want Soma Coal

What makes the infrastructures of Soma coal more than means of production and relations of coercion and patronage on the one hand, and ideological interpellation on the other? What makes it a pedagogical infrastructure? Since the Soma mine disaster, Soma coal has reshaped the bodies and desires of workers in the basin in four interconnected ways: labor, debt, social prestige, and land.

What happened and continues to happen in the Soma coal basin, including the disaster, is more than the transformation of the dominant mode of production (from agriculture to mining) under a neoliberal and authoritarian state. Nor can this process be understood by supplementing the coercive forces of an emerging mode of production under neoliberalism with a story of ideological subsumption. There is no single subjectivity, or static or progressing consciousness that can represent miners and their families as implicitly and explicitly argued by those who accuse miners and their families of being ideologically complicit in their own exploitation and suffering. Some were, and possibly still are, dedicated supporters of President Erdoğan and the AKP government. Others expressed that they know very well what the AKP rule has cost them, their land, and the country, but all the same (Mannoni 1969, 69), they support it due to a lack of an alternative that can fulfill their desire for the stability of coal mining in the region, currently maintained by the AKP and the mining capital close to the party. Yet, the coal-bound desires of miners and their family members are not limited to the continuation of the material status quo either.

The subjectivizing effects of Soma coal became discernible to me through my interlocutors' resembling and diverging opinions about coal extraction in the region—including the differences of opinion among young, middle-aged, and old (sometimes retired) miners; among migrant and nonmigrant miners; and among those who lost their immediate family members in the disaster and those who have not. Coal mining is still the only viable and desirable option for young men who don't want to leave their hometown.[31] My older miner-interlocutors who experienced their own changing prospects and witnessed the transformation of the aspirations of younger men and women had deeper insights on the effects of Soma coal. Natives of the region knew the comfort of family farming (mostly tobacco) prior to TEKEL's privatization. In their narratives, Soma coal appeared as desirable not for the social prestige it generates, but for the income and benefits attached to it. Migrant miners and their families were immersed in other dynamics. They sought and continue to seek mining jobs due to the lack of good jobs or sources of income in their home regions. While some of them bestowed symbolic value on the "black diamond" and mining that runs industries through electricity and heats homes, some others merely emphasized their material well-being in the Soma basin, and the fact that they couldn't have led better lives back in their villages or towns.

Soma coal as pedagogical infrastructure exceeds coercion, patronage, and ideology not only in its materiality and movement as a substance and an energy infrastructure but also in its relatively autonomous capacity to mold working-class and low-income subjects and their desires. Soma coal subjectivizes miners and their family members in four interconnected ways that pertain to labor, debt, social prestige, and land.

Soma coal is a source of labor that is desired by low-income residents of the basin and surrounding regions. Mining jobs pay significantly better than other working-class jobs and bring stability and other social advantages, such as the ability to take credit from banks. As I mentioned earlier, the miners' wages were raised from minimum wage to two minimum wages after the disaster. This drastic change in household incomes amplified credit indebtedness among mining families. After May 2014, miners and their family members were increasingly exposed to consumer credit ads (Mişe 2022) and began to be targeted by local banks as potential credit seekers, both of which played a significant role in the expansion of their wants. Since the disaster, indebting has been forcefully operating "as a medium for producing the subject of capitalism" (Morris 2016, 62). In other words, after the 2001 economic crisis accelerated the levels of credit indebtedness in low-income households (Karaçimen 2014, 161, 2016, 257; also see Ayhan 2019), the disaster became the second turning point in debt accruement in the Soma coal basin with which my miner interlocutors agreed.

In the winter of 2019, I was invited by Aliye, a miner's wife, to their single-family house in the town of Savaştepe, which she likened to a *gecekondu* [slum, shanty, or squatter's house]. She expressed the resemblance she experienced with the following rhetorical question: "Look around you, sister. Does this look like a miner's house to you?" I later found out that her husband refused to take any type of loan or credit from banks, including a mortgage. Her husband, Macit, said that he was afraid of losing his job and remaining indebted without a proper income. Aliye nodded sarcastically and told me that her husband was right in being worried because he was lazy and kept skipping workdays whenever he felt a little down or under the weather. She seemed resentful and angry toward her husband and expressed these feelings throughout the hours they hosted me. For her, the matter of debt was a crystallization of their marital problems.

Another manifestation of Soma coal as pedagogical infrastructure, social prestige, is very much interwoven with mining labor and indebtedness. However, this prestige surpasses the visible fulfillment of material wants via wages and debt. There is the added component of masculine pride, manifesting mostly through mid- and high-level workers in mining, and small business owners who depend on the coal industry. According to two of my middle-aged interlocutors whose sons had recently secured mining jobs thanks to party connections or favors, young men too share this pride, especially in the earlier years of their work life during which most of them get married. The advantages of being a miner were often brought up among family members who hosted me in their homes when the person in question was a young man at the cusp of marriage. In the words of Ülkü, the mother of one of the 301, "Now is the time to be a miner [*Şimdi madenci olmak vardı*]. Our children died and *these ones* are reaping the benefits of the 301." Her disdain denoted multiple addressees, including the "ungrateful widows" of the 301, the "spoiled and ignorant" miners and their families who lead lives they do not deserve because they support the AKP, and the residents of the basin who sold their lands to mining companies. The three-year-long compensation struggle and strikes initiated by Soma miners—led by the Independent Miners' Union, between 2019 and 2021—has added a different, politicized quality to this largely masculine social prestige. Whether this added political quality has the force to allure non-politicized miners and their families is yet to be seen.

Finally, intensifying coal extraction required the land dispossession of the native residents of the Soma basin who owned land in extractable areas. Many sold their lands—inside or near their hometown villages—to mining companies. These sales have caused rifts and conflicts between family members since some of those who lost their loved ones in the disaster—such as my interlocutor Ülkü and her husband who lost their son—did not want their family members to sell any land to mining companies. Nonetheless, most of those who had the opportunity to sell did sell, including several families who lost their immediate family members on May 13, 2014. I met two such families in Kınık where families who had land inside or around the Elmadere village sold their lands to Polyak Mining Co. Some of those who didn't have the opportunity to sell in other parts of the basin expressed their wish to do so if a prospect presents itself.

In their home near Polyak Mining Co., I was interviewing the sixty and seventy plus year old parents of a young miner who died on May 13, 2014. Their ten-year-old grandson—one of their deceased son's children—interrupted our conversation when his grandmother, Melek, was telling me about her son's working conditions before the disaster: "It's all because of him [pointing at his grandfather], isn't it? He sold our fields to the company [to Polyak]. Would a mine pass through here if he hadn't [*Satmasaydı maden geçer miydi buradan*]?" Polyak Mining Co. had not yet existed in 2014, when his father died in the Eynez coal mine, but his narrative connected the process leading to his father's death and the process through which a big part of their village became a coal mine. Melek responded to him by saying, "It was all for you [referring to him and his siblings], for your education." The boy had the last word, "I've learned enough [*Okudum ben yetti*]."

Deserving or Undeserving, "Not for Sale"

The case of Soma coal is a deeply enmeshed net of material, political, and social infrastructures that together operate as a pedagogical infrastructure, which was enabled by the Soma mine disaster. It is a microcosm of the AKP's social, political, and economic projects that bring together neoliberal statism, authoritarian populism, and extractivist developmentalism. Through their labor as well as their needs and desires, miners and their family members are producers of and subjected to Soma coal. They are hailed by it, and taught by it how to deal with the existing labor networks and the welfare regime. These labor networks and the welfare regime together constitute a "disorganized mix" that ties together employment, benefits, and deserving and undeserving subjects. Miners produce Soma coal as a resource and an energy infrastructure and receive it as employment-based social aid from their employers. Meanwhile, they have been accused by Kemalist and anti-AKP groups of journalists, public figures, and social media users of selling their votes to the AKP in exchange for coal aid and other welfare provisions. They have also been perceived and represented by the same groups as an ignorant working-class bunch that is ideologically subsumed by their exploiters. Miners produce, materially embody, and are subjected to Soma coal.

At the same time, the bodies and subjectivities of miners and their family members continue to become more than what is expected of them within capitalism and under the ideological forces of an authoritarian state. In many ways, the play, "Not for Sale," is an expression of the unexpected "unplanned sensibilities"[32] of people who are entrenched in and exploited through the structures and infrastructures in place. Not only people's exploitation, oppression, and tacit knowledge about the workings of their political and economic conditions, but also their capacities for transgression are at stake in the interwoven stories of the play's characters. While some of the truths of everyday life and forms of embodied and living labor are represented on stage, subjects exceed or attempt to exceed expectations and structural limits. The play is a very long, fragmentary, and dolorous tale of harsh working conditions, injurious work accidents, the behaviors of abusive and disdainful superiors, and the events that followed the Soma mine disaster. The text has a cathartic finale, and the theater group's performance had seemingly clichéd styles of directing and acting. Still, at each step, miners and their loved ones "find and lose parts" of themselves, as I quoted from the play at the beginning of the chapter. To those who are open to learning from it, "Not for Sale" is a rich representation of the production process—packaging, distribution, and receiving of Soma coal as heating aid—and of the ways in which people's subjectivities and bodies have become part of this stream. The first person to appear on stage is the foreman who is on the phone, reporting to his superior with a submissive, or as called by some miners, *yalaka* [ass-kisser] cadence. And, as in the case of this foreman who later treats miners unjustly, the role of subjective particularities and transgressive interpersonal relations in the operations of Soma coal are a central aspect of the play.

Toward the end of the play, the miners whose deaths in the disaster were dramatized on stage begin to speak to the audience. The unplanned sensibilities, words, and actions of the oppressed and exploited subjects do not match the mainstream representations of, and the enforced infrastructures available to the "deserving" miner. They exceed what is expected of them in death. The posthumous words of three main miner-characters (Mehmet, Levent, and Şafak), and of Mehmet's daughter Fatmanur conclude the play and will also conclude this chapter.

[In her long monologue, Fatmanur is at the graveyard, and speaks both to her father, and to an elderly man who is also visiting the graveyard.][33]

"Allah brought the coal to our village," my grandmother prays in gratitude. Allah also killed my dad. That's what that uncle just said. Allah made my mom sick. She will be better if I pray. Allah is also the one who will give me a long life [referring to traditional prayers for children to live long lives]. But I don't want a long life without my dad. Without the smell of his socks. I don't want a long life without the 1 Lira he gave me every day. [. . .] My cheek on my dad's sweaty socks, pulling at the pants of the bearded uncle, staring into his eyes, I told him: "Uncle, tell Allah not to come to our neighborhood again, will you?"

I will be back, daddy. You left us alone, but I won't leave you alone. I love you so so so much.

(Levent and Şafak enter the stage with a sack full of coal)

Levent: NOT

Şafak: FOR SALE

Methmet: ITS COST/BLOOD MONEY HAS BEEN COVERED IN SOMA.

[*DİYETİ SOMA'DA ÖDENMİŞTİR.*]

(Lights go down)

Author: SOMA

Dramatization by Mehmet ve Tolga
(inspired also by Ayşegül K.'s short story, "Olmaz mı [Wouldn't it be possible]." Thank you.)

Acknowledgments

I am indebted to Prof. Dr. Rosalind C. Morris for her insightful and challenging feedback on earlier versions of this chapter. Her comments have significantly enhanced both my thought processes and the quality of this writing. I am also grateful to Başaran Aksu, Barış Altun, and my late friend Tahir Çetin, the first president of the Independent Miners' Union. Their unwavering support and willingness to answer my questions about specific details have been invaluable in enriching the ethnography.

Notes

1 Pseudonyms have been used for all of my interlocutors, except for Mehmet and Tolga, whose names are publicly associated with the theater play.
2 "İhtiyaç sahibi ailelere kömür yardımı bu yıl da devam edecek [Coal aid will continue to be distributed to families in need]." *Yeni Şafak*, January 13, 2022. https://www.yenisafak.com/ekonomi/ihtiyac-sahibi-ailelere-komur-yardimi-bu-yil-da-devam-edecek-3729983. Accessed on June 20, 2022.
3 The Soma coal basin consists of four towns that fall under the jurisdiction of three cities: Kınık (İzmir), Savaştepe (Balıkesir), and Kırkağaç and Soma (Manisa).

4 Due to the scope of lignite coal production in Soma and the operations of the two thermal power plants in the basin, among fifty-five cities in which air pollution measurements have been made, the city of Manisa had the highest yearly average of SO_2 (Sulfur Dioxide) in 2019 (Dark Report 2020, 33).

5 For a description of the function and legal status of "*Sosyal Yardımlaşma ve Dayanışma Vakıfları* [Social Aid and Solidarity Foundations]" on the official website of the Ministry of Family and Social Services, please see https://www.aile.gov.tr/sygm/genel-mudurluk/sosyal-yardimlasma-ve-dayanisma-vakiflari/. Accessed on August 9, 2022.

6 Here, I borrow from Rudolf Mrázek, who wrote that infrastructures create "a moving and a sensing of the modern as much as the colonial," in the Dutch colonial and postcolonial Indonesia (2010, 107).

7 The full quote from *Grundrisse*'s "Chapter on Capital" is as follows: "The only thing distinct from *objectified* labour is *non-objectified* labour, labour which is still objectifying itself, *labour* as subjectivity. Or, *objectified* labor, i.e. labour which is *present in space*, can also be opposed, as *past labour*, to labour which is *present in time*. If it is to be present in time, alive, then it can be present only as the *living subject*, in which it exists as capacity, as possibility; hence as *worker*. The only *use value*, therefore, which can form the opposite pole to capital is *labour* (to be exact, value creating, productive labor)" (Marx 1993, 272).

8 *Milliyet* Newspaper Archive, May 30, 1986. http://gazetearsivi.milliyet.com.tr/Arsiv/1986/05/30. Accessed on August 12, 2022.

9 Ardıyok, Şahin, and İlker Kıl. 2022. "Turkey's mining regulations: Overview of the legal framework and key considerations." *dentonsmininglaw.com*, August 4. URL: https://www.dentonsmininglaw.com/turkeys-mining-regulations-overview-of-the-legal-framework-and-key-considerations/. Accessed on August 12, 2022.

10 For the figure created by Coşku Çelik based on the data collected by the Institute of Statistics of Turkey [TUİK], see Çelik (2021, 8). The figure shows the decrease in tobacco production in the four towns that make up the Soma basin.

11 For the traces of the late Ottoman legacy of poor relief, and the *waqf* (Ottoman philanthropic institutions) tradition in the transformation of the Turkish welfare regime, please see Buğra and Keyder (2006, 12); Yörük (2022, 46, 144).

12 See also Özel and Yıldırım's article on the impact of social assistance policies on Turkey's transition to a presidential system (Özel and Yıldırım 2019).

13 While the approximate amount of cash relief provided by the state was 150,000 TRY (68,625 USD with an average exchange rate of 0.4575 USD in 2014), Yumbul writes that the total of relief funds and donations—from the state and from private actors—amounted to approximately 50,000 USD per family (Yumbul 2017, 219). See also Ercan (2023).

14 In December 2014, approximately six months after the disaster, 2,831 miners were laid off by Soma Mining Co. Their severance pay and compensations were usurped by the company. Former and active Soma miners organized several protests and marches to the capital Ankara in demand of what they were due between October 2019 and July 2021.

15 The social security system reached one-third of the entire population, according to the 2,685-respondent survey designed by Erdem Yörük and KONDA research company, and as of 2019, more than 40 percent of the population has received social assistance at least once in their lifetime (Yörük 2022, 64).

16 This was coincidentally a year before coal miners in the United States, once again, took their place among the scapegoats, this time for the election of Donald Trump as president in 2016 (Moran-Thomas 2017).

17 "Almost exclusively" because there is an informal business formed around the predesignated coal waste sites [*kömür döküm sahaları*] in the basin, which move periodically. Unemployed men and women whose primary occupation is housework and childcare, who live near these sites, scavenge for pieces of coal they can use for heating, or sell through informal channels.

18 "Of the remainder, 30.4% came from fossil gas, 19.7% from hydro, 6.5% from wind, 2.5% from solar PV, 2.3% from geothermal, with smaller contributions from biofuels, waste and oil. Turkey, through its "Vision 2023 strategy" [*Hedef 2023*] that marks the 100th anniversary of the Republic, aims to increase its domestic electricity production by constructing more lignite-fired power plants and raising the shares of wind and geothermal power, setting a 30% capacity target for renewables" (EUROCOAL 2018). In the same year, the country's import dependency rate was 72 percent. In 2018, Turkey imported 38.3 million tons of hard coal for thermal power plants, steel production, industry, and domestic heating purposes (EUROCOAL 2018). Coal imports continued to increase in Turkey even though the General Directorate of Mineral Research and Exploration (MTA) had an ambitious exploratory drilling program—1.0 million meters in 2017, and even more in 2018. The increase was even more drastic than expected as indigenous coal production decreased due to COVID-19.

19 TKİ is the state institution in charge of all matters related to indigenous coal extraction and production.

20 "As part of social aid programs, 30 million tons of coal have reached those in need in 17 years." *Turkish Coal Enterprises*. https://www.tki.gov.tr/sydv. Accessed on June 20, 2022.

21 Out of 3,605.094 tons of lignite coal that has been sold by the Aegean Lignite Enterprise [*Ege Linyit İşletmesi*—ELİ] in 2020, 2,286.462 tons have been used in industrial production, and 1,318.632 tons have been used for heating (General Directorate of Turkish Coal Enterprises—2020 Annual Report, 66). For the prices per ton of lignite coal sold to thermal power plants, and more, please see "Türkiye Kömür İşletmeleri Genel Müdürlüğü—2020 Faaliyet Raporu [General Directorate of Turkish Coal Enterprises—2020 Annual Report]." http://www.sp.gov.tr/upload/xSPRapor/files/82KiO+TKI_20_FR.pdf, 65-66. Accessed on June 20, 2022.

22 The royalty system in Turkey is shaped around the price per ton of coal, instead of the amount of production. The state does not require the companies to produce more than the minimum amount specified in their contract. On behalf of the Turkish state, Turkish Coal Enterprises purchases the entirety of the extracted coal, unwashed and unprocessed (TBB 2014; Ersoy 2015; TSBD 2016).

23 Coşku Çelik notes that the Chairperson of Soma Mining Co. [*Soma Holding*]—which ran several coal mines in the basin, including the Eynez underground mine where the disaster took place—Alp Gürkan shared in an interview for *Hürriyet* Daily News that the profits of Soma Mining Co. increased thanks to the company's ability to reduce production costs from $130–140 to $23.80. This news article, which was dated May 14, 2014 (one day after the disaster), and accessed by Çelik on June 19, 2020, is no longer accessible on *Hürriyet Daily News* website: https://www.hurriyetdailynews.com/soma-mine-operator-praised-lucrative-cost-reductions-in-previous-interview-66448.

24 The lignite coal of the Soma coal basin has a slightly higher quality than the lignite extracted elsewhere in Turkey. The quality of Turkish lignite is, in fact, relatively poor: "only around 5.1% of existing reserves have a heat content of more than 300 kcal/kg (12,500 kJ/kg)" (EUROCOAL 2018). The Soma basin is the second-largest lignite

mining area after the Afşin-Elbistan lignite basin in southeastern Anatolia. Soma coal has a higher quality than the lignite coal extracted elsewhere, with a range of 2,500–3,500 kcal/mt, which is poor compared to international standards. It is classified as "hard lignite" in some sources.

25 Animal sacrifice—which ideally includes the distribution of the meat to those in need—is the central ritual of Eid al-Adha. People may also pray and wish for something to take place by promising to sacrifice an animal if their wish comes true. Even without having wished for anything, after something unexpectedly good happens, the person's family may sacrifice an animal to express gratitude to God.

26 "Dağıtılacak Kömür Yardımları Yola Çıktı [Coal aid takes off from Soma to be distributed]." 2018. *CNN Türk*, December 11. https://www.cnnturk.com/turkiye/dagitilacak-yardim-komurleri-somadan-yola-cikti. Accessed on June 20, 2022.

27 This practice exists in other coal mines in different parts of the country as well, but the amount of "yearly coal ration" and processes of distribution differ from region to region—even from company to company.

28 The expression of "yellow union"—or "yellow trade unionism"—originates in the history of right-wing politics and working classes in France and goes back to the founding of *Les Jaunes* [The Yellows] as a workers' movement in July 1900 (Mosse 1972, 193, 206).

29 Monthly union due is in the amount of one day's pay, which equals 1/30 of two minimum wages at any given moment since 2014.

30 In 2022, the price of 1 ton of coal is approximately 4,000 Turkish Liras, while the monthly fee deducted from miners' wages by Turkey's Union of Mineworkers [*Türkiye Maden İşçileri Sendikası*] is 508 Turkish Liras.

31 When someone named a second option, it was almost always joining the Turkish Armed Forces as—depending on one's formal education level—a specialized sergeant, contracted private, or contracted soldier [*uzman çavuş, uzman erbaş, uzman er*] under temporary contracts.

32 Italian art critic and feminist activist Carla Lonzi's notion of the "unplanned sensibility of the unplanned subject" refers to "the creation of something that exceeds mainstream representations and clichés," and thus, something that is in excess of what is socially expected and structurally rendered possible (Fontaine in Petrossiants and Rosales 2022, 11).

33 Translations and bracketed explanations are mine. The bolded and capitalized words and sentences appear here as they do in the original text in Turkish.

References

Adaman, Fikret, Bengi Akbulut, and Murat Arsel. 2019. "Neoliberal Developmentalism, Authoritarian Populism, and Extractivism in the Countryside: The Soma Mining Disaster in Turkey," *The Journal of Peasant Studies* 46 (3): 514–36.

Adar, Sinem, and Ayşe Buğra. 2008. "Social Policy Change in Countries without Mature Welfare States: The Case of Turkey," *New Perspectives on Turkey* 38 (Spring): 83–106.

Ark-Yıldırım, Ceren, and March Smyrl. 2021. *Social Cash Transfer in Turkey: Toward Market Citizenship*, Cham: Palgrave Macmillan. https://doi.org/10.1007/978-3-030-70381-3

Atalay, Zeynep. 2019. "Partners in Patriarchy: Faith-Based Organizations and Neoliberalism in Turkey," *Critical Sociology* 45 (3): 431–45.

Aydın, Zülküf. 2010. "Neo-liberal Transformation of Turkish Agriculture," *Journal of Agrarian Change* 10 (2): 149–87.
Ayhan, Berkay. 2019. "Constituting Financialized Subjectivities: Cultural Political Economy of Financial Literacy in Turkey," *Turkish Studies* 20 (5): 680–707. http://doi.org/10.1080/14683849.2018.1520103
Bartu Candan, Ayfer and Biray Kolluoğlu. 2008. "Emerging Spaces of Neoliberalism: A Gated Town and a Public Housing Project in İstanbul," *New Perspectives on Turkey* 39: 5–46.
Biehl, João G., Byron J. Good, and Arthur Kleinman. 2007. *Subjectivity: Ethnographic Investigations*, Oakland, CA: University of California Press.
Buğra, A. and C. Keyder. 2006. "The Turkish Welfare Regime in Transformation," *Journal of European Social Policy* 16 (3): 211–28.
Chu, Julie Y. 2014. "When Infrastructures Attack: The Workings of Disrepair in China," *American Ethnologist* 41 (2): 351–67. https://doi.org/10.1111/amet.12080
Çelik, Coşku. 2017. "Kırsal Dönüşüm ve Metalaşan Yaşamlar: Soma Havzasında İşçileşme Süreçleri ve Sınıf İlişkileri [Rural Transformation and Commodified Lives: Class Relations and Processes of Proletarianization in the Soma basin]." *Praksis* 43: 785–810.
Çelik, Coşku. 2021. "Extractivism and Labor Control: Reflections on Turkey's 'Coal Rush' in Local Labor Regimes," *Critical Sociology* 49 (1): 59–76.
"Dark Report 2020." 2020 (August). Prepared by *Temiz Hava Hakkı Platformu* [The Right to Clean Air Platform]. https://turkiyedekomur.org/wp-content/uploads/2021/06/Kara-Rapor-2020.pdf (accessed June 20, 2022).
Dinç, Tarık Nejat. 2025. "Assembling Gold, Manufacturing Risk: Technopolitics in the Age of the Third Gold Rush," in Duygu Kaşdoğan, Ekin Kurtiç, and Mehmet Ekinci (eds.), *Material Politics in Turkey: Infrastructure, Science, and Expertise*, 233–54, London: Bloomsbury.
Dogan, Evinc and Aleksandra Stupar. 2017. "The Limits of Growth: A Case Study of Three Mega-Projects in Istanbul," *Cities* 60: 281–8. https://doi.org/10.1016/j.cities.2016.09.013
Economic Policy Research Foundation [TEPAV]. 2015. "Türkiye Kömür Madenciliği Sektöründe Sözleşmesel Düzenlemeler: Gerçekleşme Biçimleri, Boyutları, Nedenleri, Yasal Nedenleri ve İSG Üzerindeki Etkileri [Contractual Arrangements in Turkey's Coal Mining Sector: Forms of Actualization, Formats, Reasons, Legal Reasons, and Impacts on Workers' Health and Safety]." Supported by the International Labor Organization. https://www.tepav.org.tr/upload/files/1457365710-2.TURKIYE_KOMUR_MADENCILIGI_SEKTORUNDE_SOZLESMESEL_DUZENLEMELER.pdf (accessed June 20, 2022).
Elyachar, Julia. 2010. "Phatic Labor, Infrastructure, and the Question of Empowerment in Cairo," *American Ethnologist* 37 (3): 452–64.
Elyachar, Julia. 2012. "BEFORE (AND AFTER) NEOLIBERALISM: Tacit Knowledge, Secrets of the Trade, and the Public Sector in Egypt," *Cultural Anthropology* 27: 76–96.
Ercan, Harun. 2023. "Disaster Management as 'Pacification': The Politics of Emergency in Turkey," *Jadaliyya*, March 2. https://www.jadaliyya.com/Details/44850/Disaster-Management-as-%E2%80%9CPacification%E2%80%9D-The-Politics-of-Emergency-in-Turkey (accessed March 12, 2023).
Erensü, Sinan. 2018. "Powering Neoliberalization: Energy and Politics in the Making of a New Turkey," *Energy Research & Social Science* 41: 148–57.
Ersoy, Nuri. 2015. "İşleneceğini Herkesin Bildiği Bir Cinayetin Öyküsü," in GE-Lİ-YO-RUM DİYEN FACİA: Boğaziçi Üniversitesi Soma Araştırma Grubu Raporu, 31–54.

https://busomarastirmagrubu.bogazici.edu.tr/sites/busomarastirmagrubu.boun.edu.tr/files/cinayetinoykusu.pdf (accessed July 1, 2024).

EUROCOAL (European Association of Coal and Lignite). 2018. "TURKEY – Country Profile." https://euracoal.eu/info/country-profiles/turkey/ -(accessed June 20, 2022).

Evyapan, Fatma. 2015. "Coal Mining in Turkey: State and Private Sector Interactions Subcontracting and *Redevance*," *Turk Thoracic Journal* 16 (1): 3–4.

Fontaine, Claire, Iman Ganji, and Jose Rosales. 2022. *Foreigners Everywhere: Diversity of Aesthetics Vol. II*. Series edited by Andreas Petrossiants and Jose Rosales. Andreas Petrossiants and Jose Rosales in collaboration with the Emily Harvey Foundation.

Foucault, Michel. 1982. "The Subject and Power," *Critical Inquiry* 8 (4): 777–95.

Foucault, Michel. 2000. "Foucault," In J. Faubion (ed.), *Michel Foucault, Aesthetics, Method, and Epistemology: Essential Works of Foucault 1954–1984*, Volume 2, 459–63, London: Penguin.

Grubbauer, Monika and Nebojša Čamprag. 2019. "Urban Megaprojects, Nation-State Politics and Regulatory Capitalism in Central and Eastern Europe," *Urban Studies* (Edinburgh, Scotland) 56 (4): 649–71. https://doi.org/10.1177/0042098018757663

Gürel, Burak, Bermal Küçük, and Sercan Taş. 2019. "The Rural Roots of the Rise of the Justice and Development Party in Turkey," *The Journal of Peasant Studies* 46 (3): 457–79.

İslamoğlu, Huri. 2017. "The Politics of Agricultural Production in Turkey," in Fikret Adaman, Bengi Akbulut, and Murat Arsel (eds.), *Neoliberal Turkey and its Discontents: Economic Policy and the Environment Under Erdoğan*, 75–102, London and New York: I.B. Tauris.

Karaçimen, Elif. 2014. "Financialization in Turkey: The Case of Consumer Debt," *Journal of Balkan and Near Eastern Studies* 16 (2): 161–80. http://doi.org/10.1080/19448953.2014.910393

Karaçimen, Elif. 2016. "Consumer Credit as an Aspect of Everyday Life of Workers in Developing Countries: Evidence from Turkey," *Review of Radical Political Economics* 48 (2): 252–68.

Kaşdoğan, Duygu and Ekin Kurtiç. 2025. "On Materiality and Politics in Turkey: An Introduction," in Duygu Kaşdoğan, Ekin Kurtiç, and Mehmet Ekinci (eds.), *Material Politics in Turkey: Infrastructure, Science, and Expertise*, 1–16, London: Bloomsbury.

Keyder, Çağlar and Zafer Yenal. 2011. "Agrarian Change Under Globalization: Markets and Insecurity in Turkish Agriculture," *Journal of Agrarian Change* 11 (1): 60–86.

Kuyucu, Tuna and Özlem Ünsal. 2010. "'Urban Transformation' as State-Led Property Transfer: An Analysis of Two Cases of Urban Renewal in Istanbul," *Urban Studies (Edinburgh, Scotland)* 47 (7): 1479–99. https://doi.org/10.1177/0042098009353629

Lacan, Jacques. 1989. *The Family Complexes*, New York: W.W. Norton.

Larkin, Brian. 2013. "The Politics and Poetics of Infrastructure," *Annual Review of Anthropology* 42: 327–43. https://doi.org/10.1146/annurev-anthro-092412-155522

Makhijani, Shakuntala. 2014. "Fossil Fuel Exploration Subsidies: Turkey," In *Oil Change International Country Study*. URL: https://cdn.odi.org/media/documents/9257.pdf (accessed June 16, 2022).

Mannoni, Octave. 1969. "Je sais bien, mais quand même . . . [I know very well but nevertheless . . .]." In *Clefs pour l'imaginaire ou l'autre scène*, Paris: Seuil.

Marx, Karl. 1993 [1939]. *Grundrisse: Foundations of the Critique of Political Economy*, trans. Martin Nicolaus, New York: Penguin Classics.

Mişe, Umut. 2022. "Two Faces of Bank Commercials in Turkey: Consumerism and Populism Advertised," *The Journal of Communication and Media Studies* 7 (2): 69–82.

http://search.proquest.com.ezp-prod1.hul.harvard.edu/scholarly-journals/two-faces-bank-commercials-turkey-consumerism/docview/2729952418/se-2

Moran-Thomas, Amy. 2017. "Mine," Hot Spots, *Fieldsights* (January 18, from the series: The Rise of Trumpism). URL: https://culanth.org/fieldsights/mine

Morris, Rosalind C. 2016. "*Ursprüngliche Akkumulation*: The Secret of an Originary Mistranslation," *boundary 2* 43 (3): 29–77. Edited by Nergis Ertürk and Özge Serin. https://doi.org/10.1215/01903659-3572418

Mosse, George L. 1972. "The French Right and the Working Classes: Les Jaunes," *Journal of Contemporary History* 7 (3/4): 185–208.

Mrázek, Rudolf. 2010. *A Certain Age: Colonial Jakarta through the Memories of Its Intellectuals*, Durham: Duke University Press.

Olds, K. 1995. "Globalization and the Production of New Urban Spaces: Pacific Rim Megaprojects in the Late 20th Century," *Environment and Planning. A* 27 (11): 1713–43. https://doi.org/10.1068/a271713

Özel, Işık D. and Kerem Yıldırım. 2019. "Political Consequences of Welfare Regimes: Social Assistance and Support for Presidentialism in Turkey," *South European Society and Politics* 24 (4): 485–511.

Özuğurlu, Metin. 2011. "The TEKEL Resistance Movement: Reminiscences on Class Struggle," *Capital and Class* 35 (2): 179–87.

Polanyi, Michael. 2009[1966]. *The Tacit Dimension*, Chicago: University of Chicago Press.

Rancière, Jacques. 2006. *The Politics of Aesthetics: The Distribution of the Sensible*, London: Continuum.

Rizzo, Agatino. 2020. "Megaprojects and the Limits of 'green Resilience' in the Global South: Two Cases from Malaysia and Qatar," *Urban Studies* (Edinburgh, Scotland) 57 (7): 1520–35. https://doi.org/10.1177/0042098018812009

Soma Belediye Başkanlığı 2015–2019 Stratejik Planı [Soma Municipality Strategic Plan (SMSP) 2015–2019]. URL: http://www.sp.gov.tr/upload/xSPStratejikPlan/files/tuMEK+2015-2019StratejikPlan.pdf (accessed June 20, 2022).

Tansel, Cemal Burak. 2019. "Reproducing Authoritarian Neoliberalism in Turkey: Urban Governance and State Restructuring in the Shadow of Executive Centralization," *Globalizations* 16 (3): 320–35. https://doi.org/10.1080/14747731.2018.1502494

TBB (Türkiye Barolar Birliği). 2014. Soma Maden Faciası Raporu. https://tbbyayinlari.barobirlik.org.tr/TBBBooks/490.pdf (accessed July 1, 2014).

Topaloğlu, M. 2015. "Rödövans Sözleşmelerinin Şekli ve Tescili [Form and Registration of Royalty Contracts]." Maden Hukuku Sempozyumu [Mining Law Symposium], October 3–4.

TSBD (Türk Sosyal Bilimler Derneği). 2016. İki Yılın Ardından Soma Maden Faciası Raporu. https://tsbd.org.tr/wp-content/uploads/2017/01/somaraporu11Nisan.pdf (accessed July 1, 2024).

Tuğal, Cihan. 2009. *Passive Revolution: Absorbing the Islamic Challenge to Capitalism*, Stanford, CA: Stanford University Press.

Tuğal, Cihan. 2023. "Politicized Megaprojects and Public Sector Interventions: Mass Consent Under Neoliberal Statism," *Critical Sociology* 49 (3): 457–73. https://doi-org.ezproxy.cul.columbia.edu/10.1177/08969205221086284.

TÜİK (Turkish Statistical Institute). 2021. "Yıllık Sanayi ve Hizmet İstatistikleri [Yearly Statistics of Industry and Service Sector]." https://data.tuik.gov.tr/Bulten/Index?p=37190&dil=1 (accessed June 20, 2022).

Uner, M. Mithat, Erin Çavuşgil, and S. Tamer Çavuşgil. 2018. "Build-operate-transfer projects as a hybrid mode of market entry: The case of Yavuz Sultan Selim Bridge in

Istanbul." *International Business Review* 27 (4): 797–802. https://doi.org/10.1016/j.ibusrev.2018.01.003.

Union of Turkish Bar Associations Human Rights Center [Türkiye Barolar Birliği İnsan Hakları Merkezi]. *Soma Maden Faciası Raporu* [Report on Soma Mining Disaster]. 2014.https://www.barobirlik.org.tr/dosyalar/duyurular/20141112_somamadenfaciasipdf.pdf (accessed June 21, 2022).

Uzmay, Asya Ece. 2025. "Fountains, Disease, Blueprints: Making the Water Infrastructure of Istanbul Visible," in Duygu Kaşdoğan, Ekin Kurtiç, and Mehmet Ekinci (eds.), *Material Politics in Turkey: Infrastructure, Science, and Expertise*, 41–56, London: Bloomsbury.

Wang, Zheng and Fulong Wu. 2019. "In-Situ Marginalisation: Social Impact of Chinese Mega-Projects," *Antipode* 51 (5): 1640–63. https://doi.org/10.1111/anti.12560

Yıldırım, Kansu. 2023. "Madencilik Sektörünün Dinamikleri: İlksel Birikim, İhracat ve Ekstraktivizm," *siyasaliktisat.com*, September 23. https://www.siyasaliktisat.com/post/madencilik-sektorunun-dinamikleri-yildirim (accessed September 24, 2023).

Yörük, Erdem. 2022. *The Politics of the Welfare State in Turkey: How Social Movements and Elite Competition Created a Welfare State*, Ann Arbor, MI: University of Michigan Press.

Yumbul, Çiğdem. 2017 (December). "Life in Soma, Turkey, After the Mining Massacre of 2014: An Autoethonographic Account of Mental Health Relief Efforts to Affected Families," Unpublished Dissertation submitted to the Faculty of Family Social Science of University of Minnesota.

4

Commentary

Canay Özden-Schilling

The Anxiety and Hubris of Infrastructures

Throughout the 2010s, I researched the economics and politics of an infrastructure: the electric grid in the United States. In many places around the world, electricity industries have been deregulated beginning with the last stretch of the twentieth century, paving the way for markets for the competitive exchange of electricity. I wondered how the experts in the United States, one of the pioneers of electricity's marketization, have come to imagine the electric grid in the image of a market (Özden-Schilling 2021). Although my focus was on the United States, the spaces of expertise I frequented were replete with internationally active experts. In the fall of 2012, it was in one of those spaces that I met a top-level electricity market designer from Turkey, employed by the government's energy market regulatory institution. Ahmet (a pseudonym) was in the United States not only as a professional but also as a scholar, to study with academic experts and develop publications. I had kept an eye on my native Turkey and its ambitions for electricity deregulation. We made plans for coffee.

Ahmet came to the meeting more professionally dressed than required by the otherwise casual university setting. He began by listing to me his educational degrees and professional affiliations, all of which were impressive. Animatedly, he caught me up to speed on Turkey's electricity deregulation. The process had begun in 2001 with a deregulation act that passed in the Parliament (about a decade after similar acts passed in forerunners United States and the UK). Since then, his organization had been responsible for the design of an electricity exchange where megawatt/hours changed hands. While similar in principle to the exchanges I studied in the United States, where prices changed daily, the Turkish exchange had a quirk; price settlements were conducted three times a month. I found this a rather curious frequency and Ahmet seemed to expect my confusion. "Maybe he will laugh when I tell him," he said, referring to the expert under whom he was going to study in the United States. "Maybe anyone will laugh." He explained that the meters widely in usage across Turkish industries predated deregulation and happened to take measurements three times a month. Since meter replacement was not prescribed after deregulation, market designers had to develop a globally unique market design to meet the meters' physical constraint. He laughed to himself while telling me this story.

"It is strange," he later remarked. The aging meters were not always punctual in their thrice-a-month measurements. And late measurements were fined to users, which constituted a source of revenue (*gelir kapısı*) for the government. Some regulators were reluctant to go ahead with meter replacement precisely not to lose this source of revenue. Some went as far as considering keeping the old meters a patriotic act, as Ahmet told me with both incredulity and a degree of understanding. Ahmet went back to reflecting on how all this might look to the eyes of an expert in the United States. "They'll know theory so well, but they won't have experienced anything like this." Ahmet said he aimed to explain this experience to US experts but didn't hold his breath that they would understand. His doubts didn't hold him back, however, from turning Turkey's experience into several scholarly articles on the subject—devoid of the juicy bits he shared with me, of course.

There is much in the way Ahmet chose to recap Turkey's electricity deregulation experience to me that illuminates the richness of infrastructural politics in Turkey. The story about designing the markets around a somewhat arbitrary physical constraint will not be surprising to scholars who know how infrastructures have sticky aspects to them that outlast, thwart, or modify political designs. One is reminded, for instance, of Stephen Collier's descriptions of centrally heated Soviet buildings, built for long Russian winters, which caused problems for post-Soviet market designers who wanted to charge consumers by usage (2011). Scholars know that such messiness between material constraints and political designs is part and parcel of how infrastructural politics works; it is not exclusive to developmentally ambiguous places like Turkey outside the Global North. Yet Ahmet was compelled to think of this situation through the eyes of a Western expert, supposedly a human benchmark for infrastructural and political excellence. Like the Japanese traders Hirokazu Miyazaki studied who constantly felt the anxiety of being behind the times (2003), Ahmet's thinly veiled embarrassment signaled a kind of worry that is found among Turkey's ambitious infrastructure builders—a worry about a lag in development that needs overcoming (Akbulut and Adaman 2013; Kaşdoğan 2017).

This worry was not the entire story with Ahmet, however. It was coupled with a certain hubris, which might also be characteristic of infrastructure builders like him. After his recap, Ahmet quickly launched into Turkey's potential to become a regional benchmark setter for energy marketization. Leading an integration of Georgia's hydro potential into Turkey's markets was on his mind, for instance. He thought that the energy market in Turkey was critical (*çok kritik*)—a system with big potential that nevertheless needed much reinforcement. He explained his personal decision to stay in the public sector despite alluring offers from the private sector in terms of that potential. There was an opportunity to achieve much growth and change in the public sector, whereas being in the private sector right now would feel almost too easy for him, as if he was taking advantage of the system's current weaknesses. As he talked, his focus switched from Turkey's inferiority in relation to Western markets to its supposed advantage. At one point, he said that Turkey's electricity market had the potential to be great precisely because it had started late—that he and his coworkers had the time to learn from the mistakes of the West. The lag in development now seemed to promise even greater heights.

As I later began to conduct research in Turkey on maritime supply chain logistics around the privatized port of Mersin, I would interview bureaucrats like Ahmet who found a renewed sense and purpose of state-making in infrastructures' marketization. But more generally, my chat with Ahmet made me reflect on how much of state-making in Turkey takes place through infrastructural politics, from the management of forest fires (Kurtiç 2022) to redesigns of landholding (Adalet 2022). Turkey is replete with infrastructure experts who are ever so self-conscious of their place in the supposed ladder of development. Infrastructure-building has long been considered an indicator of that place, and such measurements have been entangled with strong emotions like anxiety and hubris. While messiness in infrastructural design is part and parcel of infrastructural politics everywhere, whether that messiness is of the appropriate nature—whether it is laughing matter or something for international experts to learn from—is something that the experts are changing their minds about in the same breath. I think that the chapters in this section showcase brilliantly the textures of this complex world—the world of state-making and infrastructures in Turkey. In that, they join the rest of this book's timely objective to tackle material politics—or how infrastructures come to matter through politics, and politics, through infrastructures.

State-Making as Scale-Making

Anthropology's twenty-first-century interest in infrastructures has no doubt been eye-opening, as this volume among many others is testament. Scholars have taken up Susan Leigh-Star's call to "study boring things" (1999, 377) and found insight in infrastructures' structure into the ways in which our interlocutors live. Star's postulation that infrastructures remain invisible until the moment of failure (1999, 382) has been challenged since by scholars who recognize a range of visibility in the way that infrastructures function, "from unseen to grand spectacles and everything in between" (Larkin 2013, 336). Scholars who study infrastructures in the context of state-making are particularly well disposed to appreciate this fact.

The visibility of infrastructures as daily matters of political concern is without a shadow of a doubt in Turkey, historically as well as at the present moment. As made clear in the introduction of this book, the making and remaking of the built environment has been central to processes of modernization in Turkey from the late Ottoman era onward. Long before the scholarly literature on infrastructures took off, sociologist Nilüfer Göle opined on the unmistakable role that engineers have played in Turkey's politics, ultimately commenting on the relationship between infrastructures and Turkish state-making, even though she did not foreground "infrastructure" as an analytic (1986). Based on research in the late 1970s, Göle diagnosed an "engineering ideology" (*mühendislik ideolojisi*) in the texture of Turkish politics which served as a curious common denominator for both radical left-wing activism and the then-rising Islamism. These drastically different political camps, she argued, both adopted a positivistic stance while being tempted by the potential of social engineering.

Reconsidering her conclusions in the depoliticized aftermath of the 1980 coup, Göle found this legacy solidified, this time in the person of Turgut Özal's generation of technocrats who considered themselves above ideologies and solely driven by numbers. Staffers from Özal's *Anavatan Party*, she showed, leveraged their engineering backgrounds to formulate a rhetoric of an action-oriented (*icraata yönelik*) politics (1986, 15). Ahmet squarely falls in this tradition of technocrats who, while clearly working for a specific administration, formulate their work in terms of technical excellence in governance. In this early work, Göle operates from within a dated modernization paradigm which attributes the sway of engineering in Turkish politics to the underdevelopment of the modernizing forces of capitalism and liberalism in Turkey. While it is no longer plausible to agree with this explanatory device, her work remains valuable for identifying the field that one might now recognize as Turkish technopolitics—a politics of infrastructure-building that operates under the guise of not being political.

The rise of *Adalet ve Kalkınma Partisi* (AKP) is surely to be seen as part of the history of Turkish technopolitics. As is well known, AKP's founding cadres used to run the nation's largest municipalities in the 1990s before the party was founded and came to power in 2001. Recep Tayyip Erdoğan's service as Istanbul mayor between 1994 and 1998 under Refah Party was what catapulted him into national politics. To this day, AKP's experience in municipal services is a proud talking point for the party's cadres in portraying their party as one dedicated to increasing citizens' material quality of life. This is best encapsulated by Erdoğan's obsession with the quality of the Turkish highway infrastructure, which, as he skips no opportunity to remind the public, has acquired more width over the course of the twenty-first century. It seems as though no oppression, destitution, or indignity is unfixable by a few more lanes in either direction of the nation's smooth great roads. AKP's tremendous embeddedness in municipal services is what makes the handover of the Istanbul and Ankara municipalities to *Cumhuriyet Halk Partisi* in 2018 a stunning turn of events, giving the new mayors of the nation's two largest provinces a unique opportunity to build up the political credentials that, many think, might one day accord them a chance at the presidential post.

The chapters in the present section of this volume lay out the historical and contemporary relationship between state-making and infrastructure-building through detailed empirical work. They illuminate the ground where governments become tangible to citizens through their work (or failure) as service providers. In other words, infrastructure is the site of encounter between the citizen and the state; it is what formats that relationship. Oftentimes, government in Turkey does not preexist infrastructural services. It is how citizens experience the concept and presence of government in the first place. And infrastructural service, in turn, constitutes the stuff of politics—whether it is demanded by citizens, forced upon them, or withheld from them; whose interests it serves; whether it is up to par, serviceable, or wanting.

Perhaps the most striking example of infrastructure as sites of encounter between state and citizen is in the history of the Turkish state's development projects in the Kurdish provinces. Here, the Turkish armed forces waged a war against Kurdish insurgents while the Turkish government simultaneously undertook a colossal infrastructure project: *Güneydoğu Anadolu Projesi* (the Southeast Anatolia Project) or *GAP*. Undertaken by *Devlet Su İşleri* (State Hydraulic Works or DSİ) between the

1970s and early 2000s, GAP was primarily a project to install several dams in Turkish Kurdistan for purposes of irrigation and electricity generation to shore up agriculture and industries. Sociologist Mesut Yeğen has written widely about the contradictions of simultaneous investment and war in the region (1999). As he documents at length, the Turkish government variably took the same Kurdish population as objects of economic development and subjects of terrorism. There seemed to be an underlying logic here that Kurdish separatism would disappear once the region had been given an opportunity to prosper, but this logic often ran into its limits. I remember being puzzled by the contradiction Yeğen delineates in much more prosaic terms as a preschool child in the late 1980s in Istanbul. Every day, as I waited for the evening broadcast of Sesame Street to come on television, I impatiently sat through a news show called *Anadolu'dan Görünüm* (The View from Anatolia), which mainly covered two topics: news from GAP and news in Turkey's war against terrorism. I vividly remember seeing shots of concrete construction stretching across Anatolian steppes right after still bodies in a ditch, unblurred. And I remember being confused by this stark shift in tone and, needless to say, horrified beyond measure.

As Aybike Alkan shows brilliantly in this section, GAP was a result of the Turkish state's efforts to claim the Kurdish provinces as an integral part of Turkey, now rebranded as Southeast Anatolia, as well as defining Kurdish insurgence as a problem of economic underdevelopment, which could then be solved within the realm of technical intervention. Ultimately, GAP was a scale-making project about tightening the grip of the Turkish government over Kurdish provinces, reformatting governance relationships in a way that the region would become subsumed by the larger scale of the Turkish state. But of course, the contradictions of this project were right beneath the surface and hard to suppress. As Alkan shows through archival reading, the experts constantly thought with separatism in mind while simultaneously denying it, lest recoding the region as Southeast Anatolia also reaffirmed the distinctness of it and justified alternative claims over it.

What makes Alkan's approach particularly illuminating about GAP's scale-making ambitions is the way she disaggregates GAP's work into its irrigation and electricity generation purposes. Based on ethnographic research as well as a close reading of documentation, Alkan is able to consider the materiality of infrastructures beyond the mere rhetoric of their makers. She shows how GAP's irrigation goals fared massively behind its electricity generation goals, in pursuance of the experts' bias in favor of electricity and the national industries it would power. Improving irrigation would have had the potential of creating wealth that would stay in the region in higher proportions than improving electricity generation would, in the form of jobs created and land irrigated. On the other hand, electricity, as I have shown in the North American context as well (Özden-Schilling 2019), is the kind of commodity that can be easily exported out of its production region, its benefits bypassing the communities its production had disturbed. As Alkan shows, centralization-minded experts found electricity more favorable to their integration goals, either overlooking irrigation or failing to achieve the alliances with the local population necessary for irrigation projects' success. Such biases, including how the irrigation benefits were mostly channeled to Arab-populated parts of the region and resettlement costs were borne by the Kurdish population, were not lost on Kurdish insurgents, to whom the contradictions of GAP were plain from the beginning.

What Alkan shows here, then, concerns infrastructure-making as state-making, as well as infrastructure-making as scale-making. Building the material conditions in which citizens will live also decides the political regimes to which they will be subject. Infrastructures have long served as a way for Turkish governments to reformat the scales through which Turkey is governed. Modernization, in Foucauldian terms, concerns the government that “makes live and lets die” replacing the government that “lets live and makes die.” The GAP case showcases the contradictions that appear when a government goes back and forth between the two.

Making Live, Infrastructurally

The other two chapters in this section richly follow similar themes while taking us to the western parts of the country, where the infrastructures are caught up in the matter of according citizens just enough health and means of subsistence. DSİ, the same government agency that managed GAP, makes an appearance in Asya Ece Uzmay’s chapter on the modernization of Istanbul’s water infrastructure beginning in the 1930s. It is striking to see how the same agency operates differently in Western Turkey, while it is focusing on the intricacies of “making live.” In this chapter, Uzmay tracks the modernization of Istanbul’s water infrastructure, with its entire network of cisterns, sewage canals, and treatment facilities. Here, we find the young republic wondering and fumbling its way through how to care for its citizens’ health just enough to avoid epidemics like typhoid. This attempt was inevitably caught up in yet another scale-making project that determined the extent of the authority of the new municipal governance of Istanbul—the erstwhile capital of the Ottoman Empire which was now to be reintegrated into the nation in the new republic’s terms. Overhauling Ottoman waterways, it appears, also functioned as the remaking of seats of power.

Uzmay takes us back to the initial decade of the republic when experts needed to decide what to do with the infrastructures leftover from late Ottoman modernization. As is the case with other large-scale infrastructures in the Ottoman Empire and elsewhere, like electric grids and ports, water infrastructures started out as private ventures undertaken by a combination of local and foreign companies. Just like in those other infrastructures, the issue of nationalization entered the agenda of the new republic in its initial decades. Uzmay reminds us that the 1930 Municipalities Law extended and centralized municipal control over city water in Istanbul. But what the experts realized quickly was that changing ownership was by no means the end of the story when the question of authority over the governance of infrastructures was concerned. Uzmay’s chapter begins with a typhoid outbreak in 1937, which most likely spread from *bostans*—the urban orchards citizens used for subsistence purposes. At this stage, the populace had no running water and depended on public fountains to which water was transported via unclean water pipes. The experts spent the postwar years attempting what Uzmay aptly summarizes as “the transition from the public fountain faucet to a private faucet in Istanbul." Many of those experts are on record considering the abandonment of public fountains a "necessity of civilization."

The experts responded to the problem in the way they knew how—by centralizing water governance and eliminating the use of the old Ottoman waterways. But as Uzmay shows, this goal consistently slipped through their fingers, especially with the rise of *gecekondu*s (informal dwellings) as a result of internal migration beginning in the 1960s. The theoretically abandoned waterways were anything but abandoned in the areas where municipal services were scarce; they still caused disease outbreaks. Once again, it appears, infrastructures remained sticky, like the enduring fountain network, as experts engaged in their various scale-making projects: incorporating Istanbul—which was historically its own metropole—into the nation; integrating parts of illegal settlements into central Istanbul governance; translating Istanbul's water problem into an international one at the level of expertise shared at global conferences. Reformatting Istanbul's scale, Uzmay shows, concerned the medicalization of the city, as well as national experts' ambitions of urbanization and modernization.

Infrastructures accord experts ways to take resources from somewhere and reroute them somewhere else. The decisions that experts make in the process, as I have argued above, create scales of governance. Another vivid example of this phenomenon comes from Irem Az's in-depth investigation of Soma, a district of coal mines in Western Turkey in the Aegean region. In Soma, a mine collapsed and claimed 301 lives in May 2014 as a result of dangerous mining conditions. Az's fieldwork tracks the region in its less turbulent times as well, identifying a sinister and systematic kind of violence that extends the horrors of the 2014 disaster. As Az shows, the lignite coal that miners in Soma carry above ground at great risk to their health and lives is the same coal that the government gives away as welfare entitlements in sacks bearing the title of Az's chapter: "Not for Sale." In 2004, AKP both enacted a state-guaranteed profit scheme for private coal extraction entrepreneurs and reformed its welfare laws and regulations. As the new coal entrepreneurs cut labor costs drastically, AKP's new welfare regime, which included the distribution of Soma coal to low-income families, served as a band-aid for worker destitution and, thus, as another indirect subsidy for the coal industry. The resulting "coal rush" has accorded coal the highest share in Turkey's energy mix in recent years. Soma coal, in other words, has been made to power not only the nation's electricity network but also the socioeconomic conditions of its own extraction.

In Alkan's case of GAP, we see how the benefit of a production process, in that case electricity, can be rerouted away from the very region that absorbs its risks. In Soma, a similar thing happens but with a twist. The coal that is produced in the region returns to the region as a welfare benefit, in the process turning the same laborers who are producers of this coal into recipients of government welfare, establishing a debt relationship between citizens and the AKP government. As Az shows so persuasively, the process also accords AKP the opportunity to establish a difference between the deserving poor and otherwise. The labor regime that Az identifies here is one that reduces laborers and their families into recipients of welfare, coagulates their poverty, and governs selectively. The redistribution in question is not merely financial; it concerns political allegiances while forcing the recipients into subject positions they might have little power to contest. But contest, they do, as they organize in an understanding that it is, in fact, allegiances that are not for sale.

Soma's case, then, joins those of Istanbul and Southeast Anatolia, as the experts attempt to integrate it materially and politically into the national scale in a way that weakens the laborers and their families, and strengthens their own rule, although not without contestation. Once again, making live, this time via welfare benefits, is tied up in a kind of letting live that all too often veers into making die, as demonstrated by the case of the 2014 Soma disaster. Infrastructures in Turkey stand on the contradictions of this process that all three chapters in this section lay bare.

Conclusion

In popular discourse, it has been commonplace to reduce the relationship between infrastructures and states to a story of privatization and neoliberalism, where states simply disappear. If experts take infrastructures to be indicators of civilization like Ahmet did, there is also a strand of scholarship that takes infrastructures' market-forward transformations to be the bellwether of neoliberalism, and not much else (for a critique, see Özden-Schilling 2018). But having found a much more complex picture in electricity's marketization in the United States than a mere story of neoliberal forces gone rogue, I suspected a similar richness unfolding in Turkey's process of electricity deregulation. Meeting Ahmet confirmed my suspicions: here he was, an expert who has found a new purpose of state-making in the privatization and deregulation of a previously state-owned and state-operated infrastructure. Today, Ahmet's anxiety and hubris can be witnessed in other government actors who have found a renewed and different sense of state-making in privatized infrastructures, as I have come to see in my current research in and around Turkey's Mediterranean ports. Even in the context of privatized infrastructures, the state is not gone; state officials themselves have taken to calling state governance as unwieldy (*hantal*) while repurposing their roles as facilitators of private initiative. Private entities are well aware that the state has not disappeared either; many, from port operators to pilot captains, have often reminded me that they are acting "in the name of the state" (*devlet adına*) while pursuing their private interests. If anything, the public–private relationship has become more complex in such settings.

Be it privatized or still decidedly government led, infrastructures are lively sites for state-making, even as the purpose and appearance of that endeavor transform. In Uzmay's chapter, we see that a change in ownership does not immediately alter an infrastructure's material characteristics in the way that experts desire; that transformation is a lengthy and always-incomplete process. In Alkan and Az's chapters, we see decidedly public infrastructures that distribute costs and benefits extremely unevenly, with costs suffered in milieus of production and benefits rerouted and enjoyed elsewhere. If states are wholly present in the daily life of infrastructures, so should they be in the scholarship of infrastructures. The three chapters in this section rise up to that occasion and showcase the ongoing complexity of the relationship between state-making and infrastructures. They demonstrate full well that electricity is never only electricity, water is never only water, and coal is never only coal.

References

Adalet, Begüm. 2022. "Agricultural Infrastructures: Land, Race, and Statecraft in Turkey," *Environment and Planning D: Society and Space* 40 (6): 975–93. Online publication: September 8.

Akbulut, Bengi, and Fikret Adaman. 2013. "The Unbearable Charm of Modernization: Growth Fetishism and the Making of State in Turkey," *Perspectives: Political Analysis and Commentary from Turkey* 5 (13): 1–10.

Collier, Stephen. 2011. *Post-Soviet Social: Neoliberalism, Social Modernity, Biopolitics*, Princeton: Princeton University Press.

Göle, Nilüfer. 2016 (1986). *Mühendisler ve İdeoloji: Öncü Devrimcilerden Yenilikçi Seçkinlere*, Istanbul: İletişim.

Kaşdoğan, Duygu. 2017. "Potentiating Algae, Modernizing Bioeconomies: Algal Biofuels, Bioenergy Economies, and Built Ecologies in the United States and Turkey," Unpublished dissertation, York University.

Kurtiç, Ekin. 2022. "Wildfires Ignite Political Debate in Turkey," *Middle East Research and Information Project*, February 22. https://merip.org/2022/02/wildfires-ignite-political-debate-in-turkey/

Larkin, Brian. 2013. "The Politics and Poetics of Infrastructure." *Annual Review of Anthropology* 42: 327–43.

Miyazaki, Hirokazu. 2003. "The Temporality of Markets," *American Anthropologist* 105 (2): 255–65.

Özden-Schilling, Canay. 2018. "Why the Lights Went Out in Puerto Rico," *Public Books*, September 20. http://www.publicbooks.org/why-the-lights-went-out-in-puerto-rico/

Özden-Schilling, Canay. 2019. "Grid Country," *Journal of North American Anthropology* 22 (2): 118–20.

Özden-Schilling, Canay. 2021. *The Current Economy: Electricity Markets and Techno-Economics*, Palo Alto: Stanford University Press.

Star, Susan Leigh. 1999. "The Ethnography of Infrastructure," *American Behavioral Scientist* 43 (3): 377–91.

Yeğen, Mesut. 1999. *Devlet Söyleminde Kürt Sorunu*, Istanbul: İletişim.

Part II

Making Material Worlds Scientific

5

The Liminal Forest[1]

Mud, Science, and Nationalism in Turkey's Forests

Hande Özkan

November 2009. Cold day in Kastamonu. My legs hurt from walking in the thick, creamy mud covering the forest floor. What a relief when the forest administration jeep I am in stops at a fountain. . . . As I splash water on my boots, I finally understand foresters' complaints. Mud is not just a nuisance; it symbolizes what states have historically tried to eliminate from the forest: disorder, unruliness, backwardness. I cannot disagree after seeing my boots destroyed. . . . Yet, I also admire mud's persistence. Months later, as I try to salvage my boots, I experience an epiphany: mud is not only an ambiguous phenomenon external to what the forest represents. Mud **is** *the forest.*

Introduction: The Color of Civilization

How can mud contribute to anthropological discussions on the ambiguous materiality of forests and the fluidity that defines interactions between citizens and states? The construction of cultural categories and the role they play in practices of meaning-making are at the core of anthropological inquiry (Douglas 1996; Levi-Strauss 1966, 1964). While earlier scholarship on classification revolved around a binary logic, recent work has prioritized the ambiguity and fluidity of social phenomena and practices (Stoler 2009; Ogden 2011). A recent example of this scholarship is anthropological work on amphibiousness (Krause and Harris 2021; Scaramelli 2021). In this chapter, I will question the rigid binaries that have been foundational in the formation of modern Turkey by analyzing the conflicting ways in which forests have been culturally constructed as well as the material consequences of such constructs. The historical record on forestry reveals two distinct narratives that interpret the materiality of forests in contrasting ways. I will refer to the conceptualization that defines forests within a land–agriculture framework as "the terrestrial narrative" and designate the discourse that presents forests as sources of water as "the aquatic narrative." As I trace the coexistence of these two narratives, I will challenge their rigid representation of forests through a binary logic, while also questioning the representation of the state and society as diametrical opposites. Instead, I will suggest seeing mud as the symbol of forests' amphibiousness and argue that forests and the states who attempt to organize the material world based on classifications that often target ambiguities like mud are, in fact, liminal categories. By deconstructing such binaries as aquatic–terrestrial or state–society, my goal is to question modernity's self-proscribed certainties and rigidities.

Resembling the binary opposition that distances the terrestrial narrative on forests from the aquatic, states are often imagined as monolithic entities that are diametrically opposed to society. Scholars of the state have debated the relationship between the state and society, with some prioritizing the state as the main actor and others concentrating on the power of social forces; yet a state–society dichotomy persists in these analyses (Abrams 1988; Mitchell 1991; Scott 1985, 1998). Recent scholarship questions this dichotomy by emphasizing the permeability of analytical categories, adopting a dialogic approach to the relationship between the state and society, and exploring the vernacularization of politics in different cultural settings (Hansen and Stepputat 2001; Sharma and Gupta 2006; Herzfeld 2005; Navarro-Yashin 2002). This approach, which resists essentialist narratives of the state and society by highlighting the simultaneity of state-making and subject formation, has been welcomed by anthropologies of the environment as well (Sivaramakrishnan 1999; Baker 2005; Moore 2005; Agrawal 2005). My analysis will build on and contribute to this scholarship by tracing the complex relationship between state-appointed forest engineers, forest guards, and forest villagers, and demonstrating that states are the outcome of negotiated practices. By discursively reframing forests through an idiom of mud and resisting their essentialization as either terrestrial or aquatic, this chapter will also contribute to the emerging literature on amphibious anthropologies.

The history of forestry in modern Turkey is a history of nation-building and state formation. The state is, to this day, the main actor in forest management and conservation, despite neoliberalizing reforms that transformed Turkey's previous protectionist economy in the period following the 1980 military coup. As I argue elsewhere, forestry has been foundational to the process of nation-state formation in Turkey (Özkan 2018); as a result, contemporary forestry practices are still shaped by the legacy of the early republican period. Therefore, a study on the negotiated relationships and complex practices that make up forestry in Turkey is inevitably a study on state-making.

The terrestrial and aquatic narratives that have defined the official discourse on forests are products of a national nature regime that emerged in the first half of the twentieth century, when Turkey's nation-building was consolidated through a secular-modernist ideology, *Kemalism*. The early republican period (1923–50) was characterized by Turkey's self-imposed break from the Ottoman past and a series of top-down, modernizing reforms. At the time, nature was a building block of nation-building, and elites reimagined nature as national patrimony (Özkan 2018), emphasizing its value at the material as well as the discursive level. Following centuries of unregulated access, in the nineteenth century, the Ottoman state recognized the fiscal value of natural resources, resulting in forests' overexploitation for revenue. A less materialist notion of nature emerged in the last years of the Ottoman Empire and was developed into the nature regime of the republic, whose official ideology evolved into *étatism* in the 1930s. The fiscal conceptualization of nature was replaced by an economic understanding whose ideological roots were embedded in a solidarist-corporatist model, which viewed the economy as an organism and forestry as one of its organs (Yiğitoğlu 1936).

As forestry was defined through an economic framework, a second, more discursive imaginary, which emphasized forests' association with the spirit of the nation, was also taking shape. "There is a strong indisputable connection between civilization and the forest," wrote veteran forester Refik Alaçam (1945, 10), while Nazım Batur, former general director of Forestry, described the connection between forests and civilization with the following words: "People who live in unforested areas are spiritually dead, weak, and unproductive. Their health is in poor shape. Three quarters of their lifetime is spent ill. Civilization and trees are so connected that there cannot be any civilization where there are no trees. Planting trees is to contribute to civilization" (Acun 1945, xiv). At times, the correlation republican intellectuals established between forests and civilization went so far as to remove forests from the realm of nature: "With their various products, forests rank second next to milk among the items that are consumed the most in the modern world" (Diker 1947, 5). Scholar and former general director of Forestry Diker's juxtaposition of forests with milk, a symbol of modernity and one of the most iconic interventions of humans into the nonhuman world (Nimmo 2010; Wiley 2014), reveals that for Kemalist elites, the constructedness of forests was based on their correlation with civilization. It is therefore not surprising when a forestry professor referred to afforestation and conservation efforts as "a national struggle against wild nature" (Kayacık 1951, 50).

Despite official Republican ideology's self-representation as a clean slate, the continuity between late Ottoman policies and the reforms implemented by the modern nation-state is evident in Turkey's current forestry policies. As scientific forestry became the dominant discourse for late Ottoman and early Republican foresters, the bureaucratization of the forestry administration was also underway. This resulted in a hierarchical organization of forest management in which forest subdistricts were defined as the smallest units. This administrative framework has not changed much to this day, and most of forest production takes place in these subdistricts.

"You need to be Superman to be able to do all that. . . . There is a man called the *şef*. His actual job is forestry, but he cannot do it."[2] These were the words of forester-scholar Yücel Çağlar as he shared with me his critique of the duties of a *şef*,[3] a forest engineer tasked with the management of these subdistricts. As we talked, subdistricts and the complex duties of these foresters surfaced as a concern, as they did in my conversations with other foresters. It did not take me long to realize that despite their position at the bottom of the bureaucratic chain, these subdistricts are the heart of forestry. In fact, I consider them microcosms of what Sivaramakrishnan (1999) calls state-making, a process wherein various actors engage in a reciprocal process of producing politics, thereby consolidating the state, while also forging citizen-subjectivities. I argue that the encounters between forest-dependent communities and state actors in these units reveal how forestry operates in Turkey and its implications about nation-building and subject formation. As Kaşdoğan and Kurtiç discuss in the introduction to this volume, material worlds are not mere backdrops to social and political processes. By analyzing the interplay between the nation-building process and forestry, I intend to contribute to the literature which highlights that material life has an agency that is not autonomous from, but integral to, the construction of political processes.

My analysis of these intertwined processes of nature-making, state-building, and subject formation builds on archival research as well as ethnographic fieldwork conducted in northern Turkey. My approach to archives is ethnographic; I analyze official state records alongside other texts that were foundational to the construction of various official discourses in Turkey. Foucault's discussion of archives as a domain in which truths about institutional realities are constructed and normalized serves as the inspiration for this ethnographic reading of archives (Foucault 1972). I utilize textbooks, popular science publications, propaganda pamphlets, newspapers, magazines, and similar texts as "para-official" archives because they facilitated the state's modernizing discourse to become hegemonic. Moreover, as anthropologists, cultural historians, and scholars of the subaltern school have shown, relying on different registers of archives is of utmost importance if our goal is to understand the complexities of national histories and to uncover untold, suppressed narratives (Guha 1997). By treating historical records as a discursive domain wherein social categories and truths were constructed and negotiated, I will demonstrate that despite states' attempts to present a strictly categorized social order, the messiness and fluidity of social and natural worlds persist in the record. Juxtaposing official documents with para-official archival material is also conducive to Laura Nader's by-now-well-received invitation to study up while being loyal to anthropology's typical subjects such as forest villagers (Nader 1972).

Bakhtin's interpretation of language as a dialogic process and Stoler's discussion of archives' epistemic uncertainty provide me with a template to uncover the coexistence of multiple meanings and to reveal the messiness and fluidity of social and natural worlds in the historical record. Bakhtin's linguistics present a struggle between diverging social forces to claim a hegemonic space. In his analysis, words do not have inherent meanings; they are defined by multiplicity: "[A]t any given moment of its historical existence, language is heteroglot from top to bottom: it represents the co-existence of socio-ideological contradictions between the present and the past, between differing epochs of the past, between different socio-ideological groups in the present, between tendencies, schools, circles and so forth" (Bakhtin 1981, 291). Almost a century later, Ann Stoler provides an ethnographic rendering of Bakhtin's work on the unfinished, unfixed nature of meaning when she explains how Dutch colonial archives attempted to organize the social world and failed. "[C]olonial administrations were prolific producers of social categories," Stoler writes; "producing rules of classification was an unruly and piecemeal venture at best" (Stoler 2009, 1). By approaching archives as a domain of deliberation wherein meaning is simultaneously constructed and contested and uncovering similar "epistemic anxieties" (Stoler 2009) in Turkish forestry, I will show that the materiality of forests cannot be reduced to a monolithic and fixed essence. As I analyze the coexistence of the competing terrestrial and aquatic narratives, I will also show that forests have historically meant different things to different social groups. For instance, for professional foresters, forests have been symbols of civilization, but at the same time, they have been treated as commodities, defined strictly by their exchange value, whereas for peasants, the usefulness of trees is inseparable from their market value. Trees have provided them with everyday needs such as housing or heating, but they have also operated as commodities, serving as forest villagers' main source of income.

I will juxtapose this archival analysis with ethnographic fieldwork experiences in Turkey's Black Sea region since 2008. Forestry has been a significant form of livelihood in this area since antiquity, and the region is home to some of Turkey's most valuable forests. I first visited a large area in the western and central parts of the region (comprising Zonguldak, Kastamonu, and Sinop provinces) in 2008. This was followed by long-term fieldwork in Sinop and Kastamonu in 2009–10, as well as shorter visits in 2016 and 2017. The archival research has been conducted continuously since 2009 in the Republican Archives in Ankara, the National Library, Beyazit Library in Istanbul, various departments within the Ministry of Forestry and the Environment,[4] and regional offices in Sinop and Kastamonu.

Science, Civilization, and Verdure

Foresters in Turkey idealize and romanticize their role by glorifying science. As I argue elsewhere, verdure is the idiom through which scientific forestry has become hegemonic in both academic and everyday discourses (Özkan 2018, 2022). For republican elites, green was the color of civilization, and this idiom was gradually embedded in the sensibility of citizen-subjects, who were encouraged to contribute to efforts to create a "green fatherland" (*yeşil vatan*) (Gökberk 1944). The discursive marginalization of non-forested landscapes as unproductive was one way through which the idiom of verdure was disseminated within the national discourse.[5] From literature to popular publications, aridity was represented as backwardness, while forests were viewed as inseparable from civilization.

State forest enterprises are where the discourse of scientific forestry materializes, where forest management and production take place, and where *şefs*, guards, and villagers perform their respective duties. At the provincial level, the General Directorate of Forestry is composed of three divisions. At the top are thirty regional directorates, which are further divided into forest district directorates. Every district directorate is composed of forest subdistrict directorates, of which there are a total of 2,062[6] throughout the country. As I explained before, these subdistricts are where timber production takes place, and where forest villagers and foresters come into contact. Therefore, the duties of the *şefs* who oversee these units are complex and require expertise in engineering, proficiency to respond to market demands, and skills to act as representatives of the state. Forest guards are uniformed officers who report to the *şefs* and are charged with enforcing the law and monitoring production daily, while forest villagers, whose status is recognized by law, are residents of villages, which are in or adjacent to state forests. Historically, their main source of income has been forest labor, and today they are hired by the state forest enterprises on an individual basis or via cooperatives for timber production.

In its November 29, 1943, issue, the forestry weekly *Ormancı Postası* illustrated state forest enterprises' embodiment of scientific forestry by announcing recent changes to existing enterprises ("Devlet Orman İşletmeleri" 1943). After a brief statement that approximately one-third of all forests were at the time managed by the state, the newspaper discussed how the location of the enterprises was based on the ecological demands of the forests in a specific area. The rest of the text was about changes to existing enterprises, specifically citing the new territories allocated to some of the smaller enterprises, and the reduction in size of others that were too big to successfully manage. These evidence-based observations are remarkable considering that the current size of subdistricts was one of the concerns Çaglar raised when I interviewed him. He explained to me that the size of a typical forest subdistrict has continuously increased in the past century, rendering them unmanageable. The observations in *Ormancı Postası* show that the scientific ethos was not only rhetorical in the early republican period; instead, it materialized in policies and management practices. In a similar vein, praising state forest enterprises, politician Esat Tekeli wrote that they were not just structures that housed personnel and through which management was conducted, and asked the reader to appreciate enterprises as complex networks and sophisticated forms of infrastructure (Tekeli 1944). Indeed, in the early twentieth century, the modern attributes of forest enterprises went beyond forestry; at times, as the main state institutions in rural areas, they brought modern amenities and a modern worldview to towns and villages (Özkan 2018).

For their part, rural communities adopted and performed the scientific forestry discourse. While emblematic of the construction of subjectivities through power (Agrawal 2005), the internalization of this discourse was as much about agentive manipulations as it was about a structural imposition, thus confirming the reciprocal, negotiated forms of state-making in the forest. An anonymous letter dated March 8, 1939, and signed by the "youth of Çukurova," a major agricultural basin in the eastern Mediterranean, perfectly illustrates the simultaneous processes of nature-making, state-building, and subject formation, and the role that the scientific forestry discourse played in the making of citizens. Addressed to the Ministry of Interior, the letter complained about extensive corruption in forests and implicated the military forest conservation units in these criminal acts (Republican Archives of Turkey, Document 030 10 183 265 4). Established following the Forest Act of 1937, these military units were controversial and generated discord between various state agencies. Despite its brevity, the letter detailed the specific rank officers involved in smuggling and ended with a warning that the nation's forests were in imminent danger and that their conservation was crucial for the welfare of the country and its treasury. The anonymous authors' reference to "emerald forests" (*zümrüt ormanlar*), a colloquialism in Turkish that denotes the value attributed to forests, resonates with the official discourse that defined forests as national treasures. If this letter was indeed written by youth from an agricultural province, their skill in adopting the official discourse is noteworthy. What is even more important is that they strategically used the official discourse to accuse those responsible for the conservation of these forests.

Rural communities' appropriation of the scientific discourse was not enough to prevent foresters from seeing them as potential threats to forests. Scaramelli (this volume) notes a similar process in the relationship between bureaucrats and local residents as she illustrates that the former's claim to the rightful use of Turkey's wetlands is premised on their scientific expertise. Placing the scientific idiom of verdure at the center of the national nature regime inevitably led to its incompatibility with traditional practices and resulted in their criminalization. The development of scientific forestry, first in the colonies and then at imperial metropoles (Peluso and Vandergeest 2006a, 2006b), was a form of enclosure aimed at cultivating forests productively throughout the world. Scholars have analyzed how this process criminalized rural communities' practices, leading to forms of resistance (Peluso 1992; Guha 1998; Fairhead and Leach 1996). Likewise, in Turkey, rural communities' everyday, material practices were discursively transformed into primitive, irrational, and criminal acts. Elsewhere, I discuss how the axe and the goat were major tropes in this criminalization discourse (Özkan 2022). *Soymuk*, the inner membrane of conifers, which was a source of nutrition for rural communities (Gençtürk 1995) and *pedavra*, a Greek term depicting a thin piece of wood used for roofing, are other examples of this criminalization (*Cumhuriyetin 50. Yılında Orman-Köy İlişkileri* 1983). Foresters considered *pedavra* as a huge threat to the forest because of the way it was obtained. As a forest guard explained in 1946, *pedavra* was not produced "by a chainsaw like ordinary wood, but rather by hacking it with an axe" (Sungar 1946, 59). Nothing must have been scarier for foresters than two evils joining hands: the *axe* and the *pedavra*. Likewise, eating *soymuk* has been a common tradition in forest villages and was considered as dangerous to forests as grazing or poaching. For instance, writing about the plight of Sinop's forests, Cafer Altay lamented that saplings, which even survived the goats, perished at the hands and mouths of forest villagers (1965). Given the goats' criminalization in the official discourse, presenting humans as an even bigger threat to forests confirms that forest-dependent communities' everyday experiences were marginalized.

In response to the categorization of rural populations as ignorant and criminal, foresters' role as champions of science acquired a pedagogical dimension. This civilizing mission was facilitated by the fact that, in the early twentieth century, foresters were often the only representatives of the state in rural areas. A similar situation prevailed in Nazi Germany, where "foresters, with their exceptionally high reputation among the German populace, were frequently called upon as local dignitaries" (Imort 2005, 54). While foresters' presence was more pronounced when the state did not have an adequate infrastructure that allowed it access to and control over people and places (Özkan 2002), as I observed on numerous occasions, the highest-ranking forestry official is still respected as one of the notables in small towns and enjoys the privileges of this status in the rituals of political life. In other words, the undesirable qualities of rural populations are partially responsible for shaping the construction of foresters' subjectivity as vanguards of society and upholders of science. In the last section of this chapter, I will show how this representation of rural populations is, in fact, an extension of the material conditions of the forest, such as mud, which in turn reinforces foresters' pedagogical subjectivity. Writing on the media in Egypt, Abu-Lughod argues that mass media has functioned as a forum for "national pedagogy" (Abu-Lughod 2005). Forestry in Turkey has functioned in a similar framework, wherein "the educated cultured individual represents the good, the law, culture, national responsibility, and pride in the greatness of the nation's heritage" (Abu-Lughod 2002, 870). This dyadic conceptualization of elites versus the people is a direct consequence of the "high modernist" elements of the Turkish nation-building project (Scott 1998). However, as the letter by the youth from Çukurova demonstrated, rural populations are not "only pedagogical objects but also performative subjects" (Abu-Lughod 2002, 257), who demonstrate their agency by adopting and manipulating the discourses imposed on them under structural constraints.

The Terrestrial Forest

As I suggested in the introduction, one hegemonic narrative through which forests were conceptualized in the process of nation-building was terrestriality. When forests emerged as major economic actors in this period, their materiality as rooted organisms generated a conceptualization that emphasized the connections between forestry and agriculture. Identifying forests as productive land, the terrestrial narrative presented them as modern, civilized landscapes and recognized them as an antidote to abject, marginal, and unproductive landscapes. Legal and administrative discussions on forests offer a glimpse into forests' terrestrial categorization. Since the late Ottoman period, forests and agricultural lands were categorized as cultivable property, and together they featured in debates on private versus state ownership. While aquatic natural resources were identified as public goods and were regulated by the state, forests were commodified (Dursun 2007) and defined through an idiom of ownership. The trope of national patrimony, which defined forests as belonging to the nation, was the driving force behind the terrestrial imaginary and gave birth to state forestry, resulting in the nationalization of forests in 1945.

When the republic was declared in 1923, Kemalist elites adopted existing Ottoman policies along with several amendments introduced during the war of independence (1919–23). It wasn't until 1937 that a new law was adopted, resulting in the drafting of the 1937 Forest Act.[7] One practice that the young republic adopted from Ottoman forestry was the contract system in which the state gave concessions to domestic and foreign businesses to manage forests for profit.[8] According to the new law, all forests, regardless of ownership, would be managed by the state, which required cooperation between these private businesses and the state. The new law was followed by the creation of state forest enterprises as the main units of forest management throughout the country. Concessions given to private initiatives were eventually replaced with state enterprises and, in 1945, a new law was drafted, nationalizing all forests in the country.[9] The nationalization of forests marked the ultimate iteration of forests' conceptualization as land, defining them as the property of the nation.

Historically, forests have been managed according to plans created by the General Directorate of Forestry, whose task is twofold: to meet the timber demands of the market and to ensure the sustainability of forests. Emphasizing forests' role within the national economy, forestry professor and politician Ali Kemal Yiğitoğlu classified Turkey's lands as either cultivable or uncultivable and placed forests in the cultivable land category alongside agricultural land (Yiğitoğlu 1941, 12). When professor and former general director of forests Mazhar Diker claimed that the primary goal of forestry was to improve soil use efficiency, he likewise confirmed forests' terrestrial conceptualization by depicting them as analogous to agricultural land (1947). Forests' terrestrial conceptualization played such an integral role in the regime's conceptualization of forestry that it was beyond party lines. Historically, Turkey's founding Republican People's Party, representative of the military-bureaucratic elite, has advocated state ownership of forests, whereas the Democrat Party, founded in 1945 with the support of center-right voters and provincial elites, has relied on a more populist rhetoric.[10] Regardless of their fundamental ideological differences, both parties espoused the terrestrial logic. The fact that there were debates over who should own forests was the ultimate affirmation of the discourse which defined forests as land. A letter written by center-right journalist Mümtaz Apaydın to Prime Minister Adnan Menderes in 1951 exemplifies the opposition's version of the terrestrial discourse. Criticizing the nationalization of forests in 1945 and advocating for its reversal, Apaydın argued that state ownership of forests was a violation of the basic right to property and that the owners of nationalized forests should be compensated for the value of their trees and their land (Republican Archives of Turkey, Document 030-0-001-000-000-80-507-12). Bureaucrats and intellectuals were not alone in defining forests through an agricultural framework; as I will show here, ordinary citizens also adopted this narrative in their complaints to the state about land use.

As tides shift and neoliberalism reshapes Turkey's economy, the state has started to redefine itself as one among various stakeholders in areas where it historically claimed a monopoly. Nonetheless, the terrestrial discourse perseveres. On a spring day in 2010, I had tea with forest villagers and a visiting bureaucrat in a small coastal town in Kastamonu. As we chatted in a coffee shop overlooking the unusually calm waters of the Black Sea, I was initially puzzled by the bureaucrat's comment: "Who knows? Maybe one day socialism in the forest will end and you will get back your forests." Shortly after, I theorized that this reference to socialism by the bureaucrat of a country that has not been socialist was a rhetorical strategy to remind us of the state's heavy-handed involvement in Turkey's economic and social life until the neoliberal shift. The misrepresentation of *étatism* as socialism is a common trope that defenders of neoliberalism utilize to legitimize the privatization of natural resources and national industries. Today, this trope is blended with a new version of populism, which conceals the neoliberal ethos while catering to citizens' everyday nationalist grievances. Even though neoliberalism has shifted the discourse from a strong state–weak society logic to one premised upon stakeholders, the two biggest political parties, AKP which, reproduces the opposition that DP relied on in the 1940s, and CHP, as Turkey's longest-standing political party, which still represents the *étatist* logic, both conceptualize forests within an idiom of property and ownership. Recent discussions on "2B lands," state-owned forest tracts defined by Article 2B of the 1956 Forest Act as having lost the qualities of forests, further illustrate this logic because these areas get redefined as land to be sold to forest villagers who have already been using it for agriculture or other purposes. The permits given by the Turkish government for mining, tourism, and other extractive industries in the last two decades further illustrate that the terrestrial materiality that defines forests as rentable property lives on today.

Afforestation is another example of the terrestrial representation of forests. For Kemalist elites, afforestation was much more than conservation; it was vital for the nation's well-being. In a context in which trees were deemed central to the country's "climate, strength of its soil, its public health, defense, sustenance and economy" (Asafoğlu 1938, 25), afforestation projects and tree festivals helped disseminate the idiom of verdure. The fact that securing the sustainability of such an essential resource as forests required the implementation of a rigorous scientific agenda allowed the Kemalist regime to bolster its secular-scientific agenda while ensuring that the wealth generated through forest management benefited the emerging national economy. Falih Rıfkı Atay, a leading intellectual of the Kemalist regime, frequently addressed forestry in his articles in various newspapers of the era. Despite his staunch faith in *Kemalism* as a unique ideology, like many of his contemporaries, Atay was infatuated with fascist and communist regimes' ability to implement rapid reforms. In his editorial for *Ormancı Postası* on February 1, 1944, Atay advocated for afforestation and argued that ultimately scientific forestry and not the gendarme would save Turkey's forests. While Atay's prioritization of afforestation over strict restrictions in forestry practices appears as a liberal option, his praise for Mussolini's authoritarian afforestation efforts is evidence of his admiration of authoritarian policies, which revealed themselves even more explicitly when he quoted Hitler at the end of his article: "When Hitler reported the successes of the second year of Nationalist-Socialism, he said 'we saved many private forests from destruction at the hands of their owners.' . . . If they need the state to save private forests even there, imagine what the role of the state can be in our Anatolia devastated by the axe" (Atay 1944, 4). Atay's aspirations reveal that the faith in science was so staunch that it could impede basic human freedoms.

Afforestation was not limited to the efforts of scientists and intellectuals; it was codified in the forest act, requiring governors to organize annual tree planting festivals in their provinces. Tree festivals were symbolic events where elites met citizens and where notions of modernity, civilization, and productivity were articulated within a national idiom. These secular rites guaranteed the reproduction of national belonging by rooting the nation in the soil,[11] while highlighting its association with rationalism and science. The April 1944 festival in Acıpayam was especially celebratory because the trees planted along the highway between Acıpayam and Kızılhisar served as a bridge, territorially joining the two towns ("Acıpayam'da" 1944). This event was not only indicative of the materiality of forests as land, but it also placed this terrestrial materiality at the very core of the nation-state, thereby connecting the formation of the state, the making of citizens, and the construction of a national nature. The year before, on April 3, 1943, the Minister of Agriculture, the undersecretary, other bureaucrats, and faculty members from the Agriculture Institute attended the tree planting festival in Kalaba, a village near Ankara, alongside residents of nearby villages ("Toprak ve Ağaç Bayramı" 1943). During the ceremony, the national anthem was followed by speeches by faculty and dignitaries, concluding with the minister's address:

> We have always been a nation that loves its fatherland and is attached to its soil. And today we are even more rooted in our soil thanks to the revolution that was made possible by our nation. The main objective of our revolutions is to achieve a new

> civilization. This civilization will be based, above all, on a culture of the soil. It will form the base of our technique and economy. And we will remain a nation rooted in its soil. ("Toprak ve Ağaç Bayramı")

Victor Turner has shown that as cultural practices charged with symbolic significance, rituals maintain and reproduce the social order (Turner 1995). In a similar vein, in the early years of the republic, tree planting rituals funneled nationalism, modernity, and civilization into everyday life while also reinforcing the patrimonial relationship between the state and citizens. Alongside tree festivals' performative and pedagogical nature, trees' material role in anchoring the nation within the soil was evident in the minister's speech. In the process, citizen-subjects acquired a certain agency that incorporated an environmental sensibility within their national ethos.

The terrestrial emphasis on trees and afforestation projects also signified the battle against marginal, unproductive landscapes such as swamps, which have historically unsettled the modernizing ethos of nation-states. In Turkey, forests were considered barriers against undesirable forms of the aquatic, while afforestation was a state policy for reclaiming marginal lands. While foresters relied on this representation to reinforce their role as scientific vanguards, forest-dependent communities purposefully co-opted this terrestrial narrative in their demands from the state. I became aware of the intricacies of the relationship between the state and forest villagers when I attended a participatory forestry meeting in a small town in Kastamonu in 2010. In response to the discursive shift toward participatory management, local forestry agencies organize events where foresters and members of the community meet and discuss forestry matters. Until the Q&A, the meeting I attended was a typical state ritual during which the "faces of the state" appeared in many guises, such as hierarchical seating or the singing of the national anthem (Navarro-Yashin 2002). When forest villagers started asking questions, I was surprised that the previously silent men became vocal, at times indignant citizens, passionately sharing their complaints with foresters, while using the official scientific forestry discourse as their weapon of the weak (Scott 1985). One man was furious about the local forestry agency's plan to cut down trees near his village, blaming the foresters for ignoring trees' role as barriers against floods. Fueled by the recent flooding of the river, which put their village at risk, he and his neighbors articulated their frustration by extracting the rhetoric of scientific forestry and land management from the realm of the state and professional forestry and using it as a counter-hegemonic narrative. Consequently, they defined forests as terrestrial obstacles that could resist unruly versions of the aquatic. In their materiality, natural resources thus acquire a certain agency and emerge as actors that mediate the relationship between the state and society.

When afforestation projects emerged as a panacea for managing marginal landscapes such as swamps throughout the last century, certain species became symbolic of efforts to tame nature. Eucalyptus, native to Australia, played a significant role in forest plantations throughout the world as a fast-growing species (Radkau 2012). In addition to its role in wood production, eucalyptus was emblematic of forests' terrestrial nature in colonial and national governments' antimalaria campaigns in the late nineteenth and early twentieth centuries. Wetland drainage emerged as a universal practice in this era (McNeill 2000, 197), and with its ability to absorb large amounts of water, eucalyptus was viewed as an ideal species (Radkau 2012, 321). Eucalyptus plantations' role in the fight against malaria was especially widespread in southern Europe and the colonies; in some cases, such as in Palestine, eucalyptus became symbolic of the nationalist project itself (Sufian 2007). Turkey's war against malaria started in 1925 and borrowed from the Italian model, which approached the disease and its eradication through a social lens and attempted to transform everyday cultural practices that were considered to contribute to its spread (Akder 2010; Gratien 2022; Evered and Evered 2011). Consequently, sanitation, land reclamation, and drainage were seen as methods to control and prevent malaria. Eucalyptus plantations occupied such a major role in these efforts that the species is colloquially known as the "malaria tree" in parts of Turkey. Scientific and popular publications on malaria in the 1930s and 1940s illustrated the negative associations between the unruly versions of the aquatic and malaria. Consequently, species such as eucalyptus were defined as a remedy for the conceptual and material dangers posed by swamps, anchoring trees' place in the terrestrial discourse. Even though the terrestrial discourse presented forests as remedies for ambiguous landscapes like swamps, later in this chapter I will show that forests are themselves liminal landscapes by focusing on mud as the symbol of this liminality. I now turn to the aquatic narrative to show that terrestriality was not the only trope through which forests were conceptualized.

The Aquatic Forest

Afforestation was simultaneously about a different discourse, which represented forests as sources of humidity and clean water. This discourse, which I refer to as the aquatic narrative, was maintained through the persistent fear of desertification, a constituting myth of Turkish nationalism. According to this myth[12] Turks' migration from Central Asia to Anatolia was the result of climate change; as water became scarce, turning Central Asia, a once fertile land, into a barren steppe, Turks were forced to leave their motherland to find a new home.[13] This migration myth and fears of desertification have been embedded within the national ethos and the hegemonic forestry discourse. A 1939 educational pamphlet reminded readers that "there is no fear of drought in forested areas" (Eryılmaz 1939, 5). Analyzing an imagined future of oil scarcity in Oman, Limbert proposes thinking of scarcity not only as an essential quality of things, but also "as an expression of a social relationship, culturally defined" (Limbert 2010, 7). The myth of desertification in Turkey has thus engendered a national policy, wherein increasing forest coverage could not be separated from maintaining healthy water supplies.

Discussing the 1937 Forest Act and afforestation, forester and author Rıdvan Pınar claimed that the successful implementation of a country's forestry and water policies was only possible if they worked in tandem: "[W]ater, which is pivotal to and the life force of a country can certainly become the source of trouble and natural disasters in conjunction with unskilled and unmethodical forestry" (Pınar 1937, 108). This statement is vital to my argument that definitions are inherently fluid and that different narratives compete in the archival record. The aquatic narrative reverses the dichotomy between the unruliness of the aquatic and the legibility provided by forests, yet it exists alongside the terrestrial narrative, reinforcing the need to move beyond binary oppositions and fixed categories toward definitions of the landscape that center on liminality, with which I will conclude this chapter. This fluidity is further stressed through the overlaps between the terrestrial and the aquatic narratives, which accompany their fundamental differences. For instance, productivity is at the center of both discourses, but while the terrestrial narrative emphasizes productivity with reference to trees' rootedness, the aquatic narrative prioritizes the water produced by forests. In its most obvious manifestation, the aquatic narrative represents forests as sources and receptacles of water and highlights their capacity to regulate climate. As highlighted by former minister Diker, forests were the main source of water needed for agriculture (Diker 1947, 72).

The connection between agriculture and rainfall acquired through forests was reiterated by German forester Franz Heske, who taught at Istanbul University in the 1950s (Heske 1952a, 6–8). According to Heske, the connection between forests and the aquatic was so significant that its absence was indicative of not only natural but also social and political problems. Discussing forests' role in combating drought, he wrote that "the . . . destruction of forests, can cause a flood of related problems. These disasters start as soil erosion, relative reduction in rainfall and an increase in steppe climate; they can conclude as poverty, backwardness, and even political and economic collapse" (Heske 1952b, 4). By correlating forests with the aquatic, Heske thus portrayed forests as the possibility of civilization: "A modern . . . monument of civilization cannot be built on the foundations of an outmoded and backwards agriculture and nomadic animal husbandry, which both rapidly lose their productivity due to the devastation of forests, soil erosion and drought" (Heske 1952a, 7). Elsewhere, Heske was more direct in representing forests through an aquatic narrative, stating that "mountain forests are a country's natural water repository. . . . Forest soil . . . absorbs water like a sponge, stores it, gradually and continuously transfers it to the soil below" (Heske 1952a, 7). It was in a similar context that botanist and author Hikmet Birand classified northern Turkey's forests as wetland vegetation, which, he argued, stood in stark contrast to Central Anatolia's arid vegetation (Birand 1945, 143). These comments illustrate that for republican elites, forests meant rainfall and humidity, placing them at the center of national imaginaries of civilization, while also connecting them with agricultural development.

The ubiquity of a discourse is best understood by looking beyond its most obvious manifestations and analyzing its less explicit appearances. An article about prisons that was published in *ÜLKÜ*, the journal of the People's Houses, which served as a semiofficial publication of the Republican People's Party and of the Kemalist regime, provides an excellent example of how hegemonic the aquatic discourse was. Discussing rational uses for prison labor, politician Hidayet Aydıner argued that prison labor could be useful for afforestation efforts. According to Aydıner, growing seedlings in prisons was not only an efficient use of prison labor but also a necessity to prevent drought (Aydıner 1937). This rhetoric continued in the multiparty era as well. According to the first five-year development plan issued in 1963, ensuring that forests have a positive impact on water basins was one of the four goals of Turkey's forestry policy (Devlet Planlama Teşkilatı 1963, 10). The plan also noted that in addition to securing adequate rainfall, forests also prevented the damage caused by destructive forms of water such as floods (74–5), a point I will revisit in the last section of this chapter when I discuss mud as the ultimate symbol of the forest's liminality.

Forests' aquatic representation was not confined to a general discussion of good climate, rain, and productivity. This discourse also represented individual trees as vessels of humidity, a stark contrast to their role as emblems of rootedness in the terrestrial discourse. In the education pamphlet I cited earlier, trees were defined with reference to their individual parts, among which the roots had a paramount role in enabling them to absorb water from the soil (Eyilmaz 1937, 4). Eryılmaz explained that the "watery wood" in a tree's bark is the "liveliest" part of the tree, thereby relying on the aquatic as the essence of trees' materiality. A treatise on eucalyptus, likewise, defined trees as vessels of not just humidity, but literally water when the author explained that a certain eucalyptus species was not profitable for timber production because the wood dried fast due to its water content (Pryor 1954, 6). A 1954 booklet warned against the dangers posed by forest degradation using a similar discourse:

> The most beautiful and striking part of a tree is its branches and leaves. Branches and leaves not only make the tree look beautiful, but also allow it to thrive. Because it is the leaves on these branches that absorb the much-needed light from the sun and expel the extra water in the trunk as sweat. . . . Especially during spring and summer when the water is moving upwards within the tree, cutting these branches at the root, or plucking their leaves is to sentence the tree to death. (Asmaz and Seren 1954, 11–12)

Later in the text, forests' aquatic benefits were visualized by the image of a clear-watered stream, whose banks were lined by trees, while the caption reaffirmed forests' inherently aquatic nature: "Forests are the biggest sources of a country's streams" (Asmaz and Seren, 24).

A more literary example of the aquatic narrative came from journalist Şakir Sungar's travelogue, detailing his observations of state forestry enterprises in the 1940s. Sungar described a beautiful scene where forests appeared as wetlands. On his way to Kızılcahamam, a town north of the capital Ankara, he stumbled across a water fountain constructed from conifers. Amazed by the water's clarity and coolness, and the trees' ability to generate this water, Sungar wrote that "[i]t is the pines that create the water" (Sungar 1943, 23). These various representations, which served to educate the public on the interdependency between forests and the nation's water sources, situated forests within an aquatic materiality. This representation is in stark contrast with the terrestrial representation; unlike the structures rooted in the land, which sustain the homeland and eliminate marginal bodies of water, in the aquatic discourse trees are defined both by the water that they retain within their own bodies and the water they attract in terms of rainfall, which contributes to the nation's overall productivity.

I witnessed the salience of the aquatic narrative on a cold winter day in 2010. As the brisk air seeped through the windows, I sat and listened to lectures during a training seminar organized by a nonprofit organization that advocates for forest cooperatives.

Aimed at providing unemployed youth with skills-based training for forest labor, this event featured lectures given by faculty from the local university as well as officials from the regional forestry office. The lectures were accompanied by experiential learning in the forest. One of the lecturers, a senior forester from the regional directorate in Kastamonu, encouraged his audience to relate their own experiences to the lecture material on the value of forests. "I don't think someone from the Black Sea [region] can live in Southeastern or Central Anatolia," he said and continued: "Imagine you have to burn cow dung as fuel. You, here don't even like fir as fuel but burn pine or oak instead." As Hasan went on to present the arid conditions of Central Anatolia in stark contrast to the plush landscapes of the Black Sea region, his account acquired an affective quality when he presented the absence of the aquatic in the Central Anatolian steppe through the tropes of anxiety and suffocation.

I experienced the aquatic narrative in an even more material way when I tasted *soymuk*, the edible sap within the cambium of evergreens which I introduced earlier in this chapter. *Soymuk* is fascinating not only because it encapsulates the aquatic nature of trees, but because it serves as an emblem of forests' polyvocal materiality in rural communities' everyday practices. For my friends who lived in forest villages, as was the case for forest villagers for centuries, trees were both forms of livelihood and a component of everyday social and cultural practices, whether it be as a source of raw material for housing or nutrition for humans and livestock. I tasted *soymuk* in a context which says as much about trees' everyday materiality for forest communities as it does about the dialogic, negotiated forms of state-making. At the end of a long workday in the forest, where I witnessed how timber is produced, my friend invited me to join two forest guards and a few forest villagers, who were chatting as they snacked on *soymuk*. Unlike the traditional way of eating *soymuk* from living trees, these men were gathered around a recently felled tree; this was officially sanctioned *soymuk* from waste material. Despite my protests that I was queasy after a long day of excessive black tea consumption, which was an excuse for my fear of ingesting something unfamiliar, my companions were adamant about the health benefits of this precious sap. *Soymuk* is very juicy and resembles a tropical fruit. Despite the initially overwhelming and appealing taste, I knew I could not eat more than a few pieces, but the juicy fleshy texture convinced me about its long-standing place in rural communities' diet. What made the moment significant was not just tasting *soymuk* for the first time but eating it in the company of forest guards and forest villagers. *Soymuk*, which mediated the relationship between peasants and the state for decades, now manifested itself in a sanctioned way, reminiscent of older conflicts but legitimate, while the intimacy between these men in such a traditional act served as a reminder of the complex relationship between guards and villagers, which I further discuss below.

The Liminal Forest

The liminal role forest guards occupy in forest practices epitomizes the dialogics of state-making and the negotiated relationship between agents of the state and forest communities. Although their title evokes enforcement, guards' main responsibility is the management of forests. They supervise timber production in the subdistricts and help to prepare the logs for sale by local forestry agencies. They also handle the subsidized wood and timber allocation to forest villagers. While *şefs* spend as much time in the office as in the field, guards are in the forest every day and develop a level of intimacy with the forest villagers that other foresters cannot acquire.[14] The best example of this is market days, which are almost rituals in small towns. The main activity on the day of the farmers' market is not only shopping; for many residents of villages this is a time for running errands in the town center or taking care of official business such as going to the bank or a government office. Therefore, forest guards' and forest villagers' day off is not necessarily on the weekend, but on market day. Nothing could serve as a better example of the dialogics of state-making than the organization of state-led forest management based on the practices of rural communities.

Forest guards are also de facto decision-makers at the local level. This is not a formal bureaucratic procedure based on laws and regulations; instead, it is a spontaneous, contingent process that depends as much on context and relationships as it does on laws. Even though forest guards have a subordinate relationship to the *şefs* due to their level of education and their position in the administrative hierarchy, they are also their unrecognized mentors. Because *şefs* work on a rotational system, they are shuffled from one region to another and cannot acquire enough experience in a locale to give them the nuanced perspective that forest guards gain over time. What makes forest guards' experience with forest villagers unique is that they often come from rural backgrounds and were, until very recently, appointed in areas close to their hometowns.[15] During my fieldwork, I witnessed countless moments when experienced guards made practical decisions that were nominally in violation of the law.

The interview I conducted with a retired forest guard, who was born in 1925 and worked in villages in the western Black Sea region in the 1950s, provides a striking example of forest guards' liminality. Prior to being employed as a guard, Mustafa worked for the local forestry agency's lawyer, an experience which he praised for teaching him the procedures and functioning of forestry.[16] His most insightful comments came from his memories of the eight years when he worked as a forest guard after this. When I asked him if there was large-scale smuggling back then, he said: "There was no large-scale smuggling in my area, but the villages were really crowded. Smuggling, it wasn't commercial, but [people] built houses. Now there is no one who builds a house from timber, it's all reinforced concrete." It was when I asked Mustafa if he often issued official reports for these "crimes" that he started to talk like an anthropologist and to unpack the multiple meanings of the law and the liminal position he occupied between the makers of the law and those who were expected to obey them: "I have three letters of commendation. And I have also been commended by judges. Now, there are colleagues who report offenses for the smallest things and bring people to court. If you start to apply the law absolutely, then to pick a single leaf is a crime. But then, there is the issue of governance." The climax of his account was when he positioned himself in relationship to forest villagers and adopted a paternalistic tone:

> If I had to file an official report, the citizen does not know the law so I would teach him. State it this way and that way and when you're in court, do it that way. For

> example, you built a home, do not ever say you fell a standing tree; felling a standing tree comes with a big penalty. I would teach them to say I gathered [the wood] from fallen trees. In other words, they would only have to pay for the value of the timber.

I then asked Mustafa if this meant that the law was inherently flawed in the first place. If picking off a single leaf is an offense, then does that not mean that the law is too rigid to apply? Mustafa's answer was firm and precise: "Naturally, the law is one thing and governing another." Mustafa's narrative is an embodiment of two distinct elements: the paternalism of the state reflected through a moral economy which forest villagers expected the forest guards to respect, and the liminality of an actor who mediates between forest villagers and higher-ranking foresters (Thompson 1971; Scott 1976). In his contribution to this volume, Tatari analyzes a similar logic of negotiation between scientific expertise and local practices in the context of artisanal cheesemaking.

As I observed on multiple occasions, forest guards rectify the inapplicable, impractical aspects of forestry on the ground. More importantly, in their role as mediators, they rely on and collaborate with forest villagers whose everyday practices are defined, among other things, by an implicit resistance to a rigid implementation of state policies. While the legalization of the scientific discourse is hegemonic, this does not mean that forest-dependent communities are passive actors. They are active agents who respond to their predicament in subtle ways, by relying on a certain moral economy of obligations in their relationship with the state and resorting to weapons of the weak to resist structures imposed on them. "Social pressure" was a phrase I heard from foresters throughout my fieldwork. As scientists, these professional foresters were experts who had the knowledge and skills to conserve and manage forests. However, as agents of the state, they also had to take into consideration the needs of forest-dependent communities, which at times contradicted the scientific approach they wished to implement in their work.

The liminality that characterizes the state–society relationship cannot be separated from the liminality of the forest itself. Mud is a material and discursive domain in which the terrestrial and the aquatic interpretations of the forest converge and coexist. In line with Stoler's call that our approach to archives should move from an extractive to an ethnographic enterprise (Stoler 2008), I interpret the archival record on mud as a discourse that has been instrumental to the imaginaries, management, and transformation of natural landscapes in modern states. Material conditions of the forest, specifically mud, have engendered a discourse of challenge and conquest that is at the core of foresters' subjectivity as I discussed earlier. As a discourse, mud has allowed the modernizing state to classify the natural and the social by attributing either a desirable or a marginal affect to landscapes and the subjectivities associated with them. This affect is what allows me to detect the discourse of mud in the archival record even in the absence of the word itself. I interpret references to heavy rains, floods, or swamps as affective utterances of mud, which present a conceptual contrast to vegetation, which the modernizing elites considered the essence of civilization. Mud takes its power from its grotesque liminality. Neither solid nor liquid; neither terrestrial nor aquatic, but somewhere between and betwixt, mud challenges classificatory systems and fixed essences such as wet and dry, thereby creating obstacles for foresters' modernist agenda to manage landscapes and civilize populations.

Writing about the dangers of deforestation in 1934, agriculturalist Ragıp Ziya described mud's abject power through an affect of terror:

> Suddenly we saw the sky darkening, rain pouring, the enormous rocky hills acquiring a pitch-black visage, stones and earth rolling towards the treeless and steep road. We were shocked at what was happening. . . . The car trembled violently and slipped because of the encroaching flood and the slimy soil that slithered and covered the road. Had it not been for an expert maneuver by the driver, we would have rolled down the cliff! (Ragıp Ziya 1934)

What makes the apocalyptic depiction of water in this account striking is Ziya's earlier affirmative approach to the aquatic when he attributed northern Turkey's fecundity to snowfall, which is gradually soaked up by the soil. Ziya then warned against desertification by arguing that in the absence of additional sources of water, forest clearings in the south posed a potential threat. By presenting two contrasting accounts of water, this example illustrates that the materiality of water was not confined to wetness. The snowfall in the north was favored as acceptable water since it retained its aquatic qualities even when it was absorbed by the soil, whereas the floods in the south were not so tame once they mixed with the soil and turned into mud, defying binaries. Having trespassed into the realm of the abject, the liminality of mud was also a threat to the subject, in whose body and mind social order is reproduced. Ziya's reference to a potential car accident and death due to flooding can, therefore, be interpreted as an offense against the modern subject, whom mud's abjectness inherently refutes.

Levi-Strauss argued that water is not inherently pure and healing; analyzing myths about celestial water, he differentiated between two kinds: "one is calm and gentle, the other violent; one is beneficent since it is refreshing and thirst-quenching, the other maleficent" (Levi-Strauss 1964, 214). Simon Schama also signaled the malleable definition of the aquatic when he discussed the nurturing, life-giving role attributed to the Nile as opposed to the destructive representation of "the Greek torrents which crashed down from a mountainous height, threatening cities like Athens with destruction" (Schama 1995, 258–9). In a more recent example, Krause and Strang illustrate the contradictions of water as being both productive and disruptive (Krause and Strang 2016). These examples illustrate that the aquatic and the terrestrial are not fixed essences which directly correlate with wet and dry or productive and marginal landscapes. Social and natural categories are fluid, and as Mary Douglas argued half a century ago, it is the liminality of "matter out of place" that makes modern states uncomfortable (Douglas 1996, 36). Mud is neither wet nor dry, neither fluid nor solid, but somewhere in between and both, presenting an amphibious challenge to the binaries via which the modern state managed the social and the natural. Intellectuals' classification of water as beneficent or maleficent in its various forms can, therefore, be interpreted as a discursive attempt to contain mud's liminality within a binary framework. That is why the benevolent aquatic associated with trees was deemed legitimate whereas the aquatic nature of floods was considered a categorical travesty.

A final example, which illustrates the amphibiousness of forests, comes from the republican discourse on coal in the 1930s and 1940s. For Kemalist elites, coal was emblematic of and indispensable for modernization and development, but more importantly, it was treasured as an alternative to wood and a remedy for deforestation. The association between coal and forests went beyond what they had in common as sources of energy. Coal is a fossil fuel because coal beds were formed by decayed living organisms, most of which were the earth's first forests that grew in swamp-like conditions (Ward and Kirschvink 2015, 192–3). Journalist Niyazi Acun's 1952 treatise on coal was built on this connection between swamps, forests, and coal. His narrative on the formation of coal takes the reader on a geological journey to ancient swamps, which absorb dead plants that then go through a process of decomposition to eventually end up as coal. Acun wrote that these coal beds are "the oldest and purest products of the plant world, the actual underground forests" (Acun 1952, 14), and concluded by reminding the reader that appreciation of contemporary forests inevitably requires a recognition of these underground forest communities (Acun 1952, 21). Acun's discussion of the grotesque process of decomposition is a prime example of what I conceptualize as the discourse of mud. While Acun does not necessarily use the word mud, it is there as a discourse; the slimy decomposed material of the "underground forests" that is both solid and liquid is, like the floods in Ziya's text, disruptive of clear-cut categories and threatens social order. Moreover, as an integral element of the forest, mud presents ambiguity and amphibiousness as the essence of forests. Giblett defines this as the "slimy swamp of embryonic life" that gave birth to all other life forms: "The world was wetland, and the wetland was the womb from which all later life sprung" (Giblett 2014, 3). Yet, Acun's reliance on what I call the discourse of mud as an explanatory framework is curious in an era when mud was demonized as an impediment to progress. At a time when swamps were seen as a symbol of grotesque backwardness and disease and became targets of modernization projects, how can we explain Acun's emphasis on the regenerative qualities associated with swamps?

I argue that this beneficent representation of swamps was possible thanks to a categorical shift. Drawing on Bakhtin's work on the grotesque, Gardiner claims that "although carnival can be demonized as unadulterated 'Otherness,' and constructed as low, uncivilized, and unspeakably carnal, it can never be entirely eliminated, only displaced. The shadow of repressed carnivalesque desire always haunts the ostensibly individual and disciplined bourgeois subject, although it tends to be interiorized and sublimated" (Gardiner 1993). In Acun's narrative, coal was textually taken from the category of mud, the abject, to be placed within the category of forest. By evoking notions of an unadulterated, idyllic nature in the form of forests, and then naming coal beds as underground forests, Acun thus displaced coal from the abjectness associated with mud and replaced it within modernity. This attempt to turn coal into a "smooth object" (Latour 2004) relied on movement between categories; coal was discursively transformed from the abject to an object, reinforcing my argument that natural landscapes cannot be defined by fixed essences.

Figure 5.1 Photograph taken by the author in northern Turkey.

During my fieldwork, mud was an everyday nuisance as well as a discourse through which the categories of the state, society, and nature were solidified (see figure 5.1). For foresters, mud is a major obstacle in terms of field duties. While most high-ranking foresters do not spend as much time in the forest as the *şefs*, even they repeatedly emphasized mud as a major actor in the forest. Forest villagers and forest guards, who spend their workday in the forest, bear the brunt of this nuisance more than any of the foresters. Access to production sites is through unpaved, muddy forest roads, making walking let alone driving—especially in spring and fall—difficult or almost impossible.

On a spring day in 2010, I accompanied two guards to a work site in the forest. The mud got thicker as our vehicle climbed up the mountain. Despite all the complaints I had heard about mud, I was mesmerized by its power when I realized that walking several feet from the jeep to the makeshift shack would be an ordeal. Every step required an effortful choreography, requiring me to forcefully pull my rubber boots out of the mud with each step. Before the senior forest guard drove off to attend to other business, he warned me and his novice colleague that if the mud was thicker by late afternoon, we would need to hike to his location, because the jeep would not be able to pick us up. While the rookie guard looked distressed by this development, I was thrilled at the prospect of an ethnographic adventure, especially since I was now prepared with my tall rubber boots. But soon I was having second thoughts. At one point, my boots were so deep in the mud that I was almost completely immobile. Over the years, I kept revisiting this memory to realize how much I had learned in one day about the nuances of mud. With its abject liminality, mud is almost magical and awes one with its abysmal strength. Even though foresters often complained about how it interfered with their work, their tone was not dismissive, but reverent; mud was their respected enemy, a form of materiality that the social has only incompletely mastered.

Despite my clumsiness, foresters praised me because I did not refrain from "getting dirty," a comment which revealed as much about them as it did about me. For them, entering the male-dominated forestry world as a woman was noteworthy. Furthermore, mud was a discursive tool in their civilizing mission to tame nature through scientific intervention, a ritual that defined their personhood and their ideas of social order. By defying mud's grotesqueness and confronting it, I had joined this ritual and become an honorary member of their community. Giblett explains the fraught relationship between wetlands and cities in a similar way: "where the city is now, there the wetland was once; where the wetland is now on the outskirts of the city, the city, or its suburbs, soon will be; where the restored, rehabilitated, or artificial wetland is in the city, a wetland or wasteland once was" (Giblett 2016, 3). In foresters' discourse, mud signifies a social distance between civilization and unruly nature, which defies states' legibility attempts (Scott 1998). Waging a war against the impenetrable abjectness of the forest represented by mud, foresters thus define their personhood through a scientific ethos, which allows them to transform the unruly into a regulated body of knowledge and resources, defined by Ferry and Limbert as "a movement from the realm of nature to the realm of culture" (Ferry and Limbert 2008, 8).

Unlike professional foresters' experience, forest guards' and forest villagers' intimacy with mud permeates their everyday experiences, especially during rainy months when felling, cleaning, and transporting trees can be challenging. Mud generates a certain habitus (Bourdieu 2017) and as an embodied experience, forest work requires specific bodily techniques (Mauss 1973). While I was easily rendered immobile, forest villagers not only knew how to navigate mud by paying attention to its nuances, but they spent their whole day working in it. Nevertheless, as I watched a guard and three workers spend all day removing thick, creamy mud from the timber they prepared for transportation, I realized that despite foresters' attempts to think of modern forestry as a categorical victory over nature's unruliness, mud was still an integral element of the landscape, imbuing it with aquatic qualities on a regular basis. I eventually saved my boots, even though it took weeks of rigorous wiping to remove the mud that had been soaked up by the leather. Yet while the boots had only been in contact with the mud for a matter of minutes, the forest was always in the mud just as the mud was always in the forest. Eventually, one day, with a towel in one hand and the boots in the other, I realized that mud *was* the forest.

Conclusion

In this chapter, I challenged two sets of assumptions. First, I questioned the idea that forests have fixed essences by analyzing how they have historically been essentialized as either terrestrial or aquatic landscapes. By centering on mud to reframe forests as amphibious landscapes, I offered to think of liminality as forests' defining feature. My second challenge was to the assumption that the state and society are divergent categories that are inherently in conflict with one another. I showed that the complex relationship between foresters and peasants reveals a negotiated reality in forestry practices and policies. Therefore, I argued that state-making is a dialogic process and that neither the state nor society can be imagined as monolithic and homogeneous categories. As economic neoliberalism and conservative populism continue to pose a threat to natural landscapes and livelihoods, understanding cultural and historical complexities is paramount to interpreting our contemporary predicaments. The rigid categories of modernity define contemporary political realities and impose an artificially binary logic on the messiness of the social. Thinking through the archival record ethnographically can therefore help to question the hegemony of such categories to recognize the liminality that is the actual face of the modern.

Notes

1 Franz Krause, Luisa Cortesi, and Alejandro Camargo were involved in the initial drafting of this chapter and offered valuable feedback on earlier versions. I thank them for their time, effort, and critique. I would also like to extend my thanks to Ekin Kurtiç and Duygu Kaşdoğan for providing me with a platform to revisit and rethink this text within a materiality framework and for inviting me to contribute to this volume.
2 Interview conducted with Yücel Çağlar in June 2010.
3 *Şef* is the Turkish translation of chief.
4 This was the name of the ministry at the time of the research.
5 Wilson's discussion of a "sylvan discourse" in Germany provides a similar account (Wilson 2016).
6 This data, based on the distribution of subdistricts, has been obtained from the website of the General Directorate of Forestry.
7 The 1937 Forest Act was replaced by new legislation in 1956. While some have criticized this law's populism as detrimental to conservation, the backbone of the state's forestry policy remained intact.
8 For an example, see Özkan (2018).
9 Even though the opposition objected to nationalization from a populist angle, most forests were already state lands at this date. The actual target of nationalization was, therefore, not peasant rights but private forest initiatives, many of which were foreign investments.
10 As I will show in a book in progress, despite rhetorical differences, the two parties' views on forestry were in fact similar.
11 For a discussion of trees' association with the soil and the nation, see Meneley (2011) and Braverman (2014).
12 Migration was a major trope in the Turkish History Thesis, which was a component of Turkish nationalism in the 1930s. Along with the Sun Language Theory, which presented Turkish as the original human language, the History Thesis claimed that Central Asia and the Turks' legacy were the backbone of civilization. While the climatic conditions that triggered this migration are undisputable, the efforts to "imagine" the nation have imbued it with a mythological tone.
13 See Behar (1992) and Copeaux (1998).
14 A similar argument has been made by Vasan about forest guards in India (2002).
15 The recruitment system for forest guards changed in recent years when the government began to apply a universal civil servant exam across the country. Whereas

guards were recruited locally in the past, today the positions are filled based on this exam, and guards can be appointed anywhere in the country.

16 Interview conducted by the author in 2010.

References

Abrams, Philip. 1988. "Notes on the Difficulty of Studying the State," *Journal of Historical Sociology* 1 (1): 58–89.

Abu-Lughod, Lila. 2005. *Dramas of Nationhood: The Politics of Television in Egypt*, Chicago: University of Chicago Press.

"Acıpayam'da Ağaç Bayramı". *Ormancı Postası*, April 15, 1944: 3.

Acun, Niyazi. 1945. *Ormanlarımız ve Cumhuriyet Hükümeti'nin Orman Davası*, Ankara: Recep Ulusoğlu Basımevi.

Acun, Niyazi. 1952. *Yeraltı Ormanları ve Linyitlerimizin Yakılması*, Ankara: Yeni Matbaa.

Agrawal, Arun. 2005. *Environmentality: Technologies of Government and the Making of Subjects*, Durham, N.C.: Duke University Press.

Akder, Halis. 2010. "Forgotten Campaigns: A History of Disease in Turkey," in Celia Kerslake, Kerem Öktem and Philip Robbins (eds.), *Turkey's Engagement with Modernity: Conflict and Change in the Twentieth Century*, 210–35, Basingstoke: Palgrave Macmillan.

Alaçam, Refik. 1945. *Orman ve Memleket*, Istanbul: Hüsnütabia Basımevi.

Altay, Cafer. 1965. "Unutulan Sinop." *Turistik Sinop*, July 2.

Asafoğlu, Fahreddin Karaoğlan. 1938. *Orman İşleri*, Ankara: Hapisane Matbaası.

Asmaz, Hasan and Haluk Seren. 1954. *Ormancılık Bilgisi*, Ankara: Güzel Sanatlar Matbaası.

Atay, Falih Rıfkı. 1944. "Ağaç ve Devlet," *Ormancı Postası*, February 1: 1 & 4.

Aydiner, Hidayet. 1937. "Yurdumuzun Agaclandirilmasi - Zirai Hapishaneler," *ÜLKÜ* 57, November: 267–70.

Baker, J. Mark. 2005. *The Kuhls of Kangra: Community-Managed Irrigation in the Western Himalaya*, Seattle: University of Washington Press.

Bakhtin, M. M. 1981. *The Dialogic Imagination*, trans. Caryl Emerson and Michael Holquist, Austin: University of Texas Press.

Behar, Büşra Ersanlı. 1992. *İktidar ve Tarih*, İstanbul: Afa Yayınları.

Birand, Hikmet. 1945. "Batı Karadeniz Kıyılarında Bir Botanik Gezisi," *Türk Coğrafya Dergisi* 7–8: 141–53.

Bourdieu, Pierre. 2017. *Outline of a Theory of Practice*, Cambridge: Cambridge University Press.

Braverman, Irus. 2014. *Planted Flags: Trees, Land, and Law in Israel/Palestine*, Cambridge: Cambridge University Press.

Copeaux, Etienne. 1998. *Tarih Ders Kitaplarında (1931–1993) Türk Tarih Tezinden Türk-İslam Sentezine*, İstanbul: Tarih Vakfı Yurt Yayınları.

"Devlet Orman İşletmeleri". 1943. *Ormancı Postası*, 29 İlk Teşrin, 1943.

Devlet Planlama Teşkilatı. 1963. *Ormancılık - Birinci Beş Yıllık Kalkınma Planı*, Ankara Basım ve Ciltevi.

Diker, Mazhar. 1947. *Türkiyede Ormancılık: Dün-Bugün-Yarın*, Ankara: Tarım Bakanlığı Yayınları.

Douglas, Mary. 1996. *Purity and Danger: An Analysis of Concepts of Pollution and Taboo*, London: Routledge & Kegan Paul.
Dursun, Selçuk. 2007. "Forest and the State: History of Forestry and Forest Administration in the Ottoman Empire,"Unpublished Dissertation, Sabanci University.
Eryılmaz, Mithat. 1937. *Agac ve Orman Sevgisi*. Ankara: Recep Ulusoglu Basimevi.
Eryılmaz, Mithat. 1939. *Orman ve Korunması Bilgileri*, Ankara: Recep Ulusoğlu Basımevi.
Evered, Kyle T. and Emine Ö. Evered. 2011. "Governing Population, Public Health, and Malaria in the Early Turkish Republic," *Journal of Historical Geography* 37: 470–82.
Fairhead, James and Melissa Leach. 1996. *Misreading the African Landscape: Society and Ecology in a Forest-Savanna Mosaic*, Cambridge & New York: Cambridge University Press.
Ferry, Elizabeth Emma and Mandana E. Limbert. 2008. "Introduction," in Elizabeth Emma Ferry and Mandana E Limbert (eds.), *Timely Assets: The Politics of Resources and their Temporalities*, 11, Santa Fe: School for Advanced Research Press.
Foucault, Michel. 1972. *The Archaeology of Knowledge*, trans. A. M. Sheridan Smith, London and New York: Routledge.
Gardiner, Michael. 1993. "Ecology and Carnival: Traces of a 'Green' Social Theory in the Writings of M. M. Bakhtin," *Theory and Society* 22 (6): 765–812.
Gençtürk, İsmail. 1995. *Orman ve Orman Köyleri*, Ankara: Prospero Yayınları.
Giblett, Rod. 2016. *Cities and Wetlands: The Return of the Repressed in Nature and Culture*, London & NY: Bloomsbury Academic.
Gökberk, Macit Ali. 1944. "Ağaçlandırma Davamız," *Ormancı Postası* 23 Birinci Teşrin 1.
Gratien, Chris. 2022. *The Unsettled Plain: An Environmental History of the Late Ottoman Frontier*, Standford: Stanford University Press.
Guha, Ranajit. 1997. *A Subaltern Studies Reader, 1986-1995*, University of Minnesota Press.
Guha, Ranajit. 1998. *Elementary Aspects of Peasant Insurgency in Colonial India*, India & Oxford: Oxford University Press.
Hansen, Thomas Blom, and Finn Stepputat. 2001. *State of Imagination: Ethnographic Explorations of the Postcolonial State*, Durham, NC: Duke University Press.
Herzfeld, Michael. 2005. *Cultural Intimacy: Social Poetics in the Nation-State*, London: Routledge.
Heske, Franz. 1952a. *Stepten Faydalanma Imkanları*, trans. Selahattin İnal, Istanbul: Kader Basimevi.
Heske, Franz. 1952b. *Türkiyede Orman ve Ormancılık*, trans. Selahattin İnal, İstanbul: Hüsnütabiat Basımevi.
Imort, Michael. 2005. "Eternal Forest - Eternal Volk: The Rhetoric and Reality of National Socialist Forest Policy," in Franz-Josef Brüggemeier, Mark Cioc and Thomas Zeller (eds.), *How Green Were the Nazis? Nature, Environment, and Nation in the Third Reich*, Athens: Ohio University Press, 43–72.
Kayacık, H. 1951. "Türkiye'de Çıplak Sahaların Ağaçlandırılması Lüzum ve İmkanları," in *Orman Davamızın Çeşitli Yönlerine Göre İlmi Görüşler*, Ankara: Türkiye Ormancılar Cemiyeti, 49–51.
Krause, Franz and Mark Harris. 2021. *Delta Life: Exploring Dynamic Environments where Rivers Meet the Sea*, New York: Berghahn.
Krause, Franz and Veronica Strang. 2016. "Thinking Relationships Through Water," *Society & Natural Resources* 29 (6): 633–8.
Latour, Bruno. 2004. *Politics of Nature: How to Bring the Sciences into Democracy*, Cambridge & London: Harvard University Press.

Lévi-Strauss, Claude. 1966. *The Savage Mind*, London: Weidenfeld and Nicolson.
Lévi-Strauss, Claude. 1964. *The Raw and the Cooked*, New York and Evanston: Harper & Row Publishers.
Limbert, Mandana. 2010. *In the Time of Oil: Piety, Memory, and Social Life in an Omani Town*, Stanford: Stanford University Press.
Mauss, Marcel. 1973. "Techniques of the Body," transl. Ben Brewster, *Economy and Society* 2 (1): 70–88.
Meneley, Anne. 2011. "Blood, Sweat and Tears in a Bottle of Palestinian Olive Oil," *Food, Culture and Society* 14 (2): 275–90.
Mitchell, Timothy. 1991. "The Limits of the State: Beyond Statist Approaches and Their Critics," *The American Political Science Review* 85 (1): 77–96.
McNeill, John R. 2000. *Something New Under the Sun: An Environmental History of the Twentieth Century World*, New York & London: W.W. Norton & Company.
Moore, Donald. 2005. *Suffering for Territory: Race, Place, and Power in Zimbabwe*, Durham, N.C.: Duke University Press.
Nader, Laura. 1972. "Up the Anthropologist, Perspectives Gained from Studying Up," in Dell Hymes (ed.), *Reinventing Anthropology*, 284–311, New York: Pantheon Books.
Navarro-Yashin, Yael. 2002. *Faces of the State: Secularism and Public Life in Turkey*, Princeton, NJ: Princeton University.
Nimmo, Ricchie. 2010. *Milk, Modernity and the Making of the Human: Purifying the Social*, London: Routledge.
Ogden, Laura. 2011. *Swamplife: People, Gators, and Mangroves Entangled in the Everglades*, Minneapolis: University of Minnesota Press.
Özkan, Hande. 2002. "Türkiye'de Tek Parti Dönemi Coğrafya ve Mekân Anlayışları: Yatay bir Dönemlendirme Denemesi," *Toplum ve Bilim* 94: 143–74.
Özkan, Hande. 2018. "Remembering Zingal: State, Citizens, and Forests in Turkey," *International Journal Middle East Studies* 50 (03): 493–511.
Özkan, Hande. 2022. "Goats, Axes, and Uncertain Narratives: Representations of Nature and People in Asia Minor," in Ştefan Dorondel and Ştelu Serban (eds.), *A New Ecological Order: Development and the Transformation of Nature in Eastern Europe*,177–99, Pittsburgh: University of Pittsburgh Press\.
Peluso, Nancy Lee. 1992. *Rich Forests Poor People: Resource Control and Resistance in Java*, Berkeley: University of California Press.
Peluso, Nancy Lee and Peter Vandergeest. 2006a. "Empires of Forestry: Professional Forestry and State Power in Southeast Asia, Part 1," *Environment and History* 12: 31–64.
Peluso, Nancy Lee and Peter Vandergeest. 2006b. "Empires of Forestry: Professional Forestry and State Power in Southeast Asia, Part 2," *Environment and History* 12: 359–93.
Pınar, Rıdvan. 1937. "Orman Kanunu ve Agaclandirma," *Orman ve Av* 10: 3.
Pryor, L.D. 1954. *Türkiye'de Okaliptus*, Ankara: Ziraat Vekaleti Orman Umum Müdürlügü.
Radkau, Joachim. 2012. *Wood: A History*, Cambridge; Malden, MA: Polity Press.
Scaramelli, Caterina. 2021. *How to Make a Wetland: Water and Moral Ecology in Turkey*, Stanford, California: Stanford University Press.
Schama, Simon. 1995. *Landscape and Memory*, New York: Alfred A. Knopf.
Scott, James C. 1976. *The Moral Economy of the Peasant: Rebellion and Subsistence in Southeast Asia*, Princeton: Princeton University Press.
Scott, James C. 1985. *Weapons of the Weak: Everyday Forms of Resistance*, New Haven: Yale University Press.

Scott, James C. 1998. *Seeing Like a State: How Certain Schemes to Improve the Human Condition Have Failed*, New Haven: Yale University Press.

Sharma, Aradhana and Akhil Gupta. 2006. *The Anthropology of the State: A Reader*, New York: Blackwell Publishing.

Sivaramakrishnan, Kalyanakrishnan. 1999. *Modern Forests: Statemaking and Environmental Change in Colonial Eastern India*, Stanford: Stanford University Press.

Stoler, Ann Laura. 2008. "Imperial Debris: Reflections on Ruins and Ruination," *Cultural Anthropology* 23 (2): 191–219.

Stoler, Ann Laura. 2009. *Along the Archival Grain: Epistemic Anxieties and Colonial Common Sense*, Princeton and Oxford: Princeton University Press.

Sufian, Sandra M. 2007. *Healing the Land and the Nation: Malaria and the Zionist Project in Palestine, 1920-1947*, Chicago: University of Chicago Press.

Tekeli, Esat. 1944. "Devlet Orman Işletmeleri," Ormancı Postası, 1 Ikinci Kanun.

"Toprak ve Ağaç Bayramı". *Ziraat Dergisi* 39: 36–37.

Thompson, E. P. 1971. "The Moral Economy of the English Crowd in the 18th Century," *Past & Present* 50: 76–136.

Turner, Victor. 1995. *The Ritual Process: Structure and Anti-structure*, New York: Aldine de Gruyter.

Türkiye Cumhuriyeti Orman Bakanlığı, 1983. *Cumhuriyetin 50. Yılında Orman-Köy İlişkileri*, Ankara: Doğuş Matbaası.

Vasan, Sudha. 2002. "Ethnography of the Forest Guard: Contrasting Discourses, Conflicting Roles and Policy Implementation," *Economic and Political Weekly* 37 (40): 4125–33.

Ward, Peter D. and Joseph L. Kirschvink. 2015. *A New History of Life: The Radical New Discoveries about the Origins and Evolution of Life on Earth*, New York: Bloomsbury Press.

Wiley, Andrea S. 2014. *Cultures of Milk: The Biology and Meaning of Dairy Products in the United States and India*, Cambridge: Harvard University Press.

Wilson, Jeffrey K. 2016. *The German Forest: Nature, Identity, and the Contestation of a National Symbol, 1871-1914,* Toronto: University of Toronto Press.

Yiğitoğlu, Ali Kemal. 1936. *Türkiye'de Ormancılığın Temelleri, Şartları ve Kuruluşu*, Ankara: Yüksek Ziraat Enstitüsü.

Yiğitoğlu, Ali Kemal. 1941. *Türkiye İktisadiyatında Ormancılığın Yeri ve Ehemmiyeti*, Ankara: Yüksek Ziraat Enstitüsü Matbaası.

Ziya, Ragip. 1934. "Bize Tahtacının Sesi Değil Ormancının Sesi Lazım", *Orman ve Av* 59–62: 37–40.

6

Pasture-Cheese Diplomacy

Carving Knowledge in Dairy Technosciences

Mehmet Fatih Tatari

It was a sunny Tuesday in the first week of July 2018, a few days before the start of the "Anatolian Cheeses Meet in Kars Festival" that was going to be organized in Boğatepe village, Kars, the northeastern border province of Turkey. Villagers were preparing to host more than thirty artisanal cheesemakers from various parts of the country. I accompanied İlhan and Şehnaz[1] during their visit to İlhan's then recently constructed dairy. Şehnaz, a PhD student in food engineering, works in the field of microbiology of milk. As part of her dissertation research, she analyzes lactic acid bacteria in Kars *kaşar* cheese in order to develop a starter culture that can later be commercialized. She had contacted İlhan and asked for his support in collecting whey samples from his dairy. İlhan had invited her to first visit the village and the dairy during the festival. While we were walking in-between old copper vats covered with stainless steel façades, Şehnaz explained that her research aimed to analyze the *thermophilic lactic acid bacteria*[2] in the whey, which, according to dairy scientists, are among the microorganisms that are crucial for cultivating the taste and texture characteristic of Kars *kaşar* cheese. She stated that her research would hopefully result in meaningful contributions to large-scale cheese production, as is the case in most food engineering departments. Her main contribution with the invention of a starter culture would be to enable cheesemakers to have a standard *kaşar* cheese that does not vary according to the seasons or microbial composition of "raw" (*çiğ*) milk.[3] For *kaşar* cheesemakers in Kars pastures, the microbial diversity of raw milk that differs according to climate and pasture conditions constitutes the distinctive taste (and its variations) of the resulting cheese. The same diversity is considered to be a threat to human health due to the pathogens it may contain, and the major obstacle for developing a standardized cheese production process in the dairy industry as well as in the dairy science research community.

İlhan answered Şehnaz with carefully chosen words. He stated that the traditional cheeses are artisanal products that reflect the conditions under which they are produced. In his words, cheesemakers use techniques to "shape the natural world into a cultural product" called cheese; and this process cannot, or rather should not, be independent of daily circumstances. Then he added that he would be glad to contribute to Şehnaz's research and emphasized its importance for him and other cheesemakers, who are eager to learn about the scientific definitions of the microbial world in pasture-heeses. However, the expected outcome of Şehnaz's dissertation research, he said, may pose a threat to the small-scale artisanal cheesemakers in rural Kars, where cheesemaking is a craft that depends on a web of relations among pastures, cows, small farmers, milk, and cheesemakers.

Unlike the small rural dairies (called *mandıra* or *zavot* in Kars), industrial dairy factories rely on various technologies that aim to standardize milk and cheese by rendering the source of milk, craft processes, and daily conditions almost irrelevant to the production process. Starter culture is one of the fundamental commodities for the factories since it enables the operationalization of pasteurization technologies in the production of standard cheeses. Rather than using (raw) milk to obtain the curd, the industrial cheesemaking process starts with pasteurizing the milk. Pasteurization minimizes the risk according to the food safety measures since it kills the pathogenic bacteria that are classified as harmful to human health. But it also kills most of the other bacteria that are crucial for the cheesemaking craft. Once the milk is pasteurized, the starter culture is added to provide the particular bacteria that can work in the curd to make the cheese. Hence, with the use of starter culture, dairy factories depend much less on the daily conditions of dairy farming or place-based microbial flora of the milk that would require particular craft processes as practiced in most *mandıra*s in villages or pastures. Şehnaz's research aimed to replace the widespread starter cultures, which are usually imported bacteria batches, with the one that makes any *kaşar* cheese into Kars *kaşar* cheese. Yet İlhan objected to this reasoning and suggested that adding bacteria cannot localize cheeses. On the contrary, he argued that this would ensure a standard cheesemaking process that no longer depends on the particular local conditions and knowledge—it would make milk and cheese *placeless*.

The disagreement between Şehnaz and İlhan epitomizes the main concern of this chapter, namely the collaboration between artisanal cheesemakers and scientists as they engage with "local" cheese and its dairy technosciences in Kars. Artisanal cheesemaking emerged as a crucial site for small farmers in their attempts to sustain rural livelihoods by certifying local cheeses as authentic products whose distinctiveness needs to be scientifically proven to the official food safety authorities. The studies that will be introduced in this chapter provided the required scientific analyses for certifications such as the Geographical Indication of Kars *kaşar* cheese and they revealed the limits of conventional dairy science research. Focusing on the recent collaborative processes of dairy science and crafts that made new connections and boundaries between pastures, dairies, laboratories, scientists, and cheesemakers, I analyze the ways in which these processes have altered dairy scientists' research agendas on artisanal cheesemaking and also destabilized the epistemic boundaries between scientific and traditional knowledges. I argue that pasture-cheeses enable a diplomacy that leads scientists to question the conventional approaches in dairy science research on "traditional" cheeses. Recent attempts at situating microbial ecologies in Kars cheeses, while following the recent trends in global microbial research, point both to the new aspirations that emerge from the collaborative processes and to the limitations in designing and practicing research in rural Kars and different universities in Turkey. I am interested in the ways in which cheesemakers' concerns can sneak into scientific research, become interwoven with the concerns of scientists, and challenge the conventional practices of knowledge production on Kars cheeses. Place emerged as a crucial variable in these collaborative research practices that seek to analyze and distinguish pasture-cheeses from industrial and/or standardized cheeses. Pastures mattered for dairy sciences and crafts in designing research on and implementing technosciences in Kars cheesemaking. As emphasized in the introduction of this volume, the material worlds of pastures "do not constitute a ground on which political relations get materialized" (p. 5); rather, they play a significant role in shaping the political processes of standardization and industrialization of dairy production.

Collaborations between dairy scientists and artisanal cheesemakers have recently been more visible, especially in local food production circles and their technosciences. Scientists, as well as cheesemakers who are trained in dairy sciences, have been influential figures in many conferences and documentaries.[4] While recent scientific studies on artisanal cheeses target the controversies behind the black boxes of the food safety regime (Donnelly 2019, 2014; Kindstedt 2012; Percival and Percival 2017),[5] various civil society organizations and artisanal cheesemaker associations have also been promoting new safety measures to protect traditional methods through different certification mechanisms. Cheese as a food heritage has become a crucial tool in various development programs through its reinvention in the heritage arena (Grasseni et al. 2014; Grasseni 2016, 2011). Anthropologist Heather Paxson (2008, 2013) conceptualizes post-Pasteurian microbiopolitics as a grid of intelligibility for humans to understand the world of microorganisms beyond a sum of particular isolated strains to be controlled or modeled in advance; microbial communities are dynamic in this microbial materiality that practitioners collaborate with (2013, 161). This approach enables her to analyze the innovative dairy science research simultaneously with the government of the encounter between humans and microorganisms (as food). This chapter contributes to these debates by investigating the making of Kars cheeses as food heritage through not only negotiations between state institutions, farmer collectives, scientists, development experts, and various advocacy groups, but also by designing and conducting research on cheeses in dairy sciences.[6] My analysis of pasture-cheese diplomacy reveals the political nature of more-than-human life in cheese. Nonhuman agents like cows, pastures, and microbes come into play when scientists attempt to understand microorganisms, their communities, and the environment(s) that make microbial life possible in local cheesemaking. Investigating the governance of the encounter between humans and microorganisms requires taking into account the nonhuman agency in the making of scientific expertise concerning local cheesemaking and food safety. As such, pasture-cheese diplomacy also contributes to one of the main aims of this volume, namely "populating the realm of politics with a variety of actors and forces" (Kaşdoğan and Kurtiç, this volume, p. 7). This chapter reveals that the technoscientific concern of standardization in dairy production can be accompanied by cultivating an attunement to the ways in which standardization may posit a threat to the small dairies and rural livelihoods of pasture-cheesemaking. This attunement then would entail considering the more-than-human life of pastures in the making of scientific expertise on cheesemaking. In other words, the collaborative research practices on local cheeses reveal the material politics of pastures in dairy crafts and sciences.

This chapter relies on my eighteen-month ethnographic research between September 2017 and February 2019,[7] in addition to my four months of preliminary research in 2015 and 2016, and my five years of voluntary work experience in dairy farmer organizations in rural Kars before embarking on this dissertation research. This chapter is mainly based on my interactions with veterinarians, microbiologists, and food engineers who study Kars *kaşar* cheeses in three different universities in Turkey. I interviewed twenty state officials and thirteen scientists and conducted participant observations in the laboratories when scientists analyzed whey or cheese samples shipped from dairies in Kars.

This chapter proceeds in four parts. First, I provide an overview of the conventional dairy science research on traditional cheeses in Turkey, and how it informs the current food safety regime that excludes small-scale rural dairies. Then I introduce İlhan's conceptualization of "implanted reason" (*koyma akıl*) and "carved reason" (*oyma akıl*), as modes of scientific research design he encountered in his attempts to collaborate with dairy scientists and state inspectors. Considering İlhan's approach as a diplomatic proposal in collaborative research, I analyze research designs and practices on Kars cheeses—for which pastures mattered. In the third section, I situate the concern of place-based differentiations in milk and cheese within the recent discussions of the "microbial turn" and "local cheese" in the United States and Europe. The fourth and final section concentrates on Şehnaz's above-introduced research and the relationship between local cheese and microbial ecologies in the case of Kars *kaşar* cheese. The collaborative research practices I analyze throughout this chapter challenge both conventional dairy science research and the institutional limits of designing and practicing research in rural Turkey by making pastures a part of the studies. Unlike Scaramelli's analysis of the failed "attempts at 'creating participation'" in this volume, my analysis highlights the participation of cheesemakers' concerns and pastures themselves in the making of dairy technosciences. Hence, this chapter contributes to the conceptualization of "material politics" as dairy crafts and the technosciences of artisanal Kars cheesemaking enact a politics of pasture through the materiality of milk and cheese.

Dairy Technosciences and Cheesemaking

Scientific studies on the concrete forms that milk takes throughout the process of its transubstantiation have long been shaping dairy production and practices of cheesemaking. Together with the industrialization of milk and dairy production in the late nineteenth century (DuPuis 2002; Smith-Howard 2014), technosciences have been introduced in various aspects of the cheesemaking craft, especially in Europe and North America (P. Atkins 2010, 2007; P. J. Atkins 2000). Food scientists and cheesemakers, as different kinds of experts, have collaborated and disagreed on various techniques and technologies of dairy production processes. Pasteurization might be considered the most famous technoscientific controversy that has been enforced and formalized by many nation-state regulations,[8] as well as supported and challenged by many cheesemakers and scientists. In other words, pasteurization is a field of expertise that can be endorsed or challenged by scientists and adopted or rejected by cheesemakers. It is a prime example of abstract scientific knowledge that is blackboxed (Sage 2007, 208; Nestle 2010) in such a way that pasteurization as technoscience hides all the disagreements and uncertainties inherent to the material processes of curdling milk and knowledge production. A few particular heating and cooling processes, defined as "pasteurization" in dairy sciences and legal documents, have become a mandatory practice in most dairy production sites around the world. The use of "unpasteurized" or "raw" milk in dairy production, as the common practice in traditional and most artisanal cheesemaking, became subject to additional food safety criteria and more scientific research.

According to the National Milk Council (*Ulusal Süt Konseyi*) of Turkey, only between 40 and 45 percent of the total raw-milk production ends up in formal dairy processing, and 57 percent of this portion is processed by the *mandıra*s (small dairies) (Kırdar and Karaca 2017). These *mandıra*s are mostly seasonal production sites in rural areas of the country. They operate when the milk supply increases significantly in spring and summer months, since a significant portion of dairy farming in Turkey relies on extensive grazing on pastures (*mera hayvancılığı*). Most of them are located in highland pastures or villages nearby the pastures that are used by herds of dairy animals during the pasture season. The usual setting involves collecting milk produced by dairy farmers in one or a few villages around the *mandıra*. Most *mandıra*s process less than 10 tons of milk per day. Their overwhelming presence is considered a sign of "backwardness" for the dairy industry in official reports and other publications in which dairy scientists have highlighted the lack of proper sanitary conditions, advanced technologies, and standardized dairy production in the *mandıra*s for many years (Üresin 1936; Çağlar 1947; Aygün 1951; Milli Prodüktivite Merkezi Tarım Şubesi 1969; Tekinşen and Tekinşen 2005; Öztek 1983; Kurt 1968; Aras 1954; Hayaloğlu and Özer 2011).

Similar to the rest of the country, dairy production in Kars is also dominated by the *mandıra*s. More than half of the registered production sites are located in villages and operate seasonally. Kars province, with more than 380 villages, is located on the northeastern border of Turkey, neighboring Georgia and Armenia. It encompasses high-altitude plateaus with rich flora in the transition zone between Anatolia and the South Caucasus. In addition to the closed land border between Armenia and Turkey for dozens of years, Kars is located at the northern frontier of the Kurdish region in Turkey where an armed conflict between the Turkish Army and the Kurdish Workers' Party (PKK) has been ongoing since 1984. Together with these conditions causing depopulation in this borderland, and in line with the neoliberalization of agriculture (Keyder and Yenal 2011, 2013; Aydın 2010) and the industrialization of dairy production in Turkey,[9] rural dairy production has declined sharply in Kars in the last twenty-five years. Pastures have always been fundamental for dairy farming in Kars where farmers and their herds reside in these high-altitude grasslands (between 1,700 and 2,600 meters) that are covered with snow during the harsh winter conditions for seven months each year. From April until October, animals are fed in the open-air pastures according to different regimes of management in different villages.

Despite the high percentage of dairy production in the *mandıra*s, legal regulations of food safety concerning dairy products do not make a distinction between them and factories in Turkey. When I met İlhan in 2009, he was already an active supporter of traditional cheese production and commerce across various regional, national, and international networks. His struggle against the imposition of industrial standards, he told me, emerged as a necessity especially after 2004 when the Turkish state, as part of its EU candidacy process, legalized the new food safety requirements that officially banned dairy production in small rural dairies that did not satisfy Hazard Analysis and Critical Control Point (HACCP) requirements. In the last twenty years, most dairies in rural Turkey were either shut down or confined to the informal markets in provincial marketplaces or small dairy shops due to the inspections, fines, and high cost of the required renovation processes. The state inspectors, most of whom are graduates of food engineering and veterinary faculties, referred to conventional dairy science studies, which informed the food safety regulations.

In most conventional dairy science publications, traditional cheeses are considered risky, if not dangerous, for human health when produced in rural *mandıra*s devoid of necessary hygienic conditions like easily cleanable surfaces, stainless steel equipment, and technosciences like pasteurization machines or milk analyzers. The bulk of the conventional dairy science research on traditional cheeses in Turkey consists of laying down the physical, chemical, and microbiological properties of a particular type of cheese based on analyses of the samples randomly collected from the local markets by the researchers. They evaluate the risk to human health posed by the pathogens identified in the studied samples. The proposed solutions are usually concerned with the amelioration of the conditions of dairy production in small *mandıra*s in order to ensure their conformity to international industrial standards such as HACCP and with the standardization of the products. This can achieved by the use of pasteurization and homogenization of the milk and use of starter cultures. When İlhan complained to me about the "implanted reason" of the scientists, he specifically targeted these conventional studies he has encountered throughout these years.

Production permits issued by the state and different certification mechanisms consist of an organization of paperwork and an appropriate food production process. Inspectors of any such audit mechanisms work with particular checklists that are assumed to rely on scientific realities about food safety, health, and nutrition. Scientific knowledge is blackboxed in these lists, like forms that pasteurization can take in the dairy craft procedures. When scientific expertise materialized in a technoscientific intervention is implanted in the dairy craft, it changes the resulting cheese and its variations while transforming labor processes and relations—both human and nonhuman. İlhan's search for collaboration with scientists, as well as inspectors, technicians, and engineers, entails accommodating local dairy craft practices within dairy science research not simply as a place of origin or a craft to be modernized but more as a necessary site of place-based practices that feed scientific abstractions while producing cheeses. Let me go back to the opening anecdote of this chapter to unpack his conceptualization of *implanted* and *carved* reason (*oyma ve koyma akıl*) and to elaborate on a diplomatic proposal for the collaborative research practice.

Carved Reason: A Diplomatic Proposal

When Şehnaz explained to İlhan that using a starter culture would save him from worrying about the effects of the daily circumstances on the taste of each batch of production or food safety measures that favor pasteurization, İlhan's unwillingness to be part of a scientific study on developing a starter culture of Kars *kaşar* cheese became clearer. He said:

> I always say that there are two types of scientists; the first type practice "implanted reasoning" (*koyma akıl*) and the second "carved reasoning" (*oyma akıl*).

The first type of scientist, according to him, thinks that whatever they learn at school is the ultimate truth that can be applied universally. İlhan emphasized that the implanted reasoning relies on the knowledge that serves industrial technologies and large-scale dairy factories, and it labels small farmers as culturally backward, economically inefficient, procedurally unhygienic, and industrially incompetent for standardizing their production. This reasoning can only offer solutions that neglect the actual needs of small farmers, their families, their animals, pastures, and immediate surroundings. Hence, the results of knowledge production on the basis of this kind of reasoning usually exterminate the traditional techniques developed in particular places under specific natural and cultural circumstances. He concluded:

> Your "starter culture" can do the same to me, my people, my animals, my pastures . . . because it is not what we really need to make life better here! We rather need to improve our understanding of how we produce this particular cheese that we already produce. I need you to tell me what else I can do to take care of pastures, cows, milk or cheese so that the microbes you will see under your microscope will thrive in the way the cheese asks from them. And this is a job only the second type of scientist can do.

The second type of scientific reasoning, "*carved reasoning*," according to İlhan, makes use of the available scientific knowledge produced and circulated in academia, but also takes extra-scientific know-how, such as tradition or artisanship, seriously so that the actual problems of the practitioners could be addressed. Carved reasoning then implies an attunement to the specific circumstances the respective scientist might encounter; an attunement that not only allows the reconsideration of the scientific knowledge that is supposed to be universally applicable, but also requires a practice-oriented knowledge production process. Such attunement can only emerge from the very process of thinking and doing with the local practitioners. For him, this approach implies that a local issue could be solved with the participation of local actors whose extra-scientific knowledge should be taken seriously. It also points to a place-based characteristic of a particular reasoning process that should take into account seemingly unrelated concerns, such as the aim of sustaining livelihoods under the same daily conditions that characterize milk and cheese. In other words, carved reasoning cannot be detached from the local conditions, actors, practices—it must be *placed*.

İlhan's claim for a distinctive contrast between *implanted* and *carved* reasoning sheds light on different ways in which scientists engage with the local knowledge of pasture-cheesemaking. On the one hand, cheesemakers like İlhan expect scientists to respect and be open to learning from the traditional methods of the cheesemaking craft in pastures. This approach requires, first and foremost, not imposing their scientific knowledge as the only bearer of the right way of milk processing, which usually contradicts and often threatens the characteristics of small-scale pasture-cheesemaking, and the whole world it emerges from. Instead, it entails articulating artisanal/local and scientific knowledge to carve out a solution to the existing problems of the practitioners, that is, cheesemakers who strive to sustain certain quality standards and a unique taste that distinguish their pasture-cheeses from industrialized ones while satisfying food safety requirements. I consider İlhan's concept of "carved reason" as a diplomatic proposal in the search for collaborative research practices.

In her manifesto for slow science, Isabelle Stengers challenges "the sharp opposition between questions defined as scientific and those that should be left to politics, or rather to ethics" (2018, 150). For scientists to reconsider the boundaries of their scientific research questions and expertise, Stengers's call to slow down science suggests the figure of a diplomat. Stengers stresses that the expert does not preempt what kind of destruction it can bring to the nonexpert. In contrast, the diplomat is aware of the obligation of thinking with the other ways of knowing that can be undone due to expert knowledge.

> [The scientists] should cultivate an active, concrete awareness of the very special and demanding character of their knowledge, and the way its reliability depends on the distribution between what they define as mattering and what can be ignored. Acquiring and maintaining such a concrete awareness, as a condition for the capacity to enter into new relations, takes time, and this may be the true challenge here. For scientists educated in modern research institutions, whatever requires slowing down mobilisation amounts to a distraction, a diversion from the scientists' one true mission of advancing knowledge. We thus need the same kind of deep change that slow food movements propose. (Stengers 2018, 150)

Stengers's figure of the diplomat considers the possible destructions that expert knowledge may bring. Her concept of diplomacy in slowing down science involves specific and dangerous ways of "weaving relations" (2018, 156). This process is neither innocent nor a harmonious one, yet it "transforms each protagonist's relations with his or her own knowledge, hopes, fears, and memories, and allows the whole to generate what each one would have been unable to produce separately" (Stengers 2005, 1001). This conceptualization has inspired me to think about the encounters between dairy scientists and artisanal cheesemakers in Kars. The latter's primary concern is that conventional dairy science research neglects the expertise of rural cheesemakers and contributes to the destruction of the pastures as a necessary site of dairy farming and cheesemaking. Borrowing the concept of diplomacy from Stengers, I conceptualize İlhan's concern as a diplomatic proposal that can enable dairy scientists in Kars to consider the destruction of pasture-cheesemaking and the everyday livelihoods of agro-pastoralism in rural Kars while designing and implementing their scientific research. The resulting collaborative practices of knowledge production, or thinking–making–doing processes, culminate and materialize in the pasture-cheeses. As the two cases below demonstrate, pasture-cheese diplomacy involves a material politics of pastures in making cheese and dairy science research.

Scientific Expertise to be Implanted

Trained as a veterinarian, Canan is an associate professor in the Department of Food Hygiene and Technology, Caucasus University, Kars. In Fall 2017 and Spring 2018, she allowed me to attend her classes on dairy processing and technologies, and food safety and hygiene requirements in dairy production. In her lectures and during our conversations outside the classroom, she never hesitated to state that a factory setting is always much better than small dairies in terms of hygiene, health, and efficiency. Yet when I asked her questions about the microbial world of raw milk and the microbial diversity of traditional dairy products, she did not hide her ambivalent feelings. While she acknowledged as an eater that a well-made pasture-cheese usually tastes better than the industrially produced ones, she insisted that she would not consciously choose to eat pasture-cheese as a food scientist. Even if her own work in the laboratory demonstrated that the pasture-cheeses are much richer in microbial composition and beneficial to humans, she argued that one cannot trust them since they always risk containing pathogens.

As part of unpublished research she conducted with her PhD thesis adviser on traditional dairy products, Canan isolated more than nine thousand colonies of microorganisms from the samples collected in Kars pastures. She stated her amazement at the microbial diversity she encountered in these traditional products. Yet she was very much disappointed by the manufacturing conditions of these products and their sensory effects; she finds them "too salty, stinky and ugly looking." Canan's laboratory analyses identified many strains of bacteria known to be pathogenic (such as *Escherichia coli* and *Brucella*) in these samples, which she associated with the "primitive" (*iptidai*) production conditions. Since her main research interest was probiotics in dairy products, more specifically the bacteriocin capability of lactic acid bacteria, she was interested in isolating the strains that are known to be beneficial to human health. "The ultimate aim would be," she explained, "to make these microbial cultures available for factories that process milk according to the modern hygiene standards and that can make use of these cultures to produce probiotic dairy products."

Canan's firm belief in the necessity of replacing small rural dairies with large-scale dairy factories does not leave any room for her collaboration with pasture-cheesemakers besides collecting samples for her research. As she also confirmed, her research does not result in any collaboration with rural cheesemakers unless they are willing to adopt industrial technologies and modern food safety standards. Hence, her approach is in line with what İlhan calls "implanted reason." While her research focuses on pasture-cheeses as the source of microbial diversity, her way of abstracting the knowledge of this diversity in her experiments does not go back to the pastures. Rather, her expertise "edits out space by abstracting it" (Raffaetà 2021, 331); it is destined for the development of new biotechnology products that can be sold to dairy factories. Scholars have already shown cases in which the local knowledge of small farmers is appropriated by companies that industrialized small-scale artisanal production of local food (Fonte 2008, 214). Canan's research points to a similar risk of expropriation of the cheesemakers' local knowledge by scientists and companies. Her expertise does not take into account the implications of her practices of knowledge production, which contributes to the destruction of the existing everyday worlds of cheesemaking in pastures. Such biotechnological innovations risk substituting rural dairies, artisanal cheesemaking, and small-scale cheesemakers with urban factories, industrial dairy production, and workers in large-scale production sites—a process I called "pasteurizing dairy infrastructures" (Tatari 2022). Similar to the experts whose aim of centralizing water distribution in Istanbul in the 1930s associated the elimination of fountains in the streets with "civilization" (Uzmay, this volume), Canan's Pasteurian concerns on food hygiene associated pasture-cheesemaking with the material sign of the "primitive" dairy infrastructures. Prioritizing the Pasteurian principles of food safety in urban industrial dairy factories has also become a project of scale-making, similar to Alkan's argument in the first chapter of this volume: namely, the prioritization of electricity over irrigation in the Southeast Anatolia Project mirrored "the prioritization of national economic growth over the welfare of people living in the project's region" (Alkan, this volume). Pasteurizing dairy infrastructures similarly prioritized a modernist understanding of food safety and national well-being over the everyday lives in pastures where milk and dairy crafts originate.

When Pastures Matter in Dairy Science Research

Canan's approach to scientific knowledge and expertise is in sharp contrast with another process of dairy science research designed by a well-known food engineer, Nuray Güzeler, and her student Firuza Koboyeva. I met Prof. Güzeler for the first time in Kars when she attended the "International Symposium of Artisanal Cheeses in Turkey and in the World: Kars Kaşar Geographical Indication" in 2016. She explained to me that she was very excited to meet İlhan at a conference back in 2014, especially because, as a small cheesemaker, he was interested in scientific knowledge not to scale up his production—which is rare, she said. Her remark revealed that it is not only the artisanal cheesemakers who are looking for like-minded scientists to collaborate with, but also careful dairy scientists are looking for "artisanal" cheesemakers to produce knowledge together. This reciprocal concern is crucial for a collaboration that can lead to *carved reasoning*.

When Güzeler expressed her interest in designing research on Kars *kaşar* cheese during a conversation with cheesemakers in 2016, she consulted artisanal cheesemakers and listened to their concerns that could inform her work—concerns that are usually not addressed in the scientific literature, she stressed, because the latter is more concerned with solutions for large-scale production in the course of industrialization. As Scaramelli puts beautifully in the next chapter of this volume, "expertise is, amongst other things, a relational social performance" (Scaramelli, this volume). Unlike her account of the complex relationship between experts (scientists, foresters, or NGO workers) and local residents of the delta which entailed a particular hierarchy of expertise, the collaboration I analyze in the remaining part of this chapter focuses on the diplomacy between specific claims to scientific and artisanal expertise of cheesemaking, which generates a new way of relating to the materiality of pasture-cheeses.

The narratives of the cheesemakers who distinguished pasture-cheeses from the industrially produced ones highlighted the use of pasture-milk and artisanal techniques in rural dairies. Accordingly, Güzeler and her student Koboyeva designed research that would reveal physical, chemical, microbiological, and sensory characteristics of cheeses that are produced at different altitudes in different seasons. Since pasture-milk is produced between May and August in Kars, the research was designed as a comparative study on the cheeses made in April and July—"spring cheeses" versus "summer cheeses." Moreover, cheesemakers explained that the production in a few larger dairies located in the Organized Industrial Zone (OIZ), situated near the city center in Kars, may breach traditional methods used in smaller rural dairies. Güzeler and Koboyeva translated this into a comparison of the altitude: while the higher altitude samples of "mountain cheeses" were collected from small dairies in pastures, the lower altitude samples of "plain cheeses" were collected from relatively larger dairies in the OIZ. These translations and the resulting research design were carved out of a collaborative process that addressed the concerns of both the artisanal cheesemakers and scientists while also challenging conventional dairy science research that would not problematize the distinctiveness of pasture-cheeses among all Kars *kaşar* cheeses.

The researchers wanted to collect samples from three different batches of cheese produced in consecutive weeks per dairy and season. Twenty-four samples from four dairies, two in Boğatepe village and two in the OIZ, were shipped from Kars to Adana. The chemical, physical, and microbiological analyses revealed that all the cheeses produced in July had distinctive properties, which can be explained by the use of pasture-milk after May. For instance, chemical analyses suggested that the dry matter and fat in both mountain and plain cheeses are significantly higher in July than in April (Koboyeva 2018, 47, 51). Another significant aspect is that both mountain and plain cheeses were found to be less bright in texture and more yellowish in July than in April (ibid., 84, 95). Pasture-milk affected the chemical composition of the milk in all the production sites; it transferred a yellowish color from pasture flowers and grass, and the cheeses became more opaque with the lower humidity level during the summer months.

The research also identified some crucial differences between mountain and plain cheeses. For instance, pH levels that were close to each other among April samples diverged significantly among the July ones: plain cheeses had a much higher pH level in July (ibid., 44). This could be explained by the fact that the milk travels a much longer distance to reach the OIZ. Due to the higher temperature in July, this causes a significant increase in the pH levels of milk and young cheeses. The greenness of the cheese rind decreases from April to July among the mountain cheeses, while the opposite is observed among the plain cheeses (ibid., 90). This was due to the climate conditions in the higher altitude rural dairies that are nearby the pastures, where the cheese dries and reaches the desired opaque color much more quickly.

The microbiological analyses also identified some important differences. Both the "total aerobic mesophilic bacteria count" and the "total lactic acid bacteria count" turned out to be higher in April and lower in July for the mountain cheeses, whereas lower in April and higher in July for plain cheeses (ibid., 100–105). In other words, the mountain cheese microbial count decreased when pasture-milk was used, while it was the opposite for the plain cheeses. Higher counts in July can be explained due to the increased temperature during the transfer of the milk to the dairy for the plain cheeses. In contrast, mountain cheeses' higher counts in April can be considered parallel to the pasture-cheesemakers' arguments about the distinctiveness of their cheeses made between May and September. In the month of April, the animals barely start to be on the pastures, and the grass they eat is very humid after months of winter and snow. This, according to the farmers and cheesemakers, affects the cows' digestion, and often gives them diarrhea, causing a particular animal scent and taste in the milk, and making the *kaşar* cheese taste more bitter than it should be.

Not only the results but also their explanations based on the characteristics of pasture-cheesemaking contributed to the artisanal cheesemakers' struggle in unraveling the distinctiveness of their *kaşar* cheeses. It also enabled the dairy scientists to offer a new approach to traditional cheeses beyond focusing on pathogens in them or possible biotechnology products that can be developed from them. This research, according to Nuray and Firuza, offers clues for future research on the divergences between altitudes and seasons in *kaşar* cheese, especially on the transformation of the microbiological ecologies in pasture-cheeses, which begs for more detailed research over a longer time interval. Collaborative research practices suggest new ways of studying the place-based distinctiveness of Kars cheeses and their microbial worlds, while providing technoscientific interventions to the practitioners of cheesemaking. Pasture-cheese diplomacy then emerges from the processes of collaboration between scientists and cheesemakers who cultivate a concrete awareness of each other's concerns and let this awareness shape the scientific studies and artisanal know-how of Kars *kaşar* cheese. Hence, pastures matter for dairy sciences and crafts as places of dairying.

Localizing Microbial Communities Diplomatically

Each dairy product materializes particular processes of scientific research and cheesemaking craft. Anthropologist Heather Paxson conceptualizes the sensibility that makes possible the collaboration between scientists and artisanal cheesemakers: "working in selective partnership with microscopic organisms, figured as agents of a nature that is not fully objectified and never fully separate from human enterprise" (2013, 161). She calls this a post-Pasteurian alternative to the Pasteurian microbiopolitics that informs the food safety regulations, which casts (raw) milk as a potentially harmful substance humans have to control. Beyond dairy science, this shift can be seen as part of a larger "microbial turn" in biology (Paxson and Helmreich 2014, 166). Scholars have argued that the representations of microbes have shifted from being sources of peril to promise, and scientific engagements with them started to consider them as "communities that matter in diverse ecosystems" instead of individual strains (Paxson and Helmreich 2014, 168). Similar shifts can be found in fields including epigenetics where new concerns such as antibiotic resistance are explained through recent theories of horizontal gene transfer instead of older theories of gene mutation (Landecker 2016, 20). The epistemology that allowed scientists to know microbes and to engineer antibiotics has also been constitutive of the emergence of what is today known as antimicrobial resistance. Building on these recent scientific theories and the crucial insight of science studies, namely that the epistemic cultures through which materialities are known closely interact with those materialities, anthropologists revisited the older constructivist arguments in their fields, like that of "local biologies" (Lock 2006). Relying on an ethnography of the physiological conditions and social experiences of menopause in a comparative study in the United States and Japan, Lock's argument had challenged the treatment of the human body as a universal object in biological sciences and biomedicine. Her innovative conceptualization brought a materialist perspective to the situatedness of the human body and its biological making. Through analyzing the entanglements which make both the biology cultural and the culture biological in the material construction of human bodies, her study contributed to an anthropological scholarship that has long challenged the nature/culture divide. Niewöhner and Lock argued that "situating biologies" would allow ethnographic practice to grasp "environment/human entanglement" as "a ceaseless process of relating . . . through which environment and human become defined as such" (Niewöhner and Lock 2018, 691). When it comes to microbial life in cheese, the complicated processes of co-construction between microorganisms and their environments need to be thought together with the practices that not only enable practitioners to know these processes but also to make sense of the "local" cheese within its environments, that is, in relation to where it is produced geographically.

Studying microbial diversity in cheeses while attempting to link particular microorganisms in some cheeses to particular geographical places has been a matter of vital controversy among scientists and advocacy groups. On the one hand, microbiologists refute the idea that microorganisms belong to a certain place. Rather than a connection that takes the place as the source, their approach highlights a connection that focuses on the conditions that make particular bacteria manifest in particular places. In other words, geographical place becomes almost irrelevant since the same bacteria can be encountered once there is an appropriate environment for its proliferation. While this undermines any inherent connection between place and bacteria, hence complicating the collaboration between artisanal cheesemakers and dairy scientists in defining the autochthonous microbial ecology of a particular local cheese, it simultaneously enables an unlimited potential for (re)invention, as Paxson observes in processes of "reverse-engineering" terroir in the United States (Paxson

2010). While Paxson emphasizes that for the US artisanal cheesemakers "culture can be retooled to generate new places" (Paxson 2010, 445), Raffaeta investigates "how fermentation participates in the composition of different human, more-than-human, and microbial spacetimes" (Raffaetà 2021, 323) in the Italian Alps. Building on these ethnographic accounts on cheesemaking as enacting a relationship between microbial starter cultures and place, this chapter problematizes collaborations of dairy scientists and cheesemakers in deciphering the *terroir*, or the taste of place (Trubek 2008), in Kars pastures.

Dairy science studies on cheesemaking increasingly de-emphasize the isolation of particular bacteria to understand their effects and focus on analyzing the formation and transformation of microbial communities throughout particular practices of cheesemaking (Donnelly 2014, 2019; Percival and Percival 2017). Marie-Christine Montel, who is a microbiologist at the INRA Research Centre in Clermont-Ferrand, France, works closely with dairy farmers in order to ensure the safety of their products without losing the diversity of the microbial communities in the milk they process. She argues that microbiological research should take into account the whole chain of cheesemaking in order to look for potential microbial transfers. Not because some "pathogens" can simply transfer from one environment to the other, but more importantly, transfers can enable the researcher to identify microbial communities that can be formed (and transformed) throughout the whole process. Challenging the Pasteurian understandings, microbial biodiversity is not a list of species but a structured community, she states. The management of biodiversity becomes crucial by collaborating with and promoting the microbial populations of interest. And this goal is mainly accomplished via artisanal techniques of the practitioners, sometimes with the help of biotechnologies and various other diary technosciences.[10]

When Montel and her collaborators analyze "natural complex consortia" of bacteria in raw milk for "anti-listeria properties," they suggest that protecting the microbial diversity that comes with raw milk can enable the inhibition of the growth of *Listeria monocytogenes* in the cheese (Montel et al. 2014). Rather than identifying the presence of individual strains, the researchers are interested in studying the dynamics of microbial communities that would inhibit or let the strains grow. As Montel also clarifies, this kind of regulation would necessarily require much closer professional contact between cheesemakers and scientists since the milk that is not pasteurized before production can host a wide range of bacteria that might have been transferred from pastures, udders, bedding, milking equipment, or human contact. Working closely with cheesemakers and listening to their concerns about food safety regulations, Montel designed a research agenda that rests on a particular diplomacy between scientific knowledge production and artisanal cheesemaking. In other words, the reasoning embedded in this study enables artisanal cheesemakers to claim the authenticity of microbial community formation in their local cheeses while simultaneously challenging conventional food safety criteria by scientific evaluations of pathogens in cheese. In the remaining part of this chapter, I will focus on the ways in which scientific studies on Kars cheeses might similarly bring together the distinctiveness of pasture-milk, food safety concerns, and scientific knowledge.

Placing Bacteria in Kars

Studying the microbial ecologies that make Kars *kaşar* cheese distinctive was an important part of the process of acquiring a Geographical Indicator in 2015.[11] Mitat Şahin is a veterinarian specialized in microbiology who led the scientific research in this process. When I met him in July 2013, he was coordinating the initial phase of this research. He was excited about a potential database for the place-based denominations of cheeses: "We should identify the microorganisms that make our cheeses distinctive. Our aim should be to create a comprehensive database of the Turkish microorganisms of all of our local cheeses in this country." Although it is very hard for me to think of nationalism at the microbial scale, Şahin was not alone in casting microbiological dairy science research in nationalist terms. Artun Ünsal, a political scientist who also wrote extensively on the traditional dairy varieties in Turkey, criticizes the naming of one microorganism, which is almost universally used in making industrial yogurt, namely *Lactobacillus bulgaricus*. He states that it is a shame for the Turks whose yogurt production dates much earlier were not able to name this microorganism with their ethnicity (Ünsal 2011, 28, 1997, 30). Fungi like *Penicillium camemberti* or *Penicillium roqueforti* are named after the places in France that have been associated with their local cheeses—Camembert and Roquefort. But these examples of naming practices are limited in the history of microbiology, and all these microorganisms, far from being indigenous to certain places, are found in many other dairy products in different parts of the world.

A small ratio of such microorganisms identified with particular dairy products are commercially produced by agrobiotechnology companies as "starter cultures" in order to be used in the production of these dairy products. Studies on agricultural history show that the use of starter cultures was a crucial step in standardizing commercial yogurt production and making it suitable for industrial production (Stoilova 2013). Similarly, the use of starter cultures also enables industrial cheese production. Yet this is a widespread practice not only in industrial dairy but also in artisanal cheesemaking, especially in Europe and in the United States where pasteurization is not mandated and usually not implemented, and the microbial flora of "raw" milk is preserved. This implies that the cheesemakers don't have complete control over the microbial communities that will emerge in the process of cheesemaking; hence the resulting microbial life in the cheese then depends on the raw milk, the added starter cultures, and the conditions in which these microorganisms proliferate. The artisanal use of the strains of starter cultures is a topic beyond this chapter, but it's worth re-emphasizing that the artisanal cheesemakers may use these cultures either to minimize the range of different characteristics of their cheeses that they label with the same name or to experiment with their craft. However, in Kars none of the pasture-cheesemakers buy starter cultures to make standard cheeses. Some have their own methods that can attract some post-Pasteurian scientific interest in the future.[12]

During our conversation in 2015, after he completed his project and the Turkish Patent Institute approved the GI of Kars *kaşar* cheese, Şahin stressed that his research findings did not provide any concrete identification marks regarding the distinctive microorganisms in the cheese. The fact that "place" cannot be articulated with microbiological analyses disappointed him. Yet, he added, the distinctive microbial characteristics of *kaşar* cheese are produced thanks to the craft of the right environment by the cows on pastures, dairy farmers who milk them, and experienced artisanal cheesemakers; an environment that can cultivate the microbial communities that are desired for *kaşar* cheese, and that is simultaneously cultivated by these communities.

Şahin's experience of not being able to identify a strain of bacteria that could be considered autochthonous suggests that bacteria are placeless in an abstract microbiological sense. Yet, they are placed in the very practices of cheesemaking craft even if the microbiological research would not be able to declare them as autochthonous. Then the question for a pasture-cheese diplomacy becomes: How to keep these two seemingly opposed suggestions together—namely, microbes as local when they are placed as cheese through particular craft processes, and microbes as

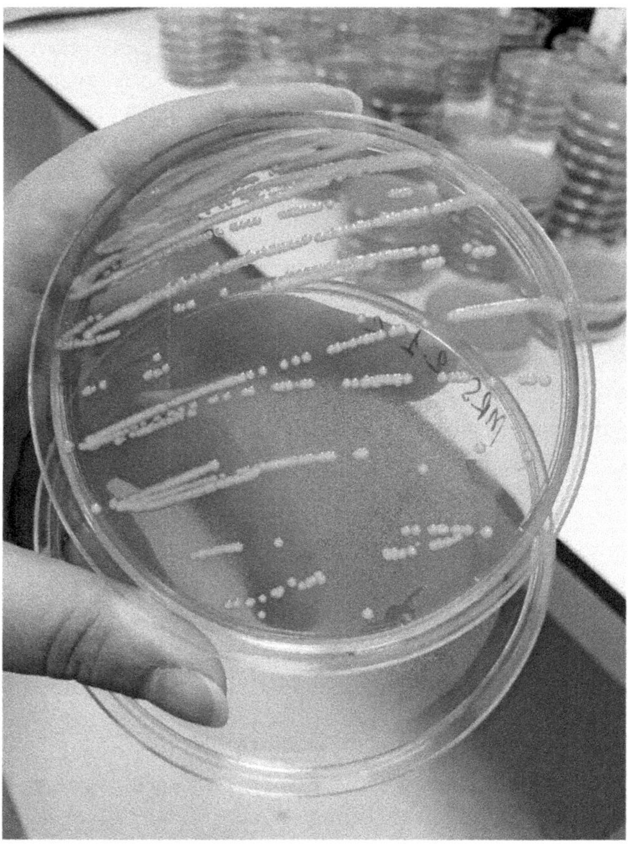

Figure 6.1 Şehnaz holding a petri dish which hosts particular thermophilic lactic acid bacteria strains that proliferated after she isolated them from the whey samples collected in Kars. Photo by the author, August 2018.

abstractly placeless when they are reproduced in the laboratory? Let me return for the final time to the opening anecdote of this chapter.

Inventing Starter Cultures for Cheesemaking

As I am writing this book chapter, Şehnaz's dissertation research project is still in progress. She collected whey samples after the (raw) milk was coagulated in the dairies. Her research practices aimed to develop a starter culture for Kars Kaşar cheese out of the thermophilic lactic acid bacteria she identified in these samples. She explained to me that after isolating different strains from the samples, she would select the ones that are most suitable to be reproduced as starter cultures. Once she decided on the possible selections, her starter cultures were expected to carry the distinctive taste of the Kars *kaşar* cheese to the cheese that is made from pasteurized milk. According to Şehnaz, this would contribute to a "definitely" healthy dairy product thanks to the pasteurization, and to a generic, standardized "local" kaşar cheese thanks to the locally sourced starter cultures.

İlhan objected to this affirmative contribution claim by arguing that such research may serve industrial producers more than artisanal cheesemakers. He stated that the need to use starter cultures in pasteurized milk to achieve standardization is an implanted truth claim by conventional dairy science and industrial factories. Yet he agreed to provide samples to Şehnaz for a few reasons. First and foremost, İlhan believed that a starter culture could not substitute the microbial composition of Kars *kaşar* cheese made from (raw, unpasteurized) milk. Second, he said that young scientists like Şehnaz, who are genuinely interested in understanding the microbiological composition of traditional cheeses, are crucial collaborators for artisanal cheesemakers. He firmly believed that both sides can inform each other with insights that the other one lacks. Last but not least, he also believed that this collaboration could potentially affect Şehnaz's approach since she might realize some of the artisanal cheesemakers' concerns in the course of her research. More than three years after this encounter, İlhan turned out to be right; not only did Şehnaz's attempt to develop a starter culture almost fail, but also she modified her research agenda to include another variable, the altitude, which she thought was irrelevant to her study before her visit to the village.

Şehnaz visited the village when the association had the yearly cheese festival in 2018. That year, the festival was entitled "Anatolian Cheeses Meet in Kars" and around fifty small cheesemakers from different cities in Turkey convened in Boğatepe village with their cheeses. The tasting workshops brought together wheels of Kars *kaşar* cheese from around thirty-five different producers in Kars. The five-day festival enabled Şehnaz to meet many artisanal cheesemakers who have their small dairies in rural Kars and different parts of rural Turkey. At the end of the festival, when we spoke about her research, she told me that while her academic interests have always been influenced by the rich microflora of raw milk and dairy products, her main focus in research concerned the particularities of food safety and standardization in Kars dairy production settings. "None of the starter cultures I can make by the end of this research can reflect the diversity that exists in pasture-milk, which is constitutive of the cheeses," she said. She expressed that her scientific expertise (*uzmanlığım*) in revealing the particularities of the biological diversity in artisanal dairy products could be brought together with the expertise of the cheesemakers, their traditional techniques, and knowledge.

While the main focus of her research—commercial starter culture—did not change in the four years following her trip, she aspired to develop a second agenda within the same research that takes into account the differential origins of the samples she collected from Kars. For each sample, we registered the altitudes of the pastures from which the milk came. Her hypothesis was that, in the course of this study, the collected whey samples might reveal possible nuances in the dominant lactic acid flora within the milk produced at different altitudes in the province. This would enable her to provide a list of thermophilic lactic acid bacteria she encountered in different samples according to their altitude, even if these would not be possibly reproduced in a starter culture trial. In other words, the database she has been creating in parallel is a larger set that would not only include the strains that are not considered suitable for being reproduced as starter cultures, but would also reflect microbial cultures of pastures at various altitudes, which shape and are shaped by the cheese as an environment and in a particular place. İlhan and Şehnaz considered this component of Şehnaz's study as an important step in the collaborations between scientists and artisanal cheesemakers in Kars, which contribute to the differentiation of pasture-cheeses from large-scale industrial producers standardized with the help of commercial starter cultures. Pasture-cheese diplomacy in Kars paves the way for enacting practices of dairy crafts and of scientific research and technosciences in pastures and laboratories.

Conclusion

Collaborations between dairy sciences and artisanal cheesemaking have materialized in a wide variety of local dairy products in Turkey. Especially since 2018, there has been increasing public interest in traditional cheese production and consumption. Many festivals and nonscientific publications paved the way for new collaborations between food engineers, microbiologists, development officials, and dairy farmers, and new cheesemaking facilities have been founded in several locations across the country. All these recent developments suggest that, along with the reproduction of the usual hierarchies of expertise, new forms of collaborations are being made and further ones could be on the horizon; new diplomatic relations between different experts, and new possibilities for carving knowledge in dairy technosciences. The material worlds of cheesemaking have been actively shaping not only the expertise in dairy crafts and sciences but also the political processes through which practices of pasture-cheesemaking may challenge the industrialization of dairy production. Hence, this chapter examined the mutual constitution of science, material, and politics by focusing on the pasture-cheese diplomacy.

As the studies I discussed in this chapter have shown, expertise in dairy science posits new research agendas when it is open to the concerns of the artisanal cheesemakers and the everyday worlds of dairy farming in Kars pastures. Paying close attention to the ethical concerns embedded in the web of relations among pastures, animals, milk, curd, cheese, dairy farmers, and cheesemakers makes diplomacy possible through pasture-cheeses. Yet this diplomacy is not only slow, but it also does not offer any guarantees for supporting pasture-cheesemaking through scientific analyses. As almost all the cases described in this chapter indicate, scientists also face many challenges along the way of cultivating awareness about the possible implications their practices might bring on pasture-cheesemaking endeavors. In this academic context, one obvious fact is that conforming to the conventional dairy science research is always safer to get published and to maintain one's professional reputation and status. Whether the scientists in question can access and utilize the technological tools needed for conducting alternative microbiopolitical protocols proposed by progressive dairy scientists such as Montel is another challenge that needs to be kept in mind. Not having an equipped laboratory in Kars dedicated to artisanal cheesemaking or the lack of DNA sequencing machines in many provincial universities also compounds the strength of the persistence of Pasteurianism in dairy science research. Meanwhile, the boundaries between Pasteurianism and post-Pasteurianism or implanted and carved reasoning can get blurred at various instances as I described in this chapter. Yet, together with the nuances, unintended consequences, or intentions of various scientific research agendas, the collaborative practices in rural Kars—and the pasture-cheese diplomacy they enact—carve out a place for the co-construction of scientific and local ways of knowing and dairying. This diplomacy, rather than suggesting a recipe for preserving and sustaining artisanal cheesemaking, simply suggests a starting point for slowing down scientific knowledge production, while it simultaneously alludes to the potential of the cheesemaker–scientist collaboration in circumventing the ongoing transformations of dairying in pastures.

Notes

1 I used pseudonyms for all the informants who did not explicitly claim to be referred by their real names in my research.

2 *Kaşar* cheese is obtained by heating the curd up to 68–72°C, and the lactic acid bacteria that can survive at these temperatures are called *thermophilic*.

3 *Çiğ* means uncooked in Turkish. Milk that is not pasteurized is called raw.

4 See Bilger (2002) https://www.newyorker.com/magazine/2002/08/19/raw-faith, and the documentaries The Cheese Nun, PBS (2006), and Cooked (2016), episode 4: Earth. The biennial conference "Science of Artisan Cheese" can also be cited as a well-known prestigious example: https://scienceofartisancheese.com/. The Slow Food Movement in Bra, Turin, Italy, also holds an important international gathering called Cheese every two years since 2001.

5 See also the works by several anthropologists and social scientists like West (2020, 2021), (West and Domingos 2012), Bowen (2010), and Fonte (2008).

6 See Nizam and Tatari (2022) and Tatari (2022, 2020) for a larger discussion of how this material politics is implicated in the certification of Kars *kaşar* cheese with a Geographical Indication in Turkey.

7 This research is funded by the Wenner-Gren Anthropological Association and the American Research Institute in Turkey.
8 While some states such as France and Italy have defined exceptional dairy processes to the mandatory pasteurization, some others such as the United States and Turkey lift the requirement in case the raw-milk cheeses are aged for a certain period of time (sixty days in the former, ninety days in the latter). For more on the recent discussions on pasteurization and raw-milk cheeses, see Paxson (2008), Donnelly (2019), and Percival and Percival (2017).
9 In a nutshell, by neoliberalization, I refer to the systematic elimination of agricultural support policies like subsidies and minimum price policies after the end of the protectionist trade regime in Turkey starting in the 1980s. The privatization of state economic enterprises in agriculture and reinstitutionalization of sales cooperatives with free-market imperatives in this process have deeply affected the dairy industry as well. In addition to the privatization and dismantling of the supply chains and production facilities of the state-owned Dairy Industry Institution (*Süt Endüstrisi Kurumu*), intensive livestock production and industrial dairy factories have been prioritized by the legislation and state subsidies that neglected not only small farmers and cheesemakers but also local breeds and the everyday life of *mera hayvancılığı* (pasture animal husbandry). Also see Özkaya and Özden (2014), Zeybek (2016), and Tatari (2020).
10 In this paragraph, I relied on Montel's presentation at the conference The Science of Artisan Cheese in 2012.
11 For a more detailed investigation of the GI of Kars *kaşar* cheese, see Tatari (2020).
12 Akin to what Raffaetà (2021) calls "heterotopia" as the local and innovative ways of enacting space-times through artisanal starter cultures, I encountered many cheesemakers in rural Kars who prepare their own starter cultures in traditional ways they learned from older masters.

References

Aras, Ali. 1954. *Kars Süt Mamuleciliği İşletmelerinin Ekonomik Yapısı*, Ankara: Ankara Üniversitesi Ziraat Fakültesi Yayınları: 58 Recep Ulusoğlu Basımevi.

Atkins, Peter. 2007. "Laboratories, Laws, and the Career of a Commodity," *Environment and Planning D: Society and Space* 25 (6): 967–89.

Atkins, Peter. 2010. *Liquid Materialities. A History of Milk, Science, and the Law*, Surrey: Ashgate.

Atkins, Peter J. 2000. "The Pasteurization of England: The Science, Culture and Health Implications of Milk Processing, 1900-1950," in Jim Phillips and David F. Smith (eds.), *Food, Science, Policy and Regulation in The Twentieth Century: International and Comparative Perspectives*, 37–51, London: Routledge.

Aydın, Zülküf. 2010. "Neo-Liberal Transformation of Turkish Agriculture," *Journal of Agrarian Change* 10 (2): 149–87.

Aygün, Cevdet M. 1951. *Peynirciliğimiz ve Peynir Standardizasyonu*, Ankara: Güneş Matbaacılık.

Bowen, Sarah. 2010. "Embedding Local Places in Global Spaces: Geographical Indications as a Territorial Development Strategy," *Rural Sociology* 75: 209–43.

Çağlar, Fikret. 1947. *Pratik Peynircilik Önemli Peynirlerimizin Yapılışı*, İstanbul: Hüsnütabiat Basımevi.

Donnelly, Catherine W., ed. 2014. *Cheese and Microbes*, Washington, DC: ASM Press.
Donnelly, Catherine W. 2019. *Ending the War on Artisan Cheese: The inside Story of Government Overreach and the Struggle to Save Traditional Raw Milk Cheesemakers*, Vermont: Chelsea Green Publishing.
DuPuis, Melanie E. 2002. *Nature's Perfect Food. How Milk Became America's Drink*, New York and London: New York University Press.
Fonte, Maria. 2008. "Knowledge, Food and Place. A Way of Producing, a Way of Knowing," *Sociologia Ruralis* 48 (3): 200–22.
Grasseni, Cristina. 2011. "Re-Inventing Food: Alpine Cheese in the Age of Global Heritage," *Anthropology of Food* 8. http://aof.revues.org/6819
Grasseni, Cristina. 2016. *The Heritage Arena: Reinventing Cheese in the Italian Alps*. Food, Nutrition, and Culture, Vol. 8. New York: Berghahn Books.
Grasseni, Cristina, Heather Paxson, Jim Bingen, Amy J. Cohen, Susanne Freidberg, and Harry G. West. 2014. "Introducing a Special Issue on the Reinvention of Food: Connections and Mediations," *Gastronomica: The Journal of Food and Culture* 14 (4): 1–6.
Hayaloğlu, Ali and Barbaros Özer, eds. 2011. *Peynir Biliminin Temelleri*, İzmir: SİDAS.
Keyder, Çağlar and Zafer Yenal. 2011. "Agrarian Change under Globalization: Markets and Insecurity in Turkish Agriculture: Markets and Insecurity in Turkish Agriculture," *Journal of Agrarian Change* 11 (1): 60–86.
Keyder, Çağlar and Zafer Yenal. 2013. *Bildiğimiz Tarımın Sonu: Küresel Iktidar ve Köylülük*, İstanbul: İletişim.
Kindstedt, Paul. 2012. *Cheese and Culture: A History of Cheese and Its Place in Western Civilization*, Vermont: Chelsea Green Publishing.
Kırdar, Seval Sevgi and Oya Berkay Karaca. 2017. "An Overview of the Turkish Dairy Sector," *Indian Journal of Dairy Science* 70 (3): 251–7.
Koboyeva, Firuza. 2018. "Dağ ve Ova İşletmelerinde Farklı Mevsimlerde Üretilen Taze Kars Kaşarlarının Bazı Kalite Özellikleri," Thesis, Çukurova Üniversitesi, Adana.
Kurt, Ahmet. 1968. *Erzurum ve Kars İllerinin Genel Sütçülük Durumları Üzerinde Bir Araştırma*, Erzurum: Atatürk Üniversitesi Basımevi.
Landecker, Hannah. 2016. "Antibiotic Resistance and the Biology of History," *Body & Society* 22 (4): 19–52. https://doi.org/10.1177/1357034X14561341
Lock, Margaret. 2006. *Encounters with Aging: Mythologies of Menopause in Japan and North America*, Berkeley: Univ. of California Press.
Milli Prodüktivite Merkezi Tarım Şubesi. 1969. *Peynir İşletmeciliğinin Teknik ve Ekonomik Sorunları*, Ankara: Milli Prodüktivite Merkezi Yayınları: 32.
Montel, Marie-Christine, Solange Buchin, Adrien Mallet, Céline Delbes-Paus, Dominique A. Vuitton, Nathalie Desmasures, and Françoise Berthier. 2014. "Traditional Cheeses: Rich and Diverse Microbiota with Associated Benefits," *International Journal of Food Microbiology* 177 (May): 136–54.
Nestle, Marion. 2010. *Safe Food: The Politics of Food Safety*, Oakland: University of California Press.
Niewöhner, Jörg, and Margaret Lock. 2018. "Situating Local Biologies: Anthropological Perspectives on Environment/Human Entanglements." *BioSocieties* 13 (4): 681–97.
Nizam, Derya and M. Fatih Tatari. 2022. "Rural revitalization through territorial distinctiveness: The use of geographical indications in Turkey," *Journal of Rural Studies* 93: 144–54.
Özkaya, Tayfun and Fatih Özden, eds. 2014. *Başka Bir Hayvancılık Mümkün*, İstanbul: Yeni İnsan Yayınevi.

Öztek, Latif. 1983. *Kars İlinde Yapılan Kaşar Peynirlerinin Yapılışları, Bileşimleri ve Olgunlaşmaları Üzerinde Araştırmalarla Bunların Diğer Peynir Çeşitleri İle Kıyaslanmaları*, Erzurum: Atatürk Üniversitesi Basımevi.
Paxson, Heather. 2008. "Post-Pasteurian Cultures: The Microbiopolitics of Raw-Milk Cheese in the United States," *Cultural Anthropology* 23 (1): 15–47.
Paxson, Heather. 2010. "Locating Value in Artisan Cheese: Reverse Engineering Terroir for New-World Landscapes," *American Anthropologist* 112 (3): 444–57.
Paxson, Heather. 2013. *The Life of Cheese: Crafting Food and Value in America*, Berkeley and Los Angeles: University of California Press.
Paxson, Heather and Stefan Helmreich. 2014. "The Perils and Promises of Microbial Abundance: Novel Natures and Model Ecosystems, from Artisanal Cheese to Alien Seas," *Social Studies of Science* 44 (2): 165–93.
Percival, Bronwen and Francis Percival. 2017. *Reinventing the Wheel: Milk, Microbes, and the Fight for Real Cheese*, Oakland: University of California Press.
Raffaetà, Roberta. 2021. "Microbial Antagonism in the Trentino Alps: Negotiating Spacetimes and Ownership through the Production of Raw Milk Cheese in Alpine High Mountain Summer Pastures," *Current Anthropology* 62 (S24): S323–32.
Sage, Colin. 2007. "'Bending Science to Match Their Convictions': Hygienist Conceptions of Food Safety as a Challenge to Alternative Food Enterprises in Ireland," in Damian Maye, Lewis Holloway, and Moya Kneafsey (eds.), *Alternative Food Geographies: Representation and Practice*, 1st ed., 203–22, Bingley; North America: Emerald.
Smith-Howard, Kendra. 2014. *Pure and Modern Milk: An Environmental History since 1900*, Oxford: Oxford University Press.
Stengers, Isabelle. 2005. "The Cosmopolitical Proposal," in Bruno Latour and Peter Weibel (eds.), *Making Things Public*, 994–1003, Cambridge: MIT Press.
Stengers, Isabelle. 2018. *Another Science Is Possible: A Manifesto for Slow Science*, English ed., Cambridge; Medford, MA: Polity.
Stoilova, Elitsa. 2013. "From a Homemade to an Industrial Product: Manufacturing Bulgarian Yogurt," *Agricultural History* 87 (1): 73–92.
Tatari, M. Fatih. 2020. "Mera Peynirciliğinin Mikrobiyopolitikası: Süt Teknobilimleri ve Kars Kaşarı Coğrafi İşareti," *Toplum ve Bilim* 153: 126–52.
Tatari, M. Fatih. 2022. "Pasturing Dairy Infrastructures in Northeastern Turkey: Pasture-Cheesemaking, Dairy Technosciences and Kars Kaşar Cheese," *Environment and Planning D: Society and Space* 40 (6): 1046–63.
Tekinşen, O. Cenap and K. Kaan Tekinşen. 2005. *Süt ve Süt Ürünleri: Temel Bilgiler, Teknoloji, Kalite Kontrolü*, Konya: Selçuk Üniversitesi Basımevi.
Trubek, Amy B. 2008. *The Taste of Place: A Cultural Journey into Terroir*, Berkeley: University of California.
Ünsal, Artun. 1997. *Süt Uyuyunca: Türkiye Peynirleri [When Milk Sleeps: Cheeses of Turkey]*, Istanbul: Yapı Kredi Yayınları.
Ünsal, Artun. 2011. *"Silivrim Kaymak!": Türkiye'nin Yoğurtları*, Istanbul: Yapi Kredi Yayinlari.
Üresin, Ekrem Rüştü. 1936. *Kars Sütçülüğü Hakkında Tetkikler*, Ankara: Ankara Yüksek Ziraat Enstitüsü.
West, Harry G. 2020. "Crafting Innovation: Continuity and Change in the 'Living Traditions' of Contemporary Artisan Cheesemakers," *Food and Foodways* 28 (2): 91–116.

West, Harry G. 2021. "Terroir Products: A Movable Heritage Feast?" *Review of Agricultural, Food and Environmental Studies*, August. https://doi.org/10.1007/s41130-021-00150-2

West, Harry G. and Nuno Domingos. 2012. "Gourmandizing Poverty Food: The Serpa Cheese Slow Food Presidium: The Serpa Cheese Slow Food Presidium," *Journal of Agrarian Change* 12 (1): 120–43.

Zeybek, Sezai Ozan. 2016. "Biyopolitika, Güvenlik ve Anti-Piyasalar: Türkiye'de Endüstriyel Hayvancılığın Seyri." *Toplum ve Bilim* 138/139: 106–25.

7

The Social Life of Environmental Expertise

Leveraging Scientific Knowledge for Remaking Bio-cultural Communities in Turkish Wetlands

Caterina Scaramelli

Introduction: Layers of Materiality

Driving around the dirt roads in the Gediz Delta's wetland conservation area with the wetland management authority and Conservation Bureau staff in 2013–14, my companions would often point to wood and metal signs planted on the ground by the roadside. The signs marked the boundary of the Ramsar Wetland Conservation area. The Gediz River Delta is located north of the bustling metropolis of Izmir, on Turkey's Aegean Sea, and is one of Turkey's fourteen wetlands that are part of the Ramsar Convention, an international agreement ratified in 1971 in the Iranian coastal town of Ramsar (Ramsar Convention 1971). Starting in the 1960s, the Turkish government sent bureaucrats to represent the country at the convention's regular conferences and technical meetings. Turkey formally joined the international convention for wetland conservation in 1994 (Arı 2006; Scaramelli 2021). In 1998, the Gediz Delta, which was already protected as a natural conservation area, was added to Turkey's list of wetlands of "international importance" (Avdan 2020).

In the Gediz Delta's wetland conservation area, the Ramsar signs staked in the ground demarcated a material boundary, one otherwise invisible in the mud, marshes, reeds, and shrubbery of the delta's lowlands. Yet, the ecological boundary of the wetland itself—indexed by the presence of hydrophyte vegetation and by soil permanently or temporarily saturated in water (Mitsch and Gosselink 2011)—is dynamic and elusive. Given the seasonal fluctuations of surface and underground water, plants, and waterbirds (which are often used as proxies for the location, importance, and health of the wetland, as I will elaborate later in this chapter), exactly where the wetland begins and ends is contested by a multitude of publics. Wetland scientists, state bureaucrats, real estate speculators, environmental managers, environment activists, and farmers all have their own understandings of what wetlands are, where they begin, and where they end (Scaramelli 2021; Schiappa 1996). To make things even more complicated, the multiple and overlapping boundaries of the Gediz Delta's formal conservation and management statuses—at local, national, and international levels, with different implications for management, development, and resource extractions—are only visible on government-sanctioned topographic and GPS maps.

The elusive materiality of wetlands, in Turkey as elsewhere, is the outcome of complex and overlapping histories of people, plants, animals, water, climate, and microorganisms, and of the varied and changing interests of state bureaucrats and experts that have sought to govern wetlands as sites of agrarian production, waste, and nature (Arı 2001; Evered 2012, 2013; Özesmi 1999). Concerted imperial and state-led efforts with terraforming have created new environments where land and water were more clearly separated: for example, irrigation and drainage canals crisscrossing agricultural fields, industrial zones, and new settlements replacing coastal marshes and swamps (Gratien 2022; Gruppuso 2018; Richardson 2016). The refashioning of environments and architecture has been a key feature of Turkish modernism from the early Republican period (Bozdogan 2001). Large-scale integrated systems of electricity production and agricultural irrigation have been the backbones of developmentalist visions from the mid-twentieth century, and have intersected with political sovereignty concerns and attempts to manage "problem" populations: ethnic minorties, rural migrants, and resettled communities (Alkan, 2025). And infrastructural megaprojects—large-scale construction projects of roads, bridges, housing, power stations, airports, bridges, canals—have been especially materially and symbolically central under AKP rule, and their ecological and social impacts have catalyzed grassroots mobilization connecting questions of environment and livelihood (Erensü and Karaman 2016; Fırat 2016; Kurtiç 2020).

The material and discursive (Barad 1999) making, unmaking, and remaking of Turkish wetlands in the twentieth and twenty-first centuries has been an important site of both state and non-state expert management that produced *national* as well as *natural* resources. Anthropologists have recently argued that such resources are always the outcomes of social, political, and cultural processes. Resources are *made* through expert practices, material ecologies and infrastructures, and forms of knowledge (Ballestero 2019; Kurtiç 2020; Richardson and Weszkalnys 2014). As Turkish wetlands have been envisioned as resources in the twentieth century, they have also become sites of nation-state making, bureaucratic control, and political repression. At the same time, wetland degradation has generated grassroots mobilizations and organizing to advance claims for democracy, community, livelihoods, and justice alongside environmental concerns (Adaman, Hakyemez, and Özkaynak 2009; Arsel, Akbulut, and Adaman 2015; Erensü 2016; Erensü and Karaman 2016; Evered 2013; Kurtiç 2020; Evren 2014; Knudsen 2009; Özkan 2018; Zeybek 2016). Wetlands, in particular, have been at the center of contestations around seemingly competing imperatives of drainage and conservation (Arı and Bekir 2011; Evered 2012). As I have argued elsewhere (Scaramelli 2021), these visions of wetland conservation and development have often been interlinked (Wilson 2011). This chapter unpacks the ways in which claims and practices of scientific expertise are used by different groups of Turkish environmental advocates, bureaucrats, and scientists to advance varied sociopolitical claims and visions of livelihood in the wetlands.

The materiality of Turkish wetlands is shaped by overlapping and sedimented layers of *material politics.* Attending to the politics of materiality entails paying ethnographic attention toward decision-makers: for example, asking who holds the power to decide how much irrigation water would be purchased to replenish the drying marshes, or which species of animals and plants would be removed and which ones encouraged to flourish. It also requires being attuned to the effects of changing agricultural policies and markets on land, water, and labor in the wetlands, and attending to infrastructural processes, poetics, and logics. Finally, the wetland's material politics is entangled with international, national, and regional policies of wetland protection, management, and development. In my ethnographic fieldwork in the Gediz and the Kızılırmak deltas,[1] I analyzed the different ways in which these regulations get implemented locally by specific individuals and institutions, through complex power and class dynamics, and advancing multiple ethical visions and social relationships (Scaramelli 2021).

In his commentary on this section, Ståle Knudsen (2025) reminds us that agency may not just be restricted to human actants but also to other organisms and materials. In doing so, Knudsen remarks, scholars have sometimes underplayed human concerns with power and identity politics, and sometimes they have failed to account for the participation of nonhumans in the making of politics. This chapter centers on human identity politics to highlight the unexpected collaborations that flourish, and oftentimes fail, between people who hold different kinds of environmental knowledge, are differently institutionalized, and leverage their expertise to speak, with moral authority, to the material worlds of wetlands. This chapter builds on ethnographic interviews and participant observation to foreground three interconnected ways in which different actors who hold scientific expertise on the wetland—NGO workers, natural scientists, and bureaucrats—stake claims on the wetland's *materiality.* They do so while naturalizing the class, gender, and ethnic lines on which their scientific expertise is both constituted and contested.

The first kind of claim-making on wetland materiality, which I exemplify with an ethnographic vignette in the next section, is staked by drawing distinctions between legitimate and illegitimate human engagement with wetland ecologies. These distinctions reproduce class differentials and related power dynamics between college-educated bureaucrats and rural and working-class residents. The second way in which actors holding scientific expertise act upon and stake claims on wetland materiality is by producing documents that imagine wetlands as sites of cultural and ethical value connected to other wetland sites across national and international scales. To exemplify this case, I draw on my own work of helping to draft a funding proposal for participatory wetland conservation. The third example of invocations of wetland materiality I illustrate in this chapter is through scientific experts' engagement with water birds and with ornithological data collection as proxies for the ecological health of the wetland.

Through these three ethnographic examples, I argue that the material politics of the wetland is simultaneously *ecological* (concerning relationships between organisms), *infrastructural* (concerning relationships between built environments and the things that these allow to move), and *ontological* (concerning people's varied understandings of what kinds of entities wetlands are).

Overall, this chapter argues that scientific expertise is at once rendered apolitical—as it becomes a seemingly objective tool for decision-making—and again re-politicized (Ferguson 1990). Claims to objectivity, I found in my ethnographic research, are articulated through discussions indexing inextricable entanglements of science, ecology, politics, and identity. Scientific expertise is not simply given by educational degrees, institutional affiliation, class position, and job titles: it is performed socially and in space. In this chapter, I examine different ways in which the performance of expertise is connected to the materiality of the wetland. I also argue that the social and cultural performance of scientific environmental expertise maps onto and reproduces class distinctions at the same time as it occasionally reveals discomfort with classed hierarchies and practices of exclusion in environmental management.

In the introduction to this volume, Duygu Kaşdoğan and Ekin Kurtiç (Kaşdoğan and Kurtiç, 2025) argue that the materiality of place—in its geological and ecological form—is key to the exercise of state power. Environmental experts can naturalize the role and emplacement of large-scale, state-sponsored, and corporate engineering projects. At the same time, they help recast landscapes into the material basis for infrastructural visions and futures. Environmental expertise, however, is also deeply contested: as an object of political claim-making, expertise often becomes a site of protest, resistance, or hosts alternative imaginations of ecology, infrastructure, and multispecies relationships. Following Kaşdoğan and Kurtiç's invitation to highlight the multiple material politics of infrastructure, expertise, and scientific knowledge as a *process*, this chapter asks how wetland knowledge comes to matter as a conduit of contested claim-making about ecology. In doing so, both state and non-state expertise claims about wetland habitats help constitute wetlands as ontologically real, material places.

Don't Shoot the Messenger: Boundaries of Legitimacy in the Wetland

Let me take you back to the Ramsar signs which occasionally demarcate the boundaries of the Gediz Delta's wetland protected area, north of the sprawling metropolis of Izmir. The wetland managers and foresters who guided me through the wetland conservation were not showing me the metal signs to illustrate the many and overlapping conservation statuses in the Gediz Delta, or to make a point about the delta's hydrography and the elusive beginning and end of the salt marshes. Instead, they wanted me to notice something tangible and striking: the Ramsar signs were covered in bullet holes.

My companions explained that these bullet holes signaled the unruly, potentially dangerous, and discontent of the delta's rural residents—farmers, livestock grazers, fishers, and hunters—who contested and resisted the restrictions on access and resource use within the Gediz Delta conservation area. As a visiting PhD student, I was to be a witness to this violation and, presumably, would write about it in my dissertation. My companions asked me if I had seen anything like this in the European and American wetlands I had visited. No, I had not, I replied. In fairness, I had not paid much attention to wetlands before starting my PhD research. Only in Turkey, a forester stated, would farmers shoot bullets into conservation signs.

And so, I realized, the social performance of pointing to bullet holes on metal signs constituted a different kind of boundary, a social–moral one. Analyzing this episode from a political ecology lens,[2] this was a boundary separating *legitimate* material interventions (sanctioned by conservation legislations, governmental protocols, and official collaborations with universities and NGOs) from *illegitimate* ones, like those of the local residents who gathered wild plants and mushrooms, fished, hunted, and grazed cattle in the conservation area (Hughes 2011; Moore 2005; Walley 2004). The bullet holes materially indexed the violation of this social–moral boundary, at least from the perspective of the environmental managers. The violation of the social–moral boundary happened at the material–administrative boundary of the wetland.

In this way, the two boundaries—that separating rightful from immoral wetland users and that separating the wetland from agricultural, industrial, and residential land—collided. I argue that both boundaries, as well as their collision, were constituted and made possible by specific claims to scientific expertise. Expertise is, among other things, a relational social performance. By positioning themselves as rightful and legitimate users of the wetland, even speaking on behalf of the wetland, the foresters were relating to wetland materiality in ways that both reflected and naturalized a hierarchy of knowledge.

As wetland managers discussed the immoral response of angry farmers shooting bullets at the Ramsar signs, they rendered the farmers who lived and worked near and beyond the boundaries of the Gediz wetland conservation area at once *homogeneous* (a multitude of generic peasants) and *invisible* in their individual and collective specificity and perspectives (Pigg 1992). In other words, the farmers were collapsed into an educated, urban, middle-class person's imagination of the "unruly" and "uneducated" peasant (Walley 2002). This image was always counterposed to that of its counterpart, the "traditional" rural subject, repository of local wisdom and environmental knowledge (Walley 2002). Both kinds of figures of rural subjects were the focus of moral reform and social commentary—rebellious hunters and livestock grazers who had to be tamed, and traditional farmers who were losing their traditions (or had already lost them) and needed to be instructed in "best practices" for soil, water, and biodiversity conservation.

The ways in which rural residents variedly knew, valued, and related to the spaces marked as "wetland" only mattered, from the environmental managers' standpoints, if they fit traditional knowledge frameworks. Through the use of surveys and structured interviews, social scientists could recover and give value to traditional environmental knowledge and ethics, and then translate them into conservation-as-development projects (West 2006). The language of environmental management since the 1990s has become one of integrative planning, stakeholder participation, and state–NGO collaborations (see also Knudsen, 2025).

The next section of the chapter draws from my ethnographic notes on a collaborative grant-writing exercise in the Kızılırmak Delta to suggest that everyday practices legitimize expertise by invoking how such expertise can travel across and connect local, national, and international scales (Choy 2011; Tsing 2005). Accentuating the materiality of the wetland as elusive and illegible without expert intervention and education, a group of middle-class professionals and scholars positioned themselves as legitimate experts and authority figures charged with the moral duty of stewarding the wetland (and defining it for other publics). Anchoring their expertise in ethical claims about and knowledge of a specific landscape worked to naturalize both expertise claims and the ontological existence of a wetland. Rather than producing an apolitical terrain, however, these practices seeped with political contestations, fissures, and debates—often underscoring bureaucrats' and farmers' class differentials and gendered dynamics.

A Failed Proposal: Visions of a Transitional Civil Society in the Wetland

In 2015, I took part in everyday farming life in a sprawling rural neighborhood in the lower Kızılırmak Delta, on the Black Sea coast of Turkey, located in the Samsun Province. The coastal marshes, lakes, sand dunes, wet meadows, and swamp forests of the lower delta were added to Turkey's Ramsar list of wetlands of international importance in 1998, after having been declared a protected area in the 1980s (Özesmi 1999; Scaramelli 2018). The rural town where I lived during my ethnographic fieldwork was part of the municipality of Bafra, a town located approximately 10 kilometers away through a winding asphalt road. Many other unpaved roads meandered through wet meadows, rice paddies, villages, and cash crop fields. I relied on riding in my hosts' car to get around where the distances were too long for me to walk or bike—which happened frequently. As a result of this dependence, and the difficulties of moving autonomously as a young, unmarried, and female guest, I usually followed my hosts around on their errands in the delta.

I lived with three different households of farmers during the course of my field research. I was the only anthropologist there during the time of my fieldwork, but many other university researchers—largely from the natural sciences—conducted field research in the delta. A tightly connected group of professors working in the natural, agricultural, and social sciences at a nearby university in Samsun routinely visited the delta as their own research field site. Besides conducting their own research, some of these professors ran a seasonal ornithological research station; others organized "open-air" classrooms and wetland camps for students—many were involved in both kinds of research and educational activities. More generally, these scientists also understood the delta's wetlands as a site for imagining and practicing participatory conservation—that is, environmental conservation that includes and benefits rural residents and other local wetland users. Governmental agencies and the local National Parks bureau charged with managing the wetland were variedly involved in these initiatives, providing official authorization, resources, and informal support. There were plenty of moments of tension and disagreement as well.

The inclusion of the rural farming communities in scientists' and (in part) state bureaucrats' visions of environmental conservation in the delta was recent. Like in the Gediz Delta, in the Kızılırmak Delta, too, I had heard ornithologists and natural scientists talk about signs marking the areas' conservation boundaries being hit by bullets after the wetland protection area had been established in the 1990s, and even stories about farmers threatening to throw stones at conservationists' vehicles. However, by the time of my ethnographic fieldwork, I had not been able to observe any of these dynamics directly. Increasingly, university and NGO advocates for the delta's wetlands often invoked, and sometimes included, the delta's farmers in their visions of conservation and sustainability.

In practice, these efforts largely involved male farmers from the largest land-owning families in the delta and a few smallholders who had participated in government-sponsored programs for ecotourism development. All three families who hosted me in the delta were routinely involved in urban residents' and university efforts to constitute a "civil society" platform to discuss development, conservation, and sustainability in the delta's protected area and its surrounding villages and fields. My presence was not incidental. I was able to lodge with these families because of a preexisting relationship with a university researcher, and I would become instrumental in these relationships, tasked with encouraging farmers' participation in various wetland education and civil society initiatives.

In the rest of this section, I draw from my ethnographic observation of how scientific experts relate to wetland materiality by translating their own ethical visions of human–ecological relations into the realm of institutional project management. During the collaborative writing of a grant proposal for a participatory conservation project, university experts reframed the Kızılırmak Delta as a place connected to other wetland sites internationally—in the process, they also legitimized their role as spokespersons for and caretakers of the wetland.

In early May 2015, the university professor who had introduced me to one of the delta residents who hosted me and who had invited me to take part in various research and educational activities in the delta told me about a new call for applications for a "civil society dialogue," a project funded by the European Union. The grant was meant to invite collaborations between European and Turkish civil society organizations. I was invited to help envision and write the proposal, and specifically to help identify and work with an Italian NGO partner.

In my ethnographic notes, I had been writing about the different ways the delta's rural residents were imagined, included, and excluded from wetland conservation activities and regulations and how, in the process, they were being constituted as homogeneous "villagers" along that boundary separating "legitimate" from "illegitimate" moral–environmental subjects. Much of that work took place in sites like wetland conferences, research activities, education programs, and civil society meetings. Working on the grant would allow me to observe the different ways in which local actors positioned themselves strategically within international networks and spheres of wetland conservation. It would also offer an ideal site to understand how the materiality of the wetland was both imagined and reconstituted through international conservation opportunities, discourses, and practices. Specifically, these scientific experts' claims on wetland materiality framed delta residents as central to the future of the wetland itself.

As with many of the other sites, activities, events, and spaces where I conducted ethnographic research, my own presence was instrumental and could not be separated from the phenomena I analyzed: as a middle-class, female, southern European student enrolled in a US higher-education institution conducting long-term research in the rural delta, I had become a resource of social capital (Bourdieu 1986) that local researchers, in turn, could leverage to pursue their own visions of sustainable conservation and wetland care. After all, I had relied on their introductions, hospitality, and networks to start my field research in the delta. My own claims of expertise, then, provided ethnographic access into this community of scientists who advocated for wetland conservation.

The work of wetland conservation—one that mutually transformed both subjects and landscapes—exceeded the confines of official wetland management plans, government directives, and zoning maps. Rather, it was located in the deep and enduring emotional commitment and care for the wetland[3] of some university professors, NGO staff, state officials, birders, and urban residents in the Kızılırmak Delta. The many overlapping, and sometimes conflicting, kinds of wetland values (Gewertz and Errington 2015) they expressed relied as much on embodied field practices (routine research, photography, ecological monitoring) as on the social, network-building ones—like those underlying the grant project.

So, in May 2015, a small group of university professors, administrators, NGO staff, and I set out to collaboratively envision and write down a grant proposal. In addition to finding and coordinating the work with an Italian environmental NGO partner, I was responsible for translating the entire project proposal into English, for designing specific activities to realize the grant's targets and objectives, and for framing these activities, objectives, and targets into a coherent program.

Specifically, our proposal aimed to "develop local residents, organizations, and authorities' awareness and intervention capacities on delta wetlands' environment, nature conservation and local opportunities for sustainable development in the Kızılırmak Delta." To do so, we set out to "enhance wetland and climate change awareness and provide sustainable development opportunities to farmers and producers," and to "enhance awareness about sustainable livelihood and environment among rural middle school students."[4] In this imagination, civil society, farmers, and governmental institutions would all work together and strengthen their collaboration around participatory and sustainable wetland management.

The backbone of the program was a year-long series of educational workshops and activities aimed at delta residents, and a visit to a similar wetland site in Italy. The project would counter the presumed "lack of awareness" of unsustainable agricultural practices and livelihood alternatives in the local rural population—whom the proposal described as viewing the delta primarily as an economic resource, and whose extractive and production activities contributed to ecological degradation in the delta. As I helped envision, write, and translate the proposal, I held back from the critiques of participatory development and political ecology tools I routinely used as analytical tools in my own research. Instead, I advocated for knowledge exchange activities and spaces that did not presume farmers were only to be the recipients of expert knowledge. I suggested that scientific questions about the wetland could be dictated by questions that residents already had been tackling. And I encouraged activities centered around humanistic engagement with wetland spaces—through art and poetry workshops for school children, for example. None of this was new or groundbreaking in this context. These holistic approaches were already at the core of my collaborators' understanding of wetland advocacy.

In practice, as I had expected, our attempts at "creating participation" from the top-down largely failed. My own embeddedness (as a researcher and guest) in the everyday life of several of the delta's rural households was expectedly not enough to disrupt the class structures and power hierarchies in place—if anything, it reinforced the idea that farmers needed an expert spokesperson/mediator to facilitate involvement, and that a foreign PhD student hailing from southern Europe could or should play that mediating role. The few meetings we held in the delta at the local school were scarcely attended by rural residents. Only my own acquaintances and hosts participated—and no female farmers attended, despite my insistence and repeated invitations over the previous few weeks. Instead, my female hosts spent an entire day making an elaborate tray of desserts to send to the meeting as a refreshment, at the request of the (male) professors leading the project-writing effort.

After one of the meetings, a local school teacher told me and the rest of the team that we had bypassed her own authority, as she had wanted the school and herself to be directly involved in and mediate the project as a primary project partner. This was not possible given the specific framing of the grant proposal, and so the teacher withdrew her direct support. Further, the Italian NGO partner begrudgingly complained to me that the Turkish partners had not provided them with overhead expenses in the project budget. The final draft of the proposal was delivered to a ministerial office in Ankara with only minutes to spare before its deadline.

Despite its many failures and shortcomings on the ground, the project had a series of incidental and productive side effects (Ferguson 1990). Specifically, it constructed the idea of separate spheres of "civil society" and "rural residents," entangled in a shared concern with sustainable futures and development in the delta, and involved in a hierarchical position of knowledge transmission. The proposal itself, however, was a success, and we were eventually awarded the grant. However, the political circumstances following the July 2016 coup attempt led to a sudden and unexpected end to this project, as two of the local partners found themselves in a position where they could no longer collaborate.[5]

It is these emplaced and mundane practices—such as those of discussing and writing a grant proposal while sipping glasses of tea around a conference table in an agricultural institute, a village school, a university office, and a shared Google document—that both create and reinforce subject positions of expertise. The legitimization of expertise operates through the social practices of envisioning the political work of "local" and "international" scales (Tsing 2005), invoking environmental subjectivities occupying presumedly different subject positions and holding contrasting values (in this context, those of rural farmers, rural students, civil society advocates, and governmental managers), and normalizing hegemonic patterns of knowledge transmission. I am not proposing a social-constructionist approach. On the contrary, I argue that the *material* presence of the wetland, as an undefined, complex ecology, and ontologically multiple environments, anchors the naturalization of expertise. The materiality of the wetland seemingly hides and conceals the class and ethnic lines on which this naturalization unfolds.

At the same time, this was not a bureaucratic exercise that created apolitical, technocratic solutions. Instead, politics was seeping through at every step of the process, and this was very apparent to the university professors, park bureaucrats, and farmers involved in the grant proposal. Rather than constructing a boundary between "politics" and "science," the grant proposal coconspirators created a social domain where political debate and disagreement could (relatively safely) occur. The class stratification perspective is also complicated by the fact that people occupy multiple class positions at once (Gibson-Graham 2006), and their life histories further complicate their class distinctions. For example, some university professors had rural backgrounds, some farmers held vast local power and economic capital, some farmers' relatives and children had gone on to white-collar professions in urban contexts, and other farmers were themselves retired middle-class professionals "returning" to their home village.

The Winter Bird Count: How Birds Become Tools of Commensurability

This section analyzes the collaborative work of National Parks staff and volunteer birders during a Winter Bird count that took place in the Aegean wetlands. My analysis focuses on the role of birds as political proxies for debates and contestations around environmental resources management, debates that also stabilize the wetland as an object of expert knowledge production and care. I suggest that the birders' *material* engagement with wetland ecologies, lived environments, and human and nonhuman dwellers, and their resulting informal and tactile, or tacit, knowledge (Polanyi 2009), is at the core of these claims and discourses. In the process, birders produced embodied knowledge—ways of knowing that rely on and reside in bodily movements, skill, and habits—that created and connected different scales of bird livelihood. In doing so, the birders rendered the wetland's complex ecology into a commensurable object, a kind of place that can be compared with other wetland places.

It is a cold, rainy morning in January 2014. I wake up at dawn, grab my backpack, a grocery store bag with my muddy plastic boots, don a bright green down jacket over a pair of gray cotton pants, walk out of my apartment building on the outskirts of Izmir and meet my companions, already waiting for me on the road in a packed jeep. Four National Parks jeeps packed with the staff and volunteers of an environmental NGO (henceforth, the NGO) are heading out for two days to conduct the mid-winter wetland bird count in the region's wetlands. Participants refer to this field activity, taking place between mid-January and mid-February, as KOSKS (Kış Ortası Kuş Sayımı), the mid-winter bird count. For the small group of volunteer birders and ornithologists participating in the count—all of us are university graduates in our twenties and thirties, I am one of two women and the only foreigner—this is a joyous occasion.

The mid-winter bird count, known internationally as the International Waterbird Census (IWC), is a global program of bird counting that monitors the health of wetlands through their waterbird populations (defined by the Ramsar Convention as "species of bird that are ecologically dependent on wetlands"). Birds provide an important proxy for the health of the wetlands and the avian flyways connecting different wetland habitats. The count is also a baseline for assessing ecological change and environmental degradation.

In a different way, the count is also a performance of how wetland management is embedded in transnational networks and established practices. It is a localized invocation of a global scale of nature-making (Tsing 2005). The first IWC, conducted by volunteers and organizations in 1967, was coordinated by the Wildfowl Trust at Slimbridge, in the UK. In the following decades, waterbird counting became an increasingly global exercise, coordinated by national and regional wetland conservation organizations (Kuijken 2006). Turkey had been a site of winter waterbird counts since the late 1960s, largely through the collaborative work of European and Turkish birders and ornithologists, and started its own national bird counts in the early 1990s under the leadership of the Turkish environmental NGO Doğal Hayat Koruma Merkezi (the Society for the Protection of Nature) (see Erciyas Yavuz and Kartal 2012).

The four jeeps, each staffed by a driver and a National Parks forester from local bureaus, all convene in a bare-bone teahouse outside of the bus station in Söke—a town located in the Büyük Menderes River Delta's agricultural plain, one and a half hours' drive south of the Izmir province. The bird counting will be conducted by a group of volunteers and staff working for an environmental NGO.[6] It is a small, tight-knit group of friends, and I am the only one lacking serious ornithological and bird identification expertise. The National Park staff—in this field expedition, they are all men—provide support and logistics, as they consider waterbird monitoring part of their official duties related to wetland conservation and management.

In my team are a conservation scientist working at the NGO, a forester from the Aydın National Parks bureau, and the driver. We are assigned Bafa Lake, just south of Söke center. The rest of the group disperses to other locations in the region. An ornithologist working for the Gediz Delta wetland management authority has prepared the plan for the day and hands out to each team a set of observation points in GPS coordinates. The forester then manually uploads onto his GPS device the thirteen coordinate points from which we are to conduct the bird count around the lake. After we park the jeep near the shores of Bafa Lake, the forester tries to prevent me from carrying the birding telescope as we make our way through fields and boulders to the edge of the lake. The conservation scientist jokingly scolds him: fieldwork (*arazi*), he lectures, is a space of gender equality, and the women, he elaborates, will insist on carrying the same load as the men.

The day proceeds in a routine. At each GPS coordinate point, the conservation scientist sets up the telescope and binoculars. In a notebook, I take note of the date, weather conditions, time, GPS position, and then write down the species of birds and approximate count numbers as the conservation scientists dictate them to me. The scientists make light fun of my spelling—some of the Turkish bird species names are new to me.

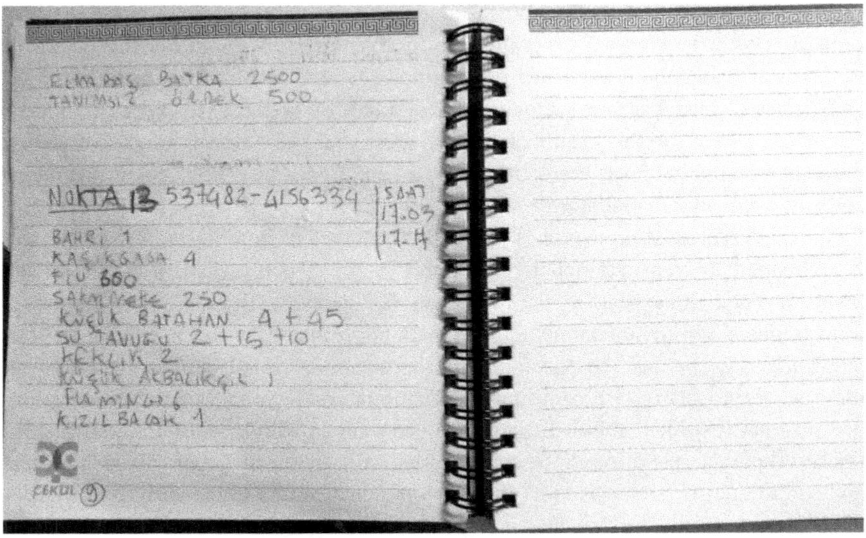

Figure 7.1 The authors' notes from the bird count, note the incorrect spelling of several bird species. Courtesy photo by the author, January 2014.

Meanwhile, the forester smokes cigarettes, takes occasional photos of us and the landscape, and is largely on the lookout for signs of (illegal, *kaçak*) hunting activities in the area. A few bottles and a plastic tarp signal a hunters' camp, rifle shots echo through the lake shores, then the hum of a motor. We watch a young man in a blue shirt and a dog on a small motorboat cross the lake, quickly disappearing in the haze and reeds by the opposite shore of the lake. The forester laments his inability to chase after them on a boat and remarks on the skillful way hunters are able to hide their weapons (and catch) in the wetland when foresters approach.

We drive and then walk from one GPS point to the next, proceeding around the lake on paved and unpaved roads, and when possible, pause for tea breaks in the village teahouses. The forester grows restless as rifle shots continue to resonate from the shallow reeds on the lake shores, and (alleged) hunters pass us. The sun is setting, and we cannot pursue them, he begrudges. A small group of male villagers driving by in a car stops our group to complain to the forester about the hunters. I hear only fragments of the animated conversation that ensues. "Why don't you do anything about it? I have been calling this number for weeks, without any answer. You should give them a fine. Have you even been here before?" Afterward, as we drive on, the forester frustratedly remarks that local residents will complain when the forestry bureau fines hunters, and also complain when they do not give out fines. The department really needs to acquire a boat to chase those hunters on the lake, he reflects out loud. And they should build more bird observation towers.

Later that night, reconvening with the rest of the team for a festive celebratory dinner at a nearby seaside town, I chat with the other volunteers in the bird-counting efforts. Two of them spell out their critique of what they understand as an "aggressive" and "ego-driven" birding culture concerned with the pursuit of rare birds. By contrast, they explain, birding culture in the Aegean region is more relaxed, more focused on passing on one's knowledge and work to others, rather than claiming ownership over it.

I participated in two-to-three-day-long winter bird counts in the Aegean region for two subsequent seasons: in 2014 and again in 2015. Each time, the dynamics were similar: local National Parks bureaus provided vehicles, drivers, food, and lodgings. The staff was invariably male (with one exception—behind her back, her colleagues remarked that after going on maternity leave, she would take on office desk duties only) and largely trained in forestry sciences. The bulk of site planning, coordinating, bird identification and counting, and record-keeping was done by the same ornithologist and the small, tight-knit group of staff and volunteers connected with the NGO—all university graduates in their late twenties and thirties, many of whom had been friends since participating in birding clubs during their university education. These informal social relationships and friendships were central to this particular material engagement with the wetland as a site for exercising bird-counting expertise. The mood of the bird count participants was often joyful, festive. Our conversations were largely about birds and birding and about environmental changes the volunteers observed from year to year on the wetlands.

Yet, the birds also provided a seemingly apolitical ground for discussing more complex and controversial issues of environmental degradation, land management, conservation, and shifting governmental legislation on environmental protection. Here, the performance of expertise did not follow strict institutional hierarchies, but rather, informal practice and socially recognized skills. The most expert birders took leadership positions handling the telescope and binoculars, an unspoken performance of status mapped onto competence and reputation (Liep 2001). In turn, they coached less experienced and capable others—like me—in more basic identification and bird-counting tasks. The National Parks staff was generally more interested in issues of hunting control than in the birds or in the results of the monitoring activities.

Different kinds of "nature" and the proper relationship between bird populations and wetland bodies were conjured in this social performance of wetland materiality (Lavau 2011). Foresters' and birders' practices and discourses revolved around the performance of particular kinds of scientific expertise, ones that relied on the premise of higher-education qualifications but were then constructed on the informal apprenticeship model of birding. This informal apprenticeship model allowed state/non-state, gender, and age distinctions and hierarchies to be temporarily suspended. For example, during one monitoring day, the youngest volunteer participant led the rest of the team because she held the most knowledge and the most bird identification experience and was also familiar with our route and sites for the day.

The bird counts generated several epistemological effects, producing the object of their analysis—the wetland—as a stable and taken-for-granted kind of object. The counts allowed participants to perform and invoke a national and international scale within which ecologies of shallow water became global objects (Tsing 2005), and, at a national and regional scale, they became ecologies comparable to one another (Choy 2011). This exercise in localizing a global category simultaneously rendered specific localities both abstract and global entities. At the same time, the birds acted as apolitical proxies for discussing the devastating effects of environmental resource extraction, real estate speculation and expansion, groundwater depletion to feed intense, water-thirsty cash crops, tourist facilities, and industrial zones, and wetland management policies and national legislation. This is a kind of mundane environmental politics on the ground, one that builds on dialogues between parties with opposing and contrasting political views. The limits of this politics are obvious: ultimately, these conversations would have no larger, structural effect. And, similarly to what I had observed in the Kızılırmak Delta, rural residents were not included in the bird-monitoring activities. In fact, with few exceptions, farmers and fishermen were hardly mentioned by the foresters and ornithologists, other than through morally laden commentary on their damaging practices of hunting, littering, and agricultural production.

Alongside the pleasure of interaction and conversation with friends, central to the bird-counting experience was the joyful pleasure of spotting a rarely seen bird, and the many pleasures of moving slowly through these aquatic environments as the changing daylight refracted on the surface of the water. At times, however, the birds themselves as individuals and collectives (van Dooren 2014) seemed unimportant to the excursion's goals. The bird count could then be interpreted as a social and ritual activity, one that materialized environmental expertise into a reading of the wetland based on a global, abstract commodity: the bird. Bird populations and data thus acted as *proxies* for the health of the wetlands, for their potential importance as habitats (at a national and international level), and as a site's change over time. They rendered lakes, reservoirs, lagoons, estuaries, saltpans, and other areas of shallow water into nodes in the international networks of birds, scientists, and environmental protection agreements.

Conclusion

In this chapter I have used three different ethnographic examples to shed light on some of the ways in which environmental materiality and scientific expertise are coproduced (Jasanoff 2004). The first ethnographic example, centered on the social and communicative role of conservation zoning signs, shows how managerial boundaries can be materialized through an implicit moral commentary about their illegitimate violation. In the process, environmental governance through expertise becomes an object of concern (Latour 2004) and a site of emotional passion and urgency, as environmental advocates emphasize the many threats faced by wetland conservation areas. The *material* anchoring of these threats—which wetland experts and managers experience by being in place, embodying the wetland and its degradation through the invocation of scientific field practices (Kohler 2002)—renders particular ecologies like the wetland into taken-for-granted objects of care, protection, and scientific management.

The second example demonstrates how ethical imaginations of place and livelihood are expressed through routine bureaucratic practices. A grant-writing exercise became the pretext and theater for different individuals and groups (university scientists, state bureaucrats, and the visiting anthropologist) to envision and thus constitute the object of their care. They devised the grant proposal as a boundary object (Star and Griesemer 1989) that held divergent meanings to different participants, while at the same time remaining coherent enough to hold them together in the collaborative practice of crafting a proposal. In the process, the grant-making activity made it possible to envision a social, collaborative space where different kinds of expertise were imagined to be equally valued and included (while, in practice, participation reproduced power differentials between university experts and rural residents). In doing so, the social performance of environmental participation could hide the class distinctions which it simultaneously mapped in its celebration of "traditional" ecological knowledge held by rural subjects. At the same time, concurrent with the erasure of class and power dynamics, the grant-writing exercise opened up a novel space for debate, disagreement, critique, and (relatively safe) political dissent in the face of top-down environmental governance and regulations.

The third ethnographic example indexed the social space of bird counting as one that held the potential to momentarily collapse boundaries of age, state/non-state distinctions, professional qualifications, gender, class, and politics. It was a performance of expertise that relied on collaborative notions of an environmental civil society and on an embodied, emplaced, and material engagement (with water, mud, plants, weather, birds, roads, mapping devices, binoculars, telescopes, notebooks, and cars). These collaborations also resulted from a conscious temporary erasure of the distinction between state and non-state experts and an emplaced approach to knowledge production, akin to a collaborative aspiration Fatih Tatari (Tatari, 2025) identifies at play among his cheesemaker interlocutors in his contribution to this volume. The personal networks, friendships, and embodied kinds of place-knowledge held by the bird count participants mattered. However, these preexisting social networks and tacit knowledge were not explicitly discussed or questioned.

The wetland, a capacious boundary object (Star and Griesemer 1989) that describes elusive watery biomes for the very purpose of creating a global category (Scaramelli 2021), is often a site where environmental politics, relations, and ethics are confounded and muddled. In this chapter, I have analyzed the coproduction of expertise and ecological materiality. In Turkish wetlands, scientists, NGO workers, and birders legitimize their own expertise by staking particular claims about the state, value, and ethics of wetland ecologies, infrastructures, and ontologies—claims that ultimately intend to transform the wetland's own materiality. At the same time, expertise is acquired, reproduced, and contested through material, embodied, and often informal engagement in and through the wetland's soils, waters, plants, animals, and infrastructures. In the process, the coproduction of expertise and materiality at once naturalizes both environmental categories and expertise, while simultaneously opening these up for being discussed, contested, improvised, and reimagined.

Notes

1 This research is based on ethnographic fieldwork and archival work conducted in Turkey between 2012 and 2018, supported by grants from MIT, the Wenner Gren Foundation, and the National Science Foundation, and approved by the IRB review process at MIT and at Amherst College.

2 I draw on Neumann's three-part formulation of political ecology: an analysis of local power dynamics between environmental managers (including both park foresters and rural residents); the international, national, and regional politics and markets that shape environmental access and use; and longer histories of land control and resource use in the context of state formation and colonial and postcolonial land management (Neumann 1992).
3 Here, I take care as a set of embodied practices (Barnes and Taher 2019), and constitutive of relational subjecthood and hierarchies (Buch 2018), as well as the violence underlying projects of biodiversity and species conservation (Bocci 2017; van Dooren 2014).
4 Unpublished Project grant submission, April/May 2015, author's collection.
5 To protect my interlocutors and collaborators, here I am unable to elaborate on the details of the conflict and political conundrum that led to this outcome.
6 I refer to this organization as "the environmental NGO" to protect the anonymity of my research interlocutors and NGO staff.

References

Adaman, Fikret, Serra Hakyemez, and Begüm Özkaynak. 2009. "The Political Ecology of a Ramsar Conservation Failure: The Case of Burdur Lake, Turkey," *Environment and Planning C: Politics and Space* 27 (5): 783–800.

Alkan, Aybike. 2025. "Water Pipes versus Power Lines: GAP Between the Promises and Practices of Infrastructure Buildup," in Duygu Kaşdoğan, Ekin Kurtiç, and Mehmet Ekinci (eds.), *Material Politics in Turkey: Infrastructure, Science, and Expertise*, 19–39, London: Bloomsbury.

Arı, Yılmaz 2001. *Visions of a Wetland: Linking Culture and Conservation at Lake Manyas, Turkey*. PhD Thesis, University of Michigan.

Arı, Yılmaz. 2006. "Ramsar Sözleşmesi'nin Doğa Koruma Yaklaşımına Eleştirel Bir Bakış," *Doğu Coğrafya Dergisi* 11 (15): 275–302.

Arı, Yılmaz and Derinöz Bekir. 2011. "How not to Manage a Wetland? The Case of Lake Marmara (Manisa) with a Cultural Ecological Perspective," *Coğrafi Bilimler Dergisi* 9 (1): 41–60.

Arsel, Murat, Bengi Akbulut, and Fikret Adaman. 2015. "Environmentalism of the Malcontent: Anatomy of an Anti-Coal Power Plant Struggle in Turkey," *The Journal of Peasant Studies* 42 (2): 371–95.

Avdan, Ataman Osman. 2020. "The Making of Consurbia: Conservation, Urbanization, and Socio-Environmental Change in Turkey's Gediz Delta," Thesis, Arts & Social Sciences: Department of Sociology and Anthropology.

Ballestero, Andrea. 2019. *A Future History of Water*, Durham: Duke University Press.

Barad, Karen. 1999. "Agential Realism: Feminist Interventions in Understanding Scientific Practices," in Mario Biagiioli (ed.), *The Science Studies Reader*, 1–11, New York and London: Routledge.

Barnes, Jessica and Mariam Taher. 2019. "Care and Conveyance: Buying Baladi Bread in Cairo," *Cultural Anthropology* 34 (3): 417–43.

Bocci, Paolo. 2017. "Tangles of Care: Killing Goats to Save Tortoises on the Galápagos Islands," *Cultural Anthropology* 32 (3): 424–49. https://doi.org/10.14506/ca32.3.08

Bourdieu, Pierre. 1986. "The Forms of Capital," in J. G. Richardson (ed.), *Handbook of Theory and Research for the Sociology of Education*, 241–58, Westport, CT: Greenwood.

Bozdogan, Sibel. 2001. *Modernism and Nation Building: Turkish Architectural Culture in the Early Republic*, Seattle, Washington: University of Washington Press.
Buch, Elana D. 2018. *Inequalities of Aging: Paradoxes of Independence in American Home Care*, New York: NYU Press.
Choy, Timothy. 2011. *Ecologies of Comparison: An Ethnography of Endangerment in Hong Kong*, Durham, North Carolina: Duke University Press.
Dooren, Thom van. 2014. *Flight Ways: Life and Loss at the Edge of Extinction*, New York: Columbia University Press.
Erciyas Yavuz, Kıraz and Esra Kartal. 2012. *Türkiye Kış Ortası Su Kuşu Sayımları 2011*, Samsun: Ondokuz Mayıs Üniversitesi Yayımları.
Erensü, Sinan. 2016. "Fragile Energy: Power, Nature, and the Politics of Infrastructure in the New Turkey," PhD Thesis, University of Minnesota, Minneapolis, MN.
Erensü, Sinan and Ozan Karaman. 2016. "The Work of a Few Trees: Gezi, Politics and Space," *International Journal of Urban and Regional Research* 41 (1): 19–36.
Evered, Kyle T. 2012. "Political Ecologies of Turkey's Wetlands and Lake Burdur: The Case of Demirel and the Duck," *The Arab World Geographers* 15 (1): 45–71.
Evered, Kyle T. 2013. "Draining an Anatolian Desert: Overcoming Water, Wetlands, and Malaria in Early Republican Ankara," *Cultural Geographies* 21 (3): 1–22.
Evren, Erdem. 2014. "The Rise and Decline of an Anti-Dam Campaign: Yusufeli Dam Project and the Temporal Politics of Development," *Water History* 6 (4): 405–19.
Ferguson, James. 1990. *The Anti-Politics Machine: Development, Depoliticization and Bureaucratic Power in Lesotho,* Cambridge: Cambridge University Press.
Fırat, Bilge. 2016. "The Most Eastern of the West, the Most Western of the East: Energy-Transport Infrastructures and Regional Politics of the Periphery in Turkey," *Economic Anthropology* 3: 81–93.
Gewertz, Deborah and Frederick Errington. 2015. "Doing Good and Doing Well: Prairie Wetlands, Private Property, and the Public Trust," *American Anthropologist* 117 (1): 17–31.
Gibson-Graham, J. K. 2006. *The End of Capitalism (as We Knew It): A Feminist Critique of Political Economy*, Minneapolis: University of Minnesota Press.
Gratien, Chris. 2022. *The Unsettled Plain: An Environmental History of the Late Ottoman Frontier*, Stanford: Stanford University Press.
Gruppuso, Paolo. 2018. "Edenic Views in Wetland Conservation: Nature and Agriculture in the Fogliano Area, Italy," *Conservation and Society* 16 (4): 397–408.
Hughes, David McDermott. 2011. "Water as Boundary: National Parks, Rivers, and the Politics of Demarcation in Chinanimani, Zimbabwe," in Joachim Blatter and Helen Ingram (eds.), *Reflections on Water: New Approaches to Transboundary Conflicts and Cooperation*, 267–94, Cambridge, MA: MIT Press.
Jasanoff, Sheila. 2004. "The Idiom of Co-Production," in Sheila Jasanoff (ed.), *States of Knowledge: The Co-Production of Science and the Social Order*, Abingdon, 1–12, Oxon: Taylor & Francis Group.
Kaşdoğan, Duygu and Ekin Kurtiç. 2025. "On Materiality and Politics in Turkey: An Introduction," in Duygu Kaşdoğan, Ekin Kurtiç, and Mehmet Ekinci (eds.), *Material Politics in Turkey: Infrastructure, Science, and Expertise,* 1–16, London: Bloomsbury.
Knudsen, Ståle. 2025. "Commentary," in Duygu Kaşdoğan, Ekin Kurtiç, and Mehmet Ekinci (eds.), *Material Politics in Turkey: Infrastructure, Science, and Expertise*, 183–90, London: Bloomsbury.
Knudsen, Ståle. 2009. *Fishers and Scientists in Modern Turkey: The Management of Natural Resources, Knowledge and Identity on the Eastern Black Sea Coast*, New York: Berghahn Books.

Kohler, Robert E. 2002. *Landscapes and Labscapes: Exploring the Lab-Field Border in Biology*, Chicago, Illinois: University of Chicago Press.
Kuijken, Eckhart. 2006. "A Short History of Waterbird Conservation," in G. C. Boere, C. A. Galbraith, and D. A. Stroud (eds.), *Waterbirds around the World*, 52–9, Edinburgh: The Stationery Office.
Kurtiç, Ekin. 2020. "Sediment in Reservoirs: A History of Dams and Forestry in Turkey," in Onur İnal and Ethemcan Turhan (eds.), *Transforming Socio-Natures in Turkey: Landscapes, State and Environmental Movements*, 90–111, New York: Routledge.
Latour, Bruno. 2004. "Why Has Critique Run out of Steam? From Matters of Fact to Matters of Concern," *Critical Inquiry* 30 (2): 225–48.
Lavau, Stephanie. 2011. "The Nature/s of Belonging: Performing an Authentic Australian River," *Ethnos* 76 (1): 41–64.
Liep, John. 2001. "Airborne Kula: The Appropriation of Birds by Danish Ornithologists," *Anthropology Today* 17 (5): 10–15.
Mitsch, William J. and James G. Gosselink. 2011. *Wetlands*, 4th ed., New Jersey: John Wiley & Sons.
Moore, Donald S. 2005. *Suffering for Territory: Race, Place, and Power in Zimbabwe*, Durham, North Carolina: Duke University Press.
Neumann, Rodrick P. 1992. "Political Ecology of Wildlife Conservation in the Mt. Meru Area of Northeast Tanzania," *Land Degradation & Rehabilitation* 3: 85–9.
Özesmi, Uygar. 1999. "Conservation Strategies for Sustainable Resource Use in the Kızılırmak Delta in Turkey," PhD Thesis, University of Minnesota.
Özkan, Hande. 2018. "Remembering Zingal: State, Citizens, and Forests in Turkey," *International Journal of Middle East Studies* 50 (3): 493–511.
Pigg, Stacy Leigh. 1992. "Inventing Social Categories through Place: Social Representations and Development in Nepal," *Comparative Studies in Society and History* 34 (3): 491–513.
Polanyi, Michael. 2009. *The Tacit Dimension*, Chicago: University Of Chicago Press.
Ramsar Convention. 1971. "Final Act of the International Conference on the Conservation of Wetlands and Waterfowl," Ramsar, Iran.
Richardson, Tanya. 2016. "Where the Water Sheds: Disputed Deposits at the Ends of the Danube," in Marjieta Bozovic (ed.), *The Poetics and Politics of the Danube River*, 308–37, Brookline, MA: Academic Studies Press.
Richardson, Tanya and Gisa Weszkalnys. 2014. "Introduction: Resource Materialities," *Anthropological Quarterly* 87 (1): 5–30.
Scaramelli, Caterina. 2018. "The Wetland Is Disappearing: Conservation and Care on Turkey's Kızılırmak Delta," *International Journal of Middle East Studies* 50 (3): 405–25.
Scaramelli, Caterina. 2021. *How to Make a Wetland: Water and Moral Ecology in Turkey*, Stanford: Stanford University Press.
Schiappa, Edward. 1996. "Towards A Pragmatic Approach to Definition: "Wetlands and The Politics of Meaning," in Andrew Light and Katz Schiappa (eds.), *Environmental Pragmatism*, 209–30, New York: Routledge.
Star, Susan Leigh and James R. Griesemer. 1989. "Institutional Ecology, 'Translations' and Boundary Objects: Amateurs and Professionals in Berkeley's Museum of Vertebrate Zoology, 1907-39," *Social Studies of Science* 19 (3): 387–420.
Tatari, Mehmet Fatih. 2025. "Pasture-Cheese Diplomacy: Carving Knowledge in Dairy Technosciences," in Duygu Kaşdoğan, Ekin Kurtiç, and Mehmet Ekinci (eds), *Material Politics in Turkey: Infrastructure, Science, and Expertise*, 119–41, London; Bloomsbury.

Tsing, Anna Lowenhaupt. 2005. *Friction: An Ethnography of Global Connection*, Princeton, New Jersey: Princeton University Press.
Walley, Christine J. 2002. "'They Scorn us Because we are Uneducated' Knowledge and Power in a Tanzanian Marine Park," *Ethnography* 3 (3): 265–198.
Walley, Christine J. 2004. *Rough Waters: Nature and Development in an East African Marine Park*, Princeton, New Jersey: Princeton University Press.
West, Paige. 2006. *Conservation Is Our Government Now: The Politics of Ecology in Papua New Guinea*, Durham, North Carolina: Duke University Press.
Wilson, Robert M. 2011. *Seeking Refuge: Birds and Landscapes of the Pacific Flyway*, Seattle, Washington: University of Washington Press.
Zeybek, Sezai Ozan. 2016. "Türkiye'de Endüstriel Hayvancılığın Seyri," *Toplum ve Bilim* 138: 7–25.

8

"Is there Oil in Turkey?"

Geology, Oil Exploration, and the Indeterminate Materiality of Resources

Zeynep Oğuz

In Istanbul and Ankara, between 2015 and 2019, when I carried out my dissertation research at multiple sites in Turkey, during conversations with strangers that often took place in cabs, cafes, grocery stores, bookstores, hospitals, and hairdressers about what I do (*social scientist*, I respond), I was also often asked what my research is about. I tell them I investigate the "cultural, social, and political story of oil in Turkey." Almost always, the person I'm talking with pauses, looks baffled, and asks: "Is there even oil in Turkey?" Sometimes, those who pose the question are simply not aware of Turkey's modest oil production. Yet others answer the question themselves: "Yes, there is, but we are not allowed to produce it." My attempts to produce evidence in my conversations about Turkey's oil are often met with a counterresponse: "That's not the whole story. There is much more than we are told. We just aren't allowed to extract our abundant oil reserves."[1]

"Is there oil in Turkey?" has been an omnipresent question in Turkish public life for decades. In contemporary Turkey, TV programs, news articles, and YouTube videos are devoted to speculations about Turkish oil. A simple search on YouTube for "oil" and "Turkey," for example, reveals hundreds of videos revolving around this unifying question. Other videos are, for example, titled "Turkey's Petroleum Truth," "Why can't we extract our petroleum?", "Turkey's Secret Oil Wells, Debunking Oil Myths in Turkey." Many of these videos feature so-called online journalists, and others are segments from national TV programs either trying to prove or debunk these speculations using a mix of historical sources, speculation, and official geological data. Yet the question about the presence of oil in Turkey is never settled but only ends up producing more uncertainty about the oil reserves' present condition and anticipation or fears about the energy-dependent Turkey's future (Oguz 2023).

In this chapter, I approach "Is there oil in Turkey?" as a crucial discourse that encapsulates the onto-epistemological relationship between the ubiquitous yet spatiotemporally differentiated geological materialities of oil and the underground on the one hand, and technoscientific practices and political–economic parameters that aim to turn it into an extractable "reserve," on the other.[2] The question about oil's absence and presence in Turkey concerns how the subsurface materiality of oil relates to the ways it is attempted to be known. In other words, what oil "is" at a particular point in time (its historical ontology) is generated through an interplay between its particular material qualities (its age, volume, depth, permeability, and porosity, for example) and how these material qualities are known or attempted to be extracted, sampled, measured, calculated, and assessed by petroleum geologists and engineers. As Dinç (this volume) notes in this exploration of Turkey's first gold mine, "gold's relative rarity is more conjectural than absolute." Gold becomes a "rare metal" as a result of the fixing of a geological space, resource economics, and technologies. Similarly, what oil is at a given time also bears upon how these technoscientific tools of rendering the underground intelligible are related to political–economic ways of translating geological knowledge into future value, such as the estimation of reserves, resource potentiality, and economic viability. This onto-epistemological interplay, however, is rarely smooth but punctuated with fluxes and flows between matter, technology, economy, and politics. I will unpack these points in the following sections.

So, *is* there oil in Turkey? A provisional answer: yes and no. Turkey *does* have some hydrocarbons under the ground, but not too much. Despite being located near rich oil fields in Iraq, Turkey remains an oil-poor state, as domestic oil production supplies about 7 percentof Turkey's annual consumption.[3] Yet even though there might be oil under the ground from a geophysical perspective, not all of it becomes refined petroleum in the end. Due to the geological properties of Anatolia, the quality of the few existing oil deposits in Turkey's southeast is poor and their extraction is often economically unfeasible (Efeoğlu 2011). Oil in Turkey is of high viscosity and thus its density and gravity are significantly higher than light crude oil, making drilling and production too costly (Derman 2014). This is to say, depending on global petroleum prices, many of the prospective oil wells drilled in Turkey are often found to be commercially unviable. People might experience the geophysical materiality of oil in different ways, through oil seepages, smells, and during exploratory drills, but in the end, these materials might never translate into what geologists call "proven reserves." Noticing such frictions and gaps between the materiality of geological matter and sets of technopolitical processes through which fossilized geological matter is enacted as a "resource," are key to recognizing the capacities and the limits of geological knowledge about the underground, and capturing the indeterminacy of oil.

As Kaşdoğan and Kurtiç state in their introductory chapter, this volume is primarily concerned with the questions of how "the different ways in which infrastructures, scientific and expert knowledges, and practices come to matter in various political contexts" and how various actors "enact politics through and with material landscapes." Limits to knowledge and material indeterminacies, this chapter discovers, are key to the enactment of politics in contemporary Turkey. To that end, in the following pages, I make three interrelated arguments about oil in Turkey as an onto-epistemological problem. First, engaging with several tensions between constructivist and the new materialist scholarship on the underground and the geologic,[4] I argue that questions and confusions regarding oil's absence or presence in Turkey stem from its particular material properties under the ground and from the inability of petroleum geology and geological engineering to fully "know" the substrata and predict petroleum potential. Next, I contend that uncertainties surrounding oil are further exacerbated by the ways in which this resource materiality is translated into the political–economic logic of reserves and reserve estimates. I analyze these modes of experience and materiality through the conceptual frameworks of "resource becoming" (Richardson and Weszkalnys 2014) and "geological indeterminacy" (Oguz 2021b). I then propose that this indeterminate character of oil, encapsulated by the question "is there oil?", engenders a myriad set of speculations about the future and anticipatory politics that the Turkish state and other actors attempt to harness for their own agendas. Picking up from my earlier argument about the inability of petroleum geology and geological engineering to fully "know" the substrata, I finally contend that the inhuman materiality of the underground might also exceed or unsettle these projects. As oil is made into a "resource" through the onto-epistemological interplay between its materiality and technoscientific attempts to render it extractable, the earthly materiality of the underground also resists, exceeds, or unsettles such attempts to fully contain and territorialize it: Oil seeps and disappears, earthquakes strike and change five-year plans, and wells dry out unexpectedly.

Below, as I unpack these arguments through a discussion of contemporary onshore and offshore oil exploration cases in Turkey, I take up a key objective of this edited volume, which is to take the materiality of politics in the making of scientific knowledge, state power, and sociopolitical imaginaries in Turkey seriously. In doing so, I also aim to contribute to recent scholarly work on the environment and resources in Turkey (see Barry 2013; Bozcali 2020; Çaylı 2021; Knudsen 2014; Kurtiç 2019; Scaramelli 2019; Schäfers 2016) by fostering a conversation between constructivist/epistemological and new materialist/ontological accounts of the underground and the geological in the fields of STS, anthropology, and geography. Further, this account also provides a more pluralistic understanding of power and politics in contemporary Turkey. Recent work on state-making, authoritarianism, and mega-projects under the AKP regime, for example, has examined how the construction of dams, bridges, power plants, and highways has been key to the production of consent and the constitution of hegemony (Bridge, Özkaynak, and Turhan 2018). As Kaşdoğan and Kurtiç (this volume) note, attention to "material politics" also allows one to rethink state–society relations and expand or populate the terrain of politics toward a recognition of active agents contesting what counts as politics.

When one takes the materiality of oil seriously, the subsurface reveals itself to be a locus of contested politics and imaginaries—a space of geological indeterminacy, and thus, a potential resource for capitalization and appropriation by the state and capital for their own developmentalist, populist, or neoliberal agendas. Yet, as I argue through a feminist geophilosophy-inspired discussion of Anatolian Plate tectonics that has shaped Turkey's subsurface and petroleum potential, the geologic also resists or even exceeds human attempts to fully harness it. Below, I discuss these frictious processes through two cases of hydrocarbon exploration in Turkey's onshore and offshore territories.

Oil Seeps and Speculations

In May 2018, three men from Hekimhan, a town in the district of Malatya, located in the Eastern Anatolia region of Turkey, noticed oil seeps accumulating in their fields around a decommissioned well and alerted the media. This so-called discovery quickly made it to local newspapers' headlines, renewing five-decades-old speculations about the hidden abundance of oil in the currently energy-dependent Republic of Turkey. The news stories were reconjuring long-held rumors in the area about the "mystery" of the fifteen abandoned wells in Akçadağ, a town half an hour away from the province of Malatya: *Why were these wells abandoned so abruptly by the state-owned oil exploration and extraction company, Turkish Petroleum Company*[5] *some fifty years ago? Why did water and sometimes gas keep leaking from them even after their capping with concrete? Were the government and the oil company hiding things from the public?* Reminding its readers about the suspicious history of the abandoned wells in Akçadağ, one local paper covered the oil seep story under the title, "Is Turkey floating over a sea of oil?" Another story, which also alluded to the same abandoned wells, asked, "Is oil being hidden?" (*Malatya Haber* 2018).

In Hekimhan, oil seemed to be both absent and present. And this presence emerged in the encounter between oil's subsurface materiality and petroleum geology's incomplete attempts to render it intelligible. As the media frenzy around oil seeps continued, for example, newspapers interviewed locals, who voiced their doubts about the nature of the sightings. A Turkish resident of Hekimhan, Ali, was quoted saying, "I can see the oil here, I can smell it, I can touch it. But they are telling me that our country lacks any oil. Which one is true — is there oil or not?" (*Malatya Guncel* 2018). For Ali, it was hard to be denied the existence of matter, while his hands were covered with it. Yet, geologists weren't denying that oil existed in its geophysical forms under *a* ground; they were questioning its existence in the very subsurface of the terrain of Hekimhan. And even if oil existed somewhere else, whether it would economically make sense to extract it was yet unknown. I take this friction between the material experience of oil's presence and geologists' inability to translate it into resource value as a crucial manifestation of the onto-epistemological relationship between the geological materiality of oil (and the subsurface) and knowledge-making practices around it.

A few days after the oil seepage news in Hekimhan, the state-owned oil exploration and production company Turkish Petroleum's (TPAO) director of exploration, Ahmet Bey, received a call from the district governor of the town.[6] I was in his office located in the main company town in Batman at the time, discussing new exploratory drilling projects planned for the quarter. After listening to the district governor for a while, Ahmet Bey told him that the oil seeps did not necessarily indicate any petroleum potential in that specific location. "They are probably traveling from some other source rock," he said. The district governor seemed to be objecting. "Yes, governor, we will look into it," Ahmet Bey murmured, rolling his eyes. He thought that oil exploration efforts should be directed at regions that already carried proven petroleum potential. Once he hung up, he drew a sigh and spurted out, "these people have no idea how the underground is structured. When they catch sight of an oil seep, they immediately assume that it means there is a big reserve under it."

In oil and gas exploration, petroleum geologists consider hydrocarbon seeps as important clues that can help estimate the migration routes of oil from their source rocks or reservoirs toward the surface (Clarke and Cleverly 1991). I thus asked Ahmet Bey if the seeps could indicate the presence of a reserve elsewhere. "Of course, that's a possibility," he responded. "But even so, it doesn't mean that it is commercially viable." Ahmet Bey's comments about "commercial viability" point to an important distinction in petroleum geology between what people in the fossil fuel industry call "proven" or "recoverable reserves" and unproven reserves, as "estimates of recoverable reserves are not a matter of geology, but of knowledge and price at a given time" (Vitalis 2020, 15). In other words, at any given time, the amount of oil or gas that can be brought to the surface is determined in relation to the technology-driven cost of extraction and economic demand. The geophysical substance under the ground, for example, might stay the same over the course of years or decades, but as technological tools to render it intelligible or global oil prices change, calculations of proven and unproven reserves also differ.

Unlike Ahmet Bey, however, the exploration geologists in TPAO's Ankara Headquarters were interested in the task ahead. Oil seepings and source rock potential studies of the Malatya region had been conducted in the past, but there were none on this particular oil seep that the geologists observed in the limestone cracks in Hekimhan (Ayyildiz 2013). Further, only one area in Malatya had been drilled before. In 1970, the Mineral Exploration and Research Institute[7] (MTA) had opened exploratory wells in the area, but abandoned them after a series of problems that made drilling very difficult and costly (Gedik and Dinçer 1970). These were none other than the Akçadag wells in Malatya, the subject of long-held speculations and conspiracy theories, which were reanimated in the aftermath of the recent seep sightings in Hekimhan.[8]

The exploration geologists in TPAO's Ankara Headquarters thought that a biomarker study in Hekimhan could be helpful to identify groups of genetically related oils, correlate oil seeps' geochemical properties with those of the potential source rocks, describe the probable source rock depositional environments, and speculate about the petroleum potential of the region. Two exploration geologists, Ufuk and Nazan, visited Hekimhan a week later. They gathered oil seep samples from Upper Cretaceous and late Eocene aged rocks and from those that could possibly be source rock shales. They collected over a hundred surface samples, mainly dark-gray and green-gray shale rocks and limestones. The samples were then sent to the main geochemistry laboratory in Ankara for an analysis of the organic elements found in the potential source rocks, their maturity, and finally, for an understanding of whether the oil seeps and the potential source rocks had any association.

The results were mixed. The shale samples were revealed to have low organic carbon values, meaning that there was no petroleum or gas source-rock potential. The limestones, however, indicated source-rock potential. Even better, the analysis of oil seeps' pre-Cretaceous age was found to be in correlation with these limestones. However, the organic material found in the oil seeps indicated what petroleum geologists call a "nonindigenous" origin, meaning that the seeps had migrated to the surface from elsewhere, likely from a deeper, older source rock beneath the Upper Cretaceous in the basin. The results of the biomarker analysis, in other words, arrived at two conclusions at the same time: there was oil, and also, there wasn't any oil. Oil was indeterminate.[9] And far from calming the public in Malatya, TPAO's geochemical analysis reports led to more unanswered questions for both the geologists about petroleum potential in the region and the local people in Hekimhan about possible hidden oil under the ground.

The Hekimhan oil seep "incident" was emblematic of the ways in which petroleum geologists were neither able to fully "know" the substrata and predict petroleum potential nor put speculations about Turkish oil to rest. I have been developing my argument that these tensions emerge from the frictions between the materiality of oil/the underground and knowledge-making practices. In the next section, I move on to a seemingly settled hydrocarbon "discovery"—the Turkish government's recent discoveries in the Black Sea—to continue tracing the emergence of such frictions and their appropriation by the state and other political actors.

Harnessing Offshore Discoveries

Although TPAO did not pursue exploration in Hekimhan, the company has been expanding its domestic onshore and offshore oil exploration activities in order to reduce Turkey's oil and gas import dependency. Turkey's offshore oil exploration efforts took a new turn in the past few years. In 2020, with the discovery of offshore hydrocarbons in the Black Sea and the massive publicity that the government generated in the aftermath of the discoveries, it *seemed* like the lingering question "is there oil in Turkey?" was finally resolved. In June 2020, Turkey's Minister of Energy made consecutive announcements of oil and gas discoveries in Turkey's offshore waters and onshore lands. Mainstream and state-owned media reported these discoveries as steps in Turkey's economic wealth and resource independence to come. The government officials' initial remarks and local media coverage purposefully exaggerated the magnitude of the discoveries. On their Twitter accounts, ministers celebrated the findings as a means of fostering Turkey's inevitable progress. Pro-government daily newspaper *Sabah*, for example, claimed that the discoveries were set to "change the energy equation" and end Turkey's resource dependency for good (Erdem 2020).

Critics of the AKP government, however, countered that the announcements were merely the AKP's and President Erdogan's political ploys to both consolidate their electoral base and detract attention from Turkey's real political and economic problems. Following the reactions on social media from Chicago at the time, I was struck by how many people seemed to think that these "discoveries" were actually fake. Many mocked the news about gas discovery in the Black Sea by sarcastically asking if there was an election on the horizon or if a bitcoin mine discovery was next in line, for example.[10] Opponent news sites such as *Bianet* and *Birgun* compiled lists of previous gas and oil discovery news in the past decade, which nobody heard from afterward (Bianet 2020; Birgun 2020; Semender 2020). The popular reaction coming from those critical of the government seemed like a reversal of the conspiracy theories about hidden oil or obstructed production that had dominated Turkish public life for decades.

Yet once again, for geological engineers and petroleum geologists I spoke to in the aftermath of the discoveries, neither position ("fake" vs. "massive" amounts of oil discovered) seemed to reflect the geophysical, economic, and technological realities. Gas was a geophysical reality, so news about its discovery was not fake. Yet its material presence did not easily translate into the language of reserves. My geologist interlocutors were highly skeptical about the reserve estimates. Contrary to the claims of government officials and pro-government media, they argued that gas discoveries in the Black Sea fell short of making Turkey energy independent. According to official sources, the total amount of hydrocarbon deposits recently discovered in the Black Sea by the state oil and gas exploration company Turkish Petroleum over the last few years amounts to 540 billion cubic meters. If these numbers are correct, theoretically, this would supply Turkey's gas demand for only ten years, which would not be considered an impressive estimate in the oil and gas industry (Algedik 2020). This is to say, only if production is commercially viable. Geologists, therefore, thought that declaring reserve estimates was not only an immature act at that point but also failed to reflect what they thought was the "modest" scale of the discoveries.

The AKP government nevertheless continued to inflate the numbers and capitalize on the indeterminacy of oil, which is at the heart of both prior speculations about hidden oil and the more recent, cynical dismissal of the offshore hydrocarbon news. The volume of hydrocarbons that Turkey claims to have discovered might not really be produced—that is, brought onto the ground. Yet this is exactly what nation-states like Turkey blur when they announce fossil resource discoveries. They capitalize on the indeterminacy that characterizes the subsoil and oil exploration (and production). They further obfuscate the distinction between deposits and reserves, or the total amount of estimated matter under the ground and the matter that can or might be recovered. It is due to these strategies of capitalization and obfuscation that there are many contradictory beliefs regarding the existence and amount of oil in Turkish public life: no oil, fake oil, hidden oil, potential oil—the list goes on. Such uncertainties that surround oil, I argue, are exacerbated by the ways in which this resource materiality is translated into the political–economic logic of reserves and reserve estimates. I analyze these modes of experience and materiality through the conceptual frameworks of "resource becoming" (Richardson and Weszkalnys 2014) and "geological indeterminacy" (Oguz 2022). To unpack these terms, below, I engage in several conversations surrounding epistemological and ontological questions regarding geology, the subterranean, and resources.

Subterranean Resources and Indeterminacy

In recent years, the subterranean, the terrain, and the volumetric have emerged as powerful concepts in geography, STS, media studies, and anthropology that theorize the relationship between materiality and knowledge and power. In human geography and cognate social science fields, underground tunnels, burial grounds, caves, mines, sewers, bunkers, ocean beds, cables, and other spaces of the Earth's subsurface are increasingly being approached as lively and dynamic social, cultural, and political sites (Childs 2020; Starosielski 2015; Pérez 2015; Oguz 2021a). Challenging the predominance of "horizontalism" in geography and cognate fields, geographers such as Stuart Elden, Stephen Graham, and Bruce Braun have attended to "vertical" and "volumetric" territories that are not captured in two-dimensional representations of cultural and social life (Braun 2000; Elden 2013; Graham and Hewitt, 2013).

Starting with the pioneering works in human geography, attention to vertical and volumetric space has examined how the state, the military, and security apparatuses territorialize and weaponize the underground as a tool of surveillance, occupation, or counterinsurgency (Adey 2010; Graham 2009; Braun 2000; Gordillo 2018; Gregory 2004; Weizman 2012). This line of research approaches the underground as a site of exploration, resistance, subversion, and subterfuge (Dobraszczyk, Lopez-Galviz, and Garrett 2015; Elden 2013; Garrett 2011). For example, the underground has emerged as a vertical space of insurgency through spaces such as tunnels, which have allowed some groups to avoid the surveillant gaze of powerful aboveground groups (Graham and Hewitt 2013). Caves have also been volumetric spaces of politics and power; in southeastern Anatolia, for example, limestone caves scattered along the Upper Tigris Valley have become objects of the Turkish state's attempts to govern Kurds and territorialize southeastern Anatolia/northern Kurdistan. As geological formations fundamental to the Turkish state's attempts to exert and secure territorial power, the caves of the Upper Tigris Valley have also been central to the ways in which Kurds in Turkey have attempted to unsettle colonial state power and territorial politics (Oguz 2021a).

In addition to political and military power and resistance, questions of expertise and technoscience are important to understanding how the underground and resources become a site of knowledge and extraction, making Science and Technology Studies' contribution to the study of the underground crucial. Scholars working at the intersection of STS, anthropology, and geography have thus examined the role of technoscientific discourses and practices, and especially the Earth Sciences, in the construction of the underground and resources as political–economic space and assets (Braun 2000; Bridge 2013; Bruun 2018; Kneas 2018; Marston 2019). Bruce Braun's pioneering work on the production of "vertical territory" in late-nineteenth-century Canada, for example, revealed how geological surveyors territorialized western Canada as a repository of natural resources by creating a new way of "seeing" the subterranean as part of the national territorial imaginary (Braun 2000). As Squire and Dodds state, "The subterranean is integral to nation-state building and geopolitical strategies of control, enclosure, and exclusion" (Squire and Dodds 2020, 9).

The control of minerals and hydrocarbons has been central to territorial projects (Bebbington 2012; Perez and Melo Zurita 2020). STS scholarship on resource exploration and extraction reveals how underground materials, such as minerals, gas, and oil, are sensed, mapped, economized, and rendered intelligible in various ways through legal regulations, techniques of surveying, calculation and measurement practices, expertise, and engineering (Kama 2016; Squire and Dodds 2020; Melo Zurita 2020; Valdivia 2015). In doing so, STS scholars reveal how resources and the underground are not given blank states or passive entities, but brought into being through particular epistemological and technopolitical discourses and practices. Resources are not natural things with essential qualities that are just sitting "out there" or "down there" waiting to be extracted. They are not purely constructs of epistemological practices and discourses, either. Instead, resources are made through complex arrangements of matter, technoscience, infrastructures, the nation-state, and political economy (Richardson and Weszkalnys 2014). Studies on "resource becoming" thus explore "the cultural, political, and scientific means through which resources are imagined, abstracted, and brought into being as natural objects" (Ferry and Limbert 2008; Bridge 2011; Kama 2016; Kneas 2018, 754; Li 2014; Richardson and Weszkalnys 2014). Territory-making and resource-making, therefore, are processes that often co-constitute each other.

In Turkey, the in-betweenness of oil figures as both a source of public confusion and a condition that the Turkish state capitalizes upon to pursue territorial and military interests within and beyond Turkey's borders. Such speculations about hidden oil and obstructed production circulate in Turkish public life, fueling a particular conspiracy theory about the significance of the year 2023 (Oguz 2023). Speculations about hidden or obstructed oil also empower conservative and Islamist projects of historical revisionism, territorial expansionism and irredentism, against the backdrop of the resurgence of "Neo-Ottomanism" in Turkey in recent decades (Çinar and Taş 2017; Karakaya 2020, 2020; Potuoğlu-Cook 2006; Tokdogan 2018; Walton 2010; Yabanci 2020; and Yavuz 2020). The political power of oil's absent presence in Turkey warrants a return to oil's geological, geophysical, and geochemical materiality and an investigation of how this absent presence itself is produced in the encounter between this materiality and petroleum geology's incomplete attempts to render it intelligible.

The socio-material frictions in the designation of proven and unproven reserves in Hekimhan reveal a crucial insight about the geological materiality of oil: that it is not a "resource" in and of itself. Kärg Kama observes that "the designation of diverse sedimentary rocks 'as oil' or 'as gas' is neither straightforward nor uniformly conducted across different geographical localities and socio-political regimes" (Kama 2019, 5; Mitchell 2010). Oil only becomes a resource when it can be extracted and turned into a commodity, which requires an interplay of economic factors and technological interventions. Rather than existing a priori, the underground and the resources in it come to be through interlinked political, economic, cultural, and technoscientific practices and processes (Richardson and Weszkalnys 2014). This "relational and spatiotemporally differentiated process" (Kama 2019, 5) through which resources come into being is what fuels further public uncertainty about Turkey's oil reserves and speculations about hidden oil under the ground. It is also what creates a fertile ground for the Turkish state, local government, and other political entities in their attempts to capitalize on this indeterminacy for their own ends.

Yet, as the indeterminacy of oil in Hekimhan suggests, nation-states' and private companies' attempts to explore or extract hydrocarbons under the ground are always prone to inherent unknowns (Bridge and Wood 2010; Kama 2020). Nazan, one of the exploration geologists in the Hekimhan biomarker analysis team, told me in a private conversation that although they were sure that there were no significant oil fields under the ground, they could not confirm the total absence of any oil on the site. She desperately added: "No matter how advanced our tools of detection and measurement are, when it comes to the underground, we cannot be absolutely certain."

Chronically faced with these gaps in knowledge and the inability of its mediating tools to fully capture the (quantitative and qualitative) materiality of the underground, geology owns up to its affordances and likens itself to social sciences and the humanities. Robert Frodeman, for example, argues that geology is a historical and interpretative science. Günel also writes about the "geologists' belief in the ultimate unrepresentability or unknowability" of the Earth's subsurface (Günel 2019, 168). As uncertainty and risk remain constitutive of the policy-making efforts of the consultants in a carbon capture and storage project in Masdar City, tension emerges between the characteristics of a single site and efforts to generalize it. Geologists and geophysicists like Nazan agree with the insights of Frodeman and Günel, confirming that uncertainty is the norm rather than the exception in the everyday practices of geology, which is a science of the particular.

Geopowers of the Earth

Since the twentieth century, when oil seeps were first identified and mapped during the Ottoman Empire, oil's indeterminacy has been fueling political imaginaries and projects in Turkey, from a myriad of speculations about its hidden abundance and conspiracy theories to anticipatory desires for wealth and territorial expansion (Oguz 2023). The widespread sense of uncertainty regarding Turkey's oil reserves partially stems from Turkey's geophysical evolution, which has determined oil's specific spatial and material qualities and quantities. The Anatolian Plate, on which most of present-day Turkey's landmass sits, is located at the convergent boundary of two giant colliding tectonic plates. Being compressed and pushed west by the Arabian Plate and pulled apart on its western margin, where it meets the Aegean Sea, the Anatolian Plate has been slowly rotating counterclockwise since this collision event that started 13 million years ago (Aitchison, Ali and Davis, 2007). The intracontinental collision has sutured the Anatolian Plate along the Bitlis-Zagros Suture Zone, which has formed as a part of the larger Alpide-Himalayan orogenic belt, while thickening the crust and uplifting eastern Anatolia. The faulting and folding of the crust in this collision zone have directly impacted the predicament of oil, its exploration, and the geographic distribution of oil fields in Turkey.

The geophysical evolution of Anatolia that has *determined*—and continues to affect—the indeterminacy of oil in Turkey encapsulates a tension between the constructivist approaches to underground resources in STS and more recent work on the inhuman[11] and the geological coming from new materialism-inspired work on matter and materiality (Bakker and Bridge 2006; Bennett 2010; Braun and Whatmore 2010; Chen 2012; Weston 2017). If the Earth is no longer understood to be a background to sociopolitical life, new materialist perspectives push these insights even further, arguing that the Earth is not an inert and immutable substrate either, but rather a dynamic socio-natural space (Barry 2013; Clark 2011; Dalby 2013; Dittmer

2014; Elden 2013, Whatmore 2006). Taking the radically inhuman alterity of the Earth seriously, then, exposes the limits of a fully constructivist understanding of the making of resources, geological matter, and the underground. As Adam Bobbette and Amy Donovan observe, the former also breaks away "from the privilege of discourse" and opens "the possibility of wresting our understanding of the geos and earth itself from the domain of the geological sciences" (Bobbette and Donovan 2019, 26). It further allows thinking about questions of epistemology and ontology together, and in relation to each other, through a historical sensibility (Donovan 2021). Ways of knowing and modes of existence are confluent processes. Relatedly, technoscientific practices of knowing the Earth are revealed to be ultimately linked to questions of political, territorial, and economic power, but are also limited and unsettled by the unstable and exuberant grounds of the geological. Herein, the "political geology" (Bobbette and Donovan 2019; Marston and Himley 2021) of the subterranean and oil also allows us to notice how the subterranean may become ungovernable, challenging states', companies', and citizens' efforts to capitalize on it (Barry 2013; Tironi 2020; Salazar and Dodds 2020).

Although I do not intend to give an authoritative account of multiple new materialisms in this chapter, it is important to clarify that the branch of new materialism I follow here is not the vitalist line of theorizing, but the "inhuman" approach to the Earth, most clearly demonstrated by the writings of Kathryn Yusoff and Nigel Clark. This body of work, drawing on speculative realism and feminist anticolonial geophilosophy, insists on the radical alterity of the geological (Clark 2011). It suggests that the Earth and its inhuman forces are not stable and passive objects: the Earth has been conceptualized as a dynamic composition of separate but entangled force fields, and the relationship between power and earthly forces is not unidirectional (Clark 2011). Elizabeth Grosz calls this dynamic and creative relationship geopower, as "the relations between the earth and its life forms, run underneath and through power relations" (Yusoff, Grosz, and Clark 2012, 945). This diagnostic is at the center of Elizabeth Povinelli's notion of "geontopower," the exercise of power that has at its core the production, government, and maintenance of the fundamental difference between life and nonlife, animation and inertia (Povinelli 2016). As Manuel Tironi contends, this approach is not meant to fall back into the figure of the geologic as an "inert, stable, taken-for-granted component of anterior (and buried) life" (Tironi 2020, 28). Rather, the attempt is to unsettle entrenched ontologies in which (soil) existence is measured solely according to the categories and in the realms of "life" (Tironi 2019; Povinelli 2016). It is acknowledging how the "world-transforming powers of human social life have always depended on the forging of relations with the inhuman potentialities of our home planet" (Clark and Szerszynski 2021). It is also thinking with the formative and destructive forces of the Eurasian-Arabian plate collision, and taking into account how the mountain ranges, fault lines, and petroleum traps, among others, have implicated geosocial and geopolitical formations in and beyond Turkey. As Amy Donovan suggests, life worlds are marked by "both the otherness of earth's activity and its participation in politics" (Donovan 2021, 11). The plate boundaries of the tectonic collision zone where Anatolia sits, for example, might also contradict and unsettle hegemonic political and regional imaginaries in Turkey (Oguz 2019).

Conclusion: Earthly Materialities

In the past decade, critical social scientific studies of the environment in Turkey have explored patterns of knowledge-making about nature, environmental destruction, dispossession, subject formation, and struggles against mining, hydroelectric power plants, and "mega projects" during periods of rapid transformation along gendered, classed, and racialized lines.

Many of these works have adopted a political ecological perspective that analyzes the social construction and material production of nature in a complex web of state–society–capital relations. In this chapter, I took a slightly different path: following multiple accounts of oil exploration in Turkey, I have fostered a conversation between constructivist/epistemological and new materialist/ontological accounts of the underground and the geological in the fields of STS, anthropology, and geography, by exploring not only how oil is made as a resource through practices of knowledge-making, but also through the frictions between such attempts to render the inhuman materiality underground intelligible and the technosocial notions of economic value (such as supply and demand) at a given time. I have also argued that the inhuman processes of the geologic and the often incomplete technoscientific efforts to render it intelligible cast the underground as a site of indeterminacy.

Attending to the "abject liminality" of mud, Hande Özkan's chapter in this volume explores how forests are themselves liminal landscapes defined by mud. Pointing out the similarities between the understanding of coal and mud in early Turkey, Özkan notes that "coal was discursively transformed from the abject to an object, reinforcing my argument that natural landscapes cannot be defined by fixed essences." In doing so, Özkan argues that state-making is a dialogic process. When it comes to oil, the topic of this chapter, we can further notice that it is also a frictious and porous process that is both reinforced and destabilized by the indeterminacies of the underground. Utilizing this geological indeterminacy, and capitalizing on the frictious ways in which indeterminate matter is enacted as a resource, the Turkish state is able to forge oil prospects as spectacles that serve specific technopolitical purposes when needed: as ploys, distractions, governance technologies, vote baits—base-consolidating, territorializing, and anticipatory devices that have concrete effects in the present (Adams, Murphy, and Clarke 2009; Anderson 2010; Bakker and Bridge 2006; Kama and Weszkalnys 2017; Kama 2019; Limbert 2015; Weszkalnys 2016).

The Turkish state harnesses the techno-economic indeterminacy of fossilized matter as an anticipatory device that fuels nationalism, territorial control/expansion, and political consolidation. It capitalizes on the very gaps between matter, resource, and reserve by obscuring the technological and economic parameters that might enable oil and gas to reach the surface and move as a commodity. But geology might also be reconfigured otherwise (Oguz 2022). Dinç argues that an analytical focus on more-than-human entanglements in the context of gold mining "enhances our grasp of extractivism's multiscalar, non-teleological character that fosters injustices, destruction, and violence, as well as resistance and solidarity." In conversation with Dinç's proposition and Özkan's insistence on taking liminal materialities seriously, I call for a serious engagement with the "unconstructable" (Neyrat 2018) and excessive

(Clark 2011) materiality of the Earth and earthly forces in the political geologies of Turkey.

Such a call may inevitably position itself in a frictious space in relation to Kaşdoğan and Kurtiç's notion of "material politics" as "a more balanced look at politics and materials" that emphasizes the coproduction of both. Instead, it emphasizes liminality and excess rather than symmetry and coproduction, and proposes to notice how political actors—workers, peasants, insurgents, activists, scientists, and others—might "conspire with"[12] mountains, fault lines, caves, the seabed, coal mines, or the atmosphere for democratic, anticolonial, liberatory, or decolonial purposes.[13] Especially in such a nation-state where environments have been systematically destroyed, exploited, and weaponized, stories that recognize the inhuman geopowers (Grosz, Yusoff, and Clark 2017) of the Earth that might exceed the debilitating and violent capacities of the state and capital are a welcome one. Such stories are also narratives of planetary multiplicity (Clark and Szerszynski 2021) from the perspective of Anatolia, Kurdistan, and the eastern Mediterranean, to name a few. They will also be stories that unsettle the temporal and spatial scales of empire and the nation-state. With its engagement with the relational and historical ontological works on indeterminacy, on the one hand, and feminist geophilosophies of the inhuman, on the other, an STS that is tuned to the indeterminacy and excesses of the Earth's geophysical processes can also diagnose spaces and times where knowledge encounters the limits of the material, where human concerns for justice conspire with the geopowers of the Earth, and finally, where resources—fossil fuels whose extraction has produced so much violence in the so-called Anthropocene—can be reassembled to become otherwise.

Notes

1 As Limbert (2015), Mazzarella (2006), and West and Sanders (2003) have pointed out in different ways, it is the very claim to transparency that produces expectations of conspiracy in political life.

2 I am in conversation with the works of Candea (2014) and Richardson and Weszkalnys (2014) in their respective discussions of onto-epistemology. Although their approaches are different from each other, these authors think about political life and social realities formed by both ways of knowing and modes of existence (and becoming). Ways of knowing (epistemology) shape modes of existence, and vice versa. As Amy Donovan notes, "how we know the world is related to the choices that we have made about understanding ourselves-in-the-world and the world itself" (2021, 102347).

3 Domestic crude oil production grew by 19 percent from 2016 to 2019, mainly due to the increased upstream activities of Turkish Petroleum Corporation (TPAO), which holds most exploration and production licenses, though demand is still predominantly met by imports. Even with growth in domestic upstream activities, Turkey remains heavily dependent on imported oil and gas to meet its consumption needs. Recently, TPAO has initiated an offshore investment campaign along with increased operations onshore, including shale oil and gas. However, Turkey's natural gas import dependence will diminish following the recent discovery of the giant

Sakarya field in the Black Sea. The field is planned to commence production in 2023, giving Turkey bargaining power in the renewal of its natural gas import contracts (MAPEG 2017).

4 These tensions mainly concern questions around the construction of reality and the reality of nature. While social constructivists argue that natural things (resources, the underground, forests, etc.) are products of human sociopolitical systems, new materialist scholarship maintains that inhuman matter exceeds human cognition and experience, as well as human scales of time and temporality. See Bosworth (2017) for a detailed account of these tensions from a feminist geophilosophy point of view. Also, see my discussion later in the text in conversation with Bobbette and Donovan (2019).

5 Henceforward TPAO.

6 Batman, a district and town in southeastern Turkey, is the main oil-producing region of Turkey.

7 Following the establishment of the Republic of Turkey in 1923, the MTA was founded in 1935 as the state-owned institute that explores mineral and hydrocarbon resources by carrying out surveys, chemical, and technological analyses.

8 Contrary to the speculations, MTA's geologists had not filled the wells with concrete, but with asphalt, the most common material used in capping oil wells found to be dry or commercially unviable in the petroleum industry.

9 See Ballestero (2016) for an account of the indeterminacies intrinsic to the Sardinal aquifer and to the technoscience by which it was known in Costa Rica.

10 Conspiratorial culture in Turkey has always been a part of Turkish society and politics, yet conspiracy theories gained new momentum during the global "turn" to conspiracy in the past decade, as well as since the AKP government's coming to power. The populist discourse of the AKP, especially President Erdoğan, often exploits conspiratorial narratives as a means of base consolidation, distraction, and warmongering. See Oguz (2022) for an anthropological account of conspiracy theories surrounding oil in Turkey. For a more general work on conspiracy theories in Turkey, see Gürpınar (2019).

11 I prefer to use "inhuman" rather than more-than-human or nonhuman, as rather than extending the "liveliness" of biological matter to the geologic, I wish to underline the alterity of geologic matter. As Clark and Yusoff (2017) note, "what is at issue is not only how to extend or enrich the composition of shared worlds but what to make of forces capable of interrupting, undermining or overwhelming the very conditions of doing politics or being social" (15).

12 I am inspired by Tim Choy's thinking of conspiracy as the affinities that breathers form together in order to unsettle present toward different relations and a different world, an "atmospheric otherwise" (2021, 250). Elsewhere, I discuss "geological solidarity" as an interscalar (Hecht 2018) mode of geopolitical relation that aims to unsettle contemporary modes of violent inclusion and exclusion. See Oguz (2022).

13 See Last (2015) for a discussion of decolonial geopoetics.

References

Adams, Vincanne, Michelle Murphy, and Adele E. Clarke. 2009. "Anticipation: Technoscience, Life, Affect, Temporality," *Subjectivity* 28: 246–65.

Adey, Peter. 2010. "Vertical Security in the Megacity: Legality, Mobility and Aerial Politics," *Theory, Culture and Society* 30: 51–67.

Aitchison, Jonathan C., Jason R. Ali, and Aileen M. Davis 2007. "When and Where Did India and Asia Collide?" *Journal of Geophysical Research: Solid Earth* 112 (B5).

Algedik, Önder. 2020. "Doğalgaz müjdesinin sakladığı skandallar!" *Gazete Duvar*. https://www.gazeteduvar.com.tr/yazarlar/2020/08/22/dogalgaz-mujdesinin-sakladigi-skandallar

Anderson, Ben. 2010. "Preemption, Precaution, Preparedness: Anticipatory Action and Future Geographies," *Progress in Human Geography* 34 (6): 777–98.

Ayyildiz, Turhan. 2013. "Source Rock Potential and Oil to Source Rock Correlation of the Upper Cretaceous (Campanian-Maastrichtian)–Lower Paleocene Units in the Malatya Basin, East Anatolia, Turkey." *Petroleum Science and Technology*, 31 (13): 1335–45.

Bakker, Karen and Gavin Bridge. 2006. "Material Worlds? Resource Geographies and the 'Matter of Nature'," *Progress in Human Geography* 30 (1): 5–27.

Ballestero, Andrea. 2016. "Spongy Aquifers, Messy Publics." *Limn* 7: 48–52.

Barry, Andrew. 2013. *Material Politics: Disputes along the Pipeline*, Malden, MA: John Wiley & Sons.

Bebbington, Anthony. 2012. "Underground Political Ecologies: The Second Annual Lecture of the Cultural and Political Ecology Specialty Group of the Association of American Geographers," *Geoforum* 43 (6): 1152–62.

Bennett, Jane. 2010. *Vibrant Matter: A Political Ecology of Things*, Durham: Duke University Press.

Bianet. 2020. "'Karadeniz'de doğalgaz bulundu' haberi ilk değil." August 21. https://m.bianet.org/bianet/siyaset/229451-karadeniz-de-dogalgaz-bulundu-haberi-ilk-degil

Birgun. 2020. "Bulunan ama daha sonra haber alınamayan doğalgaz ve petrol rezervleri . . . ." August 8. https://www.birgun.net/haber/bulunan-ama-daha-sonra-haber-alinamayan-dogalgaz-ve-petrol-rezervleri-312804

Bobbette, Adam and Amy Donovan, eds. 2019. *Political Geology: Active Stratigraphies and the Making of Life*, Cham: Palgrave Macmillan.

Bosworth, Kai. 2017. "Thinking Permeable Matter through Feminist Geophilosophy: Environmental Knowledge Controversy and the Materiality of Hydrogeologic Processes," *Environment and Planning D: Society and Space* 35 (1): 21–37.

Bozcali, Firat. 2020. "Probabilistic Borderwork: Oil Smuggling, Nonillegality, and Technolegal Politics in the Kurdish Borderlands of Turkey," *American Ethnologist* 47 (1): 72–85.

Braun, Bruce. 2000. "Producing Vertical Territory: Geology and Governmentality in Late Victorian Canada," *Cultural Geographies* 7(1): 7–46.

Braun, Bruce and S. J. Whatmore 2010. *Political Matter: Technoscience, Democracy, and Public Life*, Minneapolis: University of Minnesota Press.

Bridge, Gavin. 2011. "Resource Geographies I: Making Carbon Economies, Old and New," *Progress in Human Geography* 35 (6): 820–34.

Bridge, Gavin. 2013. "Territory, now in 3D!" *Political Geography* 34: 55–7.

Bridge, Gavin, Begum Özkaynak, and Ethemcan. Turhan. 2018. "Energy Infrastructure and the Fate of the Nation: Introduction to Special Issue," *Energy Research & Social Science* 41: 1–11.

Bridge, Gavin and Andrew Wood. 2010. "Less is More: Spectres of Scarcity and the Politics of Resource Access in the Upstream Oil Sector," *Geoforum* 41 (4): 565–76.

Bruun, Johanne M. 2018. "Enacting the Substrata: Scientific Practice and the Political Life of Uraniferous Rocks in Cold War Greenland," *The Extractive Industries and Society* 5 (1): 28–35.

Candea, Matei. 2014. "The Ontology of the Political Turn," *Cultural Anthropology, Theorizing the Contemporary*. January 13. https://culanth.org/fieldsights/the-ontology-of-the-political-turn

Çaylı, Eray. 2021. "The Aesthetics of Extractivism: Violence, Ecology, and Sensibility in Turkey's Kurdistan," *Antipode* 53 (5): 1377–99.

Chen, Mel Y. 2012. *Animacies: Biopolitics, Racial Mattering, and Queer Affect*, Durham: Duke University Press.

Childs, John. 2020. "Extraction in Four Dimensions: Time, Space and the Emerging Geo(-)politics of Deep-sea Mining," *Geopolitics* 25 (1): 189–213.

Choy, Timothy. 2021. "Externality, Breathers, Conspiracy: Forms of Atmospheric Reckoning," in D. Papadopoulos, M. P. de la Bellacasa, and N. Myers (eds.), *Reactivating Elements: Chemistry, Ecology, Practice*, 231–56, Durhan: Duke University Press.

Çinar, Alev and Hakki Taş. 2017. "Politics of Nationhood and the Displacement of the Founding Moment: Contending Histories of the Turkish Nation," *Comparative Studies in Society and History* 59 (3): 657–89.

Clark, Nigel. 2011. *Inhuman Nature: Sociable Life on a Dynamic Planet*, Los Angeles: SAGE.

Clark, Nigel and Bronislaw Szerszynski. 2021. *Planetary Social Thought: The Anthropocene Challenge to the Social Sciences*, Cambridge: Polity Press.

Clark, Nigel and Kathryn Yusoff. 2017. "Geosocial Formations and the Anthropocene," *Theory, Culture & Society* 34 (2–3): 3–23.

Clarke, R. H. and R. W. Cleverly. 1991. "Petroleum Seepage and Post-accumulation Migration," *Geological Society, London, Special Publications* 59 (1): 265–271.

Dalby Simon. 2013. "The Geopolitics of Climate Change," *Political Geography* 37: 38–47.

Derman, Ahmet Sami. 2014. "Petroleum Systems of Turkish Basins," in L. Marlow, C. Kendall, and L. Yose (eds.), *Petroleum Systems of the Tethyan Region*, 469–504, AAPG Memoir 106.

Dittmer Jason. 2014. "Geopolitical Assemblages and Complexity." *Progress in Human Geography* 38 (3): 385–401.

Dobraszczyk, Paul, Carlos A. Lopez-Galviz, and Bradley Garrett. 2015. Digging up and digging down: Urban undergrounds. *Journal of Contemporary Archaeology* 2 (2): 26–30.

Donovan, Amy. 2021. "Colonising Geology: Volcanic Politics and Geopower." *Political Geography* 86: 102347.

Efeoğlu, Tayland. 2011. "Petrol Efsaneleri," *Jeofizik Bulteni*, August, Ankara: Jeofizik Muhendisleri Odasi, 17–23.

Elden, Stuart. 2013. "Secure the Volume: Vertical Geopolitics and the Depth of Power," *Political Geography* 34: 35–51.

Erdem, Faruk. 2020. "Enerjide denklem değişiyor!" *Sabah*. 19 November. https://www.sabah.com.tr/galeri/ekonomi/enerjide-denklem-degisiyor-dogal-gaz-kesfi-ile-hem-devlet-hem-vatandas-kazanacak

Ferry, Elizabeth and Mandana Limbert. 2008. *Timely Assets: The Politics of Resources and their Temporalities*, Santa Fe, NM: School for Advanced Research Press.

Garrett, Bradley. 2011. "Shallow Excavation, a Response to Bunkerology," *Society and Space*. http://societyandspace.org/2011/06/10/shallow-excavation-a-responsetobunkerology-bradley-l-garrett/ (accessed April 23, 2019).

Gedik, Abdullah and Ali Dinçer. 1970. Malatya Akçadağ Kuyu Bitirme Raporu. Rapor no: 4644 Ankara: MTA Enerji Hammadde Etüd ve Arama Dairesi Başkanlığı.

Gordillo, Gastón. 2018. "Terrain as Insurgent Weapon: An Affective Geometry of Warfare in the Mountains of Afghanistan," *Political Geography* 64: 53–62.

Graham, Stephen. 2009. "Cities as Battlespace: The New Military Urbanism," *City* 13 (4) : 383–403.

Graham, Stephen and Lucy Hewitt. 2013. "Getting off the Ground: On the Politics of Urban Verticality," *Progress in Human Geography* 37 (1): 72–92.
Gregory, Derek. 2004. *The Colonial Present: Afghanistan, Palestine, Iraq*. Oxford: Blackwell.
Grosz, Elizabeth, Kathryn Yusoff, and Nigel Clark. 2017. "An Interview with Elizabeth Grosz: Geopower, Iinhumanism and the Biopolitical," *Theory, Culture & Society* 34 (2–3): 129–46.
Günel, Gökçe. 2019. *Spaceship in the Desert: Energy, Climate Change and Urban Design in Abu Dhabi*, Durham: Duke University Press.
Hecht, Gabrielle. 2018. "Interscalar Vehicles for an African Anthropocene: On Waste, Temporality, and Violence," *Cultural Anthropology* 33 (1): 109–41.
Kama, Kärg. 2016. "Contending Geo-logics: Energy Security, Resource Ontologies, and the Politics of Expert Knowledge in Estonia," *Geopolitics* 21 (4): 831–56.
Kama, Kärg. 2020. "Resource-making Controversies: Knowledge, Anticipatory Politics and Economization of Unconventional Fossil Fuels," *Progress in Human Geography* 44 (2): 333–56.
Kama, Kärg and Magdalena Kuchler 2019. "Geo-metrics and Geopolitics: Controversies in Estimating European Shale Gas Resources," in A. Bobbette and A. Donovan (eds.), *Political Geology*, 105–45, Cambridge: Palgrave Macmillan.
Kama, Kärg and Gisa Weszkalnys. 2017. "Resource Temporalities: Anticipations, Retentions and Afterlives," Work paper presented at the 'Anticipating Abundance' workshop, University of Durham, May 12.
Karakaya, Yağmur. 2020. "The Conquest of Hearts: The Central Role of Ottoman Nostalgia within Contemporary Turkish Populism," *American Journal of Cultural Sociology* 8 (2): 125–57.
Kneas, David. 2018. "Emergence and Aftermath: The (un) Becoming of Resources and Identities in Northwestern Ecuador," *American Anthropologist* 120 (4): 752–64.
Knudsen, Ståle. 2014. "Multiple Sea Snails: The Uncertain Becoming of an Alien Species," *Anthropological Quarterly*, 87: 59–91.
Kurtiç, Ekin. 2019. "Sediment in Reservoirs: A History of Dams and Forestry in Turkey," in T. Ethemcan and I. Onur (eds.), *Transforming Socio-Natures in Turkey*, 90–111, London/New York: Routledge.
Last, Angela. 2015. "Fruit of the Cyclone: Undoing Geopolitics through Geopoetics," *Geoforum* 64: 56–64.
Li, Tania Murray. 2014. "What is Land? Assembling a Resource for Global Investment," *Transactions of the Institute of British Geographers* 39 (4): 589–602.
Limbert, Mandana. 2015. "Reserves, Secrecy, and the Science of Oil Prognostication in Southern Arabia," in Hannah Appel, Arthur Mason, and Michael Watts (eds.), *Subterranean Estates: Life Worlds of Oil and Gas*, 340–53, Ithaca, NY: Cornell University Press.
Marston, Andrea. 2019. "Strata of the State: Resource Nationalism and Vertical Territory in Bolivia," *Political Geography* 74: 102040.
Marston, Andrea and Matthew Himley. 2021. "Earth Politics: Territory and the Subterranean–Introduction to the Special Issue," *Political Geography* 88: 102407.
MAPEG. 2017. "Orta Dönemli Petrol ve Doğal Gaz Arz-Talep Projeksiyonu." https://mapeg.gov.tr/Uploads/PetrolRaporlarFormlar/Orta_Donemli_Petrol_ve_Gaz_Arz-Talep_Projeksiyonu.pdf
Mazzarella, William. 2006. "Internet X-Ray: E-Governance, Transparency, and the Politics of Immediation in India," *Public Culture* 18 (3): 473–505.

Melo Zurita, Maria de Lourdes 2020. "Challenging Sub Terra Nullius: A Critical Underground Urbanism Project," *Australian Geographer* 51 (3): 269–82.

Mitchell, Timothy. 2010. "Future Measures: How to Calculate for a World without Oil. Annual public lecture at the Forum for Research on Law, Politics, and the Humanities." Available at: http://www.ustream.tv/recorded/4241044 (accessed March 20, 2022).

Neyrat, Frédéric. 2018. *The Unconstructable Earth: An Ecology of Separation*, New York: Fordham University Press.

Oguz, Zeynep. 2019. "Sedimenting Territory: A Political Geology of Oil, Earth, and Spatial Politics in Turkey," Unpublished Doctoral Dissertation. The City University of New York Graduate Center. New York.

Oguz, Zeynep. 2021a. "Cavernous Politics: Geopower, Territory, and the Kurdish Question in Turkey," *Political Geography*, 85: 102331.

Oguz, Zeynep. 2021b. "Harnessing Indeterminacy: The Technopolitics of Hydrocarbon Prospects," Platypus, July 20. https://blog.castac.org/2021/07/harnessing-indeterminacy-the-technopolitics-of-hydrocarbon-prospects/

Oguz, Zeynep. 2022. "Denaturalizing Gas and War: On Energy Humanities and the Cyprus Gas Conflict," *Energy Humanities*, March 2. https://www.energyhumanities.ca/news/denaturalizing-gas-and-war-on-energy-humanities-and-the-cyprus-gas-conflict

Oguz, Zeynep. 2023. "Speculative Undergrounds: Petro-politics, Territorial Imaginaries, and the Indeterminate Earth," *Cultural Anthropology* 38 (3): 411–37.

Önal, Mehmet. 2009. "Organic Geochemical Properties of Marine Oligocene Unit in the Malatya Basin, East Anatolia, Turkey," *Energy Sources, Part A* 31 (15): 1406–14.

Perez, María Alejandra and María de Lourdes Melo Zurita. 2020. "Underground Exploration Beyond State Reach: Alternative Volumetric Territorial Projects in Venezuela, Cuba, and Mexico," *Political Geography* 79: 102144.

Pérez, María Alejandra. 2015. "Exploring the Vertical: Science and Sociality in the Field among Cavers in Venezuela," *Social & Cultural Geography* 16 (2): 226–47.

Potuoğlu-Cook, Öykü. 2006. "Beyond the Glitter: Belly Dance and Neoliberal Gentrification in Istanbul," *Cultural Anthropology* 21 (4): 633–60.

Povinelli, Elizabeth A. 2016. *Geontologies*, Durham: Duke University Press.

Richardson, Tanya and Gisa Weszkalnys. 2014. "Introduction: Resource Materialities," *Anthropological Quarterly* 87 (1): 5–30.

Salazar, Juan Francisco and Klaus Dodds. 2020. "Geosocial Polar Futures and the Material Geopolitics of Frozen Soils," in J. Salazar, C. Granjou, M. Kearnes, A. Krzywozynska, and M. Tironi (eds.), *Thinking with Soils-Social theory and Material Politics*, 123–40, London: Bloomsbury.

Scaramelli, Caterina. 2019. "The Delta is Dead: Moral Ecologies of Infrastructure in Turkey," *Cultural Anthropology* 34 (3): 388–416.

Schäfers, Marlene. 2016. "Ruined Futures: Managing Instability in Post-Earthquake Van (Turkey)," *Social Anthropology* 24 (2): 228–42.

Semender, Arzu. 2020. "Daha Önce Müjdelenip Bir Daha Kendisinden Haber Alınamayan Doğalgaz Rezervlerinin Haber Manşetleri," Onedio, August 21. https://onedio.com/haber/daha-once-mujdelenip-bir-daha-kendisinden-haber-alinamayan-dogalgaz-rezervlerinin-haber-mansetleri-914726

Squire, Rachel and Klaus Dodds. 2020. "Introduction to the Special Issue: Subterranean Geopolitics," *Geopolitics* 25 (1): 4–16.

Starosielski, Nicole. 2015. *The Undersea Network*, Durham: Duke University Press.

Steinberg, Philip and Kimberley Peters. 2015. "Wet Ontologies, Fluid Spaces: Giving Depth to Volume through Oceanic Thinking," *Environment and Planning D: Society and Space* 33 (2), 247–64.
Tironi, Manuel. 2020. "Soil Refusal: Thinking Earthly Matters as Radical Alterity," in J. Salazar, C. Granjou, M. Kearnes, A. Krzywozynska, and M. Tironi (eds.), *Thinking with Soils-Social Theory and Material Politics*, 175–90, London: Bloomsbury.
Tokdogan, Nagehan. 2018. *Yeni Osmanlıcılık*, Istanbul: Iletisim.
Tuğal, Cihan. 2023. "Politicized Megaprojects and Public Sector Interventions: Mass Consent under Neoliberal Statism," *Critical Sociology* 49 (3): 457–73.
Valdivia, Gabriela. 2015. "Oil Frictions and the Subterranean Geopolitics of Energy Regionalisms," *Environment & Planning A: Economy and Space* 47 (7): 1422–39.
Vitalis, Robert. 2020. *Oilcraft: The Myths of Scarcity and Security That Haunt US Energy Policy*, Stanford: Stanford University Press.
Walton, Jeremy F. 2010. "Practices of Neo-Ottomanism: Making Space and Place Virtuous in Istanbul," in D. Göktürk, L. Soysal, and I. Tureli (eds.), *Orienting Istanbul*, 104–19, London: Routledge.
Weizman, Eyal. 2012. *Hollow Land: Israel"s Architecture of Occupation*, New York: Verso.
West, Harry and Todd Sanders, eds. 2003. *Transparency and Conspiracy: Ethnographies of Suspicion in the New World Order*, Durham, NC: Duke University Press.
Weston, Kath. 2017. *Animate Planet: Making Visceral Sense of Living in a High-tech Ecologically Damaged World*, Durham, NC: Duke University Press.
Weszkalnys Gisa. 2014. "Anticipating Oil: The Temporal Politics of a Disaster yet to Come," *The Sociological Review* 62: 211–35.
Weszkalnys, Gisa. 2016. "A Doubtful Hope: Resource Affect in a Future Oil Economy," *Journal of the Royal Anthropological Institute* 22 (S1): 127–46.
Whatmore, Sarah J. 2006. "Materialist Returns: Practising Cultural Geography in and for a More-than-human World," *Cultural Geographies* 13 (4): 600–9.
Yabanci, Bilge. 2020. "Fuzzy Borders Between Populism and Sacralized Politics: Mission, Leader, Community and Performance in 'New' Turkey," *Politics, Religion & Ideology* 21 (1): 92–112.
Yavuz, M Hakan. 2020. *Nostalgia for the Empire: The Politics of Neo-Ottomanism*, Oxford: Oxford University Press.
Yusoff, Kathryn. 2013. "Geologic Life: Prehistory, Climate, Futures in the Anthropocene," *Environment and Planning D: Society and Space* 31 (5): 779–95.
Yusoff, Kathryn, Elizabeth Grosz, Nigel Clark, Arun Saldanha, Kathryn Yusoff, Christine Nash, and Elizabeth Grosz. 2012. "Geopower: A Panel on Elizabeth Grosz's Chaos, Territory, Art: Deleuze and the Framing of the Earth," *Environment and Planning D: Society and Space* 30 (6): 971–88.

9

Commentary

Ståle Knudsen

Forests, marshes, cheese, and hydrocarbons are the materials at stake in the chapters in Part II of this book. These materials are representative and indicative of the range of "matters of concern" globally, be it energy, natural resources, conservation, food, climate change, and more. Such matters of concern are typically surrounded by controversies related to risk and uncertainty, and experts often play particular and crucial roles in attempts to settle such controversies. This ultimately relates to how knowledge is produced and made to count. And to wider questions about, on the one hand, truth, and on the other hand, the social relations between the actors involved.

The chapters here do not work from a shared perspective or theory, but the ethnographies and discussions all make gestures in the same direction. They all elaborate forms of collaboration between scientists and other experts, on the one hand, and nonexperts, on the other hand, outlining the contexts that facilitate (and sometimes hinder) such collaboration, as well as the strategies and motives of the experts.

In recent scholarship in anthropology and related disciplines, collaboration can mean different things. In the new materialism, or relational ontology, of Latour (e.g., Latour 1993) and allies such as Callon (1984), Law (2004), and Mol (2002), "collaboration" is used to signify the way different "actants" (aka "actors") come together in the enactment of an object, technology, or fact. A major claim in Latour's Actor–Network Theory (ANT) is that these actants are heterogenous and that there is in principle no reason to distinguish between human and nonhuman actants. This is to avoid the two evils of (1) the Cartesian divide (between mind and body, humans and nonhumans) and of (2) forms of social constructivism/idealism that allow for no role of the material. Thus, nonhumans are accorded agency on par with humans. While the networks described by ANT can avoid preconceived rigidities of more structural and idealistic approaches, ANT has also been criticized for being unable to account for power, politics, hierarchies, and so on (Knudsen 2023). Also easily ignored in ANT accounts are lived (human) experiences as well as identity politics.

The materiality discussions in the chapters in this part differ from the ANT perspective and are closer to a line of discussion exemplified by Andrew Barry's book *Material Politics* (2013). Thus, the chapters do engage the material or nonhuman, but they do not describe bacteria, the earth, birds, or mud as participants on par with humans. The collaborations, and sometimes also contestations, recounted here take place between human actors and are played out in (often political) fields of national scale. At this juncture, it is pertinent to mention that the title of this book is a nod toward Andrew Barry's book *Material Politics* (2013), which recounts and theorizes the role of the material in political conflict. Although loosely situating himself in the ANT tradition, his position is also influenced or tempered by the post-/neo-Marxist "radical democracy" approach of Chantal Mouffe (e.g., Mouffe 2005) and others. While Barry discusses "ways in which diverse events and materials come to be matters of public dispute" (Barry 2013, 8), and stresses—contrary to proponents of "radical democracy"—"how the properties and behaviour of organic and inorganic materials . . . themselves participate in such controversies" (Barry 2013, 12), he does not take "participation" to correspond to "agency." In Barry's account, only humans have the capacity to be actors. Humans take the initiative to enlist nonhumans so that they come to participate in political contestations. But the properties and behavior of the nonhumans are not trivial. So too in the chapters in this part.

Although Zeynep Oğuz is inspired by new materialist approaches, especially what she terms the "'inhuman' approach to the Earth," and engages alternative ontologies, her approach and conceptualization are oftentimes very much in line with Barry's. She argues, for instance, that "questions and confusions regarding oil's absence or presence in Turkey stem from its particular *material properties*" (emphasis added) and, further, that "resources and the underground are . . . brought into being through particular epistemological and technopolitical discourses and practices."

In her account of two wetland areas in Turkey, Caterina Scaramelli notes their elusive materiality, which she describes as "the outcome of complex and overlapping histories (of people, plants, animals, water, climate, and micro-organisms)." She argues that "the materiality of the wetlands is shaped by overlapping and sedimented layers of *material politics*" (emphasis in original). While being sensitive to the material quality of the marshes, the actors shaping these natural–social assemblages are humans: "Attending to the politics of materiality entails ethnographic attention towards decision-makers." Thus, her ethnography primarily focuses on "individuals and groups claiming to hold different kinds of wetland 'expertise.'"

Hande Özkan is concerned to show how the material properties of mud afford (and thus implicitly exclude) certain symbolic elaborations (e.g., the foresters' "imaginary of challenge and conquest"), and how the forest—as an organic–symbolic construct—came to "mediate the relationship between the state and society." More than the other chapters, in Özkan's chapter, classical anthropological concerns from symbolic anthropology and structuralism are revitalized in order to discuss the possibility of material politics.

For Fatih Tatari, *kaşar* cheese, milk, whey, and microbes are primarily materials *on which* scientists work, but which sometimes resist the experts' attempts to manipulate them. For example, it proved impossible to identify an autochthonous (Turkish) microbe involved in the production of the cheese. Material properties count and are not trivial. Overall, Tatari does not elaborate much on the participation of the material but does note that it will be important to pay "attention to the ethical concerns embedded in the web of relations among pastures, animals, milk, curd, cheese, dairy farmers, and cheesemakers."

All but Özkan's chapter consider the material to participate in webs of relations, or assemblages, and engage, though in different ways, with material properties and behaviors. Notably, they limit agency to a human capacity. Their analyses include the material, but it is not their contribution to the exploration of the material in "material politics" that is most remarkable. I think it is fair to say that these chapters are more concerned about politics than the material, and it is also here I find their more interesting contribution. The chapters to a larger or lesser extent address issues such as experts and knowledge, the state, the nation, civilization, and morals. The ethnographic findings here that most surprise and interest me is the fact that despite the Turkish state's increasingly authoritarian approach since approximately 2005, scientists and experts seem to seek and find ways to collaborate, to be "diplomats" between state institutions and citizens. The cases also show, however, that such collaboration often faces considerable challenges, especially related to narratives about the nation. Importantly, it is ethnography that makes these observations possible. Before discussing this further, let me first briefly contextualize these issues.

Scientists have taken on and been accorded special and important roles in modernization processes. Michel Foucault focused on scientists' and other experts' production of truths, often as means of control, surveillance, and self-management, especially emerging in association with a shift to new ways of configuring polities—what Foucault has called governmentality. Environmental anthropology and political ecology have drawn on these insights to show how experts have contributed to defusing environmental conflict by transmuting issues from political conflict to technical issues (see, e.g., Brosius 1999). Related, yet distinct, James Scott's approach in *Seeing Like a State* (1998) is more concerned about experts' roles in what he calls "high modernity": large-scale schemes with the ambition to improve the human condition. Experts, often within state institutions, were tasked with producing simplifications that made society legible in order for the social engineering state institutions to effectively act on society and create the new, modern society with economic development and material flourishing. In some respects, such schemes were utopian, and were often executed with violence and resulted in widespread suffering. Oftentimes such high-modernist schemes failed simply because the mismatches between experts' knowledges and visions, on the one hand, and the realities on the ground, on the other hand, were so significant that the schemes and plans simply could not be realized. Scott gave experts a bad press, and his perspectives found fertile ground among anthropologists whose sympathies usually lay with the nonexperts.

Scott's book has also informed studies of the Turkish modernization process, especially of the republican period up until 1980, but is also seen as relevant for understanding more recent large-scale projects (Belge 2011; Evered and Evered 2012; Üngör 2013; Akıncı et al. 2020; Knudsen 2009; Bozdoðan 2001; Harris 2012). It is common to associate governmentality and the high-modernist policies in Turkey with (especially the early) republican period and the nation-state with its ambition to modernize and standardize/homogenize society, including identities. However, as I have noted elsewhere, "there was no sudden change from sovereignty to governmentality with the establishment of the Republic . . . this change . . . took place well before the development of Turkish nationalism" (Knudsen 2009, 62). Thus, the desire for legibility, standardization, and large-scale projects, in which experts were allocated new and privileged roles, were initially independent of the idea of the nation. But "the new Republican state elite went much further than those of the late Ottoman Empire in envisioning a 'new' society, an ideal nation, and new kinds of men and women to populate it. The elite went so far as to design policies that were directed at reshaping subjects' selves" (Knudsen 2009, 63). As Kaşdoğan and Kurtiç mention in the introduction to this volume, this shift can be seen as a transition from a "shy modernity project" to a "radical modernity project," with the latter "going beyond the framework of high modernism" to nationalize the modern.

Scott inspired and legitimized anthropological studies of non-state/nonexpert knowledge, which to a large extent came to draw on ethnomethodology, cognitive anthropology, phenomenology, and studies of indigenous or traditional knowledge. Scott himself suggested the term "metis" for nonscientific, nonformal, situated and practical knowledge (Scott 1998, Chapter 9). Although not acknowledged by Scott himself, this framing of knowledge, which sometimes romanticizes nonscientific local knowledge, roughly overlaps with Tim Ingold's phenomenological approach, which distinguishes between being and seeing, seeing denoting the gaze from the outside, being the lived, practical knowledge that is often difficult to articulate (see, e.g., Ingold 2021). In Scott's rendering, metis becomes a particular mode of reasoning, often tacit, and distinct from scientific modes of reasoning. In effect, a veritable barrier is erected between science and other knowledges, based upon the way in which knowledge is held and used.

Both Scott and Ingold largely ignore the ways knowledge—including "being" or metis—becomes institutionalized. Furthermore, approaches as different as ANT and cognitive anthropology are critical of any unsymmetrical division into two major kinds of knowledges, supposedly being employed by scientists and laypeople, respectively. There is no Great Divide between science and other ways of knowing (Latour 1993), and all humans have the same cognitive capacities, and scientists employ the same cognitive registers as other humans, including practical, tacit skills (e.g., Shore 1996). While Scott's *Seeing Like a State* certainly provided novel and important theorizing of the dynamic between states and their populace under "high modernity," it also contributed to forming a rather limited picture of the expert as being arrogant, top-down, and uncooperative.

Now, it is long since the state seemed to have a monopoly on expertise and planning. Critical studies have to some extent argued that the shift to neoliberal policies since around 1980 resulted in a shift in the role of expertise. The state is no longer the last resort of authoritative knowledge. Knowledge production and science have to a larger extent become outsourced and distributed, for example by being embedded within large corporations or private think tanks. Consultancies emerge as "producers" of knowledge and managers of standards, metrics, and audits. Thus, knowledge, expertise, and scientists have increasingly come under the sway of capital. Sometimes, large NGOs also take on important roles in cultivating expertise. This does not mean, of course, that the state has disappeared, only changed its role. The neoliberal order is overseen by state institutions, and the state is in many respects at least as authoritarian as under "high modernity." Turkey comes to mind as an "exemplar" case of these developments (see, e.g., Öktem 2011).

With this shift away from the state as the primary mover of development and agent of modernization toward neoliberal ways of governance, a language of "responsibilization" has emerged or become intensified. The vocabulary and instruments of cooperation, collaboration, users, participation, stakeholders, and dialogue are spreading from development institutions and UN bodies to corporations and government agencies. This can, on the one hand, be considered a new turn of the governmentality screw and, on the other hand, as providing a real potential for empowerment (Callon, Lascoumes, and Barthe 2009).

In republican high-modernist Turkey, scientists—together with bureaucrats, teachers, the higher professions, and the military—became representatives and operators of the guardian state and state-led modernization. While experts, especially scientists, are generally held in high esteem in Turkey today, their authority is not as self-evident as it used to be, and their position in society is often pegged to nonprofessional identities within an increasingly politicized identity landscape. The consequences of this are clearly seen in Oğuz's chapter, which tells the story of how geologists become caught up in national narratives and conspiracy theories about oil and the nation. Especially telling is how their professionally informed commitment to be honest about uncertainty and the limits of their knowledge results in an "indeterminacy [that] has been fueling political imageries and projects in Turkey." In this context, geologists could only remain professional by maneuvering skillfully and diplomatically, so to speak, between different positions.

In her chapter, Scaramelli also describes how the natural scientists and experts from NGOs she worked with coped with a contested landscape as they had to relate to various forms of local resistance. Yet, the experts were also influenced by the international space within which they operate to try to cooperate with local farmers in the delta. Writing an "application for a civil society dialogue project funded by the European Union," Scaramelli together with other experts designed a proposal where they imagined "civil society, farmers, and governmental institutions would work together and strengthen their collaboration around participatory and sustainable wetland management." However, as local realities and national politics made such cooperation difficult, and as the experts worked to uphold a social–moral boundary between themselves and the ignorant rural population, the ideals of participation and cooperation were difficult to realize. There seems to be tension between internationally circulating ideals of participation and collaboration, on the one hand, and the codes and mundane practices that reproduce "subject positions of expertise" and moral boundaries between experts and nonexperts.

While cooperation is uncertain and difficult in the cases related by Oguz and Scaramelli, in Tatari's chapter, the scientists emerge as skillful and often successful "diplomats," creating new knowledge in cooperation with farmers and others—in effect destabilizing "the epistemic boundaries between scientific and traditional knowledges." Tatari convincingly describes in detail how scientists work at the interface between different scientific traditions and the knowledges involved in traditional cheesemaking. Tatari's approach does not discredit scientific knowledge nor romanticize traditional cheesemakers' practices, but does emphasize the need for scientists to be nonrigid and curious about other ways of knowing—what one of his (nonscientist) interlocutors terms "carved reasoning."

Özkan shows how "forestry in Turkey is still shaped by policies and practices established in the early republican period," in effect demonstrating the continued importance of state expertise as agents of modernization and civilization. To some extent, this seems to be the case also in the stories told by the other chapters, although experts now to a larger extent seem to have to relate directly to internationally circulating models and knowledges, whether EU-backed programs for local participation or international dairy or geological science. However, the shift from an early Republican period with a hegemonic state with its all-powerful experts to a more fluid or heterogeneous contemporary situation may have been exaggerated. Using archival material, Özkan demonstrates that even during the early Republic, local populations were not passive recipients of state policies but creatively challenged the elite. What made this counter-hegemonic move possible, she argues, is the polyvocality or indeterminacy of language, its lack of fixed meaning. Thus, distancing herself explicitly from Scott's "dyadic conceptualization of elites versus the people," Özkan sketches a discursive space that facilitates resistance, interaction, and participation.

Thus, in all these chapters, we see scientists, experts, and nonexperts maneuvering and negotiating their knowledges and identities within cultural and material landscapes, which more often than not stimulate collaboration, adaption, and flexibility, like the forest guard who chose not to interpret the law literally because that made governance difficult. Yet, moral landscapes and knowledge landscapes continue to overlap, and experts' status and roles are inextricably bound up with identity politics, whether as state missionaries of civilization or as representatives of secularism. One major argument in my work on fishers and marine scientists (Knudsen 2009) was that identity framed the way experts and laypeople interact over knowledge, with scientists typically denigrating laypeople as uncivilized and ignorant, while fishers considered scientists—as a class—as corrupt "eaters." It is notable that this did not relate so much to the secular-Islam divide, although science for some was equated with the Kemalist modernization project. Now, increasingly, it seems to be the narrative about the nation that constitutes the primary frame of reference.

These chapters demonstrate that experts in Turkey clearly find room to collaborate with nonexperts. But if there is a shift toward better scope for collaboration, what has caused that, and what are the consequences? Is it the neoliberal context that causes the experts to seek cooperation, to be diplomats? Has the curtailing of the secular Kemalist hegemony opened new roles for experts and created new conditions for interaction between experts and nonexperts? Or has the cooperation been there all the time but not been visible—as indicated by Özkan? Also, the chapters demonstrate the continued importance of state-employed experts despite the neoliberalization of knowledge.

When it comes to what effects experts' efforts at collaboration have, two observations are in place. First, it seems to be primarily at the level of mundane, everyday practices that collaboration seems to have a real effect, such as in dairy experts' interaction with dairy farmers, or forest guards' flexible accommodation in the space between the state and the rural population. This is in line with Scott's thinking: invisible social processes of accommodation and silent resistance made society work despite and beyond the wild ambitions of large-scale modernizing projects. But another take on this is also possible. Without experts and nonexperts necessarily having the same interests or sharing the same fundamental truths, maybe collaboration is not necessarily "balanced," and the result is in the "middle" (as in a compromise). Like Özkan, Erdem Evren (2022) argues against Scott's dichotomous thinking. Yet, his aim is to show that "capitalist development works on and through the desires of its target communities" (Evren 2022, 4). The local residents he worked with in Yusufeli in effect participate in and speculate on the destruction of the very land on which they have previously relied for their livelihoods. He argues that it is the hegemony established by the successful conservative-nationalist political project that makes this a rational strategy. Hardly any topic relating to material politics in today's Turkey is unaffected by debates about the motherland, separatism, and traitors (Knudsen 2016). We can only speculate, but it may seem reasonable to think that collaboration between experts and nonexperts is easier in the case of cheesemaking than in the more politicized fields of oil geology or conservation sites in deltas. However, even "microbial dairy science [is cast] in nationalist terms," indicating the almost all-pervasive character of the nationalist narrative in contemporary Turkey.

References

Akıncı, Zeynep S., Arda Bilgen, Antònia Casellas, and Joost Jongerden. 2020. "Development through Design: Knowledge, Power, and Absences in the Making of Southeastern Turkey," *Geoforum* 114: 181–8.

Barry, Andrew. 2013. *Material Politics. Disputes along the Pipeline*, Chichester: John Wiley & Sons.

Belge, Ceren. 2011. "State Building and the Limits of Legibility. Kinship Networks and Kurdish Resistance in Turkey," *International Journal of Middle East Studies* 43 (1): 95–114.

Bozdoğan, Sibel. 2001. *Modernism and Nation-Building. Turkish Architectural Culture in the Early Republic*, Seattle: University of Washington Press.

Brosius, J. Peter. 1999. "Green Dots, Pink Hearts: Displacing Politics from the Malaysian Rain Forest," *American Anthropologist* 101 (1): 36–57.

Callon, Michel. 1984. "Some Elements of a Sociology of Translation: Domestication of the Scallops and the Fishermen of St Brieuc Bay," *The Sociological Review* 32 (1): 196–233.

Callon, Michel, Pierre Lascoumes, and Barthe, Yannick. 2009. *Acting in an Uncertain World. An Essay on Technical Democracy*, Cambridge, MA: The MIT Press.

Evered, Kyle T. and Emine Ö. Evered. 2012. "State, Peasant, Mosquito: The Biopolitics of Public Health Education and Malaria in Early Republican Turkey," *Political Geography* 31 (5): 311–23.

Evren, Erdem. 2022. *Bulldozer Capitalism. Accumulation, Ruination, and Dispossession in Northeastern Turkey*, New York: Berghahn Books.

Harris, Leila M. 2012. "State as Socionatural Effect: Variable and Emergent Geographies of the State in Southeastern Turkey," *Comparative Studies of South Asia, Africa and the Middle East* 32 (1): 25–39.

Ingold, Tim, 2021. *The Perception of the Environment. Essays on Livelihood, Dwelling and Skill*, London: Routledge.

Knudsen, Ståle. 2009. *Fishers and Scientists in Modern Turkey. The Management of Resources, Knowledge, and Identity on the Eastern Black Sea Coast*, Oxford: Berghahn Books.

Knudsen, Ståle. 2016. "Protests Against Energy Projects in Turkey: Environmental Activism Above Politics?" *British Journal of Middle Eastern Studies* 43 (3): 302–23.

Knudsen, Ståle. 2023. "Critical Realism in Political Ecology: An Argument against Flat Ontology," *Journal of Political Ecology* 30 (1): 1–22.

Latour, Bruno. 1993. *We Have Never Been Modern*, trans. C. Porter, New York: Harvester Whetsheaf.

Law, John. 2004. *After Method. Mess in Social Science Research*, London: Routledge.

Mol, Annemarie. 2002. *The Body Multiple: Ontology in Medical Practice*, Durham: Duke University Press.

Mouffe, Chantal. 2005. *On the Political*, London: Routledge.

Öktem, Kerem. 2011. *Angry Nation. Turkey since 1989*, London: Zed Books.

Scott, James C. 1998. *Seeing Like a State. How Certain Schemes to Improve the Human Condition Have Failed*, New Haven and London: Yale University Press.

Shore, Bradd. 1996. *Culture in Mind. Cognition, Culture and the Problem of Meaning*, Oxford: Oxford University Press.

Üngör, Uğur Ü. 2013. "Creative Destruction: Shaping a High-Modernist City in Interwar Turkey," *Journal of Urban History* 39 (2): 297–314.

Part III

Translating Techniques and Expertise

10

Smoking under a Volcano

Cold War Base Life in Turkish Thrace

Sertaç Şen

I met Sermet for the first time at the local Hunters Club in Çorlu, my field site in Turkey. After a barrage of questions he asked to gauge my social background, political coordinates, and personal motivations, Sermet's stoic expression broke into a sanguine smile before he rolled out an apology: "Sorry, I did not mean to pry; but it is just a conditioning that the job brings: one has to get clearance every time, all the time."[1] His job was the reason why I sought an interview with him. A houseman who followed American troops from one installation to another for almost thirty years, he is a rare member of a generation still alive to tell the days of the Americans in Turkey during the Cold War. In our interview at the same spot a few meetings later, I asked Sermet about the nature of his job on the military base in Çorlu. At one point in his response, he leaned as if to whisper: "They stored nuclear weapons down the airfield. It was a secret, none of our business. I was just supposed to do my laundry, get my Salems, and wait for my yellow envelopes [checks]. That's all there is to it."

Imparted with a furtive pleasure still extant three decades into retirement, Sermet's words chart out the complex affective landscape that many civilians who worked on US military bases in Turkey navigated: confusion, material expectation, the pleasure of access, the burden of secrecy, the sting of infantilization, and the schizophrenic experience of fulfilling chores at the geopolitical seams of the Cold War, which could burst at any time. More importantly, his reference to nuclear weapons, laundry, and foreign cigarettes signals how his life and the lives of communities adjacent to overseas US military bases are shaped by the material encounters that the Cold War occasioned and circumscribed.

Hosting an American custodial detachment from the late 1950s to the early 1990s, the setting of this research, Çorlu, is an important garrison town in Turkish Thrace where such encounters played out. Around the time Daniel Lerner published his infamous *The Passing of Traditional Society*, in which he found in the transformation of the small Turkish village of Balgat a parable laying the foundation of his modernization theory (1958), Çorlu, another modest Turkish settlement of about twenty thousand people, welcomed its first American troops to their new base.[2] Along with the base came high hopes for the contributions it could bring to the town's socioeconomic outlook, the Turkish military capabilities, and the country's modernization. More modest in scale, at least at first glance, was the primary mission of the American detachment stationed at the airbase, Det-74, which was to provide field artillery training for Turkish units and oversee the nuclear-capable Honest John rockets in Çorlu.[3]

Using archival records and interviews with Turkish and American soldiers as well as civilian base employees who worked on the base, this research pieces together the story of the US–Turkish partnership in Turkish Thrace to trace "the co-production of materials and politics" during the Cold War (Kaşdoğan and Kurtiç, this volume). In reconstructing the story from multiple perspectives and beyond the confines of methodological nationalism, it engages with the local ramifications of global US military presence and discusses the ways in which everyday relations between a constellation of transnational actors comprising nuclear hosts and guests inform political subjectivities and local socioeconomic orders. The chapter argues that the materiality of the atom and the technopolitics of nuclear weapons defined the terms of the nuclear partnership between Turkish and American actors on the ground and informed new political subjectivities. It demonstrates how the translation of technical expertise and nuclear logics across political and institutional borders was a process fraught with uncertainty, tension, and contestation. It also argues that the immaterial and illicit exchanges generated by the Cold War were as consequential in shaping local socioeconomic structures as the material and licit relations authorized by the nuclear partnership.

Yet, to understand these products of the Cold War, one must first answer a basic question: What warranted the extension of the US baseworld and nuclear power to a seemingly innocuous and unprepossessing Turkish town like Çorlu? To contextualize the expansion of the US military enterprise with its attendant products, I will make a detour into the history of Turkish–American relations while situating the significance of the Turkish Straits and Thrace within this historical trajectory.

Securing an Imperial Chokepoint

The diplomatic ties between the United States and Turkey date back to the early nineteenth-century Ottoman Empire (Howard 1976). However, it was only after the Second World War that the United States and Turkey were drawn to one another as strategic allies on the international stage. Although Turkey was made a beneficiary of the 1941 Lend-Lease Act, whereby the United States released war supplies to countries deemed vital to its national security, Turkey's "active neutrality" during the war constrained the scope of cooperation between the two countries (Deringil 1989). However, the shifting balance of power in postwar Europe cemented their rudimentary bond.

As the postwar West celebrated the defeat of the Axis with great fanfare, Turkey was dreading possible Soviet aggression against its territorial integrity. The war-torn British were slowly withdrawing from the global stage to mend their domestic wounds, and nothing spelled worse news for the Turkish ruling elite than an emboldened Soviets with greater capacity for diplomatic and military maneuvering around Turkey's territorial edges. Coming from a generation that played an active role in the ten-year war between 1912 and 1922 that left the debris of an empire in its wake, the Turkish elite were trained to be cautious when the imperial pecking order was being reshuffled. The postwar Soviet actions soon confirmed their doubts.

The first diplomatic shots were fired on March 19, 1945, when the USSR informed Turkey with a note that it would not renew the 1925 Soviet–Turkish Non-Aggression Pact beyond its expiration date in November, announcing the onset of a Soviet war of nerves.[4] On June 7, 1945, Selim Sarper, Turkey's ambassador to Moscow, visited Vyacheslav Molotov, the Soviet minister of foreign affairs, to sway the Soviet decision. In the meeting, Molotov verbally intimated to Sarper that Turkey had to commit sacrifices on the altar of friendship,[5] including a favorable change in the Turkish Straits regime, the joint defense of the Straits, and land concessions near the Turkish border with the Caucasus.[6] A month later, at Potsdam, Stalin himself stoked the Turkish fear that a Soviet pincer movement was in play as he put out feelers to Churchill and Truman about border rectification and the Straits Question.[7]

The crisis escalated to a boiling point when the USSR delivered two diplomatic notes in July and September 1946 to formalize what had hitherto remained unofficial Soviet demands. The Soviet requests for a modification of the Montreux Convention and the establishment of joint defense installations in the area of the Straits fully fanned into flames the dormant cinders of a sovereignty crisis in Turkey.[8] With the red threat looming large, neighboring Bulgaria falling under the Soviet sphere of influence, Greece devolving deeper into civil war, and Iran barely avoiding a drawn-out Soviet occupation with the backing of the UN, Turkey hardly felt more secure in the postwar period than it did during the war. The regional instability was so palpable that the Turkish military had not fully demobilized to assume its postwar peace posture as late as 1948, with the bulk of its forces concentrated on Turkey's northwestern and eastern borders with the USSR.[9] The Turkish political and military elite understood that they had to navigate in a postwar gravity that weighed heavily around the Straits Question. To steer clear of troubled waters and clashing rocks, they sought to recruit Western allies.[10]

Fortunately for the Turkish elite, their efforts to insert the country into the good graces of Western powers coincided with a critical turn in US foreign policy, through which traditional American isolationism regarding the affairs of the Old World gave way to global interventionism. Accordingly, the number of US overseas military bases, which tallied at a meager fourteen in 1938, skyrocketed to two thousand in 1948 (Lutz 2009, 10). In light of the new policy, Turkey increasingly began to feature in US policy documents due to its possession of territories with immense geopolitical value, most notably the Straits (Kuniholm 2014 [1980]). If Turkey represented to American policymakers a prospective strategic partner for containing Soviet influence and securing global hegemony, the United States began to represent to many Turks a benevolent ally who could stave off Soviet bullying, one who would also potentially be less intrusive in domestic affairs than the Great Powers of the Old World.

In this context of public trepidation, sovereign anxiety, and imperial aspirations pivoting on the Straits Question, a classical act of American gunboat diplomacy found great purchase in Turkey.[11] In April 1946, the battleship USS *Missouri* showed up on the Bosporus under the official pretext of bringing home the body of a Turkish ambassador who had passed away two years earlier. The *Missouri* visit was a bellwether for the policy convergence between the two countries around the Straits problem. It was followed by US support to Turkey against the Soviet notes of 1946.[12] The American response was also swift when the British informed them of their intention to cease financial aid to Turkey and Greece on February 21, 1947.[13] Nearly a month later, President Truman delivered his historic speech before a joint session of Congress, asking for the release of $400 million and the deployment of material as well as technical assistance to Greece and Turkey: a small investment with tremendous implications, Truman envisioned, for world peace and freedom. The Joint American Military Mission for Aid to Turkey (JAMMAT) was inaugurated on July 12, 1947, to oversee the American material and technical assistance Congress authorized.[14] When Secretary of State George Marshall announced the Marshall Plan at Harvard University in the same summer, Turkey was also included in the program for the economic recovery of war-torn Europe, no small feat for a country that entered the war at its eleventh hour.[15]

To further cooperate with the United States and obtain membership in the nascent NATO, Turkey reciprocated these acts of American magnanimity by sending an infantry brigade to help the war effort in Korea.[16] The bonding that the Truman Doctrine, the Marshall Plan, and the Korean War solidified culminated in an invitation to Turkey to join NATO in October 1951, foreshadowing Turkey's official entry into the alliance on February 18, 1952. The following years saw a flurry of legislative activity in the Turkish parliament to bring the country into accord with NATO.[17] While the ratification of multilateral agreements ensured compliance with NATO structures, a series of bilateral agreements[18] and letter exchanges[19] paved the way for the foreign basing of American troops and nuclear weapons in Turkey.

From its embryonic beginnings in the 1940s to its maturation under NATO, the Turkish Straits remained a focal point for the Turkish–American rapprochement. Being a naval chokepoint that obstructed Soviet power projection to the Mediterranean and the Middle East, the Turkish Straits was the soft underbelly of the USSR, hence the crown jewel of the newfound partnership (Vali 1972). From the Soviet standpoint, the Turkish Straits were what the Panama Canal was to the United States or the Suez to the British.[20] It was a geographical bottleneck without the possession of which, in Stalin's words, "a small state [like Turkey] . . . held a great state [like the USSR] by the throat and gave it no outlet," or much earlier in Tsar Alexander's words, Russia could not become a "master in [its] own house."[21] All in all, the Straits constituted an imperial frontier where Soviet aspirations met American containment. Therefore, all key NATO strategy documents from Turkey's NATO accession through the 1960s, without exception, prioritized the denial of the Straits to enemy forces as a strategic objective of "overriding importance."[22]

If the Straits marked a huge geopolitical gain in allied hands, the narrow strip of land spanning Turkey's northwestern borderlands between the Bosporus and Dardanelles, Turkish Thrace, marked a major liability for its defense. Contiguous with Bulgaria and Greek Thrace through a narrow corridor, flanked by water, elongated in form, and lacking natural barriers, depth, and infrastructure for adequate defense,

Turkish Thrace gave many headaches to international defense planners. Early military assessments of the land ranged from completely indefensible to liable to withdrawal and delaying action with little hope of retention under pressure.[23] Upon Turkey's NATO entry, high-ranking NATO commanders, including SACEUR Matthew Ridgway himself,[24] paid inspection trips to Thrace one after another,[25] all anticipating withdrawal and evacuation in the event of a Soviet attack. Even then, they feared that withdrawing elements would be exposed to the enemy's exploitation forces for near lack of defensive positions to fall back on in a narrow peninsula with limited infrastructure for evacuation, and a reprisal of Dunkirk in the Turkish Straits with Turkish fishermen could hardly form the basis of a solid exit strategy. Ultimately, the Turkish Straits and Thrace presented defense planners with a dilemma, for they were both indispensable and indefensible.

However, the military balance of power that occasioned the reservations of early NATO commanders about the Straits and Thrace on the principles of conventional warfare shifted with the adoption of a nuclear-oriented forward defense strategy in the mid-1950s.[26] As early as December 1955, Ridgway's replacement as SACEUR, Alfred Gruenther, entertained the idea of a nuclear solution for the defense of the Straits by recommending the earmarking of two Honest John and two Corporal battalions to Western Turkey.[27] In March 1957, his successor and the chief architect of the NATO atomic stockpile, Lauris Norstad,[28] pressed for the urgent deployment of a minimum of one Honest John battalion to establish a ground atomic delivery force in what he deemed the southern flank's most vulnerable portion, the Turkish Straits.[29] The decision to establish a NATO atomic stockpile under SACEUR's command at the Paris Summit of December 16–19, 1957, lifted the last bureaucratic hurdle for the widespread nuclearization of Turkey and the rest of Europe.[30] Turkey accepted the deployment of an Honest John battalion on March 24, 1958.[31] With the acceptance of a nuclear fix to the problem of the Straits' defense, a new atomic gaze recast the attenuated landmass of Thrace from a defensive liability to a corridor of temptation convenient to the corralling of enemy forces for atomic destruction.[32] Accordingly, a few months after the first atomic deployments to Turkey, nuclear-capable Honest Johns were shipped to Çorlu in May 1959.[33]

Material Politics of Nuclear Power

The American presence in Çorlu predates the dispatch of Honest John. Yet, it was not the Americans themselves but their machinery and goods that first appeared in Çorlu throughout the 1940s and 1950s. After a government announcement for building a workshop to oversee the maintenance of agricultural machinery transferred to Thrace via the Marshall Plan, American tractors began to roam the streets and farmyards of Çorlu.[34] Catching wind of the opportunities agricultural mechanization might bring about, local entrepreneurs opened gas stations to refuel vehicles and workshops to repair and sell farm equipment. Schoolchildren consumed copious amounts of American powdered milk at school for nutrition, and the only local newspaper of the town, *Çorlu Ekspres*, pulled content from United States Information Service (USIS) to fill its meager four pages before the arrival of Americans.[35]

Despite the proliferation of the material and visual signs of American life, the Americans largely remained absent in Thrace until the late 1950s.[36] The notable exceptions were oil companies prospecting the Thracian soil for natural resources and the military personnel flying to the region for inspection trips and NATO exercises. However, the Honest John deployments to Turkey for the defense of the Straits and Thrace ushered in an influx of American personnel to the region. The Americans were primarily tasked with training the Turkish Army in nuclear field artillery and taking custody of nuclear weapons. With their deployment, Çorlu became a nuclear storage site and a training ground for the newly minted Honest John rocket battalions.[37]

Frank was a member of one of these earliest training teams, FTT-1A1.[38] He arrived in Çorlu in July 1958 after a long island-hopping trip across the Atlantic. An artillery weather observer by training, he was one of some twenty members of the American training section who worked with Turkish soldiers. Besides the training section, nearly a hundred Americans functioned in the support and munitions security sections, and another dozen staffed the Coast Guard unit at the nearby town of Ereğli. Billeted in Belgian Quonsets with intermittent heating, little sanitation, poor insulation, and no potable water, the living conditions on the base remained harsh until the 1980s. Frank described his transition from his temperate post at Fort Bragg to the frigid flatlands of Thrace as one "from rags to rags, and damp ones in that." For the enlisted and officers alike, Çorlu deserved its status as a hardship tour.[39]

On the receiving end of the training effort stood the newly formed Honest John battalions, manned by mandatory Turkish conscripts and led by idealist officers.[40] Quickly coming under the spell of "the nuclear sublime," that is, the awe and fear nuclear technologies are likely to evoke in spectators, the officer class, in particular, was enthused about Honest John (Masco 2006). Viewing nuclear weapons as a transcendental signifier of modernity, most officers ascribed poetic significance to the emergent nuclear infrastructures in Turkey, including Honest John, in the belief that their delivery meant not only a revolutionary step for the now-nuclear Turkish military but also a nod from the civilized West for Turkey's acquired status of modernity and Western identity.[41] The high morale and the spirit of camaraderie that nuclear deployments animated among the troops thus carried over to routine military drills, target practices, and war exercises. For most officers who served in a rocket battalion in Çorlu, the atmosphere surrounding those early days of American assistance was one of friendly competition, intense learning, and zealous determination.

However, from the outset, the nuclear partnership between Turkish and American troops was marred by problems of a technopolitical kind. First, Honest John fell short of many Turkish soldiers' initial expectations despite its awe-inspiring destructive capabilities. A product of the Surface-to-Surface Missile development program that the US Army had inaugurated in the 1950s in response to an existential crisis it underwent under Eisenhower's presidency, Honest John was essentially a nuclear-capable technology for battlefield use.[42] Powered by a solid propellant, it was a tactical nuclear weapon with low yield, little maneuverability, long assembly time, and, worst of all, short range.[43] What is more, Honest John was rather a free rocket than a guided missile. As Frank's expertise indicates, its effective delivery depended on a series of meticulous calculations about the weather and battlefield conditions. Even then, the effects of radioactive fallout would be difficult to estimate, with grim possibilities for proximate troops and civilians.[44] Honest John's technical shortcomings, which, from the perspective of Americans, did not necessarily nullify its deterrent capability, thus sparked many questions for Turkish soldiers about its reliability and practicability.[45] For Honest John comprised not only wires, metals, and fissile materials that went into its making but also a complex world of assumptions and nuclear logics, most notably that of deterrence, that proved difficult to transfer across national and institutional boundaries.

Second, the deployment of Honest John under NATO atomic stockpile arrangements stipulated that the nuclear warheads would remain in the custody of American troops while delivery systems would remain in the possession of the host nation. These weapons also came with locking security systems such as Permissive Action Links that were devised to prevent unauthorized detonations, including their use by host nations without US approval.[46] That nuclear sharing was not unconditional and came with many strings attached was a point that initially eluded and eventually alienated many Turkish soldiers.[47] Many locations on the base, most importantly Special Ammunition Storage Sites where nuclear munitions were stored, remained out of bounds for them, and consequently, many felt that they were trained in a technology they were astronomically unlikely to access and use themselves. For the disillusioned camp, the emergent nuclear infrastructures in Turkey—with their attendant launchers, missiles, nuclear warheads, and storage sites—carried a paternalistic politics based on spatial segregation and hierarchy, the infantilizing and disempowering effects of which ran counter to their expectations and aspirations.[48] Providing an exception in American technical assistance where a more hands-on approach to the cultivation of expertise was encouraged, in this case, it appeared that a hands-off approach to learning was preferred. Unlike other forms of civilian and military assistance, where Americans often urged their Turkish counterparts to get their hands dirty, nuclear technical assistance sought to discipline Turkish soldiers to keep their powder dry.[49] As such, the materiality of the atom set an internal limit to the promise of nuclear modernity it signified.

Yet, the material politics of nuclear power in Turkey did not concern only the conduct of politics under the specter of nuclear destruction or the scripting of politics into atomic artifacts and infrastructures from above. Instead, similar to politics and technoscientific processes enacted through expert collaboration and encounters in cheesemaking (Tatari, this volume), these artifacts and infrastructures also generated politics on the ground, which reverberated back into larger political processes. For example, Hasan Kıyafet, who served in the late 1960s as a translator for a custodial detachment, described his time with Americans as a turning point for his political becoming.[50] "I came to Çorlu as an unexperienced leftist," he told in our interview, "and left it as a seasoned socialist." Similarly, Sami, an NCO who worked with Americans in the 1970s, expressed how his experiences in an Honest John battalion inspired his nationalist creed: "If you tell Turkish soldiers 'Here, take this celery stalk,' then they tell you in turn 'Hey Mister, take a walk.'" Thus, nuclear cooperation trained Turkish soldiers not only in weapon proficiency or military expertise in the nuclear age. It also trained many in new political subjectivities aligned with nationalist and leftist ideologies.

A Town Goes Nuclear (?)

John Tumpane was a family partner in the Tumpane Company, which won the base maintenance contracts to support the American personnel in Turkey from the late 1950s to the 1970s. He came to Turkey in July 1958, just like Frank, but he was to work in a civilian capacity under his brother, who acted as the company's general manager. In his autobiography, Tumpane recounted his endeavors to issue a driving license in Turkey, a mighty bureaucratic struggle at which his Turkish aide Abdul scoffed. Abdul suggested that his American driver's license and a carton of Salem cigarettes from the PX would suffice, but Tumpane was adamant about keeping his business untarnished by bribery or quid pro quo.[51] After a few visits to the traffic bureau, however, his friends congratulated Tumpane teasingly for switching to Salems (1981, 15–21). Tumpane's story is illustrative of two points about technical military assistance. First, American assistance to Turkey generated a cobweb of relations that went beyond military encounters on and around the base. Second, it set into motion unintended flows and illicit exchanges that the original contract had not prioritized, foreseen, or even allowed.

The deployment of nuclear weapons, training teams, and custodial detachments had consequences reaching beyond the base, differentially incurring costs and benefits for civilian populations. The impacts widely varied along the axes of class, gender, profession, social capital, and site of residence. For agricultural populations in the countryside, Honest John brought few opportunities and much trouble. Field maneuvers, military convoys, and artillery practice left razed fields, damaged crops, broken roads, unexploded ordnance, and mutilated bodies in their wake.[52] Military traffic and collateral damage from artillery fire became significant causes of unnatural death in Thrace, with the latter causing havoc in the countryside where most firing ranges were located. Some injuries were due to poor villagers scavenging for ordnance scrap.[53]

For urban inhabitants, the influx of salaried military classes to operate the town's military bases compounded the existing housing problem. Because the nuclear partnership was essentially a military enterprise among men of different nationalities, it provided little, if any, direct benefits to women.[54] Local women in Çorlu remained, somewhat surprisingly, insulated from the gendered violence that overseas military bases often bring to host communities due to the town's proximity to Istanbul and its dearth of entertainment facilities available to soldiers (Akibayashi and Takazato 2009; Cheng 2010; Enloe 2000). "You need girls, clubs, hotels to get people out of the base," an enlisted interviewee asserted, and Çorlu had almost none of these. However, as troops rotated in and out of the field, the base also presented a boon for males in certain businesses and local labor markets.

Because base maintenance was contracted to American firms, such as the Tumpane Company, local military contractors could not tap into much of the resources unlocked by the nuclear partnership.[55] However, these firms recruited employees from the local labor force, and soon after the arrival of Americans, a small civilian platoon of cooks, aides, janitors, houseboys, barbers, tailors, and drivers began to commute to the base to maintain day-to-day operations. The job's appeal, first and foremost, was financial because the wage gap between the local civilian and military markets was vast. In the most dramatic case, Sermet remembered that his first payment for houseboy services was a hundred times more than what he used to get as an apprentice tailor. Upon receiving his first paycheck, he was shocked to see that "a man like himself, who used to hustle for a few liras a month, could earn that much money on the base without breaking a sweat." In the words of Sabri, another base employee who worked as a tailor, the base gave some locals bread—of the unsliced, rich, and colossal sort (Figure 10.1).

However, the spoils of Cold War nuclear readiness did not neatly trickle down to the town. Instead, they were channeled through kinship and neighborhood ties, creating and remolding patronage networks within the community. In contradiction to the principles of modern bureaucracy that American personnel preached to their Turkish colleagues, nepotism was in full force in decisions regarding base maintenance. Base commanders and managers relied on word-of-mouth and existing patronage networks whenever there was a job opening. Gatekeeping and mobbing were rampant, with sometimes local employees leading the charge. As a result, nearly all base employees were from the same neighborhood, most being first- and second-degree kin. Nuri, a

Figure 10.1 Base employees at a dinner. Courtesy Image was acquired by the author from the private archives/records of a deceased base employee and is published with his permission.

kitchen aide, succinctly put the centrality of kinship to employment as follows: "It was like the days of the sultanate; if your father left, you replaced him."

Yet the boundaries between the base and the town were not only porous to a select group of people. Along with people, material goods moved in and out of the base. Although nuclear weapons formed the material basis of technical assistance, many civilians and soldiers were more interested in the quotidian materials that the American military presence made available in Çorlu. Most of these goods, like adult magazines, filtered cigarettes, soft beverages, liquors, and canned food, were officially slated for American use only. However, they were routinely and illicitly obtained through quid pro quo relations, traveling along elusive itineraries contingent on unauthorized relations of exchange. For this reason, when Hasan Kıyafet started his duty on the base as a translator, he was warned by a Turkish NCO that he should prepare himself to become a tradesman in addition to his military duties because a man in his position would leave Americans "with either money or honor, not both."

In a period when Turkey had not fully transitioned to a liberal market economy, American goods that the base introduced to Çorlu carried a charm beyond their use-value. Many Americans were quite cognizant of the power of ordinary items like a carton of cigarettes. They frequently used these fetishized commodities to curry favor, lubricate bureaucratic cogs, and preempt resistance. For instance, a base commander interviewee conceded that he provided whiskey to the local head of the police on more than one occasion to extricate his personnel from delicate legal situations, affirming the routine violation of regulations concerning material exchange. Similar to Bergama locals' navigation of the extractive uncanny and slow violence resulting from transnational processes (Dinç, this volume), exchanges of American goods in Çorlu also caused divisions within the local community. For example, as the Harb-İş labor union's liaison on the base, Nuri once attempted to organize workers to secure union protection and benefits for all the civilian base employees.[56] However, he was "sold out" by some of his fellows "for a pack of cigarettes from the PX." Similarly, Sermet confirmed the power of quotidian goods in getting Americans what they wanted, narrating: "Say, a guy is coming to take over watch duties, and an American wants to be left alone. He throws at the guy [guard] the May issue of the [Playboy] magazine, and the guy looks at it all day. Yeah! Throw in a can of Coke too. How much does Turkey cost?"

Yet the locals were not simply hapless natives spellbound by shiny trinkets and cargo cult objects thrown at them. It was not only American goods that traveled across civil–military boundaries. Instead, an unstructured network of petty smuggling ran both ways. Many base employees and even regular civilians followed Americans to barracks, firing ranges, and NATO exercises to peddle merchandise appealing to soldiers' personal needs and curiosities. They curated rugs, jewelry, food, and clothing to incite Americans' consumerist and orientalist sensibilities. In turn, they sought and often secured access to the world of American goods circulating across the base exchange network.

Once these items trespassed civil–military boundaries, their travels often continued along indeterminate and unpredictable trajectories. On the one hand,

Americans usually treated the objects they procured from locals as gifts and keepsakes. On the other hand, the goods that traveled out of the base were often caught in larger networks of exchange in which various civilian and military actors deployed them to different social, economic, and political ends. Many base employees and civilians brokered the allure of American goods into local power and prestige, exchanging cigarettes, alcohol, and insider information for money, patronage, status, and favors. For example, Mustafa, a base driver, boasted how he exchanged an American bicycle for the first refrigerator ever entering a Çorlu household. Another employee confided that his political debut happened over drinks he supplied to the local head of a political party. Yet another acknowledged how he frequently utilized foreign cigarettes to settle political and legal disputes. Many locals were not even privy to the nuclear buildup within a few kilometers of their houses. Nevertheless, that did not stop them from regularly visiting the local Hunters Club, where illicitly obtained American goods were periodically auctioned. While Honest John, the material linchpin of the nuclear partnership in Thrace, lay dormant, other objects that the base introduced to local lives animated a whole world of transactions around which the Cold War in Çorlu played out.

Honest Johns were discontinued in Turkey in the 1980s. The last American units left Çorlu in 1991. The nuclear cooperation in Çorlu produced neither bunkers nor haunting memories of civil defense exercises against nuclear detonations, nor any visible signs of "the nuclear uncanny" unsettling the lives of locals living around nuclear facilities (Masco 2006).[57] However, it has left behind significant social, political, and infrastructural legacies. The airbase where Americans were stationed has been repurposed to a new end, becoming the only airport in Thrace following its conversion to a joint-use facility for civilian and military purposes. The nuclear partnership opened channels for the negotiation of local authority through the circulation of ordinary objects, which derived their social efficacy and material worth from their foreign origins (Sahlins 2010). The only object that proved challenging to harness to the local political economy, Honest John, is but a fleeting memory in today's Çorlu except for a few people who are old or epistemically privileged enough to remember. By contrast, many of my interviewees still reminisce about how ordinary objects that the Cold War thrust upon their lives took on indeterminate trajectories of exchange, attesting to the primacy of ordinariness in the politics of the nuclear world (MacKenzie 1990, 404).

Yet, if one still insists on seeking out a proverbial Grocer, in the manner of Lerner, to dramatize the local transformation of Çorlu, perhaps one needs to look no further than Irfan. Irfan was the owner and manager of the first "modern" supermarket in Çorlu. His success as a businessman was rooted not so much in individual psychic mobility, restless sensibility, or greater capacity for empathy as Lerner would have us believe. Instead, the supermarket's success primarily owed to the military contracts Irfan secured for the provision of consumables during periodic NATO exercises in Thrace. Everyday relations and on-the-ground material transactions that the Cold War wittingly or unwittingly jolted into existence have changed his fortunes—and the fortunes of Çorlu, which has transformed from a modest garrison town to the most populous settlement in contemporary Thrace.

Acknowledgment

The author wishes to thank all the Çorlulu interlocutors, both Turkish and American, in this study for generously sharing their life histories and time. He is also grateful to the editors of this volume, as well as to Matthew Gutmann, Catherine Lutz, Jessa Leinaweaver, Ali Sipahi, Yasemin Bavbek, Erhan Çifçi, Rehan Rafay Jamil, Ani Adhikari, and Mariz Kelada for their intellectual support at various steps of the project.

Notes

1 All translations from Turkish to English belong to the author.
2 See Adalet (2018), Bah (2008), and Shah (2011) for critical evaluations of Lerner's work.
3 Later 21st USAFAD (U.S. Army Field Artillery Detachment).
4 The treaty had formed the basis of amicable relations between the USSR and Turkey during the interwar years. See Hurewitz (1956, 142–3) for the treaty text.
5 Later in his memoirs, Molotov denounced the postwar Soviet policy regarding Turkey and the Straits as "an inopportune, impossible affair," and ultimately, "a mistake" (1993, 72–4). Considering Molotov's reputation as a hardline Stalinist, his remarks illustrate Stalin's brinkmanship in foreign policy toward Turkey.
6 The Montreux Convention of 1936 has regulated the passage of civilian and war vessels in the Turkish Straits by specifying a wide array of conditions to be applied discriminately for the vessels of the riparian Black Sea Powers and other countries in peacetime and wartime. See Meray and Olcay (2020) for the full text of the Montreux Convention and conference proceedings.
7 See Vali (1972, 238–44) for Stalin at Potsdam. The Soviet media also sustained pressure on Turkey, with the most notorious example from the period being the publication of a letter claiming historical rights to Turkey's northeastern borderlands. For the full text of the letter, see Simon Janashia and Nikoloz Berdzenishvili, "Письмо в редакцию газеты Коммуниста О наших законных требованиях к Турции," *Pravda*, December 20, 1945, 2 and *Izvestia*, December 20, 1945, 3.
8 The Soviet notes of 1946 jettisoned earlier demands for land concessions and instead focused solely on the Straits. See Soysal (1991) for the Soviet notes of 1946 and the Turkish response. See also the memoirs of Feridun Cemal Erkin (1968, 270–1), the author of the Turkish response to the second Soviet note and later minister of foreign affairs, for the diplomatic atmosphere in Turkey upon the receipt of the Soviet notes.
9 See TC Başbakanlık Devlet Arşivleri Genel Müdürlüğü (2009, 14) for postwar force levels in Turkey.
10 See also Isci's recent overview of Turkish–Soviet relations in the aftermath of the Second World War (2023), where he counters the revisionist claim that postwar Turkish fears were strategically overblown and thus not wholly genuine, so as to engineer an alignment with the West.
11 Soysal notes that shops, bars, and restaurants named "Missuri" mushroomed in Turkey after the visit (1997, 23).
12 The US support of the Turkish position against the USSR was a remarkable policy reversal, considering how less than a year ago, on November 2, 1945, an American note to Turkey had suggested the revision of the Montreux Convention.

13 The official note was delivered on February 24. See McGhee (1997, 26–8) for the American reception of the British withdrawal plan.
14 JAMMAT was to become the largest US advisory group in the world by 1951. It was renamed the Joint United States Military Mission for Aid to Turkey in 1958.
15 See Huston (1988, 190–4) for the history and scale of American assistance to Turkey.
16 See the memoirs of Erkin (1986), Turkish ambassador to Washington, for a firsthand account of the early Turkish efforts to join NATO and the decision to participate in the Korean War.
17 See Law 6375, Law 6427, and Law 6860, which were ratified by the Turkish parliament, respectively, on March 10, 1954, June 30, 1954, and December 5, 1956. With these laws, NATO charters like the Status of Forces Agreement, Military Facilities Agreement, Agreement on the Status of NATO National Representatives and International Staff, and Protocol on the Status of International Military Headquarters came into effect.
18 Bilateral agreements encompass a series of treaties signed by the United States and Turkey during the Cold War. Most importantly, these treaties granted the United States basing rights in Turkey. They remained largely outside public scrutiny and parliamentary approval. Holmes notes that forty-one of the fifty-four Turkish–US bilateral agreements between 1947 and 1965 were secret (2014, 61). Vali records the existence of fifty-five bilateral agreements from 1954 to 1964 (1972, 96). See Tunçkanat (2018) for the complete text of some bilateral agreements and the negative sentiments their secret nature instigated among leftist and/or nationalist military circles.
19 See "Turkish - United States Arrangements for Introducing Modern (including atomic) Weapons into NATO Defense Forces" September 18, 1959, and October 28, 1959, DNSA, for the most significant letter exchange that allowed for the stationing of Jupiter missiles in Turkey, which later contributed to the Cuban Missile Crisis.
20 This was a parallel that Stalin and Molotov repeatedly drew at Potsdam to push for imperial consistency regarding the regulation of international waterways.
21 See Vali (1972) for the historical consistency of Russian and Soviet aspirations for the Straits.
22 See "Strategic Guidance," December 9, 1952, MC 14/1-FINAL, NATO; "Overall Strategic Concept for the Defence of the NATO Area," October 14, 1956, MC 14/2, "NATO Strategy," November 29, 1966, MC-MCM-142-1966, NATO; "Measures to Implement the Strategic Concept for the Defence of the NATO Area," December 8, 1969, MC-48/3-FINAL, NATO.
23 See "Strategic Guidance," July 21, 1952, MC-SG-13-23-DRAFT, NATO for the indefensibility of Thrace due to its topography. Subsequently, written and verbal remarks to the effect that Thrace was indefensible were toned down to make defense planning more palatable to Turkey and Greece in view of the pushback from Turkish and Greek officials who feared that their Thracian territories would be sacrificed without resistance. The official statements and documents thereafter avoided defeatist language and prioritized technical and military terms like "withdrawal" and "delaying action" under pressure that afforded more flexibility and optimism. See Ridgway (1956, 251–2) for the Greek reaction to Field Marshal Bernard Montgomery's off-hand remarks about the indefensibility of Greek Thrace. For similar Turkish sensibilities about Turkish Thrace in NATO defense planning, see "Military Committee Meeting in Paris, France on Tuesday, 9 December 1952 at 1000 Hours," December 11, 1952, MC-RECORD-MC/CS-7, NATO and Hüseyin Rahmi Apak,

"Başbakana Açık Mektup [Open Letter to the Prime Minister]," *Özdilek*, February 12, 1953, 1.

24 SACEUR is the commander of Supreme Headquarters Allied Powers Europe (SHAPE), overseeing all planning and execution of NATO operations in Allied European territories.

25 See "Visit of Field Marshal Montgomery to Greece and Turkey, 7-15 May 1952," May 16, 1952, FM-63, NATO and SHAPE Secretariat (1953, 378–85) for Deputy SACEUR Field Marshal Bernard Montgomery's visit to Thrace. See Ridgway (1956, 251–4) for SACEUR Matthew Ridgway's tour the same year.

26 See "The Most Effective Pattern of NATO Military Strength for the Next Few Years," November 18, 1954, MC-48, NATO; "Capabilities Study for the Allied Command Europe (ACE) 1957," November 18, 1954, MC-49, NATO; and "Measures to Implement the Strategic Concept," March 15, 1957, MC-48/2, NATO, for the new forward defense strategy based on nuclear weapons.

27 See "Ground Atomic Support Command for Defence of the Turkish Straits," April 17, 1957, MC-SGWM 263-57, NATO.

28 See Jordan (2000) for Norstad's SACEUR term and nuclear diplomacy.

29 See MC-SGWM 263-57; "Ground Atomic Support Command for Defence of the Turkish Straits," May 2, 1957, MC-SGM-295-57, NATO; and SHAPE Secretariat (1967a, 64–6).

30 See "Verbatim Record of Meeting—Final," February 5, 1958, NAC-C-VR-(57)82-FINAL, NATO for the Paris Summit and Turkish push for nuclearization on the heels of the 1956 Suez Crisis and the 1957 Syrian Crisis.

31 See SHAPE Secretariat (1967b, 53) for Norstad's direct involvement in negotiations with Turkey.

32 See SHAPE Secretariat (1976, 36–8).

33 See "History of the Custody and Deployment of Nuclear Weapons July 1945 Through September 1977," February 1, 1978, NSA and "Report on the 1958 Annual Review - Chapter on Turkey," December 6, 1958, NAC-C-M-(58)141-PART2-TU, NATO for the first nuclear deployments to Turkey.

34 See "Tarım Alet ve Makinelerinin Tamiri İçin Atölyeler İnşa Ediliyor [Workshop Construction for the Repair of Agricultural Equipment and Machinery]," *Cumhuriyet*, June 2, 1949, 3.

35 The USIS was a US public diplomacy and propaganda instrument geared toward winning hearts and minds overseas.

36 The US Army Corps of Engineers, who embarked on their mission in 1947 under JAMMAT for base construction and infrastructural capacity building across Turkey, largely bypassed Thrace (Grathwol and Moorhus 2009).

37 These battalions would receive training in Çorlu and leave to populate the artillery cadres of other Turkish Army Corps stationed elsewhere. At one point in the early 1960s, Çorlu hosted four Honest John Battalions at the same time, all at full strength and equipped with tactical nuclear weapons. These were the 420th, 551st, 611th, and 690th Honest John rocket battalions. Correspondingly, Çorlu was home to four different US detachments at its peak in 1962, those being Det-57, Det-67, Det-74, and Det-155. Following the relocation of the main group, Det-67, from Çorlu to Çakmaklı in 1963, Det-74 provided the backbone of the US military presence in Çorlu. Like other US custodial detachments, namely Det-97 in Köseköy (Izmit), Det-98 in Erzurum, and Det-155 in Ortaköy (Çanakkale), Det-74 was subordinate to Det-67, later the 528th USAAG (US Army Artillery Group) in Çakmaklı,

Istanbul. See "Medical Service Activities Report, Report Control Symbol MED-41 (R4) (U)," January 10, 1963, RG112, 390/18/29/04, Box 68, Turkey-Tuslog 67, NARA for the US force concentration in Çorlu at its heyday. See "Medical Service Activities Report, RCS MED-41 (R4) (U)," January 31, 1964, RG112, 390/18/29/04, Box 68, Turkey-Tuslog 67, NARA for the relocation of the main group from Çorlu to Çakmaklı.

38 FTT-1A1 stands for Field Training Team, 1st Turkish Army, 1st Training Team.

39 The military classification of hardship tour entitled soldiers to better pay in compensation for poor living conditions. Overall, the facilities in Çorlu and Thrace remained in very poor condition by American standards, even as late as the 1980s. The infrastructural conditions on the base remained so underwhelming by American standards that during a subcommittee hearing for military construction appropriations in 1983, Maj. Gen. Norman G. Delbridge presented his audience with a picture of a decrepit building from the base, flagging the conditions at Çorlu as "of particular concern . . . due to poor lighting and no heat." See "Hearings on H.R. 1816 (H.R. 2972) To Authorize Certain Construction at Military Installations for FY84," March 15, 1983, HRG-1983-ASH-0004, CONG.

40 The roster of early Honest John Battalions involves some famous military figures, like Mehmet Hikmet Bayar, commander of the Turkish Land Forces from 1994 to 1996, and Hüseyin Kıvrıkoğlu, chief of the Turkish General Staff from 1998 to 2002. See Bayar (2006, 301–53) for an account of his service days in Çorlu.

41 See Dalakoglou (2010), Larkin (2013), Khan (2006), and Schwenkel (2013) for the poetics of infrastructures. See the memoirs of Kocatürk (1999, 442–5) and Bayar (2006, 304–5) for examples of the atomic poetics in Turkey.

42 See Bacevich (1986) for the military and political context of tactical nuclear weapon development in the United States, including the Honest John.

43 See Arkin, Cochran, and Hoenig (1984, 282–3) for the technical features of Honest John and nuclear warheads that were likely to be paired with them.

44 See Masco (2006, 2014, 2021) and Gusterson (1996) for the US debates over nuclear testing and radioactive fallout.

45 See MacKenzie (1990) for a discussion of the reliability of nuclear weapons.

46 See Feaver and Stein (1987) for the development of PAL and other security devices to ensure US control of nuclear weapons.

47 See Sabri Yirmibeşoğlu's memoirs (1999, 181–2; 394) for the Turkish confusion about custodial arrangements regarding nuclear weapons, which was prevalent even among the highest ranks.

48 See Joerges (1999a, 1999b), Mitchell (2011), Winner (1980), and Woolgar and Cooper (1999) for a long-running discussion about whether artifacts have politics and vice versa.

49 See Adalet (2018, 107–15) for American attitudes toward Turkish engineers in the context of the Turkish road program, and American incitements for a more hands-on approach.

50 Hasan Kıyafet later became an author of moderate fame who produced in the genre of social realism. His breakout novel, *Komunist İmam*, is now in its sixtieth edition. He attempted to publish his memoirs about his mandatory service in an Honest John battalion in Çorlu twice, yet the publication process was interrupted because he was indicted on both occasions. See Kıyafet (2015) for his Çorlu memoirs.

51 PX stands for post exchange, referring to retail stores in American military installations. The provision of PX goods to host-country personnel and civilians is forbidden by law.

52 Local newspapers from the period are replete with news of military accidents and collateral damage. For a very small sample of military-related injuries and deaths, see "Roket Parçalandı Üç Kişi Öldü [Three died in rocket explosion]," May 15, 1965, *Çorlu*, 3; "Kırklareli Pazarında Patlayan Havan Mermisi 8 Kişinin Ölümüne Sebep Oldu [Mortar Fire Hit the Marketplace in Kirklareli, Eight Died]," April 29, 1967, *Devrim*, 1; "Ulaş'ta Patlayan Bombadan İki Kişi Öldü [Bomb Exploded in Ulas, Two Died]," May 27, 1963, *Çorlu Ekspres*, 1.

53 See Bayar (2006) and Kıyafet (2015) for the link between rural poverty and artillery-related injuries in Thrace. See Kim (2016) for a similar link in the Korean context.

54 None of my interlocutors remembers female employment on the base.

55 These contractors mainly served the V Army Corps headquartered in Çorlu.

56 Broadly, there were two types of base employees. Those who tended to private needs, like barbers, houseboys, tailors, and shoe shiners, were not unionized, and they were paid on a piece-rate basis. Kitchen personnel, drivers, and janitors were unionized under Harb-Is, and they were paid regular salaries. In either case, the earnings of the two groups were comparable and their job security was virtually guaranteed, barring major transgressions.

57 This local indifference to the possibility of mass destruction inherent to nuclear infrastructure is due in large part to the regional history of Thrace, where nuclearization forms an episode of a much longer and continuous history of militarization. See Orsini (2022, 33–7) for similar local attitudes toward nuclear infrastructure in Cold War Italy.

References

Archives

NATO Archives Online

Newspapers

Cumhuriyet
Çorlu
Çorlu Ekspres
Devrim
Özdilek

Primary Sources

Bayar, Mehmet Hikmet. 2006. *Yarim Asirlik Asker: Askeri Ogrencilik ve Subaylik Donemi [Soldier For Half a Century: Cadet and Officer Years]*. 2 vols. Vol. 1, Istanbul: Okuyan Us.

Erkin, Feridun Cemal. 1968. *Turk-Sovyet Iliskileri ve Bogazlar Meselesi [Turkish-Soviet Relations and the Question of the Straits]*, Ankara: Basnur Matbaasi.

Erkin, Feridun Cemal. 1986. *Disislerinde 34 Yil: Vasington Buyukelciligi [34 Years in Foreign Service: Ambassador to Washington]*. Vol. 2-1, Ankara: Turk Tarih Kurumu.

Hurewitz, Jacob C. 1956. *Diplomacy in the Near and Middle East, V2: A Documentary Record, 1914–1956*, Princeton, NJ: D. Van Nostrand Company, Inc.

Kiyafet, Hasan. 2015. *The Asker: Amerikan Ussunde Anadolulu Bir Subay [The Asker: An Anatolian Officer on An American Base]*, Ankara: La Kitap.

Kocaturk, Kenan. 1999. *Bir Subayin Anilari, 1909–1999 [Memoirs of an Officer, 1909–1999]*, Istanbul: Kastas Yayinevi.

McGhee, George C. 1997. *On the Frontline in the Cold War: An Ambassador Reports*, New York: Praeger Publishers.

Meray, Seha and Osman Olcay. 2020. *Montro Bogazlar Konferansi: Tutanaklar-Belgeler [The Montreux Straits Conference: Minutes, Documents]*, Istanbul: Is Bankasi Kultur Yayinları.

Molotov, Vyacheslav. 1993. *Molotov Remembers: Inside Kremlin Politics, Conversations with Felix Chuev*, Chicago: Ivan R. Dee.

Ridgway, Matthew B. 1956. *Soldier: The Memoirs of Matthew B. Ridgway*, New York: Harper & Brothers.

Soysal, Ismail. 1991. *Turkiye'nin Uluslararasi Siyasal Bagitlari (1945–1990): Kesim A (Cok Tarafli Bagitlar) [Turkey's International Treaties (1945–1990): Part A (Multilateral Treaties)]*. Vol. 2, Ankara: Turk Tarih Kurumu.

Soysal, Ismail. 1997. *Soguk Savas Donemi ve Turkiye: Olaylar Kronolojisi (1945-1975) [Cold War and Turkey: A Chronology of Events (1945–1975)]*, Istanbul: Isis.

TC Basbakanlik Devlet Arsivleri Genel Mudurlugu. 2009. *1. Ordu Komutanligi Tarihcesi [The History of the 1st Army]*, Istanbul: T.C. Basbakanlik Devlet Arsivleri Genel Mudurlugu.

Tumpane, John D. 1981. *Scotch and Holy Water*, Lafayette, CA: St. Giles Press.

Yirmibesoglu, Sabri. 1999. *Askeri ve Siyasi Anilarim, 1928–1965 [Military and Political Memoirs, 1928–1965]*. Vol. 1, Istanbul: Kastas.

Secondary Sources

Adalet, Begum. 2018. *Hotels and Highways: The Construction of Modernization Theory in Cold War Turkey*, Stanford, CA: Stanford University Press.

Akibayashi, Kozue and Suzuyo Takazato. 2009. "Okinawa: Women's Struggle for Demilitarization," in Catherine Lutz (ed.), *The Bases of Empire: The Global Struggle Against U.S. Military Posts*, 243–69, New York: New York University Press.

Arkin, William M., Thomas B. Cochran, and Milton M. Hoenig. 1984. *Nuclear Weapons Databook: U.S. Nuclear Forces and Capabilities*, Cambridge, MA: Ballinger Publishing Company.

Bacevich, Andrew J. 1986. *The Pentomic Era: The U.S. Army Between Korea and Vietnam*, Washington, DC: National Defense University Press.

Bah, Umaru. 2008. "Daniel Lerner, Cold War Propaganda and U.S. Development Communication Research: An Historical Critique," *Journal of Third World Studies* 25 (1): 183–98.

Cheng, Sealing. 2010. *On the Move for Love: Migrant Entertainers and the U.S. Military in South Korea*, Philadelphia, PA: University of Pennsylvania Press.

Dalakoglou, Dimitris. 2010. "The Road: An Ethnography of the Albanian-Greek Cross-Border Motorway," *American Ethnologist* 37 (1): 132–49.

Deringil, Selim. 1989. *Turkish Foreign Policy During the Second World War: An 'Active' Neutrality*, Cambridge: Cambridge University Press.

Enloe, Cynthia. 2000. *Maneuvers: The Intersectional Politics of Militarizing Women's Lives*, London: University of California Press.

Feaver, Peter D. and Peter Stein. 1987. *Assuring Control of Nuclear Weapons: The Evolution of Permissive Action Links*, Thousand Oaks, CA: Sage Publications.

Grathwol, Robert P. and Donita M. Moorhus. 2009. *Bricks, Sand, and Marble: U.S. Army Corps of Engineers Construction in the Mediterranean and Middle East, 1947–1991*,

Washington, DC: Center of Military History and Corps of Engineers United States Army.
Gusterson, Hugh. 1996. *Nuclear Rites: A Weapons Laboratory at the End of the Cold War*, Berkeley, LA: University of California Press.
Holmes, Amy Austin. 2014. *Social Unrest and American Military Bases in Turkey and Germany Since 1945*, Cambridge: Cambridge University Press.
Howard, Harry N. 1976. "The Bicentennial in American-Turkish Relations," *Middle East Journal* 30 (3): 291–310.
Huston, James Alvin. 1988. *Outposts and Allies: U.S. Army Logistics in the Cold War, 1945–1953*, Selinsgrove: Susquehanna University Press.
Isci, Onur. 2023. "Turkey at a Crossroads: The Soviet Threat and Postwar Realignment, 1945–1946," *Diplomatic History* 47 (4): 621–46.
Joerges, Bernward. 1999a. "Do Politics Have Artefacts?" *Social Studies of Science* 29 (3): 411–31.
Joerges, Bernward. 1999b. "Scams Cannot be Busted: Response to Steve Woolgar and Geoff Cooper, "Do Artefacts Have Ambivalence? – Moses' Bridges, Winner's Bridges and Other Urban Legends in STS"," *Social Studies of Science* 29 (3): 450–7.
Jordan, Robert S. 2000. *Norstad: Cold War NATO Supreme Commander, Airman, Strategist, Diplomat*, New York: St. Martin's Press.
Khan, Naveeda. 2006. "Flaws in the Flow: Roads and Their Modernity in Pakistan," *Social Text* 24 (89): 87–113.
Kim, Eleana J. 2016. "Toward an Anthropology of Landmines: Rogue Infrastructure and Military Waste in the Korean DMZ," *Cultural Anthropology* 31 (2): 162–87.
Kuniholm, Bruce R. 2014 [1980]. *The Origins of the Cold War in the Near East: Great Power Conflict and Diplomacy in Iran, Turkey, and Greece*, Princeton, NJ: Princeton University Press.
Larkin, Brian. 2013. "The Politics and Poetics of Infrastructure," *Annual Review of Anthropology* 42: 327–43.
Lerner, Daniel. 1958. *The Passing of Traditional Society: Modernizing the Middle East*, London: Collier-Macmillan.
Lutz, Catherine. 2009. "Introduction: Bases, Empire, and Global Response," in Catherine Lutz (ed.), *The Bases of Empire: The Global Struggle Against U.S. Military Posts*, 1–44, New York: New York University Press.
MacKenzie, Donald. 1990. *Inventing Accuracy: A Historical Sociology of Nuclear Missile Guidance*, Cambridge, MA: The MIT Press.
Masco, Joseph. 2006. *The Nuclear Borderlands: The Manhattan Project in Post-Cold War New Mexico*, Princeton, NJ: Princeton University Press.
Masco, Joseph. 2014. *The Theater of Operations: National Security Affect From the Cold War to the War on Terror*, Durham: Duke University Press.
Masco, Joseph. 2021. *The Future of Fallout, and Other Episodes in Radioactive World-Making*, Durham: Duke University Press.
Mitchell, Timothy. 2011. *Carbon Democracy: Political Power in the Age of Oil*, London: Verso.
Orsini, Davide. 2022. *The Atomic Archipelago: US Nuclear Submarines and Technopolitics of Risk in Cold War Italy*, Pittsburgh, PA: University of Pittsburgh Press.
Sahlins, Marshall. 2010. "Infrastructuralism," *Critical Inquiry* 36 (3): 371–85.
Schwenkel, Christina. 2013. "Post-Socialist Affect: Ruination and Reconstruction of the Nation in Urban Vietnam," *Cultural Anthropology* 28 (2): 252–77.

Shah, Hemant. 2011. *The Production of Modernization: Daniel Lerner, Mass Media, and the Passing of Traditional Society*, Philadelphia: Temple University Press.
SHAPE Secretariat. 1953. *SHAPE History: Origin and Development of SHAPE*, Brussels: SHAPE.
SHAPE Secretariat. 1967a. *SHAPE History: 1957*, Brussels: SHAPE.
SHAPE Secretariat. 1967b. *SHAPE History: 1958*, Brussels: SHAPE.
SHAPE Secretariat. 1976. *SHAPE History: The New Approach, 1953–1956*, Brussels: SHAPE.
Tunckanat, Haydar. 2018. *Ikili Anlasmalarin Icyuzu [The Real Face of Bilateral Agreements]*, Istanbul: Alaca Yayinlari.
Vali, Ferenc A. 1972. *The Turkish Straits and NATO*, Stanford, CA: Hoover Institution Press.
Winner, Langdon. 1980. "Do Artifacts Have Politics?" *Daedalus* 109: 121–36.
Woolgar, Steve and Geoff Cooper. 1999. "Do Artefacts Have Ambivalence? Moses' Bridges, Winner's Bridges and Other Urban Legends in S&TS," *Social Studies of Science* 29 (3): 433–49.

11

Undoctoring Sport

Constructing Liberal Bodies in Postwar Turkey

Can Evren

Founded in 1938 and headquartered in Ankara, the public administration *Beden Terbiyesi Genel Müdürlüğü* (General Directorate of Physical Education, GDPE) had ambitious goals to reform the leisure-time habits of the republic's citizens. Envisioned as an organ of biopolitical nation-building, GDPE aimed to create an exercising population, considering regular physical exercise central to public health, military preparedness, and industriousness (Akın 2004). GDPE and Law No. 3530 that created this public administration in 1938 were continuous with broader efforts to institute public health as a critical interface of nation-building and state-employed public health specialists as nation-builders (Dole 2004, 259–61; Alemdaroğlu 2005). To that end, the law foresaw staffing the directorate with bureaucratic cadres allocated to credentialed experts in biomedicine and physical education, who closely followed technoscientific discourse and practice in Europe, particularly in France and Germany. The law also announced plans for the establishment of "a higher institute of physical education in Ankara that would determine the medical and technical rules of sports and physical education, train qualified sports teachers, trainers, and supervisors to work for the Directorate, the army, and the Ministry of Education, and implement regular medical controls of athletes."[1] The institute would, in other words, accredit a new profession specialized in the intersections of sports, medicine, and physical education.

The role model for this planned higher institute was the *Deutsche Hochschule für Leibesübungen*, which was founded in Berlin in 1920 during the Weimar era and framed by the concept of "human economy that aimed at the conservation, restoration, and rational utilization of human resources" (Hau 2008, 383). In 1933, the Republican People's Party (RPP) invited the school's founding director Carl Diem to visit Turkey and draft blueprints for "state leadership in physical education." These blueprints eventually materialized in Law No. 3530.[2] GDPE was initially an independent administration tied to the Prime Ministry, but later placed under the Ministry of Education in 1942. During the Second World War, GDPE bylaws introduced the controversial concept of *mükellefiyet* (obligation), foreseeing daily hours of physical exercise to be mandatory for every young citizen across the nation—males between twelve and forty-five years and females between twelve and thirty years—and thus situating daily physical exercise, primarily for military preparedness, on the same footing as other citizen obligations such as compulsory schooling and male conscription. These obligatory visions included, at its most radical, bureaucratically drafted weekly exercise schedules to be implemented uniformly by schools, the army, sports clubs, People's Houses, and workplaces across the nation (Akın 2004, 157–71).

Beden Terbiyesi Merkez İstişare Kurulu (Central Advisory Committee of Physical Education, CAC-PE), a ministerial committee defined by law as the highest decision-making organ of GDPE, was a hybrid institution, however, and cut across the state–society divide. The ten-person committee consisted of five Ankara-based bureaucrats who were physical education or public health liaisons for their ministries or for the General Staff of the Armed Forces and five civilian appointees affiliated with sports clubs and federations whose activities centered more in Istanbul. While sports clubs and Olympic federations were legally mandated to contribute to public health goals, they were also tasked with representing the nation-state in the Olympics where victories and defeats of a specialized class of athletes mattered more than population-level health. Sports clubs' primary activities focused less on organizing daily physical exercise as preventive medicine than on winning-oriented Olympic competitions.

In larger city centers, competitive sports events attracted middle-class spectatorship and partisan identification with contestants, received press coverage, and served as commercialized entertainment for urban fans, thus fueling a sports market. Throughout the interwar years, competing logics of sports and physical education entered politicized conflicts (As 2016), often mapping onto the cleavage that would later mark the partisan division of parliament into Democrat and Republican camps. The very concepts of sports and physical education denoted two distinct halves of a sociopolitical field that stood uneasily integrated by GDPE statutes, while both targeted the material body through their means and philosophies and for distinct but related ends. A key reason why GDPE hardliners and state-affiliated public health doctors were averse to competitive immersion in sports, above all in football matches, was the frequent injuries strenuous sportive exertion caused when the main drive of the activity was beating opponents. GDPE ideologues considered this overcompetitive culture of leisure as wasteful squandering of human resources for short-term pleasures of one-upmanship rather than long-term developmental goals of keeping the national physical stock healthy and fit on a daily basis. GDPE's founding cadres and executives, in short, viewed sportive competition as a questionable method for achieving population-level health and building an industrial nation. Some even believed noncompetitive gymnastics or calisthenics could replace competitive sports.

On July 2, 1945, as the end of the Second World War was in sight, Minister of Education Hasan Ali Yücel joined the meeting of CAC-PE and called the ten-person committee to plan a national congress that would be a more populated version of CAC-PE. The minister knew well that bringing together GDPE cadres and sport club affiliates was not an easy task in a political context that would soon see the Parliament split into Democrat and Republican parties. Until the promulgation of Law No. 3530, sports club notables had developed routines of federative self-governance, and by the end of the world war in 1945, those same sports club circles voiced demands for abolishing GDPE or rolling back public administrative jurisdiction over sports governance. Between 1945 and 1950, GDPE critics were vocal in Istanbul's popular sports press and frequently utilized early Cold War discourse, identifying unpopular statutes on obligatory exercise and GDPE's administrative expansion as smacking of the totalitarian zeitgeist.[3] Nonetheless, Yücel and GDPE director Vildan Aşir Savaşır asked CAC-PE to convene a motley crowd of physicians, academics, sport club delegates, physical educators, public health technocrats, and sports journalists for the national press. CAC-PE compiled a list of 150 individuals and invited them to a six-day congress in Ankara in February 1946. The invitees were to discuss the nation's postwar future in sports and physical education and reforms to GDPE statutes. The event was named *Birinci Beden Eğitimi ve Spor Şurası*, which I shall render here shortly as the Sports Council (Aydın, Geyik, and Ayçiçek n.d., 67–80). Thanks to Yücel's penchant for books and publishing,[4] the minutes of the Sports Council's deliberative assembly were meticulously recorded in the manner of parliament sessions, including parenthetical marks of booing and applause, leaving behind a four hundred-page document printed in 1947 (T.C. MEB BTGM 1947).

This chapter delves into and analyzes the minutes that document the Council Assembly as members negotiate the technoscientific paradigms of building, governing, and modernizing the national athletic body. In this six-day event, rival factions fought over many issues, but I focus on a contentious issue that speaks to the concerns of this edited volume. This contention concerned the institutional source of expertise and knowledge that should be authorized to make technical, managerial, and governmental decisions in the realm of sports, such as devising training schedules or nutritional programs for athletic bodies, guiding youngsters to various sports branches they would excel in, legislating regulations on sports administration, and, critically, caring for the athletic plasticity of citizen bodies—not only their malleability and enhancement through practice but also their vulnerability to injury and death. To quote the editors' introduction, council members took the athletic citizen body as "a material entity—entwined with meanings, values, and power relations" (Kaşdoğan and Kurtiç, this volume) and as a material site for concocting visions of technoscientific regulation and development. This chapter consists of a close reading of these entwinements to explicate the material politics of athletic nation-building. Despite ambitious proposals for biomedically and bureaucratically regulating the athletic body through the leadership of sport medicine experts, a recipe voiced particularly by state-affiliated doctors, "vernacular practices of expertise and competing visions of development persisted" (Adalet 2018, 13) as the sporting world relied on its practical norms and discourse of athletic excellence, technique, training, and well-being.

Critically, council members were weighing these contending narratives when ideological parameters of nation-building were reinterpreted in Turkey at the dawn of the Cold War. Minister Yücel explicitly contextualized the council in this postwar democratic transition when, in his opening speech, he asked invitees to work "with a fully liberal mentality [*tam hür anlayışla*]" and explained that the government favored "principles and methods of physical education and sport as they are practiced in a democratic society" (*demokrat bir cemiyette beden eğitimi ve spor nasılsa, aynı prensip ve metotları*) (T.C. MEB BTGM 1947, 51). Sports narratives in the council were, therefore, narratives on state–society relations that treated the materiality of the athletic body and its governance like an experimental laboratory for validating or invalidating liberal democratic norms. These narratives, I argue, negotiated key political concepts of liberalism, such as the public–private divide, as possibly embodied materially by athletic bodies. I show how most of the participants—against the dismay of the doctor and physical educator minority—refused the biomedical reduction of the athlete-citizen to an anatomical and physiological object. Instead, critics conjured a vision of athletic personhood that normatively safeguarded the divide between its private and public domains, pointing to subjectivist categories like taste, eagerness, and will as constituting the private domain of athletic selfhood that must be defended against technoscientific dirigisme by doctors, who equated those same subjectivist categories with irrationality, excessive ambition, or hedonistic self-harm.

In this historical conjuncture, the sports community viewed GDPE-driven biomedical projections skeptically, as overreach of a bureaucratic power alien to sports, and countered them with rival notions of technicity and expertise, which they grounded in forms of sportive knowledge shared by insider practitioners, captured by the term *ampirik*. The same word, however, was used derisively by physicians with various superimposed meanings that connoted unsystematic, backward, unscientific, and unregulated action. The coalition of athletes, Olympic federation executives, and sports journalists—among them public figures like Burhan Felek—reacted to anthropometric and physiologic guidelines as restrictive of sport's private autonomy rather than positively contributing to sportive performance. My story, then, is the story of a contentious encounter, perhaps a boxing match, between biomedical sport science and *ampirik* visions of development as members of differing professional domains articulated rival understandings of technoscientific authority in matters of sports governance. In doing so, the contestants partook in the broader remaking of state and society as well as cultures of governance, a remaking process to which scholarship in Turkish Studies has recently been paying closer attention (Aytürk 2015; Brockett 2009; Erken 2019; Örnek and Üngör 2013).

Similar to Özkan's contribution to this volume, which unpacks the binary oppositions that informed the material politics of forestry and nation-building, I read the archive with an anthropologist's hat, analyzing the sociohistorical emergence of an emic binary opposition pitting *ampirik* against *sportif-tıbbi*, thickly describing how this emic opposition symbolically consolidated group boundaries between athletes and doctors and organized rival theories of the relationship between materiality, techniques of training and care, competitive performance, and athletic nation-building. Contentious debate in the Sport Council recombined opposing categories of expert science and lay practice, as the community of athletes rallied around the notion of an athletic trainer's *ampirik ihtisas*, which could be rendered as the expertise of autodidacts or old-timers, ex-practitioners turned into trainers and managers. The notion implied a mode of organization in which biomedical expertise assimilates to the logic of athletic practice rather than athletic practice being organized according to measures designed by sport science experts. This recombination, this chapter shows, not only constructed a dualistic view of liberal athletic personhood, separating an athlete's free inner self from an accidental external physique. The concept of autodidact expertise also functioned as a Cold War analogy that mapped this dualistic personhood onto a similarly liberal society–state dualism. In conversation with Şen's (this volume) invitation to conduct ethnographies of political subjectivities shaped in the context of the Cold War, I show how the sport community responded to doctors' embrace of transnationally circulating paradigms of biomedical sport science by creatively adopting rival paradigms in transnational circulation in the world of sport, preaching the Olympic superiority of liberally governed nations that safeguard the autonomy of athletic bodies and organizations from the administrative interference of bureaucratically organized scientific authority.

Round 1: Doctors versus Athletes

The procedural organization of the council itself became entangled in rival technoscientific metaphors during the opening session. As the organizing hosts of the council, the Ministry of Education handed out a program with five predetermined commissions focusing on different themes and expected the invitees to break out into those commissions for three days before reconvening for a deliberative assembly. But some members thought it necessary to start with a deliberative assembly rather than blindly follow the ministry's program. These objections frustrated ministry insiders. "In every national congress," opposed Niyazi Erkin, bacteriologist and chief public health technocrat who spent the war years managing epidemic outbreaks in small towns, "commission work should precede general assembly meetings." Erkin used a hygiene infrastructure analogy: "If we were carrying water to an urban area," he said, "the Ministry handing us a program is like building the waterways first and then letting water flow in it. But the other proposal [to deliberate the program first] is like letting the water flow first and then digging canals later." To which Burhan Felek, the eminent sports journalist, wittily replied with a liberal narrative on private doctor–patient consultation: "When you see a doctor, does the doctor first examine you and then ask to hear your symptoms or does the doctor first ask to hear your symptoms and then start examining you?" Lurking behind the witty response was a political discourse about sport governance as better targeting issues petitioned from the bottom-up, so to speak, by sportive constituents, rather than implementing the dictates of an authoritarian public health doctor. One of the following speakers, sports journalist and former Galatasaray and boxing federation executive Eşref Şefik Atabey, backed Felek's call for a preliminary assembly but cautioned against excessive deliberation given time considerations, precisely because he saw the doctors' worldview and that of the sports community as irreconcilable. "Many esteemed doctors present among us advocate theories that outright oppose sports," Atabey said, and mulling over "[contradictory] formulas, does sport lead to health or does health lead to sports, would consume too many hours of fighting" (T.C. MEB BTGM 1947, 57–61).

A group of invited doctors was discontent with the program for their own reasons. They petitioned the chair to authorize a separate commission on Sports Health and Sports Medicine. Petitioners felt left out by the Ministry of Education, interpreting this omission to mean that a separate biomedical jurisdiction was not welcomed in sport governance. The petitioners were two physicians, Prof. Dr. Muhterem Gökmen and Dr. Raşit Serdengeçti. Radiologist Gökmen had assisted the German émigré physicist Friedrich Dessauer in importing X-ray machines and setting up radiology centers during the remaking of Istanbul University Medical School. His name loomed large in programs for public investment in medical imaging infrastructure, a prerequisite for sports medicine too (Dinc 2007). But the chief protagonist in attempts to doctor sport governance was Raşit Serdengeçti, who undersigned the commission's policy draft alongside his ally, physical anthropologist Şevket Aziz Kansu. Specialized in internal medicine, Serdengeçti was the leading advocate within the doctor community for the recognition and institutionalization of sports medicine as a distinct expertise, a public role he performed for decades until passing away in 1979.

Born in 1903, Serdengeçti had come of age in post-First World War Istanbul and participated in the city's Olympic sports craze in the 1920s. In 1940, two years after the establishment of GDPE, Serdengeçti was appointed to lead the newly created GDPE Health Department (*BTGM Sağlık Dairesi*). In his first five years in this position, Serdengeçti enjoyed amicable relations with the wartime director General Cemil Taner, who allocated budgets to fund publications on sports medicine and equip the health department with imported spirometers and ergometers, which were considered cutting-edge technology in sports medicine. With Taner as general director and Serdengeçti as head of health, GDPE published half a dozen translated booklets on sports medicine, and Serdengeçti followed these translations with radio lectures, newspaper columns, and manuals he wrote in Turkish throughout the 1940s, including the publication of lecture notes for his exercise physiology seminars at *Gazi Eğitim Enstitüsü* in Ankara to candidate teachers. Moreover, with backing from politically influential social hygiene puritans like Fahrettin Kerim Gökay, sports medicine was chosen as the main theme of the 8th National Turkish Medical Congress in 1943. The initiative produced three long booklets on sports' public health, surgical, and pathological aspects. Serdengeçti hoped to use the 1946 Sports Council as a platform to take his vision further and develop the GDPE Health Department into a more complex organization that would both regulate sport culture medically and instrumentalize biomedical technoscience to enhance the competitive performance of national athletes. But he was also cognizant of the sociopolitical limits of implementing this vision in a context of widespread discontent with GDPE among Olympic athletes and sport club representatives. In a book he wrote in 1964, Serdengeçti describes General Taner as an ally but complains that postwar GDPE administrators yielded to pressures from sport club notables. Expecting a more extensive budget allocation for 1947 following the council, Serdengeçti was frustrated to face budget cuts and resigned after a conflict with GDPE director Savaşır. The Health Department would be disbanded after the Democrat Party came to power in 1950 and shelved until the 1960s (Serdengeçti 1964, 29–37).

The sports medicine draft presented by Serdengeçti and Kansu proposed a GDPE-run bureaucratic certification system that would require every licensed athlete participating in any official regional, national, and international competitions to carry GDPE-authorized health cards (*sağlık fişi*) and athletes would be asked to present these cards before matches as eligibility certificates. The proposed certification system had two dimensions. Doctors differentiated these two dimensions as *sıhhi muayene* or *sıhhi kontrol* (health examination or medical control, used interchangeably), and *sportif-tıbbi muayene* (sport-medical examination). The medical control in question consisted of two requirements: (1) Every official sport event under GDPE jurisdiction was required to hire a certified matchday doctor responsible for medical oversight and care for on-site injuries. (2) All competing athletes were required to undergo annual health screenings so that life-threatening conditions or infectious diseases could be detected. Results would be printed on the athlete's GDPE-authorized health card. In short, medical control prioritized athlete safety.

Doctor members of the council criticized sports club executives for overlooking health risks and blindly pushing their athletes to compete for glory at the expense of well-being or consulting uncertified caretakers when athletes are injured. Serdengeçti, for instance, recalls his time in Ankara when he was unable to prevent Ankaragücü sport club executives from fielding their star winger Şükrü Gülesin in the football derby against Gençlerbirliği, despite the athlete being diagnosed with jaundice (*sarılık*) (Serdengeçti 1964, 35). During the assembly, doctors narrated stories of a long-distance runner who collapsed on the track, the former Olympic wrestler Koç Ömer who wrestled while infected with tuberculosis and died, wrestlers relocating their opponents' dislocated shoulders on the podium, or the footballer Muhteşem who broke his leg during a match and ended up amputated due to nonexpert intervention gone wrong (T.C. MEB BTGM 1947, 89–94). The doctors asked for funding for more staff and equipment for the GDPE Health Department, where athletes and clubs could pay affordable fees to get tested. The policy draft also required clubs to hire matchday doctors and pay those doctors from ticket sales revenues. This measure could be interpreted as a workplace safety regulation in the spirit of occupational medicine.

Often bringing up the derisive concept of *ampirizma* when referring to nondoctor care, doctors expressed their professional expectations from GDPE regulations by identifying with the alliance between doctors and the Ministry of Health against traditional healers and the longer history of bureaucratically backed "professional closure" since Ottoman modernization efforts in the mid-nineteenth century (İlkan Rasimoğlu 2021). While doctors knew that implementing absolute control over sports was impossible in the short term, they expressed wishes for exclusive expert jurisdiction (Starr 2009) through being favored by supportive state elites and state-certification schemes (Abbott 1991). Wishful demands for exclusive jurisdiction were explicitly articulated in doctor societies, for example, when one professor of medicine, in the 1943 National Turkish Medical Congress, likened "the work of non-doctors in the sports world" to "healer-cum-frauds and non-certified surgeons and doctors of the old times." The professor demanded a "law, like that passed by the Ministry of Health banning [traditional healers] from practicing, which would similarly ban non-doctors from sports work" (Sekizinci Milli 1944, 144). Not only healers but also sports club masseurs were frequent objects of doctor criticism. In his booklets, Serdengeçti fumed against the widespread practice of athletes getting "massaged by whoever offered one" (*aklına esenin yaptığı masaj*) as pain-relieving remedies after intensive effort (Serdengeçti 1946, 46–8).

When the council gave the green light to a separate sport medicine commission, Eşref Şefik Atabey dismissed the very idea of a sports doctor, "a form of medicine that lets its order and rules to be shaped by the rules and regulations of sport" (*malûmdur ki spor doktorluğu diye henüz nizamlarına kaidelerine spor talimatlarını hâkim kılmış bir doktorluk yoktur*) (TC MEB BTGM 1947, 76). With this statement, he was calling out existing medical practice for not understanding the specialized athletic body, for being unfamiliar with sportive habitus, "the increasingly intense inculcation of specific dispositions that prepare one for athletic competition" and which "extricate themselves from social conventions and norms of ordinary conduct," thus creating new kinds of material bodies and injuries (Defrance 2013, 304). This extraordinary materiality of athletic bodies had provoked a medical language that pathologized them as abnormal. In criticizing intensive training without doctor oversight, Serdengeçti used the French concept *sur entrainement* rendered *aşırı idman* in Turkish. Overtraining caused deformities. In *Hekim Gözüyle Tenis,* Serdengeçti describes a whole collection of abnormalities such as "a footballer's knee," "a wrestler's shoulder," or "a tennis player's elbow" (Serdengeçti 1946, 46–8) all of which he pathologizes with the concept *arıza*, impairment. This conceptualization by Serdengeçti shows medical suspicion for sportive physicality, for the ways bodies are plastically shaped by specialized habitus and stand out from the ordinary workforce. The contrast between ordinary and extraordinary physicality mapped onto the jurisdictional divide between doctors and athletes. While Dr. Gökmen called for "collaborative dialogue between *sporcular* and *hekimler,*" conceiving the 1946 Council as a platform for translation across these fields, the frequent juxtaposition of categories *sporcular* and *hekimler* attests to difficult-to-permeate professional boundaries between sportive and biomedical domains. It also shows that both doctors and athletes perceived clear boundaries between these domains (T.C. MEB BTGM 1947, 75–8).

Round 2: Military–Clinic Complex versus Practical Rehab

Positioned on the sports side of this boundary, Atabey and Felek suspected doctors to be unfamiliar with sport-specific injuries, but journalists were not passive recipients without positive projects of their own. As leading contributors to sports pages in newspapers and specialized sports magazines printed in Istanbul and Ankara and circulated across the nation-state since the 1920s, Atabey and Felek were part of a media infrastructure that disseminated not only sports news but also sportive forms of knowledge about the materiality of bodies that claimed the word "science" in other ways. In popular sports publications of the time, the adjective "scientific" rarely implied biomedical discourse. Instead, the term distinguished rule-based play from informal or casual gaming, denoting competitions organized according to rules and regulations set by international sports federations.[5] Books with titles like *The Science of Soccer* described either rule-based organization or systematized technical exercises and tactical formations used by globally renowned athletes and teams (see, e.g., Currie 1919). Until the 1950s, academic discourses by doctors were rarely published in the popular press. But the sports press featured accessible self-care recipes on nutrition or exercise which were more likely written by athletes, active or retired. When Raşit Serdengeçti started publicizing physiologically grounded advice on training and nutrition in the 1940s, the media outlets he chose were either the state-owned radio, GDPE publications, or RPP-affiliated political newspapers like *İstiklal*, which reserved little space for sports coverage and were negligible players in sports publicity.[6]

Popular sport weeklies like *Spor Alemi* and *Kırmızı-Beyaz* connected their readers with the transnational sport public, and these magazines also disseminated discourse on physical therapies and training. In his autobiography, the prominent solider-athlete of the period, Sahir Gürkan (n.d., 18–39), shares a detailed account of his experience with a severe football injury and the non-biomedical methods of rehabilitation he practiced as a boarding student in the Kuleli military high school in Konya in the 1940s. After being injured in a football game and walking around "with an inflamed foot, in pain," the school's military doctor judged Gürkan's foot to be irrecoverably injured. The doctor initially ordered his dismissal from a military career altogether, pushing the pupil into despair, but eventually released him from duty for a recovery period of six months. The youngster returned to his Aegean hometown, Ödemiş, for this period, moving from state-governed military space to familial town life. In Ödemiş, Gürkan first sought an appointment with a surgeon in the big city, İzmir, who he accessed through bourgeois acquaintances, but recalls not being cared for by the doctor who told him there was nothing to be done.

Soon after futile encounters with doctors, Gürkan's older brother, the narrative goes, guides him to a *çıkıkçı*, a traditional healer/bonesetter who had earlier miraculously healed the older brother's football-caused knee injury. In the narrative, the bonesetter tightly wraps Gürkan's foot with some homemade balm and orders him to rest for fifteen days. While resting, Gürkan "practiced with hardcover books in a style he had seen in one of the magazines." At the end of fifteen days, the healer unwraps the foot and suggests at-home exercises, including sunbathing for the foot. Gürkan follows the healer's advice while also practicing with "hardcover books." Eventually, his foot feels pain-free and "back to normal." On his return to military school in Konya, Gürkan is examined by the school doctor, who is surprised to see him recovered but orders the pupil never to play football again. Gürkan watches his schoolmates play, envying his peers in this more-than-a-year hiatus from football. Repeating a leitmotif in the narrative, Gürkan, this time, comes across the Ankara-based popular sports magazine *Kırmızı-Beyaz*, where he reads about "a form of training practiced by the celebrity striker Tommy Lawton of Arsenal [London]" that involves walking on toes in an upright position in 20-minute sets.

"Feeling ashamed" for practicing these drills and "fearing someone will see him," Gürkan nonetheless secretly follows the advice and "before long, my calves were rock-strong and my feet back in power." After the world war ends and Gürkan moves to the War Academy, he once again bypasses military hierarchies to pursue football popular culture. The college student accepts an invitation from the city's bourgeois notables to play for a civilian football team representing Konya against visitors Kasımpaşa from Istanbul. Gürkan impresses the public and makes the news after this popularly spectated match, but now faces military sanctions for violating army rules against cadets appearing in civilian sports events. However, his fame saves him from sanctions, and Gürkan eventually gets selected for both the civilian and the military national football teams in 1949. He goes on to represent the Turkish military squad that wins the inter-army games in France that year (Gürkan n.d., 18–39).

Regardless of the veracity of Gürkan's memoir, the narrative sequence that moves from prohibitive military doctors and surgeons to the enabling small-town healer and then to rehabilitation through drills devised by English footballers he encounters in the popular sports press suggests the structural role these binary oppositions play in the formation of athletic subjectivity and corporeality in the social context at the time. The walk-on-toes method developed by a professional footballer in England could be considered as an accurate example of what doctors called "the state of *ampirizma* in sport affairs" (T.C. MEB BTGM 1947, 87). In the narrative, moreover, the practical therapy of rural healers, despised by the medical professional community, is mapped on the same plane as the practical therapies of celebrity athletes one finds in the sports press. Both serve applied sportive goals in shorter-term time frames. Together, the healer and the footballer constitute the young cadet's private world of small-town family and magazine readership, as well as secret pleasures hidden from military oversight, culminating in the narrator's autodidact coming-of-age as a celebrity footballer parallel to his military career. These sportive pathways comprise the *ampirik* embodiments of play, training, healing, and self-care. Critically, these pathways are not reducible to "the traditional" that precedes "the modern" but constitute a coevolving *ampirik* modernity nurtured by sources of authority and inspiration outside the purview of doctor-soldier or clinic-barracks complexes. These sources are backed by the powers of publicity, popularity, and practicality—and professional specialization in sports.

Round 3: Occupational Physiology versus Popular Fitness

Different than testing and treatment, in the futuristic vision of Raşit Serdengeçti and Şevket Aziz Kansu, *sportif-tıbbi muayene* would be conducted by a committee of experts in "sports physiology, physio-pathology, sports anatomy, anthropometry, and sports psychology." Sports medicine grew out of the physiological science of muscle fatigue that dominated the worldview of social hygienists and liberal reformers since the late nineteenth century, who sought to rehabilitate laboring bodies against the ills of industrial work technocratically. As demonstrated in Anson Rabinbach's classic *Human Motor* (1990), the science of fatigue viewed the laboring human body as a living motor that should be well maintained rather than overworked. It was a technocratic discourse for managing capital–labor conflict: if workers were assigned tasks according to aptitude, they would be more efficient. According to the science of fatigue, if workers could regularly rest, muscle and nerve fatigue could be minimized, and labor could be energized back to efficiency. The study of fatigue recognized limits to human productivity but replaced psychological explanations like laziness with the search for the physiological causes of those limits. Fatigue scientists were often social reformers who favored capping working hours and debilitating effort. They saw these reforms as necessary policies for the national good in the long run. Immersed in this literature, Serdengeçti published numerous books describing the physiology of fatigue (*yorgunluk*) and rest (*dinlenme*) (Serdengeçti, 1948, 1951). His sports-medical discourse was similarly prophylactic and aimed to correct the irrational uses of athletic human motors.

While preventive in origin, global developments in the 1920s had invented ways to put theoretical muscle physiology in the service of performance-enhancing technoscience in sports, especially for runners. One of the prominent examples was the work of British Nobel Laureate A. V. Hill, who experimented on elite athletes during high-intensity training and popularized new explanations of injury or below-par performance. His reasoning focused on metabolic changes during exertion, such as muscle cell deoxidation. Combined with technical innovations worldwide that allowed periodic monitoring of metabolic changes during the whole course of strenuous exertion, Hill's experiments gave birth to new concepts like the oxygen plateau, maximal oxygen uptake, and oxygen debt. These indicated metabolic patterns and benchmarks during intense exertion and which were visualized in the scientific language of diagrams, graphs, and tables. This new science of high-performance physiology soon informed endurance drills to increase athletes' aerobic capacities and training schedules that combined the goals of injury prevention and performance enhancement (Wrynn 2010; Krüger 2015; Heggie 2011). These developments are today accepted as the origins of the applied science of exercise physiology, which developed into a full-fledged academic discipline only after the 1960s.

Physiological representation of sports performance involved a critical optical shift, which Hikmet Dilevurgun nicely described in his paper at the 1943 National Turkish Medical Congress. Physiological assessment of fitness penetrated beyond what teammates, trainers, or spectators could see with the naked eye. Dilevurgun wrote that "the sports show played in front of our eyes might appear like an epic of strength [*kudret destanı*], but in reality, [the sports show] obeys a metabolic drama that takes place in the interior of the cell." According to the doctor, "the protagonist [in this metabolic drama] is not the athlete's strong muscles but the presence or absence of oxygen. Ninety percent of sports injuries follow the scarcity of oxygen" (Dilevurgun 1943, 10). As the doctor's discourse implied, accepting muscle physiology (cell oxidation) as the decider of endurance went against the centrality of photographic representation and journalistic rhetoric in the popular reception of athlete celebrities and the commercial routines of the sports press. Photo portraits of topless athletes centering on biceps were the primary media for popularizing athletic masculinity in late Ottoman urban culture as masterfully demonstrated by Murat Yıldız (2015). In the interwar period, too, popular weeklies reached audiences with photographic representations, and improvements in photographic technology helped adorn the popular press with snapshots of games-in-action. In this context, it is worth noting that Burhan Felek himself was one of Babıali's first sports photographers. To paraphrase Dilevurgun, if journalistic narratives or photographic compositions represented fitness in dramatic frames to appeal to mass audiences, figures like Felek were seasoned experts in this rhetoric. But sports medicine manuals did not speak this "athletic vernacular" (Wrynn 2010, 134). These manuals included not photographs but tables, graphs, and diagrams that represented the results of spirometer measurements or illustrated heart X-rays (see Figure 11.1) . The physicians' policy draft in the 1946 Council aimed to expand this infrastructure of biomedical representation.

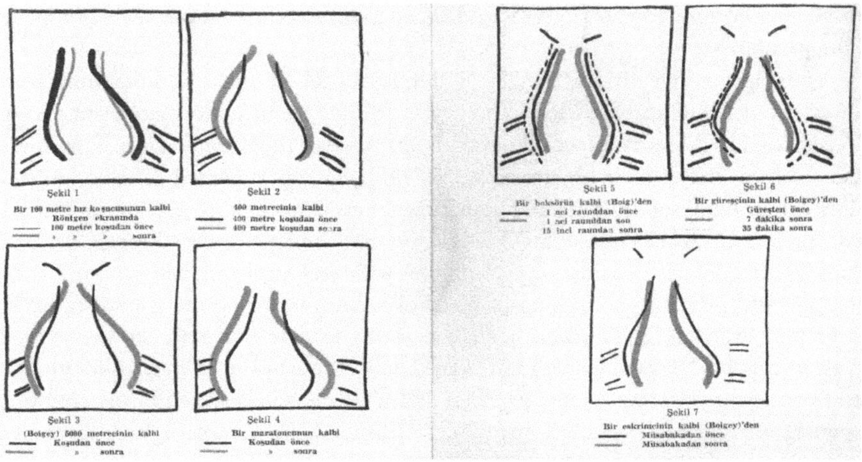

Figure 11.1 Serdengeçti's biomedical illustrations of athletic fitness (Serdengeçti 1949, 15–16).

Discontent against physiological sport technoscience should also be contextualized in this representational dissonance between the sport-medical gaze, on the one hand, and the commercial compact between athletes, former-athletes-turned-trainers, sports journalists, sports clubs, and popular consumption on the other. The verbose but playful and rich-in-analogy rhetoric used in the 1946 Council by skillful journalists Atabey and Felek as they argued against the scientific discourse of doctors at the time testifies to the social content of uneasy relations between the sportive and biomedical domains I analyze here. It is not surprising that Serdengeçti expressed his disapproval of the sportive domain with phrases connoting sophistry and religion, calling journalists *spor ulemaları* "who create literary phrases such as the love of sports and admire and name those athletes as heroes who sacrifice and wear out their bodies for ambitions of championship" (Serdengeçti 1942a). Adapting the logic of occupational health to the sports world, Serdengeçti also diagnosed the social obstacles that made it impossible for regulators to treat sports clubs and venues as workplaces. According to the physician, industrial conceptions of sports were obstructed by the commercial compact between athletes seeking fame, journalists marketing sportive rhetoric, and popularity-seeking sports executives who "have turned their back on science" and "exploit a few champion athletes with God-given talent and harm them for purposes of quick glory" (Serdengeçti 1947d). This compact made it impossible to treat club executives as employers. On the side of labor, "ambition for fame makes the athlete forget about the hardships involved." If sports could be treated by occupational medicine, that would "benefit both the worker and the boss" (Serdengeçti 1942c). Using the same analogy used by the military hygienist Sırrı Alıçlı that equated the barbarism of world wars with fatigue-caused nervous restlessness (Alıçlı 1947), Serdengeçti, in his wartime column, argued that sports turned into barbarism when the sports world was not regulated by rational limits set by experts of fatigue science. According to Serdengeçti, sports medicine, with its ennobling characteristics, "bridled the barbaric habits of modern civilization" and "rescued sports from blood-thirsty sadistic pleasures of spectacle" where the athlete's material body became human sacrifice (Serdengeçti 1942c).

Round 4: Anatomic Police versus Liberal Men of Practice

Whereas Serdengeçti represented the physiological component, Kansu's persona was central to the anthropometric element in this expert planning. Anthropometrics would classify every candidate-athlete in the nation by "body structure and body type" and inscribe this classification on GDPE-authorized health cards (T.C. MEB BTGM 1947, 90). As a physician-turned-physical anthropologist who spent the interwar period racializing ethnoreligious boundaries (Maksudyan 2005), Kansu was silent on race taxonomy in the 1946 Council. Anthropometry, here, is embedded in the broader sports science vision for rationalizing the allocation of limited human resources to specialized athletic challenges according to individual physical aptitude. In the years leading to the council, Kansu had been commissioning anthropometric surveys to former students who took his anthropology courses at the Faculty of Language, History, and Geography and now taught at Village Institutes. Working like field researchers under Kansu's direction, these teachers measured their pupils' anatomic dimensions and had them compete in athletic events serving as small-scale experiments, tabling sportive records according to the Manouvrier Index, a simple, leg length to trunk length ratio (see, e.g., Özden 1946).

These experiments focused mainly on Olympic track and field games and claimed to tell long-distance potential from sprint potential or high-jump potential from long-jump potential. Kansu published the results of these experiments in the DTCF *Journal of Anthropology and Ethnology* and referenced them in the council as baby steps toward his future vision. With more state funding and staff for sportive anthropometry, he hoped to ultimately build a center in Ankara that regularly updated data from competitions nationwide and tracked progress (or decline) in the national record. The center, he hoped, would analyze population-level data in every Olympic branch. The more this scientific knowledge accumulated in the academic annals published in Ankara, the more the center would be able to coordinate, or perhaps dictate, decisions by coaches in sports clubs and physical education teachers in public schools nationwide who deal day-to-day with young bodies, guiding them to athletic endeavors. Centralized guidance would help scientifically economize the work of athletic human motors by assigning adolescents to the sport branch in which the pupil had a shot at excelling. This expert-guided allocation would prevent "youthful energies to be wasted in irrational venues of effort" (T.C. MEB BTGM 1947, 90).

Key advocates of rolling back state interference in sport governance, such as journalists Burhan Felek and Eşref Şefik Atabey, objected every time the possibility of anthropometric mandates was raised. "I am not in principle against anthropometric indexes," Felek joined the debate, "but I wonder whether the report's authors are themselves convinced of the absolute truth of these categories." Felek presented a narrative in recent sports history, a rhetorical method best employed by career sports journalists that performatively asserted and defended the sociopolitical boundary between the world of sports and doctors. Giving the example of two different sprinters who won gold medals in the same event in the 1924 Paris and 1928 Amsterdam Olympics, Felek voiced skepticism about the infallibility of equating anatomy with sportive aptitude. "Abrahams was a thin and tall man. But before that, the world champion sprinter Paddock was a short, stocky man." By contrasting the body types of two consecutive champions of the same competition, Felek warned that "we, those who practically work in this profession [*bizim gibi pratik olarak bu işte çalışanlar*]," sense danger. Felek continued,

> a doctor can tell a man, "You should become a sprinter." And then, among those who apply these [classifications], a bigot or, how should I say, a functionary who has too much respect for expertise [*bir mutaassıp veya nasıl söyleyeyim, ihtisasa fevkalade hörmeti olan bir memur*] can tell this man "I classify you as a sprinter and you cannot become a long-distance runner. I will not license you to sprint." I propose to accept the policy draft [by the physicians committee] on the condition that these [anthropometric classifications] will remain mere recommendations [Bravo sounds and applaud]. (T.C. MEB BTGM 1947, 99)

Felek, here, underlined an affinity between anthropometric classification and bureaucratic rigidity and defined an opposition between scientific experts and obedient state functionaries on one side, and "those like us who practically work in sports," on the other. Felek proposed to keep these as separate professional jurisdictions without allowing executive meddling by biomedicine or attempting to discredit sports medicine.

Felek's cautious discourse, "how should I say," a tone he preserved throughout the council, signals his unwillingness to antagonize GDPE bureaucrats. But his speech was followed by applause loud enough to be noted in the transcripts. Published minutes contain other signs of antipathy to anthropometric decision-making. When Kansu's field researcher, Village Institutes teacher Osman Özden, took the stage to insist on the correlation between anthropometric assignment and superior athletic records, the teacher had to conclude his remarks amid commotion from the audience, likely telling him to cut it short. Felek's compromising attitude was not unexpected. He had been appointed to CAC-PE in 1938 to mediate between the sports community in Istanbul and GDPE bureaucracy in Ankara. Between 1945 and 1952, though, Felek was one of the three sponsors of a draft bill to replace Law No. 3530. The other two sponsors would become Democrat Party deputies in 1950: Fenerbahçe club member/former athlete Zeki Rıza Sporel and Konya deputy Saffet Gürol. During the 1920s, Felek and Gürol were executives in *Türkiye İdman Cemiyetleri İttifakı* (Union of Sports Societies of Turkey, TICI), the highest governing authority in sports between 1924 and 1936 before the union was replaced by GDPE. In the same decade, Sporel had risen to become a soccer celebrity not only in homebase Istanbul but also across Turkey as the nation's top scorer and sports apparel merchant. With one foot in the world of sports and one foot in the world of bureaucracy, Felek retained his mediating rhetoric throughout the council, but he advocated on the side of the sports community on almost all contentious issues, which attests to the defeated position of GDPE hardliners who could not even convince the friendliest Olympian. In fact, staunch critics of GDPE in Istanbul's sports press regularly blamed Felek for being a GDPE lackey, while GDPE hardliners did not trust him.[7] Unlike the bill's other sponsors, Felek did not seek a political career in the Democrat Party. For these reasons, I find Felek's position significant. It suggests the conflicts in 1946 did not merely reflect party politics but were refracted through sportive discontent with GDPE based on a broader professional cleavage.

In a personal letter to the council, TICI-era national athlete Firüzan Tekil demanded that "the state sponsors (*himaye*) but not administers (*idare*) sport," a consistently used categorical opposition by TICI leaders (T.C. MEB BTGM 1947, 283). TICI statutes acknowledged state sponsorship of sports as *himaye* while retaining the private law status of TICI as a civil society federation formed according to the law of associations and governed according to self-drafted bylaws. Discontent with visions of technoscientific administration of the athletic body that materialized in the physicians' proposal should be seen as the micro-managerial correlate of this conceptualization of governance at the macro-level. Bureaucratically backed scientific managerialism crossed the boundary from sponsorship to administration if guidelines were not recommendations, as Felek suggested they should be, but executive orders legitimated by the state-certified status of scientific truths. It is important to underline that in this early Cold War moment, the sport-political language of autonomy was part and parcel of a global dividing line between liberal democratic regimes, on one side, where sports affairs were governed autonomously by private law federations, and totalitarian regimes, on the other side, where sports affairs were embedded in administrative state hierarchies. This binary language was quickly evolving into a global discourse of the emerging cultural Cold War between democratic and antidemocratic sport regimes (Beck 2005; Keys 2006). *Himaye,* as distinct from *idare,* was a local version of this global discourse.

Round 5: The Container versus the Contained

Sportive refutations of anthropometric assignment also produced liberal narratives of athletic personhood. Eşref Şefik Atabey, the loquacious rhetorician, took the stage to share a father–son allegory that undermined the preventive medicine-driven paternalism implicit in Kansu's and Serdengeçti's discourse of scientific decision-making. Based on "his physical form, I tried to encourage my son to practice swimming and even bought him fashionable apparel, but the kid won't swim," Atabey said. Similarly, "a high schooler might get classified as a runner because of his physical form but not have a taste [*zevk*] for that sport. Just like my son didn't. What will he do? He will start boxing." Decisions based on "physiological formations," he continued, "prioritize the cover but what makes us practice a sport is our inside" (*formasyon fizyolojik ile seleksiyon yapılırsa kılıfa ehemmiyet vermiş oluruz. Halbuki bize sporu yaptıracak olan içimizdir*). Atabey not only created a binary opposition between personalized interiors and impersonal exteriors, but he also rhetorically amplified this language with poetic metaphors. For Atabey, the athlete was not reducible to the *kılıf* (cover) but had an *iç* (inside); the athlete's driving elan was not the *zarf* (the envelope) but the *mazruf* (the enveloped), inaccessible to this science of covers. With his binary rhetoric, the journalist invented a liberal discourse on athletic personhood, divided between a private sphere of subjective difference and a public sphere of objective similarity (T.C. MEB BTGM 1947, 145).

Atabey's discourse rejected decision-making based on medical generalizations and defined athletic ontogenesis as the free play of subjective inclinations and preferences. Moreover, Atabey also inverted the pathologizing discourse of doctors like Serdengeçti, who described anatomic or physiologic outcomes of extraordinary effort and exertion as *deviations* from population-level norms, in other words, as abnormalities. For Atabey, in contrast, the material, bodily outcomes of intensive specialization and effort in a sport branch are plastic *adaptations* of one's cover to what is dictated by the inside of the body. "Every adaptation is a deformation: even if this takes ten years, in the end, physical form will no longer matter." Disregarding the question of whether such adaptations can be harmful, Atabey's discourse called out the genetic determinism of anthropometric assignment for violating liberal boundaries and meddling in the private sphere of playful self-discovery and self-realization at one's own risk—for interfering in zones of entrepreneurial, competitive selfhood (T.C. MEB BTGM 144–45). Atabey's use of the concept *zevk* (taste) is particularly important as the GDPE hardliners frequently used the same term when criticizing leisurely sport and defining physical exercise as a citizen's duty to remain fit for the nation. Atabey's defense of allocating young bodies to whichever sport types they enjoy was followed by an English-centric historical metanarrative by civil law professor Bülent Davran, who refuted romantic histories that equated modern sports with Platonic physical education. Davran argued sports to have been born in modern England as part of liberal struggles against the Anglican Church, which banned "play for play's sake" for being sinful—equating GDPE with puritanism. In what must have sounded scandalous to GDPE administrators, Davran argued that sports had no utility for political or industrial ends. The legal scholar defended the citizens' right to harm themselves at their own risk in their freely chosen leisure activities, since "*zevk* need not be moderate" (154–8).

Unlike Felek, Atabey had been a vocal critic of TICI's amateur code and was the protagonist in the dramatic split of Galatasaray Sports Club into two separate organizations and the formation of *İş Bankası* sponsored Güneş in the early 1930s. Refuting the sports medicine report, according to which nation-states with sports medicine organizations outcompete those who lack biomedical sports bureaucracies, Atabey not only defended the technical superiority of *ampirik* methods of training but went further to claim health screenings were futile. Once again, relying on journalistic narration of episodic sports history, Atabey declared *ampirik* methods victorious in recent world history by citing the 1921 title match in New Jersey where American champion Jack Dempsey triumphed over his French rival Georges Carpentier. French physicians had trained Carpentier "engrossed in their strict theories," but he was weaker than Dempsey, Atabey recounted. For Atabey, *ampirik* drills were based on "mechanical methods" and improved technique and physicality simultaneously through the repetition of moves specific to that sport's gaming rules. These drills were designed with a "knowledge intrinsic to sports." According to Atabey's narrative, "the United States earlier tried to raise champions by anthropometric means but later reverted to mechanical methods," representing the triumph of *ampirik* worldwide. In this *ampirik* modernity, physical fitness follows technique (rather than the other way around) as athletes build strength and endurance through repeating technical drills and playing more practice games (103).

Moreover, this professional technical immersion improves intuitive judgment on physical fitness. Atabey argued that fielding sick runners should be blamed on the trainer rather than explained by a lack of medical oversight. These incidents follow from the "incompetency of an *ampirik* expertise, the incompetence of the trainer" (*ampirik bir ihtisasın, yani antrenörün ehliyetsizliğinden ileri gelir*), which implied that an experienced specialist could intuitively notice fitness problems. In this narrative, the source of both authority and responsibility should remain inside the sports community rather than be externalized to a bureaucratic overseer if athlete safety measures are to be effective. Dangerously asserting exclusive jurisdiction of athletes and former athletes in assessing medical eligibility, Atabey praised the proverbial "[wrestler] Suyolcu Ahmet, who is one hundred years old and still retains his will" and "can tell the fit from the unfit if he was presented with thirty young candidate wrestlers" (103–4). While not going as far as Atabey, Burhan Felek nonetheless also criticized existing testing procedures as "wholly theoretical" (*tamamen nazari*), as not having applied value for athletes (77).

In both Atabey's and Felek's discourses discussed above, the binary opposition theoretical versus practical incorporates multiple layers of ideological meaning on technicality and scientificity. They echo Cold War discourse on "applied and experiential" models of expertise associated with American philosophies of technoscientific managerialism that claimed to overcome scholastic distinctions between experts and nonexperts and used sportive metaphors of teamwork to imagine cohesion between experts and workers in goal-oriented projects (Adalet 2018, 111). Atabey's idealized vision of *ampirik* culture, embodied by trainer-boxer cohesion, similarly imagines the nation as a cohesive team united by the technical dictates of goal-oriented competition. This team's cohesion relies on fraternal senior–junior ties (*abi-kardeş*) between successive generations of retired and active male athletes, excludes the expert-stranger, and undermines the hierarchy between the scientific and the practical. In doing so, this *ampirik* vision delegitimizes the position of the biomedical expert as a praetorian guardian over an irrational, potentially self-harming athlete. By the same stroke, Atabey's discourse forecloses the possibility of treating athletic effort as labor or club–athlete relations as workplace relations involving commerce-driven risks of injury and harm, central tenets of Serdengeçti's sports medicine discourse. The tension thus hints at class-political implications of how and where technoscientific authority and expertise of sport governance would be located, as the image of cohesive teamwork erases the image of the occupational workplace.

Conclusion: Cold War's Victory

This chapter focused on a critical moment of transition in the political history of Turkish nation-building when a flagship institute of interwar nation-building, the

GDPE, was critically evaluated and directions for postwar development were fiercely debated. I showed how political discourse on the athletic body involved more than one metanarrative of modernization. While GDPE-affiliated biomedicine experts had ambitions to manage the sportive nation scientifically, a coalition of sportive democrats with powers of publicity were pushing to truncate those visions. I describe this tendency as "undoctoring sport" in the sense that these brewing formulations of privately governed athleticism foreshadow a broader vision of "bottom-up" governance that decentered projects of bureaucratic doctoring. This sportive vision blended with democratic, liberal, and populist tendencies that would crystallize in the Democrat Party hegemony to come but was grounded first and foremost in tensions over professional jurisdiction. Focusing on the year 1946, I tried to work on a historical cross-section when entanglements of the athletic body, biomedicine, technoscience, and governance were signaling transformative articulations in the language of the cultural cold war.

Notes

1 *Beden Terbiyesi Kanunu, No. 3530*. Official Gazette no. 3961, 29 June 1938.
2 "Beden ve gençlik terbiyesi teşkilatı kurmak için Almanya'dan gelecek olan Dr. Carl Diem'in gelişi hakkında yazışmalar." 14 November 1938. BCA 490-1-0-0. 116-75-2; "Rahmi Apak, Naili Moran ve Carl Diem'in gençlik teşkilatları ve spor eğitimi üzerine hazırladıkları raporlar." 18 November 1937. BCA 490-1-0-0. 1107-43-1.
3 A powerful text is Fikret Adil, "Türk Sporu: Yükselme için yeni veçhe verilmesi lazımdır," *Futbol*, issue no. 1, 17 September 1945, p. 1, 8.
4 Taha Toros Archives, Folder No. 109—Hasan Ali—Can Yücel. Details about recording and printing the council transcripts are mentioned by Vildan Aşir Savaşır after Hasan Ali Yücel's death. Savaşır was the GDPE director and an ally of Yücel during the 1946 Council, but both figures were soon replaced.
5 For a review of the early Republic's prominent national sport journal *Spor Alemi*, where both Burhan Felek and Eşref Şefik rose to prominence as sports journalists, see Eroğul (2010). In almost all references, the word *fenni* referred to systematized technical or tactical routines of training and gaming, not to biomedical knowledge.
6 On the fate of print entrepreneurs who had skeptical views of popular sports for their unhealthiness, see Haldun Taner's recollections on the newspaper *Yeni İstanbul*'s commercial failure in the late 1940s (Bali 2011, 50).
7 This is based on the minutes of CAC-PE (Aydın, Geyik, and Ayçiçek n.d., 370–8).

References

Abbott, Andrew. 1991. "The Order of Professionalization: An Empirical Analysis," *Work and Occupations* 18 (4): 355–84.

Adalet, Begüm. 2018. *Hotels and Highways: The Construction of Modernization Theory in Cold War Turkey*, Stanford, CA: Stanford University Press.

Akın, Yiğit. 2004. *"Gürbüz ve Yavuz Evlatlar": Erken Cumhuriyet'te Beden Terbiyesi ve Spor*, Istanbul: İletişim.

Alemdaroğlu, Ayça. 2005. «Politics of the Body and Eugenic Discourse in Early Republican Turkey,» *Body and Society* 11 (1): 61–76.

Alıçlı, Sırrı. 1947. "Mesleğimize Dair Konuşmalar," *Dirim*, July: 198–200.

As, Efdal. 2016. "İktidar-Spor Kurumları İlişkileri Bağlamında İki Dünya Savaşı Arasında Türkiye Cumhuriyeti'nin Katıldığı Olimpiyatlar (1924 Paris, 1928 Amsterdam, 1936 Berlin)," *CTAD* 12 (24): 156–204.

Aydın, Zübeyt, Cafer Geyik, and Halil İbrahim Ayçiçek. n.d. "Spor Hizmetleri Genel Müdürlüğü," *Yayınlar*. Accessed February 28, 2022. http:// https://sgm.gsb.gov.tr/Public/Edit/images/SGM/dokumanlar/MDKK_1942_0953.pdf

Aytürk, İlker. 2015. "Post-post-Kemalizm: Yeni bir paradigmayı beklerken," *Birikim*, November: 34–47.

Bali, Rıfat N. 2011. "Unutulmuş Bir Tüccar ve Gazete Patronu: Habip Edip Törehan," *Toplumsal Tarih*, May: 46–53.

Beck, Peter. 2005. "Britain and the Cold War's 'Cultural Olympics': Responding to the Political Drive of Soviet Sport, 1945-58," *Contemporary British History* 19 (2): 169–85.

Brockett, Gavin D. 2009. "Provincial Newspapers as a Historical Source: Büyük Cihad and the Great Struggle for the Muslim Turkish Nation (1951-53)," *International Journal of Middle East Studies* 41: 437–55.

Currie, F. Davison. 1919. *The Science of Soccer*, London: G. Routledge & Sons Ltd.

Defrance, Jacques. 2013. "The Making of a Field With Weak Autonomy: The Case of the Sports Field in France, 1895-1955," in Philip S. Gorski (ed.), *Bourdieu and Historical* Analysis, 303–26, Durham, NC: Duke University Press.

Dilevurgun, Hamdi. 1943. *Sekizinci Milli Türk Tıb Kongresi: Sporun Tıbbi Arızaları*, Istanbul: Kader Basımevi.

Dinc, Gulten. 2007. "Friedrich Dessauer's (1881-1963) Contributions to the Development of Radiotherapy in Turkey," *Radiotherapy and Oncology* 82: 239–42. https://doi.org/10.1016/j.radonc.2006.12.003

Dole, Christopher. 2004. "In the Shadows of Medicine and Modernity: Medical Integration and Secular Histories of Religious Healing in Turkey," *Culture, Medicine, and Psychiatry* 28: 255–80.

Erken, Ali. 2019. *America and the Making of Modern Turkey: Science, Culture and Political Alliances*, London: I. B. Tauris.

Eroğul, Ali. 2010. "Spor Alemi (1919-1929): A Turkish Sports Magazine in the Transition Period From the Ottoman Empire to the Turkish Republic," MA Thesis, Boğaziçi University.

Gürkan, Sahir. n.d. *Sahir Gürkan Belgeseli*, Istanbul: Türkiye Futbol Vakfı Yayınları.

Hau, Michael. 2008. "Sports in the Human Economy: 'Leibesübungen,' Medicine, Psychology, and Performance Enhancement during the Weimar Republic," *Central European History* 41: 381–412.

Heggie, Vanessa. 2011. *A History of British Sports Medicine*, Manchester: Manchester University Press.

İlkan Rasimoğlu, Ceren Gülser. 2021. "Introduction of the Modern Physician and the Debate on Medical Professionalism in the 19th Century Ottoman Empire," *Dynamis* 41: 473–501.

Keys, Barbara J. 2006. *Globalizing Sport: National Rivalry and International Community in the 1930s,* Cambridge, MA: Harvard University Press.

Krüger, Michael. 2015. "History of Sports Medicine in Germany. Some Preliminary Reflections on a Complex Research Project," *Historical Social Research / Histrorische Sozialforschung* 40 (4): 331–49.

Maksudyan, Nazan. 2005. "The Turkish Review of Anthropology and the Racist Face of Turkish Nationalism," *Cultural Dynamics* 17 (3): 291–322. https://doi.org/10.1177/0921374005061992
Örnek, Cangül and Çağdaş Üngör. 2013. *Turkey in the Cold War: Ideology and Culture*, New York, London: Palgrave Macmillan.
Özden, Osman. 1946. *Türk Atletleri Üzerine Antropometrik Araştırmalar.* Ankara: İdeal Basım ve Cilt Evi.
Özkan, Hande. 2025. "The Liminal Forest: Mud, Science, and Nationalism in Turkey's Forests," in Duygu Kaşdoğan, Ekin Kurtiç, and Mehmet Ekinci (eds.), *Material Politics in Turkey: Infrastructure, Science, and Expertise*, 93–118, London: Bloomsbury.
Rabinbach, Anson. 1990. *The Human Motor: Energy, Fatigue, and the Origins of Modernity*, New York: Basic Books.
Sekizinci Milli Türk Tıb Kongresi, Ankara 18-20 Birinciteşrin 1943. 1944, Istanbul: Kader Basımevi.
Serdengeçti, Raşit. 1942a. "Hekimlik ve sporda ihtiras," *İstiklal*, 12 April.
Serdengeçti, Raşit. 1942b. "Spor faaliyetlerinde tuzun ve şekerin rolü . . . ." *İstiklal*, 28 March.
Serdengeçti, Raşit. 1942c. "Spor Hekimliği," *İstiklal*, 3 April.
Serdengeçti, Raşit. 1946. *Hekim Gözüyle Tenis,* Ankara: T.C. Milli Eğitim Bakanlığı Beden Eğitimi Genel Müdürlüğü Yayın Müdürlüğü.
Serdengeçti, Raşit. 1947a. "Bizde Spor Hekimliği II," *Dirim*, June: 168–9.
Serdengeçti, Raşit. 1947b. "Bizde Spor Hekimliği III," *Dirim*, September-October: 269–73.
Serdengeçti, Raşit. 1947c. "Spor Hekimliği," *Dirim*, January-February: 16–18.
Serdengeçti, Raşit. 1947d. "Yabancı memleketlerde ve bizde 'Spor Hekimliği'," *Dirim*, March: 73–5.
Serdengeçti, Raşit. 1948. *Dinlenme,* Ankara: Milli Eğitim Basımevi.
Serdengeçti, Raşit. 1949. *Spor Hekimliği: Sporun Fizyololojisi, İjyeni, Biyometrisi, arızaları ve tedavileri*, Istanbul: T.C. MEB BTGM, İbrahim Horoz Matbaası.
Serdengeçti, Raşit. 1951. *Sağlık Meselelerimiz,* Ankara: Milli Eğitim Bakanlığı.
Serdengeçti, Raşit. 1964. *Spor Hekimliği Nedir, Ne İçindir, ve Nasıl Teşkilatlanmalıdır?* Istanbul: Türkiye Milli Olimpiyat Komitesi Yayınları, Güneş Matbaası.
Starr, Paul. 2009. "Professionalization and Public Health: Historical Legacies, Continuing Dilemmas," *Journal of Public Health Management Practice* 15 (6): S26–S30.
Şen, Sertaç. 2025. "Smoking Under a Volcano: Cold War Base Life in Turkish Thrace," in Duygu Kaşdoğan, Ekin Kurtiç, and Mehmet Ekinci (eds.), *Material Politics in Turkey: Infrastructure, Science, and Expertise*, 193–211, London: Bloomsbury.
T.C. MEB BTGM. 1947. *Birinci Beden Eğitimi ve Spor Şurası: 18-24 Şubat 1946: Çalışma Programı, Raporlar, Konuşmalar*, Istanbul: İbrahim Horoz Matbaası.
Wrynn, Alison M. 2010. "The Athlete in the Making: The Scientific Study of American Athletic Performance, 1920-1932," *Sport in History* 30 (1): 121–37.
Yıldız, Murat C. 2015. "'What is a Beautiful Body?': Late Ottoman 'Sportsman' Photographs and New Notions of Male Corporeal Beauty," *Middle East Journal of Culture and Communication* 8: 192–214.

12

Assembling Gold, Manufacturing Risk

Technopolitics in the Age of the Third Gold Rush

Tarık Nejat Dinç

The world has witnessed an unprecedented proliferation of mining activities over the past four decades. From the mid-1980s to the turn of the century, more than a hundred countries changed their mining codes, primarily through the World Bank's Structural Adjustment Policies to attract private and foreign investments in mining. Gold mining lies at the heart of this extractive moment, accounting for nearly half of all new mining investments (Bridge 2004). Consequently, more gold have been produced since 1980 than all gold ever produced up to then. I call this the *third gold rush*, following the colonial gold rush in sixteenth-century South America and the settler-colonial gold rushes in nineteenth-century US, Canada, South Africa, and Australia.

Within the third gold rush, the turn of the twenty-first century witnessed a significant obstacle to the Turkish government's extraction-based neoliberal development strategy aiming to transform the country into a major gold producer: a cotton- and olive-farming community mobilized against Turkey's first proposed gold mine in Bergama, Izmir. The conflict centered on the technopolitics of risk regarding the cyanide use for extraction, the construction of a toxic-waste dam, and acid mine drainage (AMD) contaminating soil and water. The ensuing decade-long resistance by Bergama's farming communities emerged as a pioneer and role model for rural environmental movements against mining and other development projects across the country. Moreover, it significantly contributed to the growing global anti-cyanide mobilization.

Exploring Turkey's first gold mine in Bergama, this chapter ethnographically traces one fundamental question: How can we theorize the relationship between global extractive expansion and risk politics shaping mining conflicts? As much as neoliberal policies and rising gold prices are significant factors underlying the third gold rush, these alone cannot fully explain its material conditions of the possibility. To address this question, I scrutinize the materialities of gold mining and more-than-human entanglements.

My query is divided into three sub-questions, each discussed in corresponding sections: (1) What are the material conditions of the possibility of the third gold rush, and what specific risks do they engender? (2) How does farmers' situated expertise on farming uncertainties and risks lead to their anti-gold mining resistance? (3) How does the corporate–state nexus attempt to govern risk and contain resistance?

Gold has an enigmatic existence, being simultaneously everywhere and nowhere. Even our living-room plant's pot soil contains some gold. Yet, its average distribution in the Earth's crust is so rare that 1,000 metric tonnes of crustal material contain only a little over 1 gram of gold (Saunders et al. 2018).[1] Gold's distribution throughout the whole planet is uneven. Gold prospectors of the nineteenth-century gold rush era used gravity to separate gold particles much denser than the sandy host medium and precipitate them at their pans' bottoms. The Earth did the same in its formative era some 4.5 billion years ago. Denser elements, including gold, moved toward the newly forming geosphere's center and became part of its melted iron core. Consequently, Earth's core is thought to contain 98 percent of the planet's total gold inventory. Indeed, the core's average gold content is comparable to the grade—the relative gold content by mass—of many recently "discovered" gold "deposits."[2]

Hence, gold's relative rarity is more conjunctural than absolute. The romantic imagery of gold as hidden wealth waiting for a lucky prospector is more fictive than real. In gold mining, the identification, demarcation, and fixing of a geological space as an ore body is a function of resource economics, price, technology, quantity, particle size and shape, and the presence of other minerals, as well as the physical and chemical interactions among them.

Hecht (2018) heeds Tsing's (2005) call to focus on political dimensions of scale-making projects, proposing *interscalar vehicles* as both analytical and political scale-making agents. Interscalar vehicles move between, and connect, spatiotemporal scales. Here, I follow Hecht and contend that a new mining assemblage developed over a century and centered on cyanidation is an interscalar vehicle, both spatially and temporally.

Thus, I argue that, contrary to public and analytic imaginaries that treat mineral "resources" and surrounding nonliving entities as inert, mining is a more-than-human endeavor that humans constantly try to navigate through the agency of nonhumans. These entangled relations between humans and nonhumans lead to a crucial aspect of (gold) mining often overlooked: the act of extraction is simultaneously an act of injection. The peculiar characteristics of this extraction versus injection constitute the risk politics that contour mining conflicts. Therefore, to theorize the interplay between the scaling of extractivism (Acosta 2013; Shapiro and McNeish 2021) at the global level and socio-environmental risk politics, we must expand our analytical focus on resources to include where and how they are materially located, and from the extraction of the resource to the production of waste as a locus of manufactured risk. This shift in focus reveals that risk assessment, as a technopolitical apparatus, acts as a vector of extractive slow violence. In line with the aim of this book volume in revealing "co-production of materials and politics in empirical terms—that is, by focusing on particular practices and processes unfolding in specific times and spaces" (Kaşdoğan and Kurtiç, this volume), this chapter will, therefore, demonstrate, first, how gold's materiality and particular material processes of assembling gold in the third gold rush rendered the issue and concept of *risk* central to sociopolitical conflicts. Second, the chapter will show the formative role of Bergama farmers' material and more-than-human relations with the landscape in shaping their risk expertise, which they extrapolate to the socio-ecological risks of gold mining. As gold mining reached an unprecedented global scale through the circulation and translation of expertise, material relations, and governmentalities, this chapter's analysis of particular frictions (Tsing 2005) through which globalized gold mining materialized in an Aegean town in Turkey will reveal the impact of Bergama's anti-gold mining struggle on both circulating resistance practices and counterinsurgent maneuvers of technopolitical risk assessment.

Material Genealogy of the Third Gold Rush

For much of the twentieth century, global gold production was mostly confined to the four settler-colonial countries subjected to nineteenth-century gold rushes. Until 1980, around half of all gold came from South African mines in that era, and the "big four" were responsible for three-quarters of the entire global gold production (Govett and Govett 1982). The third gold rush is, however, truly global in scale. Between 1990 and 2001, a period corresponding to the Bergama mining project and other international gold mining investments in Turkey, nearly one-third of $90 billion global investments in mineral mining was allocated to gold alone (Bridge 2004). As a result, at the turn of the new millennium, the share of the "big four" dropped below 50 percent. Currently, it sits at only one-quarter of global production (GFMS 2002; Thomson Reuters 2018).

What are the material conditions of possibility of the third gold rush? What enabled it to expand from four countries to almost the entire Global South, including Turkey? Equally important, what made gold mining situated within the field of technopolitical risk?

My account of gold's materiality is located within Science and Technology Studies scholarship informed by Actor–Network Theory (ANT) (Callon 1984; Callon, Rip, and Law 1986; Latour 2005; Jensen et al. 2017). Appadurai's (1986) suggestion to follow things as they circulate through social relations, when combined with ANT's intervention transcending the modernist epistemological binary hierarchically separating subject from object (Latour 1999), birthed a vast new area, termed "new materialisms" (Bennett 2010; Coole and Frost 2010; Harvey, Hansen, and Nustad 2019). I use "new materialisms" loosely to denote the heterogeneous scholarship problematizing the modernist binaries of subject versus object, nature versus culture, and body versus mind, through symmetrical and relational epistemologies that do not privilege humans a priori. As this volume suggests, in these analyses, nonhuman species, things, objects, and minerals become active, agentive—though not completely autonomous—participants in making reality (Bauer and Kosiba 2016).

Latour's primary interest in dismantling the modernist settlement results in too much of a shortcut between the here-and-now contingency of the empirical world and the philosophical inquiry of modernity, leaving many conjunctures populating the intermediary realm between the two unattended, hence constituting ANT's Achilles' heel. In this chapter, I focus on that intermediary realm rich with political contestations. I attune to new materialist studies addressing "extractive" industries, minerals, and resources, and to works combining new materialisms with other social theories, including political ecology, technopolitics, and governmentality, such as Mitchell's (2002) exploration of technopolitics through the entangled relationship of mosquitoes, humans, dams, rivers, and epidemics.

Thus, my work resonates with Li's (2015) analysis of conflicts around corporate mining in Peru. Combining the political ecological perspective with ANT-informed analysis, Li brings together human and nonhuman actors; she historicizes the material and technological conditions of corporate mining and unpacks technoscientific practices that create pollution as a problematization for expert intervention. Similarly, I will provide a historical account of how cyanide use emerged as a result of mining engineers navigating specific minerals' material agency. This process led to what Romero calls the chemicalization of mining (2018): cyanidation—the new mining assemblage's key component—became the material infrastructure for the global expansion of gold mining. However, waste dams—another infrastructure crucial for containing cyanide-laced slurry—emerged as contested objects of the technopolitics of risk.

Recent scholarship in anthropology and human geography calls for attending to inorganic substances to expand the analytical and empirical reach of more-than-human scholarship (Povinelli 2016; Cohen 2015; Ferry, Vallard, and Walsh 2020) and for incorporating new materialisms into resource geography (Richardson and Weszkalnys 2014; Bakker and Bridge 2006). As Field (2020) highlights, gold rarely suffers from a lack of agency in scholarship or Eurocentric public imaginary. Gold's "preciousness" offers a more complex picture of nonhuman agency. Gold's "allure" is naturalized through a seemingly perfect combination of the inalienable physical and chemical properties of gold-as-element and its scarce distribution as material, prompting a supposedly inalienable, transhistorical, intrinsic value that grants it agency as money and wealth. However, gold's properties are not unique. Other elements, some even more scarce, possess similar properties. Thus, Field argues that gold's agency in Eurocentric scholarship and imaginaries is closer to commodity fetishism. Silenced in this ontological imaginary are the pre-Columbian ontologies in the Americas, where gold possessed no value as money, nor signified a Eurocentric notion of wealth. Field rightly asserts that gold's agency does not stem from its inherent properties. There are no transhistorical properties detached from sociocultural components that give gold a priori agency (Field 2020, 182–3).

In this section, I start from where Field finishes. Field looks at the physicochemical properties of gold-as-element and different ontologies of gold-objects to argue that there is no singular gold-as-actor. Conversely, I focus on mining and examine what happens in the time frame between gold-as-element and the creation of gold-objects. Aligned with Richardson and Weszkalnys's (2014, 8) arguments that "natural resources are inherently *distributed things* whose essence or character is to be located neither exclusively in their biophysical properties nor in webs of sociocultural meaning," I show that gold's story, and the particular ways it became globalized to include Turkey, is not a story of being but of more-than-human becoming.

By tracing this process, I challenge the imaginary of inertness underlying the term "extraction." The substances encountered in "extraction" are imagined as inert, passively waiting to be extracted. This imaginary of inertness encompasses three simultaneous realms. First, the material to be extracted—gold in our case—is imagined as possessing a pre-mediated, lifeless, inert existence. Second, the material substances from which gold is extracted are cast as lifeless and inert. Finally, the environmental properties of the landscape where these substances exist—whether above or underground—are imagined merely as décor for mining practices. As I will show, the imagery of the a priori presence of gold as hidden wealth waiting to be "extracted" starkly contrasts with the realities of so-called extractive industries in general and gold mining in particular. In modern mining, gold is never "discovered"; it does not lie inert, waiting for "extraction." Rather, I argue, gold is assembled. This section shows that the material processes configuring the particular ways in which gold is assembled in the third gold rush shape socio-ecological conflicts, as in Bergama, that center on the risks of gold mining.

In order to trace the material conditions of the third (global) gold rush, I suggest returning to the second gold rush era in the later nineteenth century and materially trace how cyanide emerged as an integral component of the new assemblage. In the California gold rush's early stages, amalgamation (an ancient technique) and gravity separation with pans and cradles while collecting gold from alluvial deposits constituted the primary techniques of gold production. As sedimented gold was depleted and prospectors moved upstream, they encountered the quartz rock formations from which the gold particles had been washed before being sedimented in riverbeds. This changing gold landscape marked the beginning of quartz mining in California in 1851 (Jung 1999).

Despite the initial hype, quartz mining turned out to be truly a rocky experience. Importantly, gold's siderophile nature, its love for iron, constituted a major obstacle for California miners. Gold in California's quartz rocks resided in pyrite ore: particles were no longer free-mill or native gold but attached to (and at times encapsulated by) pyrite, or iron sulfide (FeS_2), also known as "fool's gold." Pyrite prevents mercury from amalgamating with gold particles. In quartz mining's earlier stages, as ore bodies were at or near the surface, most of the sulfur in the ore body would have oxidized naturally, enabling satisfactory levels of amalgamation. However, as mines became deeper, no natural sulfur oxidation occurred (Lougheed 1989). For miners, unoxidized pyrite meant a diminished gold "recovery rate," which denotes the percentage of gold particles in the ore body actually assembled. Gold production figures in California steadily declined from 1854 onward, despite all efforts.

Similar problems occurred in Australia and South Africa. In South Africa, even though Witwatersrand's gold deposits were unique, with a completely different geological genesis, the ore was pyritic. The initial mining took place in outcrops, where gold-bearing rock formations meet the land surface. Thus, the iron pyrites were oxidized and liberated gold particles in the outcrops; gold assembly was easy, requiring little capital investment. Beyond depths of 200–300 feet and below water level, however, oxidation ceased, gold concentration diminished, and the ore became pyritic. With a sudden drop in recovery rates to below 50 percent, a profitable assemblage of what was then considered low-grade ore became impossible (Fivaz 1988).

Thus, mining companies started to explore better ways to assemble gold from iron pyrite ores. Chemist John Stewart MacArthur and the Forrest brothers advanced the idea of chemically dissolving gold in pyritic ores with potassium cyanide and then precipitating it with zinc.[3] Cyanidation's impact on gold mining cannot be overstated. Compared to pre-cyanidation figures, gold production in South Africa increased tenfold within ten years. More importantly, cyanidation also allowed for the assemblage of low-grade gold,[4] and, by enabling the recovery of gold particles from pyritic ores in quartz rock formations, expanded the potential geological and geographical scope of gold mining and initiated an era of chemicalization (Romero 2018).

Further, new techniques, devices, and materials have contributed to the socio-material assemblage of gold, particularly in the last several decades. The patented *carbon in leach* process developed by using charcoal coconut shells increased gold recovery rates while reducing costs. Also introduced was high-density polyurethane (HDPE)—ordinary plastic used in shopping bags—that triggers *heap leaching*. Heap leaching is primarily an open-pit, bulk-processing method of extremely low-grade (as low as 0.5 grams per tonne) ore with mediocre recovery rates, favoring quantity over quality. It requires very low investment and development cost. The presence of easily accessible, extremely large volumes of ore is the only prerequisite. These techniques, devices, and materials dramatically decreased the initial capital cost, continuously lowering ore grades that can be profitably processed. Consequently, when gold prices increased in the 1970s and temporarily reached an all-time high in 1980, the socio-material assemblage of gold mining engendered the third gold rush in the Global South.

While the global expansion of extractive industries has been heavily scrutinized in critical studies of extractivism, the socio-ecological significance of ore grades is often overlooked. This is partially due to the disproportionate focus on extracted material, or "resource"—a focus that risks reproducing the extractivist logic. If one shifts focus from the minerals extracted to what they are extracted from and how, the socio-ecological implications of changes in ore grade become apparent. The new gold mining techniques, together with political–economic changes such as increasing gold prices, ushered in the third global gold rush, where the production of toxic waste has become a key issue for socio-ecological resistance and environmental justice mobilizations. The Bergama gold mine, with its grade of 9 ppm, was designed to produce more than 100,000 grams of toxic waste per gram of gold. Put differently, this exceeds five times more waste than what Witwatersrand produced a century ago. Toxic-waste production and its risks became a central site of contestation, shaping the politics behind the expansion of gold mining in Turkey. In 1992, Eurogold,[5] the subsidiary of a mining consortium formed by three Australian, French, and Canadian companies, obtained its operation license near the village I call Sırmalı.[6] Eurogold started to acquire land from villagers who were initially excited by the prospect of gold mining. Then the Environmental Impact Assessment (EIA) study commissioned from Dokuz Eylül University brought gold mining's hitherto unknown aspects to the farmers' attention. The facts and figures unearthed by the EIA were mind-boggling. For the 24 tonnes of gold to be produced over eight years, 2.4 million tonnes—a 100,000-fold amount—of rock would be removed, crushed, and milled to a size of 38 micrometers (smaller than what a naked human eye can detect), washed with cyanide solution, then dumped into a waste dam reservoir. To this end, a 30-meter-high dam would be built to create a reservoir with a surface area of 16 hectares, capable of holding 2 million cubic meters of toxic waste.

The act of extraction, I contend, is simultaneously an act of injection. The enormous amounts of earth processed to assemble gold constitute only half of the toxic waste pumped into the reservoir. The remaining half consists of water injected into the system to "extract" gold. Hence, for every gram of gold, a 100,000-fold amount of earth removed is matched with a 100,000-fold amount of water. Furthermore, for every gram of gold, 83 grams of cyanide would be injected into the system. Over the mine's life cycle, a total of almost 2,000 tonnes of cyanide would be used. When the EIA's results reached Bergama, the Sırmalians' initial excitement started to fade. At the core of the conflict in Bergama, as in many other gold mining conflicts around the world, therefore, was not the extraction and depletion of the intended "resource" but the mind-boggling amounts of materials injected into the system, producing disproportionate amounts of toxic waste.

The presence of a toxic-waste dam—or tailings dam, in the mining industry's parlance—for decades to come after mining operations cease, with all its socio-ecological risks, emerged as a primary cause for concern among Bergama farmers. Tailings dams are interscalar vehicles of slow violence (Hecht 2018). They transform the direct, immediate socio-environmental violence of mining waste—as with the Ok Tedi Mine in Papua New Guinea, which dumped chemically processed toxic waste directly into rivers, destroying the livelihood of Indigenous communities (Kirsch 2014)—into slow violence (Nixon 2011) and turn manufactured disasters into manufactured risks.

The vibrancy of the mined minerals is not limited to their relationship with the assembled material. The rocks from which gold is "extracted" and the minerals they contain come alive through "extraction." Once heavy metals in gold-bearing rocks and gold-bearing ore are exposed to air and moisture through excavation, milling, and cyanidation, they move from a (chemically) stable state to an active (or reactive) state. In the latter, they more readily enter into contact with other chemical elements and form new compounds with toxic characteristics.

The threat of heavy metals is further compounded by AMD, another primary environmental contamination. AMD entails a similar process: exposed sulfur-bearing minerals, such as pyrite, are transformed into sulfuric acid. Gold's siderophile nature results in gold particles' tendency to reside in pyritic ore. As a result, pyrite exists in relative abundance in gold-mine pits and waste dams, ready to be transformed into sulfuric acid. The latter, when mixed with flowing water, causes severe surface acidity that dissolves activated toxic heavy metals such as lead, mercury, and arsenic.

Mining ontology is fixated on the "extracted" mineral, while everything else is dismissed and discarded as gangue (or overburden and tailings). This asymmetry is replicated in the production of knowledge on AMD. "We cannot talk properly about the dynamics of acid mine drainage because we know very little about it," sighed Derya Zeki, a professor of metallurgy at Istanbul Technical University, in one of our conversations. He drew attention to uncertainties due to the deliberate lack of knowledge: "There are thousands of scientific articles on every aspect of mining imaginable, but there are barely a handful of articles on acid mine drainage. Because nobody explores it; because nobody provides funding for such research. If you are a graduate student in mining and want to study acid mining drainage, you won't be able to find funding."

A quick WorldCat search confirmed Zeki's statements. Between 1931, when AMD first appeared in an article, and 1990, when the global expansion of gold mining went full steam ahead, the ratio of articles on mining to articles on AMD was more than one thousand to one. Scientific literature on the AMD potential of waste dams, mainly of gold mines, is virtually nonexistent. Such manufactured ignorance (Proctor and Schiebinger 2008) is then translated into uncertainties—the raw material of the risk apparatus (Dinç 2021).

Manufactured ignorance is not limited to AMD. The authors of the EIA report on the Bergama mining project pointed to a lack of information and geographical knowledge about the region, diverse and conflicting data, and lack of independently scrutinized and verified data beyond what Eurogold had supplied. Such shortcomings resulted in great uncertainty regarding the mine's potential impacts on the socio-material environment. Similar uncertainties stemming from manufactured ignorance also concerned the effects of the landscape transformation due to mining. A risk assessment report[7]—commissioned by the government to validate Eurogold's cause—indicated a significant drop in groundwater levels due to constant groundwater discharge into the pits. The report's author admits that Eurogold's conflicting assumptions, due to lacking proper knowledge quantifying specific soil and underground water behavior in the mining landscape, cause great uncertainty about the mine's effects on the subterranean aquifer.[8] The manufactured uncertainties of gold mining in Bergama therefore constituted a risk infrastructure—something with which the villagers have long been familiar, thanks to their farming expertise.

"Who are they to know?"

When the Ministry of Environment approved Eurogold's project in 1994, 657 villagers filed a lawsuit against the ministry to revoke its permit. The late autumn of 1996 marked the conflict's turning point. As soon as the local administrative court ruled against the villagers, Eurogold, within a few days, uprooted more than three thousand olive and pine trees on the mine site. This uprooting constituted the moment of truth for all villagers and, in quick succession, triggered mass mobilization, ranging from rallies and sit-ins to road blockades, both locally and nationally in metropolitan centers. "Bergama's peasants" became a role model for many rural environmental movements, as well as a symbol of civil disobedience in Turkey (Arsel 2016; Adaman and Arsel 2016).

Their innovative protests brought the farmers to national attention and gold mining, a highly contested environmental issue, to the national agenda. While Bergama's farming communities persistently protested Eurogold and the government, a public forum concerning the perils of gold mining emerged. National TV channels covered the protests and the conflict, which became one of the most debated political issues (Çoban 2004; Kadirbeyoğlu 2016; Koçer 2007).

In one TV program, a well-known toxicologist, who throughout his career never missed an opportunity to side with corporate interests in publicly controversial projects, became upset about "lay people's" involvement. He burst out: "Everyone with a mouth talks about this issue. A bunch of ignorant people is just brainwashed, and they keep saying 'We don't want it [. . .].' Who are they to know? We are the ones who know these things. We know the science behind this. Let us do the talking. But nobody asks us." His hands shook with anger. The moderator tried to appease him: "Well . . . We are asking you, and you are on a national channel." The scientist relaxed somewhat and continued explaining at great length the technicalities of gold mining through quantitative data.

This section takes seriously the toxicologist's dismissive question "Who are they to know?" State representatives and pro-mine technoscientific experts portrayed the farmers as ignorant and brainwashed by environmentalists and leftists, while the latter romanticized them as inherent ecologists. I refrain from either stereotype. Here, I focus on more-than-human agencies from the gold landscape to the farming landscape, showing that Sırmalıans have developed elaborate risk assessment and management expertise through farming. The more-than-human similarities between the two realms enable them to extrapolate their expertise to the socio-ecological risks of gold mining and to forge alliances with scientists who oppose gold mining. Moreover, as historical subjects of the modern industrial agriculture assemblage, I argue, they are both agents and victims of extractivist agricultural slow violence. This experience has given them the capacity to apprehend gold mining's potential future slow violence on their socio-material landscape. In her analysis of coal extraction in Soma, another Aegean town only 43 kilometers away from Bergama, Az (this volume) states that "Soma coal is a material and symbolic presence in the work and everyday lives of Soma residents (in different forms among different groups) as a determinant of their experiences of labor, and as a heating source, which means it is ambient in the air that they breathe, and thus, present in their bodies." While Az powerfully explains the extracted material's role in shaping the everyday socio-material landscapes, this section will reveal how Bergama farmers' long-existing daily material entanglements with the landscapes shape the socio-material ground in which they understand and experience the risks entailed in gold mining.

Bergama Town has a population of fifty thousand, with another seventy thousand in surrounding villages. In the 1950s, reclamation of the Bakırçay River Delta's vast swamps created rich farmlands. The villagers' primary economic activities consist of olive production on the hills and cash crop farming on the plains. The intercity road demarcating the plains' eastern edge and connecting İzmir to Çanakkale on the northern Aegean coast separates the mine from rich cotton fields. The gold mine is less than 15 kilometers from the town center. Three villages—which I call Kıyıcak, Sırmalı, and Esenköy—immediately surround the gold mine. Although all three villages were most active in the movement, Sırmalı, where I conducted ethnographic fieldwork between 2000 and 2003, is considered its ground zero.

Historically, cotton constitutes the main cash crop in Bergama, as in most of Western Anatolia's plains[9] (Figure 12.1). Corn is another major cash crop, followed by sunflowers, tomatoes, legumes, and clover. Wheat is also regularly produced, primarily for subsistence. Almost no farmer grows a single cash crop, preferring instead a mixture of two or more crop types, with a primary crop cultivated more extensively and a secondary one on a smaller plot.

Bergama is Turkey's northernmost major cotton plain. Autumn rains can quickly ruin crops, affecting this region earlier and more intensely than the southern regions where summer lasts longer. As cotton is hand-harvested in Bergama, in three consecutive rounds lasting several weeks, depending on the cultivar, a considerable portion falls to the ground and loses most of its economic value when it rains. Moreover, rain delays harvesting until the fields have dried up, making harvesting even more vulnerable as it is further prolonged into the rainy season. Therefore, relying solely on cotton carries extensive risks for Bergama farmers, who manage this risk by producing another cash crop less affected by rain.

Crop diversity has long been considered a risk aversion measure, portrayed as a defining characteristic of subsistence farmers in rural and economic anthropology (Scott 1976; Cancian 1980; Cashdan 1990; Henrich and Mcelreath 2002). Such analysis misses the fact that it is a mechanism of risk assessment and management strategy, rather than mere aversion, that considers the agency of nonhumans, such as crops, soil, and weather conditions.

Figure 12.1 Cotton cultivation in Bergama under the shadow of the gold mine (the mine site is in the upper left corner of the photo). Photo taken by the author in 2004.

An essential component of industrial agriculture is the use of so-called hybrid seeds. These commercially developed and marketed cultivars often replace older versions to which farmers are accustomed. Thus, farmers' expertise is always contingent and dynamic. "The field is a farmer's laboratory," says Abdullah Aysu, a cereal farmer and former head of Turkey's Farmers' Union. Farmers constantly experiment with changing environmental conditions, crops, and seed varieties, revising and sharing their knowledge and expertise with their peers.

Sırmalıans do not immediately start using new cultivars. Rather, they let well-off farmers test them first or allocate only a minuscule portion of their land as an experiment. Therefore, poor yield or unexpected infestation with some disease or pest is contained and does not harm the overall yield and revenue. Regardless of how convincing new cultivars' lab results may appear on paper, Sırmalıans understand that local environmental conditions cannot be replicated under laboratory conditions. Although never dismissive of new cultivars, they like to see actual results in their own "laboratories" before fully committing.

Sırmalıans' attitude toward new cultivars is a risk assessment and management strategy that they extrapolate to gold mining. As they cautiously approach the claims of experts—whether state agricultural officials or agribusiness companies—concerning new cultivars when handed favorable results on paper, Sırmalıans take any favorable risk assessment results provided by Eurogold or state officials with a grain of salt. Their entangled experiences with nonhumans make them well aware of the discrepancies between the discursive and the material, which engender a level of uncertainty to be closely monitored and continuously assessed.

Just like gold particle sizes, the characteristics of the rock formation in which they are embedded and their interactions with other minerals and compounds determine specific gold mining practices. In farming, a very complex interplay of various factors goes into planning which cultivars will be sown. Four main cotton cultivars are common in Bergama: black-seeded "163" (Nazilli M-163), white-seeded "503" (Nazilli M-503), "Şahin Bey," and, newly, "Karmen."[10] One factor influencing cultivar selection is the plot's location. Soil characteristics are not homogeneous across the plains. The outer parts feature *kır toprak* (light soil), a less fertile soil type that is easier to irrigate but loses moisture faster. The soil gradually gets thicker, darker, and more fertile toward the center. Finally, the plains' center has *kara toprak* (dark soil). As the soil thickens, it absorbs more water per decare and keeps moisture longer. Consequently, cultivars requiring more water, such as 503, better suit the dark soil toward the center.

503 is a relatively late-blooming variety, with larger cotton balls loosely attached to the branches, very suitable for hand-harvesting. However, for the very same reason, they are also very susceptible to weather. They can easily fall to the ground in heavy wind or rain, creating a major disaster for small farmers. On dark soil, 503 cotton balls washed off by rain firmly stick to the mud. Also, since dark soil remains moist for longer, it takes longer for farmers to reenter the fields for harvesting. This situation delays harvesting well into the rainy season, causing a chain reaction. By contrast, 163, although more laborious to hand-harvest, is a relatively early bloomer and more resistant to adverse weather. Hence, farming takes place within a matrix of uncertainties based on the simultaneous involvement of multiple actors, including

crops and their varied characteristics, soil, soil's minerals and bacteria, and weather patterns. Farming for Sırmalıans is not merely a human activity. Nor is it an act of absolute mastery over nature; it is the activity of a more-than-human collectivity. As in gold mining, a seemingly simple decision such as cultivar selection requires mastery, not of "nature," but of navigating multilayered uncertainties involving nonhuman agents. Such mastery makes Sırmalıans expert risk managers.

Particularly in cotton cultivation, Sırmalıans tend to sow more seeds more tightly than needed, instead of sowing them equidistantly at the optimum plant distance. Each farmer has their own way of sowing cotton, but the average ranges from 2.5 to 4 kilograms of seeds per decare. The state agricultural office's experts deem this irrational—a waste of resources and money. Once the seedlings emerge, they need to be thinned out if they are too close together—the most laborious work within the entire life cycle of cultivation. Thick sowing gives state agricultural experts ammunition to label farmers as ignorant.

However, thick sowing makes perfect sense from a risk management point of view when the role of nonhumans in uncertainties and risk is considered. During sowing and harvesting, weather conditions become particularly important. For farmers, the greatest risk lies in the seeds' failure to germinate or the seedlings' failure to emerge. This would have devastating effects: farmers would not only have to reinvest in seeds but also start from scratch, losing crucial time, missing optimum conditions for cultivation, and pushing the harvest well into the rainy season. Rainfall between sowing and the seedlings' emergence is never desirable, and for farmers, those days are the most anxiety-ridden since they determine the season's course. Heavy rainfall rots the seeds and prevents germination; light rain creates a thin, grease-like layer on the soil, called *kap* or *kaymak*.[11] *Kap* makes it difficult for seedlings to emerge, causing *kalınbacak* (thick-leg), where seedlings grow inside the soil instead of surfacing. To counterbalance this risk, seeds are thick-sown. The germinated seeds' combined efforts help crack the *kap* and facilitate the seedlings' emergence.

Investing in the collective power of seedlings against the risk of *kap* is not the only reason for sowing thick. It also effectively serves as what the risk management discipline calls "building redundancy." Redundancies (such as dual sensors on airplanes) are incorporated into critical nodes of a process to prevent a component's failure from causing critical system failure with catastrophic consequences. For farmers, the total number of emerging seedlings establishes a yield cap for the remaining season. Thick sowing, therefore, serves as redundancy at a critical node in the cultivation process, acting as an insurance policy that balances the loss of ungerminated seeds. "Plentiful has a remedy, sparse has none," wisely notes Mesut, one of my interlocutors. Moreover, more seedlings than necessary give farmers the chance to select stronger ones during thinning. Thick sowing, far from being an act of ignorance, constitutes an effective risk management strategy to cope with material uncertainties.

Within this agricultural resource assemblage, farmers develop a farming calculus to constantly navigate more-than-human agencies with the "market logic" of agricultural capitalism. Their entangled relationship with varied cotton seeds and soil, each imposing different characteristics, is negotiated through a matrix of local land-tenure regimes, irrigation technologies, agricultural chemicals, weather, seed commodity chains, and kinship relations. Navigating these constantly changing relations in the agricultural landscape means constant experimentation within uncertainty, rendering farmers risk experts. The modern agricultural landscape in Bergama as a risk landscape and farmers as risk experts are co-constituted.

The risk expertise developed in the fields is a dynamic knowledge form constantly shared with peers. Such sharing was replicated in novel forms of expert meetings between farmers and scientists opposing the gold mine. It also shaped the ways in which they mobilized against the mine.

If fields are farmers' laboratories, coffeehouses are their debriefing rooms. In the coffeehouses during rummikub sessions, farmers compare, discuss, and disseminate newly obtained information about current weather conditions, their possible impacts on crops, new pest infestations typical of monoculture, evaluation of new devices, and results of ongoing experimentation with new crop or seed varieties. Depending on the issue's importance, debriefings may become heated. Other times, they are shared casually, combined patchwork-like with other daily topics.

Sometimes, a farmer from a distant village in the same or nearby region visits Sırmalı, and a particularly inquisitive conversation starts as the visitor sips the glasses of tea offered. The socio-ecological landscapes of the visitor's village are distinct enough to provide novel information and perspective, but familiar enough to generate correspondence between the visitor and Sırmalıans. This makes the evaluation and translation of new information relevant. Once the visitor leaves, the new information is disseminated in the coffeehouse over the coming hours or days. Similar to any expert conversation in any debriefing room, conversations occur at lightning speed, in a language that to a stranger appears like shortened, encrypted codes.

In these coffeehouses-cum-debriefing rooms, Bergama farmers in the resistance's early days started to regularly meet with scientists who wanted to warn them about the risks of gold mining. Two sets of experts, with expertise in different realms, met over tea and inquisitively wandered through olive groves, cotton fields, and the mine site. Their expertise, developed based on their respective socio-ecological landscapes, was gradually juxtaposed. "We all became chemists," said Mesut in our first conversation. He then recited a lengthy account of heavy metals' effects on freshwater, soil, crops, humans, and animals. The juxtaposition of expertise in farming and mining landscapes engendered new forms of layered knowledge for both the farmers and scientists visiting their villages—similar to the destabilization of the epistemic boundaries between "scientific" and "traditional" forms of knowledge Tatari examines in this volume. This collaboration revealed how underground streams—running north–south and feeding on the Geyikli Mountain, with Sırmalı in its southern foothills—ran the risk of being laden with higher-than-average arsenic, mercury, lead, and antimony content while passing underneath the gold mine. The heavy metals in the "overburden" and the "ore" would become soluble by the AMD due to sulfide oxidation in the ore. The streams feeding the aquifer that the farmers use for irrigation and through their wells would eventually contaminate it.

Such contamination, however, is neither immediate nor sudden; instead, it is prolonged into the future. AMD slowly develops as more rocks and soil are exposed to air and water in the pits, and toxic waste accumulates in the aging, temporarily impermeable dam reservoir. Over time, AMD builds up in the aquifer to noticeable or measurable contamination levels, and AMD-caused heavy metals circulate through wells, fountains, and irrigation.

How can one presently apprehend the significance and severity of such slow violence scheduled for a distant future? For Sırmalıans, the same aquifer—bearer of another slow violence from two generations ago, prolonged into their present—becomes a pivot for such apprehension. The Bakırçay River Delta's mid-twentieth-century transformation into fertile plains was intended to introduce cash crop-oriented, heavy-input-dependent industrial agriculture. Replacing subsistence-based cereal fields with cash crop cotton necessitated intensive irrigation. As elderly Sirmalians recall, water was aplenty, and digging several meters sufficed to build a well in the early years of cotton cultivation. Over the years, they had to dig deeper and deeper. Half a century later, 70 meters was no longer deep enough to reach underground water. As both object and subject of industrial agriculture, Sırmalıans inflicted slow violence upon themselves and their socio-ecological landscape. The aquifer, soon to experience slow violence due to mining waste, has long been object, mediary, and embodiment—both literally and figuratively—of agricultural slow violence. Sırmalıans' historical relationship with the aquifer entangled in slow violence enabled them to extrapolate a potential future slow violence. "Who are they to know?" the toxicologist asked insultingly, regurgitating the long abused trope of 'ignorant farmers.' Indeed, Sırmalıans know the slow violence of extractivism, not despite but because of being farmers—as they were subjects of another form of extractive slow violence (McKay, Fradejas, and Ezquerro-Cañete 2021).

New knowledge about the hybrid landscape of cotton, olives, and gold was then disseminated in coffeehouses across the region. In the six months after the İzmir–Çanakkale intercity road's blockade in November 1996, which marked the first mass protest, Sırmalıans were particularly busy harvesting olives during the day and visiting other villages at night.

On April 22, 1997, more than five thousand farmers from a dozen villages, after shutting down phone and power lines, marched to the mine site, flattened the fences with tractors, and occupied the mine. After several hours of confrontation between protesters and military security forces, Izmir's mayor drove there, negotiated with the protesters, and agreed to close the mine for thirty days due to security concerns.

The occupation pushed the conflict onto Turkey's political agenda. Even worse for a globalist government aspiring to attract foreign investment, the international press, including the *Wall Street Journal* (Dorsey 1997), covered the mine's occupation in-depth. Canadian gold mining company Cominco, with 152 out of 558 permits controlling the second-largest number of exploration rights in Turkey, announced a temporary suspension of operations. As damage control, then-president Süleyman Demirel infamously stated in support of international gold companies: "We will let the gold mines work. We will not be poor guardians of rich deposits." Two weeks post-occupation, Minister of Energy and Natural Resources Rıza Güneri visited the mine site and talked to the villagers. On his way to Bergama, he stated:

> Bergama's people are under the influence of biased information. Tomorrow, with bureaucrats and scientists, we will provide them with the truths. We came here to

> say that, thanks to the measures taken, it is impossible for the locals to be harmed by the cyanide extraction process. We came to embrace our citizens in Bergama to save them from the effects of biased information.

Despite the president's words and the minister's visit, only three days later, the Council of State, the highest administrative court, revoked the Ministry of Environment's permit to Eurogold in a court case filed by the villagers and supported by scientists' testimonials and expert reports. The court decided that the risk factors involved in cyanide leach technology violated the constitutional right to life and to live in a healthy, intact environment. The verdict condemned the cyanidation technique rather than a mere mining project. The verdict shocked both mining companies and the national government, whose globalist aspirations involved making Turkey part of the world gold production market by attracting foreign investment. Instead, it saw the world's first de facto legal ban on cyanide use in mining. Soon thereafter, the Czech parliament banned cyanide use in mining, followed by Wisconsin and Montana in the United States—an essential step toward the current global anti-cyanide campaign. Consequently, the global gold mining industry was forced to devise the *International Cyanide Management Code* "intended to promote and help ensure the safe and environmentally responsible management of cyanide used within the gold and silver mining industries." The Cyanide Code is but a PR attempt by the global gold mining industry; however, it showcases the increasing global pressure, and Bergama played a significant role therein. The Turkish government's globalist desires were achieved, albeit in reverse.

Risk Assessment as Vector of Slow Violence

The Council of State's verdict revoking the Ministry of Environment's license granted to Eurogold created a standstill. On one side were the higher court's decision and a highly mobilized village community with widespread public support demanding the mine's dismantling. On the other side stood a gold mining company and a national government eager to oversee the proliferation of gold mining in Turkey, for which the Bergama project served as a gatekeeper.

Shortly after the verdict, Eurogold made minor changes to its facility design and commissioned from Golder Associates, an international consultancy agency with expertise in the mining industry, a quantitative risk assessment of its tailings dam's design. In Golder's 76-page-long report, only half a page is dedicated to the site's geographical, social, economic, and agricultural characteristics. This is particularly astonishing—one would expect detailed analysis of all the social, economic, agricultural, and environmental factors to assess realistically the potential negative impacts of a tailings dam failure. Instead, Golder's risk assessment allocated only one paragraph to the lives and livelihoods of Bergama's villagers, under the heading "Project Setting," as if they were merely a painting's background. This reveals the political aspect of technical risk assessment: the risk assessment's performed reality draws on the erasure of Bergama villagers' reality.[12]

The report enacted yet another erasure: Golder excluded overtopping from its calculations. Overtopping refers to water levels exceeding the reservoir capacity due to excessive rain, causing water to overflow from the dam wall and resulting in dam failure. Golder justified this exclusion with the rationale that "recirculation of the tailings water is an integral component of the process and other inflows into the dam, i.e., rainfall and runoff, are insignificant" (23). However, overtopping is the number-one cause of active tailings dam failures (Foster, Fell, and Spannagle 2000).

Golder mobilized its networking power for Eurogold in 1998, roughly when it produced its risk assessment. Golder included Eurogold's Bergama tailings dam in the joint publication by the International Council on Metals and the Environment and the United Nations Environment Programme, titled *Case Studies on Tailings Management*—a compilation of twenty-one risk management cases of mine tailings around the world "to promote good environmental practices" (ICME and UNEP 1998, iii). But at the time of writing, the Bergama mine had not yet started operating, and the Council of State had revoked Eurogold's operation licenses. Nevertheless, this did not prevent Eurogold's Bergama mine from appearing in the compilation.

Domestically, the ICME and UNEP joint publication came to Eurogold's rescue: Eurogold urgently needed new PR tools to convince the public about the safety of its gold mining operations in Bergama. Eurogold representatives and supporters used the publication to snub critics immediately upon its release, confidently arguing that Eurogold deployed the best technologies and that its facilities were "state-of-the-art," such that the UN had "selected" it as an example for mining companies worldwide. Eurogold reciprocated Golder's favor by making it the inspector for the integrity of the waste dam's impermeability.[13] Upon Golder's submission of the tailings dam's quantitative risk analysis, which concluded "with a good degree of confidence that the risk posed by the TMF[14] in Ovacik is negligible" (1998, 31), Eurogold applied to the Ministry of Environment and the Prime Ministry to reevaluate its operations, claiming that their additional measures would "eliminate" all risks associated with their operations. As "one of the world's most trustworthy audit firms" (Eurogold Madencilik 1999, 2), Golder had provided proof that "all the risk factors were effectively eliminated" (ibid., 7).

After receiving this application, the Prime Ministry requested Turkey's highest scientific body, Türkiye Bilimsel ve Teknolojik Araştırma Kurumu (TÜBİTAK), to form a committee to "evaluate whether, after the extra measures taken in the Bergama gold mine, the risks factors were acceptable" (TÜBİTAK-YDABÇAG 1999, 2). A panel of eleven university professors from various disciplines—environmental engineering, chemistry, seismology, mining, hydrogeology, geology, and law—was to produce yet another risk assessment. At stake for the government was to make Turkey a gold mining country. Hence, Turkey's highest scientific body was introduced into the conflict, not to save one gold mine, but to neutralize the nationwide barricade by the community in Bergama and the Council of State.

Golder still played a role in TÜBİTAK's evaluation. In August, the panel chair and another panel member visited Colorado, US, for meetings with the Environmental Protection Agency and Golder. Contrary to what one would expect, the Golder meeting was not to scrutinize the specific methods and outcomes of their risk analyses. Instead, it took the form of a consultation, with the TÜBİTAK delegation asking technical questions about the specifics of gold mining. Golder, a consultancy agency, whose highly problematic risk analysis for Eurogold had led to TÜBİTAK's risk assessment in the first place, therefore de facto became a consultant for TÜBİTAK, supposedly appointed to assess Golder's risk assessments. In the meeting, Golder admitted that the HDPE-liner system, the impermeable plastic layer at the dam reservoir's bottom, would eventually leak and suggested the need for a contingency plan.[15] "At some point, they do leak," read the meeting minutes kept by Golder (Appendix XI). This blunt admission starkly contrasted with its own risk assessment of the waste dam, which claimed quantitatively negligible risk.

The 500-page-long TÜBİTAK report was nothing more than an exculpation of the Bergama gold mine and cyanidation in general. Compellingly, the main report starts with a legal assessment of how the Council of State's verdict should not be interpreted as condemnation of a widely used gold production technique. The report concludes that it would be appropriate to allow this and other similar ventures to operate. Four years after the council's verdict and two years after Eurogold's petition to the Prime Ministry, the government granted Eurogold a temporary one-year operating license, based on TÜBİTAK's report. Eurogold finally succeeded in starting operations in April 2001.

The Bergama waste dam's material reality surfaced years later: as usual, heavy rains hit Bergama in the winter of 2009. On February 8, continuous rainfall poured into the tailings dam, already nearing maximum capacity after eight years. When floodwater levels approached a critical level, mine operatives diverted water from the dam reservoir to the adjacent creek to prevent overtopping, as they would whenever heavy rains hit the region. However, this time the dam reservoir had too little excess capacity. Also, there was too much floodwater to be diverted, as the creek was already loaded (Evrensel 2009). Eyewitness accounts vary, but either the overloaded creek or the overtopping rainwater flooded the open pit and underground mine shafts. Fortunately, no casualties occurred, and the tailings dam remained intact. Regardless, the flooding unquestionably countered Golder's assessment that overtopping was no risk factor for the toxic-waste dam. As an ad hoc emergency measure, the toxic slurry filling the open pit and underground shafts was haphazardly pumped out by mineworkers, further flooding the surrounding areas, fields, and roads with the toxic waste.

Petryna (2009) reminds us how risk and disasters are much more tightly intertwined than the distance that the risk analysis enterprise establishes between the two. Moreover, Fortun's (2001) account of the Bhopal disaster shows that, far from being the result of "human errors," disasters are not instantaneous events but events-in-the-making due to structural factors and design decisions. This is particularly significant because consultancy agencies' risk assessments are seldom mere discursive practices entirely independent of industries' materiality. As the Bergama gold mine shows, consultancy agencies are often simultaneously involved in the design, construction, and maintenance of the industrial facilities for which they produce risk assessments. To the extent that disasters are always-in-the-making, risk assessments are always part of disasters-to-come.

Conclusion

Eurogold changed hands—and names—several times throughout the Bergama saga. In 2002, it became a subsidiary of Newmont, the world's largest gold producer. The international negative publicity caused by the Bergama movement, with lengthy articles in international newspapers, including the *Wall Street Journal*, *Financial Times*, and *New York Times*, was too considerable for Newmont relative to the size and profit from the Bergama mine operation. Moreover, the villagers took their case to the European Court of Human Rights, which in 2004 ruled in their favor. In 2005, the US Ambassador to Turkey kindly requested then Prime Minister Recep Tayyip Erdoğan to help find a company to take over the Bergama mine from Newmont.

A Turkish entrepreneur in the printing business, with close ties to Erdoğan's ruling party (AKP), bought the mine in 2005. However, after the failed coup attempt in 2016, he was accused of serving as banker to the religious Gülen movement, accused of attempting the coup; his possessions and holdings were seized by the state. Today, Bergama's gold mine is operated by the state-run Savings Deposit Insurance Fund of Turkey. In thirty short years, a World Bank-guided extraction-based neoliberal development strategy that had started with the privatization of a state-run silver mine project in 1987 ended with the nationalization of Turkey's first gold mine.

The Bergama villagers' movement slowly faded after 2002. A feeling of defeat lingered. Its legacy of resistance was so strong that, until 2009, only one more gold mine entered operations in Turkey. Since then, only fifteen, mostly small projects, have been implemented, a small figure compared to the hundreds of permits acquired over the past two decades. Only three global gold mining companies remain in the country.

Nevertheless, the gold mining threat is still very real. The current ground zero of conflict is the forest-mountain ecosystem complex of Mount Ida, which lies only 100 kilometers north of Bergama, where reportedly 300,000 trees were cut to establish a gold mine before the Canadian company's operations were suspended by court order. A recent report revealed that mining companies acquired operation or exploration licenses for nearly half of the land area between Bergama to the south and the Dardanelles Straits to the north, an area comparable to the land area of Hawai'i (TEMA 2020).

Similar to other cases of transnational circulation of knowledge, expertise, and materialities analyzed by Şen and Evren, Bergama's story showcases that, despite immense power asymmetries and a devastating capacity for socio-ecological exploitation, global extractivism does not have a predetermined, teleological course. In this chapter, building on Hecht's argument, I have shown that the cyanidation-based mining assemblage is an interscalar vehicle, as both a technopolitical practice and an analytic, a vehicle that simultaneously connects (and disconnects) different spatiotemporal scales. It pivots between the simultaneous production of gold as a resource expressed in grams and that of toxic waste expressed in tonnes. It is also a temporal interscalar vehicle: the time frame of mining activity is measured in years, whereas the socio-ecological threats posed by its toxic waste, collected in dam reservoirs, are measured in decades, if not centuries. Moreover, it is a spatial interscalar vehicle operating simultaneously on multiple levels. It constitutes the material conditions for a provincial activity confined locally to expand to the entire globe. However, through its risk politics, it paves the way for local resistances to turn into global movements that prevent extractivism from assuming a teleological character. Yet, the same risk framework also leads to the global circulation of counterinsurgent technoscientific expertise, acting as a vector of slow violence. An analytical focus on more-than-human entanglements, which necessitates expanding our view from the materialities of extractivism to incorporate nonhuman agencies, enhances our grasp of extractivism's multiscalar, non-teleological character that fosters injustices, destruction, and violence, as well as resistance and solidarity.

Notes

1 Although earlier estimations put gold's crustal abundance around 4 or 5 ppb (parts per billion), recent estimations range from 1.2 to 1.5.
2 See McDonough (2003, 556) for the composition of Earth's core.
3 The dissolution of gold by cyanide has been known for more than a century. Scheele, the chemist who identified oxygen and many other elements, also experimented with hydrogen cyanide, which he discovered in the eighteenth century. Many other chemists throughout the nineteenth century were already aware of this chemical process. MacArthur applied this knowledge directly to gold ores and patented it.
4 For instance, from earlier gold grades in the vicinity of ounces per tonne, the average grade in Witwatersrand dropped to 20 ppm during its first half century (Prentice 1936) and ultimately to 5 ppm in 2016 (Neingo and Tholana 2016).
5 To avoid confusion, I use the name Eurogold throughout.
6 Sırmalı is a pseudonym.
7 To be discussed further below.
8 See Babidge (2019) for a case from Chile where deliberate ignorance and subsequent uncertainties about underground water serve the perpetuation of mining.
9 See Sirman (1988) and Çalışkan (2010) for excellent ethnographies of cotton production in Turkey's Aegean Region.
10 The state-owned Nazilli Cotton Research Institute developed most of these cultivars. An epitome of the state's modernist agricultural development projects, they received their names mostly from their referral codes in the labs (Nazilli M-163, M-503).
11 Literally translated, *kaymak* means clotted cream.
12 I discuss elsewhere in detail how risk analysis is a performative apparatus in the Callonian sense. However, it is necessarily incomplete in containing the reality it enacts, yielding counter-performative outcomes (Dinç 2021).
13 While the article mentions the detection and repair of "a number of holes and tears" up to 3.5 meters wide in the impermeable layer as an example of Golder's quality control process, critics consider them proof that toxic leaks are inevitable.
14 Tailings Management Facility: the mining industry's PR term to sugarcoat the toxic-waste dam.
15 "[I]sn't the preparation of such contingency plans expensive?" responded the TÜBİTAK delegation to this suggestion (Appendix 11:1).

References

Acosta, Alberto, 2013. "Extractivism and Neoextractivism: Two Sides of the Same Curse," in M. Lang and D. Mokrani (eds.), *Beyond Development: Alternative Visions from Latin America*, 61–86, Amsterdam: Transnational Institute.

Adaman, Fikret, and Murat Arsel, eds. 2016. *Environmentalism in Turkey: Between Democracy and Development?* New York: Routledge.

Appadurai, Arjun, ed. 1986. *The Social Life of Things: Commodities in Cultural Perspective*, Cambridge University Press.

Arsel, Murat. 2016. "The Bergama Imbroglio," in F. Adaman and M. Arsel (eds.), *Environmentalism in Turkey: Between Democracy and Development?* 277–90, New York: Routledge.

Babidge, Sally. 2019. "Sustaining Ignorance: The Uncertainties of Groundwater and Its Extraction in the Salar de Atacama, Northern Chile," *Journal of the Royal Anthropological Institute* 25 (1): 83–102.

Bakker, Karen and Gavin Bridge. 2006. "Material Words? Resource Geographies and the 'Matter of Nature,'" *Progress in Human Geography* 30 (1): 5–27.

Bauer, Andrew and Steve Kosiba. 2016. "How Things Act: An Archaeology of Materials in Political Life," *Journal of Social Archaeology* 16 (2): 115–41.

Bennett, Jane. 2010. *Vibrant Matter: A Political Ecology of Things*, Durhan, NC: Duke University Press.

Bridge, Gavin. 2004. "Mapping the Bonanza: Geographies of Mining Investment in an Era of Neoliberal Reform," *The Professional Geographer* 56 (3): 406–21.

Çalışkan, Koray. 2010. *Market Threads: How Cotton Farmers and Traders Create a Global Commodity*, Princeton: Princeton University Press.

Callon, Michel. 1984. "Some Elements of a Sociology of Translation: Domestication of the Scallops and the Fishermen of St Brieuc Bay," *The Sociological Review* 32 (1): 196–233.

Callon, Michel, Arie Rip, and John Law. 1986. *Mapping the Dynamics of Science and Technology: Sociology of Science in the Real World*. London: Macmillan Publishers.

Cancian, Frank. 1980. "Risk and Uncertainty in Agricultural Decision Making," in Peggy Barlett (ed.), *Agricultural Decision Making: Anthropological Contributions to Rural Development*, 161–76, New York: Academic Press

Cashdan, Elizabeth. 1990. *Risk and Uncertainty in Tribal and Peasant Economies*, Westview Press.

Çoban, Aykut. 2004. "Community-Based Ecological Resistance: The Bergama Movement in Turkey," *Environmental Politics* 13 (2): 438–60.

Cohen, Jeffrey. 2015. *Stone: An Ecology of the Inhuman*, Minneapolis: University of Minnesota Press.

Coole, Diana and Samantha Frost. 2010. "Introducing the New Materialisms," in Diana Coole and Samantha Frost (eds), *New Materialisms: Ontology, Agency, and Politics*, 1–43, Durham: Duke University Press.

Dinç, Tarik Nejat. 2021. "Incomplete: Risk Topographies and Conflict Landscapes in Turkey in the Age of The New Gold Rush," PhD Thesis, Stanford University.

Dorsey, James. 1997. "Grass-Roots Protest Clouds Mining Prospects in Turkey," *Wall Street Journal*, April 29. Front Section.

Eurogold Madencilik. 1999. "Ovacık Altın Madeni İnsan Sağlığı ve Çevre Yatırımları Tam Güvenilirlik Raporu."

Evrensel. 2009. "Zehirli İhtimal," *Evrensel*, February 10, 2009. https://www.evrensel.net/haber/210363/zehirli-ihtimal
Ferry, Elizabeth, Annabel Vallard, and Andrew Walsh, eds. 2020. *The Anthropology of Precious Minerals*, Toronto: University of Toronto Press.
Field, Les. 2020. "Gold, Ontological Difference, and Object Agency," in Ferry, Elizabeth, Annabel Vallard, and Andrew Walsh (eds), *The Anthropology of Precious Minerals*, 164–88, Toronto: University of Toronto Press.
Fivaz, C. 1988. "Presidential Address: How the MacArthur-Forrest Cyanidation Process Ensures South Africa's Golden Future," *Journal of the Southern African Institute of Mining and Metallurgy* 88 (9): 309–18.
Fortun, Kim. 2001. *Advocacy after Bhopal: Environmentalism, Disaster, New Global Orders*, Chicago: University of Chicago Press.
Foster, Mark, Robin Fell, and Matt Spannagle. 2000. "The Statistics of Embankment Dam Failures and Accidents," *Canadian Geotechnical Journal* 37 (5): 1000–24.
GFMS. 2002. "Gold Survey 2002." Gold Fields Mineral Services Ltd.
Golder Associates. 1998. "Report on Probabilistic Risk Assessment, Ovacık Mine Tailings Dam, Turkey."
Govett, M. and G. Govett. 1982. "Gold Demand and Supply," *Resources Policy* 8 (2): 84–96.
Harvey, Penny, Christian Krohn-Hansen, and Knut Nustad. 2019. *Anthropos and the Material*, Durham, NC: Duke University Press.
Hecht, Gabrielle. 2018. "Interscalar Vehicles for an African Anthropocene: On Waste, Temporality, and Violence," *Cultural Anthropology* 33 (1): 109–41.
Henrich, Joseph and Richard Mcelreath. 2002. "Are Peasants Risk-Averse Decision Makers?" *Current Anthropology* 43 (1): 172–81.
ICME and UNEP. 1998. *Case-Studies on Tailings Management*. International Council on Metals and the Environment.
Jensen, Casper Bruun, Andrea Ballestero, Marisol de la Cadena, Michael Fisch, and Miho Ishii. 2017. "New Ontologies? Reflections on Some Recent 'Turns' in STS, Anthropology and Philosophy," *Social Anthropology* 25 (4): 525–45.
Jung, Maureen. 1999. "Capitalism Comes to the Diggings: From Gold-Rush Adventure," in James Rawls, Richard Orsi, and Marlene Smith-Baranzini (eds.), *A Golden State: Mining and Economic Development in Gold Rush California*, 52–77, Berkeley: University of California Press.
Kadirbeyoğlu, Zeynep. 2016. "The Transnational Dimension of the Bergama Campaign against Eurogold," in Thomas Faist and Eyüp Özveren (eds), *Transnational Social Spaces: Agents, Networks and Institutions*, 37–58, New York: Routledge.
Kirsch, Stuart. 2014. *Mining Capitalism: The Relationship between Corporations and their Critics*, University of California Press.
Koçer, Banu Aysu. 2007. "Eight Karats of Justice: Analysis of the Grassroots Resistance Movement Against Goldmining in the Villages of Bergama, Turkey."
Latour, Bruno. 1999. *Pandora's Hope: Essays on the Reality of Science Studies*, Cambridge: Harvard University Press.
Latour, Bruno. 2005. *Reassembling the Social: An Introduction to Actor-Network-Theory*, Oxford: Oxford University Press.
Li, Fabiana. 2015. *Unearthing Conflict: Corporate Mining, Activism, and Expertise in Peru*, Durham, NC: Duke University Press.
Lougheed, Alan L. 1989. "The Discovery, Development, and Diffusion of New Technology: The Cyanide Process for the Extraction of Gold, 1887–1914," *Prometheus* 7 (1): 61–74.

McDonough, William F. 2003. "Compositional Model for the Earth's Core," *Treatise on Geochemistry* 2: 547–68.

McKay, Ben M., Alberto Alonso-Fradejas, and Arturo Ezquerro-Cañete. 2021. *Agrarian Extractivism in Latin America*. Routledge Critical Development Studies. Abingdon: Routledge.

Mitchell, Timothy. 2002. *Rule of Experts: Egypt, Techno-Politics, Modernity*, Los Angeles: University of California Press.

Neingo, P. and T. Tholana. 2016. "Trends in Productivity in the South African Gold Mining Industry," *Journal of the Southern African Institute of Mining and Metallurgy* 116 (3): 283–90.

Nixon, Rob. 2011. *Slow Violence and the Environmentalism of the Poor*, Cambirdge: Harvard University Press.

Petryna, Adriana. 2009. *When Experiments Travel: Clinical Trials and the Global Search for Human Subjects. When Experiments Travel*. Princeton: Princeton University Press.

Povinelli, Elizabeth. 2016. *Geontologies: A Requiem to Late Liberalism*, Durham: Duke University Press.

Prentice, T K. 1936. "Presidential Address: The Witwatersrand Gold Mining Industry and Its Metallurgical Development." *Journal of the Southern African Institute of Mining and Metallurgy* 37 (2): 27–37.

Proctor, Robert and Londa Schiebinger. 2008. *Agnotology: The Making and Unmaking of Ignorance*, Stanford: Stanford University Press.

Richardson, Tanya and Gisa Weszkalnys. 2014. "Introduction: Resource Materialities," *Anthropological Quarterly* 87 (1): 5–30.

Romero, Adam. 2018. "Beyond the Mother Lode: Synthetic Cyanide and the Chemicalization of California Gold Mining (1885–1905)," *California History* 95 (1): 2–24.

Saunders, J. Edward, Norman Pearson, Suzanne O'Reilly, and William Griffin. 2018. "Gold in the Mantle: A Global Assessment of Abundance and Redistribution Processes," *Lithos* 322 (December): 376–91.

Scott, James. 1976. *The Moral Economy of the Peasant: Rebellion and Subsistence in Southeast Asia*, New Haven: Yale University Press.

Shapiro, Judith and John-Andrew McNeish. 2021. *Our Extractive Age: Expressions of Violence and Resistance*, Abingdon and New York: Taylor & Francis.

Sirman, Ayse Nükhet. 1988. "Peasants and Family Farms: The Position of Households in Cotton Production in a Village of Western Turkey," PhD Thesis, University of London.

TEMA. 2020. "Kaz Dağları Yöresi'nde Madencilik."

Thomson Reuters. 2018. "GFMS Gold Survey 2018."

Tsing, Anna Lowenhaupt. 2005. *Friction: An Ethnography of Global Connection*, Princeton and Oxford: Princeton University Press.

TÜBİTAK-YDABÇAG. 1999. "Eurogold Ovacık Altın Madeni TÜBİTAK-YDABÇAG Komisyon Değerlendirme Raporu." İstanbul.

13

Commentary

Begüm Adalet

The place of matter and materiality in politics has received much attention from scholars of science and technology studies, anthropology, history, sociology, and political theory, among others in recent years. By bringing questions of materiality to bear on the study of power, political rationality, subjectivity, and knowledge production, these works have revealed the ways in which material objects, technologies, and infrastructures, such as railways, electric grids, checkpoints, telegraph lines, and ports, have served as important sites of colonial governance, territorial control, and capitalist consolidation (Mitchell 2002; Goswami 2004; Larkin 2008; Tawil-Souri 2011a; Tawil-Souri 2011b; Barry 2013; Barak 2013; Meiton 2019; Khalili 2020). Moving away from more deterministic variants of materialist theories and instead situating material worlds in their context of social relations and political economic entanglements, these literatures scrutinize the relationship between matter and power, while also showing how material politics are always immersed in human relationships, agency, and intentionality.

Infrastructures, for instance, are built networks that make movement, circulation, and exchange possible, facilitating the flow of goods, people, and ideas (Larkin 2013; Mitchell 2014). As structures that alter the environment, they do not simply function as the mediums, facilitators, and material expressions of authority, but are conduits that materialize and territorialize power and resistance, raising questions about the specific nature of the relationship between their designers, builders, and users. They can be the site of political rationality, occasion the enactment of political subjectivity, and facilitate claims to citizenship, but also act as "semiotic and aesthetic vehicles" that generate and transmit the ambient conditions of everyday life, such as desire, anxiety, fear, uncertainty, and frustration (Larkin 2013, 333). As Bonnie Honig has argued, infrastructures are the types of public things that help bring durability and permanence to the world and yet they also remain the terrain and object of political contestation because "one community's public things" can be "the product of an act of theft and dispossession to another" (Honig 2017, 3). While public things such as bridges are expected to "interpellate us into democratic citizenship," then, the histories they conjure and the futures they promise may be complicated if they are built by colonizers, are privatized under neoliberalism, are subject to differential access due to white supremacy, or are the "result of prior thefts and appropriations" (Honig 2017, 5–6, 24, 89). Indeed, the uneven allocation of infrastructure has historically differentiated populations, subjecting some to processes of subordination and racialization, and facilitating the construction of unequal classed, sectarian, and gendered relations and subject positions, among others (Von Schnitzler 2016; Nucho 2017; Nemser 2017; Anand, Akhil, and Hannah 2018; Hetherington 2019). But the breakdowns, failures, and glitches of infrastructures also render them visible and may reveal fragilities in imperial and capitalist power, occasioning us to imagine alternative "commons" and assemblies of resistance (Star 1999; Elyachar 2014; Berlant 2016; Butler 2018; Chua 2018).

In Turkey, a growing literature has documented the material forging of the nation-state through the construction of architectures and infrastructures, such as railroads, roads, dams, and irrigation canals (Bozdoğan 2001; Tekeli and Ilkin 2004; Bozdoğan and Akcan 2012; Kezer 2015; Adalet 2018; Kurtiç 2019; Oğuz 2021; Adalet 2022). Turkey's project of engineering a homogenous modern nation-state historically rested on spatial and material interventions, such as the transformation of the nonhuman environment, projects of dislocation, forced migration and resettlement, and the destruction and reorganization of rural and urban landscapes (Gambetti and Jongerden 2011; Okçuoğlu 2019; Biner 2020; Binboğa 2020; Scaramelli 2021; Yildirim 2024). These projects' "political address," in Larkin's terms (2013), extended the promise of modernity, but in practice, they facilitated processes of dispossession, accumulation, and marketization, producing and exacerbating racialized, gendered, and class inequalities and dependencies. As these studies have demonstrated, attention to material politics can help move us away from top-down discussions of the state toward the study of how states are engineered, assembled, and configured. However, these infrastructures and other material artifacts can also become sites of mobilization and contestation, given the fragile aspects of the planning and construction of the built environment (Gündoğan 2011).

This volume, and in particular, the chapters in this section, build on this rich literature and open up new venues of interrogation in the study of material politics. Bringing together original archival research with interviews and oral histories, they collectively and convincingly make the case for the bottom-up and contextualized study of material politics. In doing so, they foreground the voices and experiences of the communities whose lives have been touched and transformed by new technologies and infrastructures of state formation, development, securitization, and the implementation of liberal and neoliberal economic models in Turkey. In that sense, the following chapters are exemplary of socially situated accounts of material politics, as they focus on the everyday experience of US military presence and nuclear infrastructures in the country, the targeting of sporting bodies as sites of cultural discourse and expert knowledge, and the politics and role of knowledge production in the contestation between extractive industries and environmental activism. By focusing on toxic, environmental, corporeal, nuclear, military, and other types of material politics, they also contribute to literatures that are increasingly attuned to the politics of translation (Babül 2017; Savci 2021) and negotiations of transnational expertise in demographic, scientific, and architectural history in Turkey (Hartmann 2016, Erken 2018, Erdim 2020, Yilmaz n.d.). In the remainder of this introduction, I will highlight the two themes that run across the chapters in this section: (i) expertise and knowledge, and (ii) transnational exchanges.

The chapters in this section show the ways in which scientific, medical, military, and environmental knowledge and attendant practices of expertise are embedded in relations of power. These networks of expertise produce facts, knowledge, and objects, and are themselves the products of contestation, thereby calling attention to the "conjunction of myriad fields and communities of practice and power" (Abu El-Haj 2001, 21). As Timothy Mitchell put it in his seminal account of twentieth-century Egypt, the expertise of "modern engineering, technology, and social science" has been deployed to reorder the social and natural environment, establish control over bodies, and "to repair the ills of society, and to fix the economy" (2002, 15). Expertise is also closely entwined with the production and measurement of knowledge. The measurements that experts use are never merely descriptive, calculative, or neutral, but bring phenomena and facts into being, generating certain realities while foreclosing others (Law 2004, x). In this exercise of creating new facts, expertise also entails cultural activity and practice, such as dialogue and exchange, along with the creation of epistemic communities through acts of exclusion and inclusion. While the conventional definition of expertise includes engineers, administrators, scientists, and doctors, the chapters in this volume collectively expand our understanding of who can be thought of as experts, identifying epistemic communities among sports trainers and resisting farmers, and situating them in unexpected locations like fields of football and agriculture. In doing so, they follow and document professional and scientific practices across a variety of actors, institutions, and, of course, materials.

Tarık Nejat Dinç's chapter is about Bergama's farming communities who successfully mobilized against the toxic infrastructures of a gold mine that was proposed for the first time in Turkey. Dinç convincingly makes the case for these farmers as experts by foregrounding their processes of risk assessment and decision-making about the land, quantities of water, qualities of soil, decisions about what crops to cultivate and when, how to protect from pests and disease, and dynamics of farming more broadly. In other words, this is an account of "risk expertise" from the bottom-up, in ways that reveal the implausibility of a binary between risk experts and "laypersons," as well as the entanglements of all varieties of expertise with the materialities of mining and farming landscapes. These landscapes are not inert matter to which expertise is applied, but the very material out of which they develop. But instead of a harder version of materialism, which can be found in some versions of Actor–Network Theory (ANT), the chapter invites us less to think about objects as full-blown actors that "overflow their makers" (Latour 2007), than to highlight how humans are always situated within material networks and technologies that create the environmental and political economic conditions of their actions. In other words, this is less an account of how technological artifacts can actually be agentic participants in the negotiations and associations that create sociotechnical systems, than of how the nonhuman world is entangled with social relationships and encounters between different communities with claims to expertise, livelihood, and power. Importantly, as Dinç puts it, the complex interactions between farmers, seed, soil, and water amount to a "particular agricultural resource assemblage," which is important to the extent that "farmers develop a farming calculus that aims to constantly negotiate more-than-human agencies with the 'market logic' of agricultural capitalism." In this account, capitalism does not become the passive background in an effort to recover the agency and vibrancy of the nonhuman world, as can be the case in some versions of ANT. Rather, it is a contradictory, shifting, and crisis-prone terrain and system with moments of vulnerability, as is revealed by Bergama farmers successfully shutting down the operations of the Canadian gold exploration and mining company in 1997.

In Can Evren's chapter, the material that becomes the site of professional contestations over expertise, authority, and knowledge production is the sporting body in Turkey in the 1940s and 1950s. On one side of the debate were politically connected biomedical scientists with intellectual roots in racist taxonomies and anthropometry, and on the other side were autodidact trainers, each with their own vision about the biomedical and bureaucratic interventions that they deemed necessary for the physical disciplining of athletic bodies. Evren's chapter is an important and historically situated contribution to a growing literature on biopolitics and the related concept of necropolitics in Turkey (Bargu 2014; Iğsiz 2018; Adalet 2022; Zengin 2022). By focusing on what he memorably calls "the material politics of athletic nation-building," Evren shows how biopolitical concerns are material in the double sense since they have to do with both material bodies and with the material of political economy and institutional history. The debates over measurement devices for athletic fatigue and performance enhancements for training, after all, were in fact debates about the centralization of state authority and whether or not to adopt liberalism with more autonomy for sportspeople and sports club representatives. The material bodies that experts fought over, in other words, belonged to athletes and to the nation-state, which was in the throes of contestations over public versus private forms of authority and economy.

Collectively, the chapters in this section open up refreshing questions about who has expert knowledge, and who shares, withholds, and interrogates it. In each of these chapters, expertise is co-constituted via its relationship to materialities, be it agricultural and mining landscapes, sporting bodies, or nuclear infrastructures, with broader implications for the adoption and contestation of political and economic systems like capitalism and liberalism. These complex interactions between knowledge and material politics occasion us to rethink the definition and scope of expertise. As Annelise Riles (2010) has shown in her study of the finance world in Japan, for instance, expertise can also be located on the margins, requiring not access to a specialized body of knowledge but "*lack* of knowledge of certain aspects of the financial markets" that renders some as legal experts (2010, 796). Furthermore, as much as experts aim for standardization and harmonization, their efforts are derailed by complications, mistranslations, and other types of "frictions" (Tsing 2005; Babül 2017). In those cases, expertise does not merely consist of certitude, mastery, and calculation, but may be open to different affective registers, as Sertaç Şen shows in his chapter on nuclear technologies.

Şen's chapter joins new histories of the Cold War in Turkey that go beyond foreign policy accounts that present international relations as taking place between distinct entities of nation-states. Instead, the approach here is "transnational," highlighting movement and exchange across and between units otherwise assumed to be insulated. As the prefix "trans" suggests, this approach foregrounds the travel and transformation of ideas, people, and political activities across, beyond, and through borders and spaces. The chapter thus joins the "transnational turn" in feminist studies, history, literature, American Studies, and other disciplines that have revealed borders to be constructed and porous (Grewal and Kaplan 1994; Kaplan and Pease 1994; Kelley 1999; Iriye 2007). More specifically, it joins studies of expertise that have highlighted the importance of transnational networks, interactions, and dialogue, rather than the external or unidirectional imposition of new forms of knowledge (Bockman and Eyal 2002; Hartmann and Unger 2016; Soloyev and Dayé 2021).

Focusing on everyday life on a US military base in Çorlu in Thrace in the 1940s and 1950s, Şen documents the oft-neglected affective components of expertise, running the gamut from confusion and expectation to pleasure and secrecy amid material encounters that are "occasioned and circumscribed" by the Cold War, which is marked by sovereign anxiety and imperial aspirations. As with technologies more broadly, which operate at the semiotic, affective, and aesthetic levels of fantasy, desire, and promise (Larkin 2013; Günel 2019), Şen's nuclear infrastructures have poetic significance. Rather than deliver the modernity that they promised, the tactical nuclear weapons, or Honest John rockets that were stationed in Çorlu, turned out to have "low-yield, little maneuverability, and short-range," and seemed to "threaten their own safety as users." Furthermore, the warheads were to remain in custody of American troops while delivery systems were in the possession of the host nation. The storage sites remained out of bounds, "and many felt that they were trained in a technology they were astronomically unlikely to access and use themselves." As with Evren's chapter where human bodies became the site of expert practice, the Turkish members of the base were kept away from access, with boundaries and limitations placed on their access to equipment, knowledge, and expertise.

Still, additional materials that moved in and out of the US base, including magazines, cigarettes, and liquor, manifested the porosity of additional borders as they "trespassed civil-military boundaries" and "continued along indeterminate and unpredictable trajectories." Once again, the material infrastructures and goods generated unexpected politics and consequences on the ground, including the radicalization of personnel at the base into leftist politics. As with Dinç's account of Bergama, where the gold mine was supposed to become a model of global extractive politics and instead emerged as a role model for environmental resistance movements globally, the meaning and terrain of "transnational politics" shift as those designated to be passive recipients of expert knowledge and technologies transform them through their uptake, unexpected usage, and dissident politics. Overall, these chapters document types of transnational conversations that occasioned contestations between political, economic, intellectual, and ecological projects, each with their networks of expertise and material politics.

References

Abu El-Haj, Nadia. 2001. *Facts on the Ground: Archaeological Practice and Territorial Self-Fashioning in Israeli Society*, Chicago: University of Chicago Press.

Adalet, Begüm. 2018. *Hotels and Highways: The Construction of Modernization Theory in Cold War Turkey*, Stanford, CA: Stanford University Press.

Adalet, Begüm 2022. "Agricultural Infrastructures: Land, Race, and Statecraft in Turkey," *Environment and Planning* 40 (6). https://doi.org/10.1177/02637758221124139

Anand Nikhil, Gupta Akhil, and Appel Hannah, eds. 2018. *The Promise of Infrastructure*, Durham: Duke Press.

Babül, Elif. 2017. *Bureaucratic Intimacies: Translating Human Rights in Turkey*, Stanford, CA: Stanford University Press.

Barak, On. 2013. *On Time: Technology and Temporality in Modern Egypt*, Berkeley: University of California Press.

Bargu, Banu. 2014. *Starve and Immolate: The Politics of Human Weapons*, New York: Columbia University Press.

Barry, Andrew. 2013. *Material Politics: Disputes Along the Pipeline*. New Jersey: Wiley-Blackwell

Berlant, Lauren. 2016. "The Commons: Infrastructures for Troubling Times," *Environment and Planning D: Society and Space* 34 (3): 393–419.

Biner, Ozlem. *States of Dispossesion: Violence and Precarious Coexistence in Southeast Turkey.* Philadelphia: University of Pennsylvania

Binboğa, Seçil. 2020. "The Soils of Turkey: Nature, Science, and Crisis (1930–1960)," in O. Inal and E. Turan (eds.), *Transforming Socio-natures in Turkey: Landscapes, State and Environmental Movements*, 11–30, New York and London: Routledge.

Bockman, Johanna and Gil Eyal. 2002. "Eastern Europe as a Laboratory for Economic Knowledge: The Transnational Roots of Neoliberalism," *American Journal of Sociology* 108 (2): 310–52.

Bozdoğan Sibel. 2001. *Modernism and Nation Building: Turkish Architectural Culture in the Early Republic*, Seattle: University of Washington Press.

Bozdoğan Sibel and Esra Akcan. 2012. *Turkey: Modern Architectures in History*, Chicago: University of Chicago Press.

Butler, Judith. 2018. *Notes Toward a Performative Theory of Assembly*, Cambridge: Harvard University Press.

Chua, Charmaine. 2018. "Logistical Violence, Logistical Vulnerabilities," *Historical Materialism* 24 (4): 167–82.

Elyachar, Julia. 2014. "Upending Infrastructure: Tamarod, Resistance, and Agency after the January 25th Revolution in Egypt," *History and Anthropology* 25 (4): 452–71.

Erdim, Burak. 2020. *Landed Internationals: Planning Cultures, the Academy, and the Making of the Modern Middle East*, Austin: University of Texas Press.

Erken, Ali. 2018. *America and the Making of Modern Turkey: Science, Culture and Political Alliances*, London: I.B. Tauris.

Gambetti Zeynep and Joost Jogerden. 2011. "The Spatial (re)production of the Kurdish Issue: Multiple and Contradicting Trajectories—Introduction," *Journal of Balkan and Near Eastern Studies* 13 (4): 375–88.

Goswami, Manu. 2004. *Producing India: From Colonial Economy to National Space*, Chicago: University of Chicago Press.

Grewal, Inderpal and Caren Kaplan. 1994. *Scattered Hegemonies: Postmodernity and Transnational Feminist Practices*, Minneapolis: University of Minnesota Press.

Gündoğan, Azat Zana. 2011. "Space, State-Making and Contentious Kurdish Politics in the East of Turkey: The Case of Eastern Meetings, 1967," *Journal of Balkan and Near Eastern Studies* 13:389–416.

Günel, Gökçe. 2019. *Spaceship in the Desert: Energy, Climate Change, and Urban Design in Abu Dhabi*, Durham and London: Duke University Press.

Hartmann, Heinrich and Corinna Unger, eds. 2016. *A World of Populations: Transnational Perspectives on Demography in the Twentieth Century*, New York: Berghahn Books.
Hetherington, Kregg, ed. 2019. *Infrastructure, Environment, and Life in the Anthropocene*, Durham: Duke University Press.
Honig, Bonnie. 2017. *Public Things: Democracy in Disrepair*, New York: Fordham University Press.
Iğsız, Asli. 2018. *Humanism in Ruins: Entangled Legacies of the Greek-Turkish Population*, Stanford: Stanford University Press.
Iriye, Ankira. 2007. "The Transnational Turn," *Diplomatic History* 31 (3): 373–6.
Kaplan, Amy and Donald Pease, eds. 1994. *Cultures of United States Imperialism*, Durham, NC: Duke University Press.
Kelley, Robin. 1999. "But a Local Phase of a World Problem: Black History's Global Vision, 1883-1950," *The Journal of American History* 86 (3): 1045–77.
Kezer, Zeynep. 2015. *Building Modern Turkey: State, Space, and Ideology in the Early Republic*, Pittsburgh: University of Pittsburgh Press.
Khalili, Laleh. 2020. *Sinews of War and Trade: Shipping and Capitalism in the Arabian Peninsula*, London and New York: Verso Books.
Kurtiç, Ekin. 2019. "Sediment in reservoirs: A history of dams and forestry in Turkey," in O. Inal and E. Turhan (eds.), *Transforming Socio-Natures in Turkey: Landscapes, State and Environmental Movements*, 90–111, London: Routledge.
Larkin, Brian. 2008. *Signal and Noise: Media, Infrastructure, and Urban Culture in Nigeria*, Durham: Duke University Press.
Larkin, Brian. 2013 "The Politics and Poetics of Infrastructure," *Annual Review of Anthropology* 42: 327–43.
Latour, Bruno. 2007. *Reassembling the Social: An Introduction to Actor-Network-Theory*, Oxford: Oxford University Press.
Law, John. 2004. *After Method: Mess in Social Science Research,* London: Routledge
Meiton, Fred. 2019. *Electrical Palestine: Capital and Technology From Empire to Nation*, Berkeley: University of California Press.
Mitchell, Timothy. 2002. *Rule of Experts*, Berkeley: University of California Press.
Mitchell, Timothy. 2014. "Introduction: Life of Infrastructure," *Comparative Studies of South Asia, Africa and the Middle East* 34 (3): 437–9.
Nemser, Daniel. 2017. *Infrastructures of Race: Concentration and Biopolitics in Colonial Mexico*, Austin: University of Texas Press.
Nucho, Joanne. 2017. *Everyday Sectarianism in Urban Lebanon: Infrastructures, Public Services, and Power*. Princeton: Princeton University Press.
Oğuz, Zeynep. 2021. "Cavernous Politics: Geopower, Territory, and the Kurdish Question in Turkey," *Political Geography* 85: 102331.
Okçuoğlu, Dilan. 2019. "Territorial Control and Minority Reforms: An Empirical Study of Kurdish Borderlands in Turkey," PhD Dissertation, Queen's University.
Riles, Annelise. 2010. "Collateral Expertise: Legal Knowledge in the Global Financial Markets," *Current Anthropology* 51 (6): 795–818.
Savci, Evren. 2021. *Queer in Translation: Sexual Politics under Neoliberal Islam*, Durham, NC: Duke University Press.
Scaramelli, Caterina. 2021. *How to Make A Wetland: Water and Moral Ecology in Turkey*, Stanford: Stanford University Press.
Soloyev, Mark and Christian Dayé. 2021. *Cold War Social Science: Transnational Entanglements*, London: Palgrave Macmillan.

Star, Susan Leigh. 1999. "The Ethnography of Infrastructure," *American Behavioral Scientist* 43: 377–91.

Tawil-Souri, Helga. 2011a. "Colored Identity: The Politics and Materiality of ID Cards in Palestine/Israel," *Social Text* 29 (2): 67–97.

Tawil-Souri, Helga. 2011b. "Qalandia Checkpoint as Space and Nonplace," *Space and Culture* 14 (1): 4–21.

Tekeli, Ilhan and Ilkin Selim. 2004. *Cumhuriyetin Harcı: Modernitenin Altyapısı Oluşurken*, İstanbul: Tarih Vakfı Yayınları.

Tsing, Anna. 2005. *Friction: An Ethnography of Global Connection*, Princeton and Oxford: Princeton University Press.

Von Schnitzler, Antina. 2016. *Democracy's Infrastructure: Techno-Politics and Protest After Apartheid*, Princeton, NJ: Princeton University Press.

Yildirim, Umut. 2024. "Decolonial Ecologies and 'Low-Intensity War' in Kurdistan." *Middle East Research and Information Project*. 311. https://merip.org/2024/07/decolonial-ecologies-and-low-intensity-war-in-kurdistan/.

Yılmaz, Seçil. n.d. "Intimate Technologies of Family Planning and Birth Control Politics in Turkey in 1960s," Manuscript on file with the author.

Zengin, Asli. 2022. "Death and Afterlives in the Middle East: An Introduction," *Comparative Studies of South Asia, Africa and the Middle East* 42 (1): 141–5.

14

Afterword

Andrew Barry

Opening this book, the editors briefly refer to two projects. One is the Yusufeli hydropower project, inaugurated by President Recep Tayyip Erdoğan on November 22, 2022. Erdoğan's address

> was a carefully crafted blend of an emphasis on the project's achievements, such as the sheer scale of the dam, the unprecedented length of its tunnels and roads, and the expanded size of the new town center, of the expression of his love for the nation, as well as his gratitude to the Yusufeli inhabitants for their praiseworthy sacrifice for the sake of the nation's future.

The other is the modernization project of the republican Turkish state, "a process defined by Tekeli and Ilkin as a transition from a 'shy modernity' to a 'radical modernity.'" They are just two of a remarkable array of projects discussed in this book. These range from specific irrigation, domestic water supply, and drilling projects to projects of urbanism and conservation, to a research project on cheesemaking, to the Southeast Anatolian project, as well as the national Turkish project of modernization. Why so many projects, and why does this term figure so frequently across the text? What does the ubiquity of this term have to say about the relations between infrastructure, expertise, and material politics? And does the idea of the project have any special significance in relation to the development of infrastructure in Turkey?

Note first that the word project has a double sense (Barry and Gambino 2022). A project refers to the organization of materials, finance, institutions, workers, and citizens. Projects are efforts to bring things together for specific purposes: whether this is the construction of a dam, a tunnel, a mine, a transport system, the development of a region, or the reconstruction of a state. Moreover, while projects are often situated, they may occur at multiple scales, in one or across many sites, and over an extended territory. Projects carve out their own spaces, disrupting existing borders, and establishing new ones. And they also have a specific temporality; they are generally only expected to exist for a period, even if their consequences may be long-lasting. They are expected to have a beginning and an end.

The philosopher Bruno Latour once proposed that the moderns were experts in what he termed "purification" (Latour 1993). In his influential account, the moderns sought to keep nature and society separate, purified, and distinct. In this way, political life was rendered free from contamination by its material base. For Latour, the modern vision of purification was, however, mistaken; for the purification practices of the moderns created—and in his view have continued to create—hybrid assemblages that disrupted the distinction between the natural and social. However, despite the evident historical importance of the scientific laboratory as a modern institution, perhaps Latour gave us a misleading account of the production of knowledge and the formation of hybrids. He was doubtless surprised by all the expert labor that went into forging and sustaining the distinction between nature and society in the confined space of the laboratory. But would he and other ethnographers of scientific practice have come to a different conclusion about the moderns if he had started his fieldwork not in the confined space of the laboratory but across the distributed space of the project? After all, those involved in projects necessarily work with hybrid materials, in varying circumstances in the field, and not at all in the purified space of the laboratory. And those who participate in projects, or who benefit from or who are forced to experience their consequences, come to know a lot about the hybridity of the world and its messy socio-material assemblages. In the context of a project, it may be exceptionally challenging to purify anything, let alone recreate laboratory conditions.

But *to project* is also a verb, as well as a noun. A projector is a person or a machine that projects or throws forward, casting light on the future.[1] No wonder that the idea of the project has been so connected to the great political movements of the twentieth and twenty-first centuries, from socialism to modernization, from development to transition. No wonder that the formation of modern Turkey has been considered a project. And no wonder, too, that politicians of all political persuasions tend to be in favor of projects. After all, projects appear to take politics out of dealing with immediate crises, problems, and events, directing populations to future possibilities rather than dwelling on everyday concerns. Projects point toward as yet unrealized futures, which may or may not be delivered in practice, futures around which a majority can come to agree and may be unified in the present. The more mundane task of sustaining infrastructures in their existing state or, for that matter, rescuing them from the state of disrepair into which they have fallen arguably offers less political promise. Older infrastructures, in Turkey and elsewhere, require maintenance, but new infrastructural projects still proliferate.

Despite the ubiquity of projects as organizational forms, project management is doubtless a challenging business. The project manager operates in the middle, mobilizing disparate skills and techniques, from engineering to finance, to public relations and law, security, and human resources. Moreover, the achievement of a project contains a myriad of apparently distinct targets that must be coordinated both in sequence and in parallel. Contracts need to be negotiated, labor hired, and land purchases organized and paid for. It is not surprising that all of this work of assembling may spill over into what is conventionally called politics, as citizens do not feel sufficiently consulted or compensated, or raise wider questions about the values that the project embodies, or the interests of those who are expected to benefit. Projects seem to be attractive to the authorities, establishing a (literally) concrete vision of the future, but, in projecting the future, they also generate expectations about what might or should be delivered. As the contributors to this book demonstrate, the state has historically been critical to the development of projects and it continues to play this role—even if, in neoliberal guise, it does not direct projects itself but serves to facilitate or catalzse the investments of private capital.

One of the challenges of assembling projects is that they involve bringing together the most technical and quantitative practices, such as engineering and finance, with the least technical and quantitative expectations, affects, and speculation. From the point of view of managers and engineers, projects may well have a clear goal and a clear timetable. But those who are not part of the project may be much more aware of how projects foster disorder and disagreement, not least because of the social divisions that a promised prospect of economic development may generate. No wonder, in disrupting the order of things, projects don't always run smoothly but tend to generate further disorder. In this light, activists and citizens develop counter projects (Dinç), while critical researchers highlight the mismatch between what a project was intended to achieve and how it has been realized in practice. If the idea of the project suggests the possibility of a process guided by reason and calculation, projects also generate expectations, passions, and anger as well as belief (Şen).

A further challenge arises that brings us to consider the significance of material politics. After all, projects are not just about management and finance, or even politics as it is conventionally understood. Materials invariably play a part in projects and, indeed, many projects are primarily concerned with the movement, rearrangement, and transformation of materials. Materials that are both strong and long-lasting, but also flexible and adaptable, such as steel and concrete, lie at the heart of many projects. But despite the ubiquity of concrete and steel, materials can't be assumed to provide a stable and solid foundation for the dynamics of projects. Their unpredictability and success do not just depend on the behavior of persons but also, necessarily, on the properties and behavior of materials. The strength and durability of materials may serve to stabilize a project, acting literally as a material base, but materials can also be both resistant and unruly, disrupting the order of the project too. Even steel may corrode or become weak through fatigue, and concrete may crack or fail when it has been poorly or cheaply made, when it is subject to excess stress, or because of the shock of seismic activity—such as that prevalent across Anatolia.

When thinking about material politics, it is not a matter of simply adding a discussion of the politics of material agency to human agency, or vice versa. Whatever humans do is always supplemented by material devices and processes. It is perhaps not surprising that materials figured so centrally in Foucault's later studies of discipline and governmentality, given the critical importance of infrastructures to economic and social life. Indeed, for Foucault, if one is to understand the political rationality of France, one needed to examine the importance of the infrastructural work of the construction engineers trained at the *l'École des Pont et Chaussées* (Foucault 1986). The study of infrastructure should lie at the heart of political analysis.

Some theorists have rightly insisted that there is a need to recognize the activity of nonhumans that occurs independently or beyond the rule of experts, pointing to the limits of scientific expertise and engineering (Oğuz). Yet, at the same time, physical and biological things, whether they are gold reserves (Dinç), wetlands (Scaramelli), or tunnels and dams (Alkan), are also increasingly supplemented by accounts of their dynamics and properties, however inaccurately and imperfectly. Indeed, there are continual attempts by corporate and government experts to bring the unruly properties of nonhumans under some form of control. In this light, the idea first advanced by Bernadette Bensaude-Vincent and Isabelle Stengers that materials have come to exist as "informed materials" is useful (Bensaude-Vincent and Stengers 1986). Materials are often not encountered in an independent state but exist in conjunction with maps, measurements, assessments, and research projects (Tatari), as well as speculations and projections about their properties, the risks they may generate, and the economic value that may be realized from their extraction. It is in this light that one can understand the critical significance of natural scientific and engineering expertise for projects, a theme that runs through this volume. Those engaged in projects seek to supplement the existence of the material components of projects with information, rightly or wrongly projecting a stable future for the material as well as the human world.

The idea of materialism has, of course, been associated with the notion that the politics of capitalism primarily center on the conflict between labor and capital. But while such conflicts between labor and capital occur in the development of infrastructure projects, the idea of the project points toward a broader terrain of contestation characteristic of capitalism and other injustices. After all, infrastructure projects routinely entail the purchase or forced appropriation of land, transforming the environment as well as the financial circumstances and everyday lives of affected populations. Indeed, as well as labor, it is land, property, and the environment that become the focus of the material politics of infrastructure. And if projects are tied to speculations and promises about the future, then the question of who will both benefit and carry future costs is also in play. It might be expected that the costs of projects are borne in the present, and benefits will be realized in the future, over a period of time, once the project is completed; but the reverse may equally be true. The benefits of projects may be realized for politicians and corporations in the present, while the long-term consequences of projects all too frequently include debt, pollution, and social dislocation.

Antonio Gramsci once sought to expand the field of materialist political analysis, recognizing both the significance of geography and the contingency of history, attending to both the emergence of the Fordist system of manufacture in the North of Italy and the internal colonialism experienced by the South. One could say that studies of material politics take his program further still, recognizing that the distribution, circulation, and behaviour of materials, as well as the movement and conduct of persons and ideas, may all become political. Following Gramsci, the sociologist Stuart Hall once wrote about the importance of conjunctures in political life; periods in which diverse historical tendencies came together to generate new political situations, which could turn out to be crises (Hall 2017). Hall was preoccupied with the historical movement of ideologies, the political emergence of neoliberalism, and the sedimented legacy of colonialism in social and political life in the UK. This volume is equally concerned with political history and colonialism, but the contributors go beyond Hall in adding to the analysis of conjuncture how it is necessary also to attend to the historical transformation of materials and infrastructure. This is a form of political analysis that may or may not focus on periods of crisis, a dispersed politics of infrastructural projects, the stability and instability of their materials, the multiple forms of expertise on which their development may rely, the subjectivities they engender, and the ways that citizens and workers continue to be affected by their ongoing existence.

All of these concerns figure in this book, which collectively weaves a critical and nuanced account of the entangled histories of materials, infrastructural projects, and politics in Turkey. Asya Ece Uzmay shows us how "Istanbul's water problem" is much more than just water, but becomes entangled with the politics of housing, public health, and disease, as well as the wider ecological relations of a rapidly expanding city. Elif Irem Az traces the simultaneous existence of coal as both a symbolic and a material resource, which becomes a critical element of a pedagogical infrastructure that is sustained after a disaster. At the same time, coal has become a "microcosm of the government's social, political and economic projects that bring together extractive neoliberal developmentalism and authoritarian populism." Aybike Alkan's critical contribution highlights the idea of the project, pointing to the ways in which *Güneydoğu Anadolu Projesi*(GAP) failed as a development project, which was "significantly affected by . . . the recognition and denial of the idea of a *region*." Indeed, in her commentary, Canay Özden-Schilling observes that the "most striking example of infrastructures as sites of encounter is in the history of the Turkish state's development projects in the Kurdish provinces"—notably GAP.

In turning to consider the significance of environmental and scientific expertise, this volume also turns to a concern with knowledge production that is the focus of earlier STS scholarship, including Latour. Hande Özkan dwells on what she calls "the national nature regime," directing our attention to the role of an afforestation project in national state-making. She, along with other contributors, points to the need to bring multiple histories, including those of land and livelihoods, with the history of neoliberalism and conservative populism in Turkey. Whereas Latour dwelt on the means through which Pasteur brought back to the farm to his laboratory in Paris, Mehmet Fatih Tatari focuses on the collaborative research practices in Kars in eastern Turkey "and the pasture cheese diplomacy they enact," which "carve[s] out a place for the co-construction of scientific and local ways of knowing and dairying." The focus here is not on mega infrastructure projects but on small research projects that establish collaborative relations between scientists and artisanal cheesemakers, "slowing down" the production of knowledge (cf. Stengers 2017). Caterina Scaramelli takes us to the Gediz Delta's wetland conservation area, interrogating what she evocatively terms the "overlapping and sedimented layers of material politics." Scaramelli, like Özkan and Tatari, delves deeper into the dynamics of materials and organisms, and the multiple ways in which their existence is both mediated and supplemented through research and educational projects that rely less on the purified space of laboratory science than on the open collaborative space of field research. In her contribution, Zeynep Oğuz considers the geological indeterminacy of Turkey's oil resources, which remain "unconstructable" and excessive, beyond the grasp of the projects of petroleum geoscientists. This is a story of political geology, and of the "earthly forces" that continue to contribute to the political history of Anatolia, while being beyond the rule of experts.

In her recent work on the history of the trade and extraction of nuclear materials in Africa, the historian Gabrielle Hecht insisted on the importance of thinking through interscalar relations (Hecht 2018). In her account of the African Anthropocene, she traces the relations between the subatomic and the planetary, and the infrastructural and the bodily, focusing on sites of uranium mining in Gabon and South Africa. In a similar vein, the final chapters of this book show, like Hecht, how it is possible to trace the interscalar. Tarık Nejat Dinç, like Hecht, highlights the importance of focusing not just on the resources that are extracted but, critically, on that which is not extracted but remains as a source of toxic waste, slow violence, and environmental injustice. Sertaç Şen likewise draws out interscalar relations over time, dwelling on the multiple ordinary legacies of the presence of a US nuclear base in Turkish Thrace, connecting the material politics of the Cold War with immaterial and localized change, "attesting to the primacy of ordinariness in the politics of the nuclear world." In turn, Can Evren's contribution also moves elegantly across scales, demonstrating how the transformation of the physical and athletic body itself became both an object of expert intervention and a critical part of the Turkish modernization project.

If the idea of the project thus runs as a thread through this remarkable collection of studies, then in each case these projects take a singular form. They are assemblages of particular materials and their transformations, situated across Turkey, associated with both infrastructural construction and environmental violence, and linked to diverse forms of political practice and expertise. What emerges from the collection, however, is much more than a set of individual case studies, each with their own necessarily particular features. On the one hand, each of the chapters offers an abductive argument, pointing from the specificity of the case outwards toward tendencies in Turkish politics from the formation of the Republic onward. On the other hand, across the chapters, the volume builds up an inductive argument, progressively establishing the significance of the politics of infrastructures, expertise, and materials in Turkey. If Turkey can be understood as a project, then this project is tracked and traced, never complete or accomplished, always leading to further projects, themselves marked by partial and local stabilizations, and ongoing instabilities.

Note

1 My observations on projects draw on an ongoing research collaboration with Evelina Gambino that has focused on infrastructure projects in Georgia and Italy (Barry and Gambino 2022). Thanks also to Eray Çaylı and Georgina Born for their comments on an earlier draft of this afterword.

References

Barry, Andrew and Evelina Gambino. 2022. "The Labour of Capitalisation," *Fixing Futures* lecture series, Frankfurt am Main: Goethe Universität.

Bensaude-Vincent, Bernadette and Isabelle Stengers. 1986. *The History of Chemistry*, Cambridge, MA: Harvard University Press.

Foucault, Michel. 1986. "Space, Knowledge, Power," in Paul Rabinow (ed.), *The Foucault Reader*, London: Penguin.

Hall, Stuart. 2017. *Selected Political Writings: the Great Moving Right Show and Other Essays*, Durham, NC: Duke University Press.

Hecht, Gabrielle. 2018. "Interscalar Vehicles for an AFRICAN Anthropocene: On Waste, Temporality and Violence," *Cultural Anthropology* 33 (1). https://journal.culanth.org/index.php/ca/article/view/ca33.1.05

Latour, Bruno. 1993. *We Have Never Been Modern*, Hemel Hempstead: Harvester Wheatsheaf.

Stengers, Isabelle. 2017. *Another Science Is Possible: A Manifesto for Slow Science*, Cambridge: Polity.

Index

Contributors

Begüm Adalet is Assistant Professor in the Department of Government at Cornell University. She is a political theorist with research and teaching interests in infrastructures and ideologies of empire, anti-colonialism, and transnationalism, with a focus on the Cold War period. She is the author of Hotels and Highways: The Construction of Modernization Theory in Cold War Turkey (Stanford University Press, 2018). Her writings have appeared in the American Political Science Review, Political Theory, Environment and Planning D: Society and Space, and South Atlantic Quarterly, among others.

Aybike Alkan is an independent researcher specializing in the sociotechnical dynamics of large-scale infrastructure projects. She obtained her PhD in sociology from Koç University in 2021, with research focused on the politics of scale-making in water and energy infrastructure development in the Euphrates and Tigris river basins. Following her PhD, she completed a postdoctoral fellowship at the History of Technology Department at TU Berlin, where she expanded her work on the intersections of technopolitics, infrastructure materiality, and technology transfer across borders. Her last publication, "Technopolitical Construction of a River Basin: Turkey's Encounters and Adventures with the 'TVA Idea,'" received the Young Author Article Prize from NTM - Zeitschrift für Geschichte der Wissenschaften, Technik und Medizin. She is also a founding member of IstanbuLab, an independent research platform on Science, Technology, and Society (STS) in Turkey, aimed at introducing STS within Turkey and contributing to broader global discourse through Turkey's unique science and technology landscape.

Elif Irem Az is an anthropologist, poet, and postdoctoral fellow in disaster studies at Harvard University's Center for Middle Eastern Studies. She received her PhD in Sociocultural Anthropology from Columbia University. Her research and multi-genre writing focus on the intersections of disability and debility, labor and the medicalization of labor processes, temporality, resource extraction, and disasters.

Andrew Barry is Professor of Human Geography at University College London. He is the author of Material Politics: Disputes along the Pipeline (Blackwell) and Political Machines: Governing a Technological Society (Athlone). His current research is on the politics of chemistry and chemicals.

Tarık Nejat Dinç is Visiting Assistant Professor at Reed College. He is a sociocultural anthropologist working at the intersection of environmental anthropology, science and technology studies, and resource geography. His research focuses on materialities of mining and toxicity, technopolitics of risk, and rural environmental justice movements. He received his PhD in Anthropology from Stanford University, and worked as a food and agriculture campaigner for Greenpeace and as Program Coordinator of the Farmers' Union of Turkey, a member of the global peasant movement La Via Campesina.

Mehmet Ekinci is a PhD candidate at Cornell University, Science and Technology Studies Department. He is a lecturer at the Academic Writing Program, Koc University, Turkey. His research interests include the political economies of knowledge making in contemporary life sciences research labs, understanding the pervasive discourses on Artificial Intelligence in contemporary societies, and developing new teaching methods of critical thinking, reading and writing in academia. During his doctoral studies at Cornell University, Ekinci taught First-Year Writing Seminars on drugs and politics, histories of human subjects in experimental biomedicine, and futuristic strains of technoscience and capitalism. He received his Molecular Biology and Genetics (BSc) undergraduate degree from Bogazici University and he studied Sociology (MA) at the same university before starting his PhD at Cornell University, 2012.

Can Evren is an assistant professor of anthropology at Ashoka University. After receiving a PhD in cultural anthropology from Duke University in 2020, he was a postdoctoral associate at Boston University's Kilachand Honors College between 2022 and 2024. He studies and writes about how the world of sports produces vernacular idioms of democracy, statehood, and government.

Duygu Kaşdoğan is Assistant Professor of Urbanization and Environmental Problems in the Political Science and Public Administration Department at Izmir Katip Çelebi University, Turkey. She received her doctoral degree in the Science and Technology Studies Program at York University, Canada (2017). She was a research fellow in the Sociology Department at Koç University, Istanbul, under the Scientific and Technological Research Council of Turkey (TÜBİTAK) Co-Funded Brain Circulation Scheme fellowship programme in 2016–17, and a visiting researcher in the Anthropology Department at MIT, Cambridge in 2013–14. She is the founding member of IstanbuLab and Transnational STS Network, and an associate editor for *Engaging Science, Technology, and Society*. Her research focuses on democratization of science, political ecology of disasters, anthropology of life, and cultural heritage.

Ståle Knudsen is a professor at Department of Social Anthropology, University of Bergen. His research is broadly situated within environmental anthropology and political ecology. Early work was based on long-term fieldwork in Turkey and covered issues such as knowledge, technology, science, seafood and consumption, introduced species, state policies, poverty, environmentalism, and common pool resources. More recent work has concentrated on Norwegian corporations' engagement with corporate social responsibility when they operate abroad. Current research addresses aquaculture and the maritime sector in Norway and Turkey with a focus on financial logics and sustainability as this is negotiated at the interface between corporations, states, international institutions, civil society, and local communities. Selected publications: *Fisheries in Modernizing Turkey* (Berghahn 2009), *Corporate Social Responsibility and the Paradoxes of State Capitalism* (Berghahn 2023), and 'Critical Realism in Political Ecology: An Argument Against Flat Ontology' (*Journal of Political Ecology* 2023).

Ekin Kurtiç is Assistant Professor at the Centre of Development Studies in the Department of Politics and International Studies at the University of Cambridge. She is an anthropologist of infrastructural politics, environment, and rural futures, with a focus on water and soil. Her writings have been published in *Cultural Anthropology, Environment and Planning D: Society and Space, MERIP*, among others.

Zeynep Oguz is Lecturer/Assistant Professor in Anthropology of Development at the University of Edinburgh. Her research interests include how political projects are entwined with earthly forces; and she examine these interactions in the context of fossil fuel extraction, energy transitions, insurgency and counter-insurgency, nationalism, and lately, right-wing environmental movements in Turkey and the United States. She received her PhD in anthropology from the Graduate Center at the City University of New York (CUNY) in 2019. She has co-edited two special volumes recently, with the first one titled "Contesting Transitions: New Directions in the Anthropology of Energy, Climate Justice, and Resource Imaginaries" (*Critique of Anthropology*, 2024), and the second one titled, "Earth as Praxis: Geology, Power, and the Planetary" (*Environmental Humanities*, 2023). Her work has also been published in *Cultural Anthropology, Journal of Cultural Economy*, and *Political Geography*.

Hande Ozkan is Associate Professor of Anthropology at Transylvania University in Lexington, Kentucky. She got her PhD at Yale University with a dissertation titled "Cultivating the Nation in Nature: Forestry and Nation-Building in Turkey." As an anthropologist with former academic training and expertise in history, she integrates ethnographic fieldwork with archival research. Her research is at the intersection of the politics of nature, state formation and nation-building with a specific focus on Turkey. She is especially interested in representations of nature and the discursive power such representations carry. Her works have been published in journals such as the *International Journal of Middle East Studies* and the edited volume *A New Ecological Order: Development and the Transformation of Nature in Eastern Europe*. Her teaching covers a wide range from political anthropology to the medical humanities. She is especially interested in pedagogies which address power in course content as well as class experiences.

Caterina Scaramelli is an anthropologist of the environment and science, trained at MIT' History, Anthropology, and Science, Environment, and Society department. Currently, she is a senior lecturer in the department of Earth & Environment at

Boston University. Her research focuses on meaning-making and politics through environmental transformation and governance. She is the author of *How to Make a Wetland: Water and Moral Ecology in Turkey* (Stanford University Press 2021), and is currently working on cultures of agro-biodiversity in Turkey and the Mediterranean.

Canay Özden-Schilling is an anthropologist of capitalism, technology, and infrastructures, with past and ongoing research projects on markets of electricity and global port logistics. Her first book, *The Current Economy: Electricity Markets and Techno-Economics* (Stanford University Press, 2021), is an ethnography of the electric grid in the United States in the age of competitive markets and smart grids. Her current book-length project explores the cultural life of maritime shipping, as seen from the port cities of Mersin (Turkey) and Singapore. She is an assistant professor in the Department of Sociology and Anthropology at the National University of Singapore.

Sertaç K Şen is a PhD candidate in the Department of Anthropology at Brown University. He works on how warfare and preparedness shape ordinary people's lives and the spaces they inhabit through a historical ethnographic lens. His research interests include civil-military relations, political economy of war, border studies, and urbanism, with a focus on Southeast Europe and the Middle East. Currently, he is working on his dissertation on the social history of Thrace, Turkey's northwestern borderlands. His publications include "Marshaling Development: Turkish Thrace in the Interwar Years" (2023) and "On the Watch: Civil-Military Relations and Affective Politics in Turkey after the Failed 15 July 2016 Coup Attempt" (2019).

M. Fatih Tatari received his PhD in Anthropology with a designated emphasis in Science and Technology Studies at the University of California, Davis. His main research interests include anthropology and sociology of agriculture and food, economies and ecologies of pastoralism, more-than-human worlds and human-nonhuman entanglements, and science and technology studies with a special focus on food. He is a postdoctoral research fellow at Politecnico di Milano, with a joint affiliation in the Department of Chemistry, Materials, and Chemical Engineering and META (Social Sciences and Humanities for Science and Technology) Research Unit. He is the co-investigator (with Ian Scoones) of the research project "Pastoralism and action for sustainability: Participatory planning for the governance of extensive grazing in Turkey" funded by the British Academy. He is also a partner of the Yerküre Local Studies Research Cooperative.

Asya Ece Uzmay is a PhD candidate in the History of Architecture and Urban Development Program at Cornell University, United States. Her research explores the architectural, urban, and environmental histories of modernism in West Asia, with a focus on technology, politics, and housing.

www.ingramcontent.com/pod-product-compliance
Ingram Content Group UK Ltd.
Pitfield, Milton Keynes, MK11 3LW, UK
UKHW020245290926
15470UKWH00002B/755